Peasant History in South India

PEASANT HISTORY IN SOUTH INDIA

David Ludden

PRINCETON UNIVERSITY PRESS

Copyright © 1985 by Princeton University Press
Published by Princeton University Press,
41 William Street, Princeton, New Jersey 08540
In the United Kingdom:
Princeton University Press, Guildford, Surrey

ALL RIGHTS RESERVED
Library of Congress Cataloging in Publication Data
will be found on the last printed page of this book
ISBN 0-691-05456-8

Publication of this book has been aided by a grant from the
Henry A. Laughlin Fund of Princeton University Press

This book has been composed in Linotron Sabon
Clothbound editions of Princeton University Press books
are printed on acid-free paper, and binding materials
are chosen for strength and durability

Printed in the United States of America by
Princeton University Press
Princeton, New Jersey

For my father, my first teacher, Allen E. Ludden,
who almost lived to see it done.

CONTENTS

LIST OF MAPS
(following page 67)

ix

LIST OF FIGURES

LIST OF TABLES

PREFACE

Few foreigners who confront village India avoid bewilderment. I certainly did not. Assumptions, preconceptions, experience, and learning clashed uncontrollably during my first year in the Tamil countryside. At twenty, after two aimless years in college, having absorbed the rudiments of public health, I arrived in Reddipalayam, a village fifteen miles west of Madras City. Eager to be useful in a small health facility there, I lived through a year of drought, among people in villages that ring the huge Ambattur irrigation tank, bone dry during the whole of the 1968 agricultural year. Nobody spoke Tamil the way my text and tutor said they should. Paralyzed by conflict, the health facility accomplished little of what I had anticipated. Worst of all, health problems I had thought could be solved by medication, care, vitamins, and education turned out to be symptoms of poverty inherited by undernourished day laborers. Frustration and confusion prompted me to begin studying in earnest for the first time.

Three sets of impressions during that year guided my thinking and research thereafter. First, the immense diversity of people, dialects, and ideas about life in that small circle of villages, close to two active commercial towns, Avadi and Ambattur, suggested to me the movements and differentiations of people over centuries that echoed in the personal energy, ingenuity, and vivacity of the individuals around me. Second, the people who animated village society seemed always to pursue their individual goals within complex social interdependence; this produced endless intrigue. Intricate webs of alliance, solidarity, distrust, and conflict bound everyone around that tank into a tight and lively social fabric, which stretched, moreover, through personal and institutional connections to towns near and far, and even overseas to Canada, the United States, Malaysia, and Sri Lanka. Third, the villagers' sense of heritage struck me deeply. Having spoken some words of greeting to a stranger, I would be treated to a discourse on the incomparable antiquity and beauty of the Tamil language. In buses hung verses from a Tamil text, the *Tirukkural*, composed some fifteen hundred years ago, which many riders could to my surprise interpret with enthusiasm if not unanimity. In everyday conversations, legends of ancient kings and quotations from medieval verses mingled with newspaper headlines and hot gossip. Family histories and accounts of longstanding feuds rolled off tongues at any provocation, especially when several tellers instigated one another. My presence seemed to stimulate recitations of the epic tale of British rule and Indian independence.

Village existence brought history to life, but the villagers' own sense of history puzzled me and seemed internally contradictory. On the one hand, villagers saw local history set firmly in the same world as their own. Their fathers and ancestors were protagonists. Critical decisions by people like themselves made their world what it is today, on the farm and in the village. Yet, on the other hand, they conceived the history of Tamil Nadu, and even more of the Indian nation, to be a drama set in an alien world, filled with virtually mythical beings, who breathed heavenly air and accomplished glorious deeds, whereas mere villagers, poor country folk, simply subsist. When villagers told stories of the village past, their tales overflowed with local folk making life-and-death decisions, carrying out intrigues, forging alliances, solving problems, and manipulating opportunities. But when villagers thought about village India in the national context, they portrayed their rustic world as one perpetually filled with darkness and ignorance, despite the best efforts of mighty national heroes.

An assumption lurks within this self-conception: villagers make no impact on the destiny of the nation, whereas leaders who make history at the national level remain powerless to change inherently inert village society. My suspicion and curiosity mounted when I discovered that scholars projected that same historical conception onto village society. I found on my return to the university that academic specialists who knew villages best—some economists, but mostly anthropologists— conceived village society to be essentially static, structured by ancient Indian civilization and by modern official attempts to develop the countryside. Historians, I found, paid little attention to the village, except to chart the impact of elite initiatives on village life. As I pursued graduate study during the 1970s, however, scholars began to search for the villagers' role in Indian history and for historical dynamics in Indian rural society. Soon they found the villagers' role significant indeed, as the role of farmers in modern Indian politics became more apparent and as agrarian problems assumed more importance in studies of the subcontinent.

When I returned to Tamil Nadu to do dissertation research in 1974, I rode a tide of agrarian studies that has risen considerably since then. My dissertation recreated in academic form a villager's style of local history: it concerned village development in the Tirunelveli region, portrayed strictly local matters in local terms, and treated rural history disjointed from Indian or even South Indian history. This book is a reincarnation of that dissertation and does not contain all the detail of its former self. Here I consider regional agrarian history and take into account as fully as possible South Indian and national history, pursuing a critique of what I call the imperial historical sensibility. Whereas the dissertation's central problem was to set out in detail events in the countryside, this book turns its focus toward the implications of putting peasants at the center of the social historiography of agrarian civilizations.

The Yale Five-Year B.A. Program funded my first trip to India. My dissertation research, financed by the Social Science Research Council and the American Council of Learned Societies, could not have been done without gracious help from staff members at the India Office Library, Madras University, the Tamil Nadu Archives, and Tirunelveli District headquarters. Writing, revision, and mapmaking were substantially funded by the departments of History and South Asia Regional Studies and the Dean of the Faculty of Arts and Sciences at the University of Pennsylvania. My massive debts to individuals defy adequate acknowledgment. Many will be clear in the following pages, but others deserve special mention here. Jacqueline and Sidney Mintz made my first trip to India much more enjoyable than it might otherwise have been. Holden Furber introduced me to Indian history. Tom Kessinger supervised my dissertation. Michael Pearson made me think about Indian history in its wider human setting. Michelle McAlpin guided me into social science history and made me at least partly an economic historian. Burton Stein, Robert E. Frykenberg, Dharma Kumar, Brian Murton, Arun Bandopadhyay, Chris Baker, Ariun Appadurai, and David Washbrook shared with me expertise and key source materials. My colleagues in the departments of History and South Asia Regional Studies at the University of Pennsylvania have constantly challenged me to make local and peasant history more meaningful; their suggestions and encouragement have maintained my enthusiasm for this book during what seem endless rounds of revision. Margaret Case, more than anyone, sustained my labor with hope that the book would someday be published and with good ideas about how to make that happen. Carl Beetz drew the final copy of all maps and figures. Gyan and Aruna Prakash, Pat Gorman, and Joan Plonksi put the typescript into machine-readable form and otherwise aided final revisions. My wife, Kathleen Galligan, drew maps and charts, proofread and commented on many parts of the manuscript, and inspired my work all along. Thanks one and all.

CONVENTIONS

All terms in italics are Tamil terms in transliteration, without diacritics. To make this book more accessible, I have used as few Tamil terms as possible and all of these are nouns critical to my presentation with no English equivalents. Such terms appear in italics only on first citation, and subsequently in normal typeface. All Tamil terms appear in the glossary with full diacritics and *Tamil Lexicon* definitions. English or Anglo-Indian terms are substituted for Tamil terms wherever possible, their equivalence having been indicated by juxtaposition, with parentheses, on first citation. Anglo-Indian terms also appear in the glossary, with definitions and derivations where known.

Proper names are not italicized. Place names are spelled as most widely recognized today, personal names as spelled by the people themselves. Capitalization has been kept to a minimum by reserving it for proper names for people, places, and institutions. Official titles are not capitalized except when they have become part of a person's name. "Tirunelveli" always denotes the territory called Tinnevelly District from 1801 to 1911, or its headquarters town, according to context.

Fasli years are fiscal years. F. 1260 began May 1, 1850 and ended April 30, 1851. For simplicity, I often locate events in fasli years in calendar years. One lakh is 100,000.

ABBREVIATIONS

References to archival sources appear in a form designed for ready reference: by series, volume, date, page, and location. This convention is necessary because a given document series may appear in more than one place with different volume and page numbers. During the East India Company period, district collectors' correspondence was usually penned about one month before it was entered into the Board of Revenue Proceedings, so that TCR and PBR dates differ; the first dates its composition in district headquarters and the second its consideration by the Board of Revenue.

Annual revenue reports for fiscal years are cited in the notes simply as "Jamabandy Reports," with their respective fasli dates; full citations appear only in the bibliography. Like some other British period records, Jamabandy Reports appear in Board of Revenue volumes both in the India Office Library and Records, London, and in the Tamil Nadu Archives, Madras; but their appended revenue accounts, with cultivation data, are preserved only in the Tamil Nadu Archives. I cite only the records I have used, though they may exist in more than one series and in more than one place.

EPIGRAPHICAL SOURCES

ARE	Government of India. Archaeological Survey. *Annual Report of South Indian Epigraphy*
SII	Government of India. Archaeological Survey. *South Indian Inscriptions*
TAS	Government of Travancore. *Travancore Archaeological Series*
TLI	V. Rangacharya, *Topographical List of Inscriptions of the Madras Presidency*, Madras, 1919

GOVERNMENT RECORDS

A.S.	appeal suit
F.	fasli year
G.O.	government order
IOL	India Office Library and Records
O.S.	original suit

PBR	Proceedings of the Board of Revenue
S.A.	special appeal suit
TCO	Tirunelveli Collectorate Office
TCR	Tinnevelly District Collectorate Records
TDCR	Transferred District Court Records
TNA	Tamil Nadu Archives
#	court case number

JOURNALS

AAAG	Annals of the Association of American Geographers
AG	Annales de Géographie
AHR	American Historical Review
AJS	American Journal of Sociology
CIS	Contributions to Indian Sociology
CSSH	Comparative Studies in Society and History
EH	Economy and History
EHR	Economic History Review
EI	Epigraphica Indica
ES	Economy and Society
HJAS	Harvard Journal of Asiatic Studies
IA	Indian Antiquary
IESHR	Indian Economic and Social History Review
IGJ	Indian Geographical Journal
IHR	Indian History Review
IJAE	Indian Journal of Agricultural Economics
IJE	Indian Journal of Economics
JAAS	Journal of Asian and African Studies
JAOS	Journal of the American Oriental Society
JAS	Journal of Asian Studies
JEH	Journal of Economic History
JESHO	Journal of the Economic and Social History of the Orient
JIH	Journal of Indian History
JMGA	Journal of the Madras Geographical Association
JPS	Journal of Peasant Studies
MAS	Modern Asian Studies
MI	Man in India
NGJI	National Geographical Journal of India
PA	Pacific Affairs
PP	Past and Present
PS	Peasant Studies
Rev	Review

ABBREVIATIONS

SA   *South Asia*
SAR   *South Asia Review*
SEHR   *Scandanavian Economic History Review*
SH   *Studies in History*
SJA   *Southwest Journal of Anthropology*

PEASANT HISTORY IN SOUTH INDIA

INTRODUCTION
A PEASANT MILLENNIUM

The nineteenth century invented much of the world we know. Industry mechanized work; science rationalized thought; geopolitics ripped old empires apart, built new ones with iron and steel, and designed the modern world map of imperialist and nationalist oppositions. When cosmopolitan minds sought the animus behind this great transformation, they found machineries in European cities, and the intellectual light cast on the metropolis left the countryside in shadow. In history's spotlight, urban industrial, proletarian, imperial, and national leaders seemed to surge into the future, as villagers clung to the past in deserved obscurity. The city symbolized modern change and the countryside traditional stasis.[1] Because those cities were European, Europe's presence hung over the globe. Europe seemed to be the source of the forces that propelled epochal change everywhere. Modern history became the epic tale of cities that transformed Europe and Europeans who transformed the world's agrarian societies.

Scholars still cast their light on the past so as to cover village societies and peasant populations with shadowy darkness. Although during this century revolutions turned parts of the world upside down and thrust peasants into history's limelight,[2] the notion that village societies are by nature inert and change only under the impact of urban initiative remains deeply ingrained in the scholarly imagination.[3] Research routines normally begin with the now classic contrast between urban and rural society.[4] Urban life bustles; open, expansive, and diverse, cities and towns are focal points for social creativity. Village life is boring; closed, inward-looking, and homeostatic, villages left to themselves repeat parochial routines unthinkingly. In light of this stark contrast, towns and cities that housed kings and elite cultural forms throughout preindustrial centuries seem logically to generate and transmit modern social change.[5] Studies of change in rural settings thus frequently proceed in three steps: they first establish a base line by describing initial static conditions; second, they identify those exogenous forces that propel change; and third, they chart the vectors and rates of resulting movement. The historian might chronicle what happened when and where. The social scientist might apply theories to explain both stasis and change. But they share an analytical premise that integrates their

3

research: forces from outside push rustics out of well-worn ruts, and village folk respond; thus village societies change.

Peasants appear in this logic to be social actors who resemble billiard balls, and those who study them concentrate on defining the most essential constituents of peasant society and culture, on describing static conditions, and on measuring changes produced by exogenous shocks. There is a running dispute within and between two major lines of theory, each developed to explain a historical fact with which no one argues: those premodern peasant societies that were most dramatically demolished lay closest to European industrial cities. Outside Europe, old peasant societies survived, and peasants multiplied in countries impoverished compared to the West and weaker on the world political scene. Two theoretical traditions, running through the work of Karl Marx and Max Weber, respectively, account for this contrast in opposing terms. Political economy argues that peasants are, in essence, family farmers, producers, and consumers, who as such would tend to respond in similar ways when struck by the same external forces, so that historical contrasts among peasantries derive from the differential impact of industrial capitalist expansion from metropolitan Europe.[6] Cultural sociology argues, to the contrary, that, as human beings in distinctive civilizations, peasants are not endowed with a single basic social character; peasant societies would thus respond to external forces so as to express the peasants' specific cultural heritage.[7] Yet both lines of theory are based on one historical premise: we can posit some set of conditions that depict inert peasant society and enable us to measure and to explain induced social change during modern times.

The whole peasant world has always been depicted and measured in comparison to European peasant experience. Because Europe's generative power would appear to arise from its own agrarian past, historians have dug deep into the rustic antecedents of the industrial revolution, and research has chiseled away at the supposition that premodern European peasants lived locked in village social stasis.[8] Where substantial peasant populations survive, however, that assumption remains in force and stigmatizes living generations. The very fact of peasant survival seems to support the assumption, and ingrained research habits, unassailed by searching historical scholarship, reiterate it unquestioningly. The billiard-ball analogy seems particularly compelling in Asian studies, for in Asia, where much of the world's peasant population lives today, European expansion provided an obvious external force to disrupt existing societies. Scholars can thus frame their detailed studies within one overarching scenario: first there were centuries of essential social stasis in villages, profound in Asia compared to Europe, under indigenous Asian rulers. Then came the Europeans and shocks to the old order, irresistible everywhere in Asia after 1800. Finally, peasants were pushed out of well-worn ruts and responded variously in social revolutions, modernization, agricultural involution, or stolid stagnation. The implicit moral in this epic tale is that peasants may become social forces of great political importance and may even make the headlines periodically, but they are people whose own way of life does not in itself generate change: peasants are, in short, "people without history," in Eric Wolf's apt phrase.[9]

Even within the Asian context, peasants of the Indian subcontinent seem especially ahistoric. Unlike their Chinese counterparts, they do not enter standard historical accounts until the period of British colonial rule, in the eighteenth and nineteenth centuries; even then they do not respond with dramatic upheaval. To scholars of political economy, from Karl Marx to Barrington Moore, Indian village society seems stolid in the extreme.[10] To cultural sociologists from Max Weber to Louis Dumont, the explanation for Indian peasant inertia lies in village traditions prescribed by the caste system, which persist and which resist assaults by capitalist urbanites.[11] The notion that ageless stasis typifies India's social and cultural forms, particularly in the countryside, underpins Indological and anthropological research; modern historians logically look to colonial capital cities and to the British for the animus that changed village India during the nineteenth and twentieth centuries. Compared to Chinese and even more to European peasants, village family farmers in India seem securely locked outside history.

One case study can but open a tiny crack in the edifice of presupposition and convention that obscures India's rich rural history. My story concerns a peasantry at the tip of the peninsula, in the Tirunelveli region of Tamil Nadu (Map 1). Because this region comprised, after 1801, the Tinnevelly District of Madras Presidency in British India (Map 2),[12] peasant history could be chronicled in this book according to the standard epic scenario, along lines dictated by cultural sociology or political economy. Setting 1801 as the epochal moment of external shock, subsequent changes could be explained as the result of British colonial rule imposed upon this part of the Tamil-speaking cultural domain in South India,[13] or as the result of industrial capitalist penetration into this one part of precapitalist, agrarian South India.[14] This overarching narrative framework has many advantages. It unifies the study of Indian history by setting off the colonial era from epochs before and after for all peoples in the subcontinent, and by creating a comprehensive image of a traditional Indian civilization subjected to worldwide forces of change. It thus enables the scholar to make suggestive comparisons between India and other world areas that can be studied within the same framework. It forges links between history and social science based on shared procedures and assumptions. It is supported, moreover, by the authors who penned documents that dominate the historical record. Official wisdom under British rule held that Indian village history, properly speaking, began with the founding of the colonial regime, when urban elites began to push their powers for the first time into isolated "village republics," which had subsisted and reproduced themselves "from time immemorial," as though sealed in a time capsule.[15] This vision permeated popular culture and scholarship during the colonial era, and remains pervasive today. To argue that after 1801 significant change in South Indian village society resulted from unilateral British imposition of foreign interests, cultural forms, law, and political power would thus seem obvious in wide circles of imperial officials, national leaders, and modern scholars, however hotly they might dispute the direction, timing, and desirability of imposed change.

Two flaws in this framework dictate that it be abandoned. First, it provides a distorted view of social process in rural history. Putting our picture of peasant society into motion at the birth of British rule implies that initiatives by colonial elites caused all change thereafter, and, conversely, that rustic commitments to traditional culture by nature resist or deflect those forces of change injected into villages by the new rulers. As the billiard-ball analogy suggests, a narrative strategy that divides "old" and "new" regimes reduces peasants as social actors; by doing so it also muddies any account of historical cause and effect. Data that might be understood to record local change caused by creative peasant decisions, conceived and executed in terms consistent with peasant culture, appear instead to reflect village responses to colonial initiative. Peasant action becomes by definition reactive, so that whatever peasants do, however actively, is necessarily an effect, not a cause, of change. This attitude toward peasant action, rooted in the colonial situation we seek to understand, constrains the historian's imagination within the conceptual framework set by colonial elites. It thus prevents a critical perspective on official documents by structuring peasant history according to the assumptions of colonial documentary evidence.

The more serious flaw in the conventional narrative framework is its proven inaccuracy as an interpretive framework for Indian history in general. Research has relegated nineteenth-century ideas about isolated village republics in changeless rural India to the status of quaint historical fiction. Before colonial times villages existed within agrarian systems that changed profoundly over the centuries.[16] Regional agrarian systems engaged urban and rural social actors, who, working within the tenets of Indian cultural tradition, forcefully effected the growth of trade, of cities, of empires, and of regional polities; all these also engaged Europeans and produced the setting within which Englishmen rose to power in the hinterlands of long-established coastal trade centers during the eighteenth century.[17] Alliances between Englishmen and Indians in these coastal settings established the colonial regime: the empire that British India became during the nineteenth century did not emerge so clearly from the unilateral imposition of European might as did colonial regimes in the Americas, Africa, and Southeast Asia. Imperialism in South Asia was an Anglo-Indian effort, from first to last; it evolved as it did because of India's participation in epochal changes across Eurasia during the millennium before 1900. India's peasantry were always involved in this process.

The colonial regime, when established in each region of the subcontinent, exerted what are now seen by historians to have been relatively weak disruptive powers in village society—weak, that is, in comparison with conventional imagery and with analogous shocks visited upon Amerindian, African, and Southeast Asian villages—not so much because the British were weak or did not want to effect massive rural transformations as because the English worked within and adapted to evolving Indian agrarian systems. The regime galvanized these systems into a massive empire and integrated them into a world capitalist economy. The closer historians have looked at village India under the Raj, the more they have found villages neither transformed nor stagnant under the imperial impact, but rather slowly changing through the colonial era on lines consistent with developments that predate the founding of British rule.[18]

Historical studies of peasant society during British rule in India thus need be set inside a narrative and interpretive framework that pays due attention to long-term trends before British rule and to peasant activity affecting those trends. Such an historical framework has begun to emerge in work devoted to South India. The major purpose of this book is to develop that framework one step further, by considering peasant history in the Tirunelveli region over the millennium before 1900, from the establishment of medieval dynasties in the Tamil country through the first century of British rule in Madras Presidency.

Evidence for agrarian history before 1800 in South India is abundant and diverse, and includes literature and folklore.[19] The great bulk consists of dispersed and often fragmentary inscriptions, carved into stone and etched in metal, which record ceremonial transactions in South Indian temples.[20] There was no central record-keeping apparatus during centuries before 1800, and everyday records were not penned on paper, but rather pressed into palm leaves, creating manuscripts that to survive had to be recopied each century. This effort was expended only on the most highly prized verbal artifacts, above all, poetry. To the surviving corpus of written evidence from centuries before 1800, which includes foreign observations, the historian can add copious information from other sources. Material evidence abounds, and as Marc Bloch taught, the land itself is an archive for scholars with eyes to see and feet to walk forest and field. Nineteenth-century records, penned on sturdy paper, survive to document outcomes of peasant activity during the centuries before 1800; they preserve old village folklore, as well. Available evidence is ample enough to substantiate major millennial trends in rural South India, if we are resigned to the fact that gaps in the evidence will always remain.

To spotlight peasant action in agrarian social history, we need to train our mind's eye to draw from available evidence facts and inferences concerning mundane affairs in everyday rural settings. We can begin by defining the peasantry in its agrarian context. Farmers, villagers, folk, and masses: all these define a peasantry, but none does so alone. Peasant family farmers work the land in small-scale communities where recurring chores, constant worries, and ritual routines suggest miniscule worlds sealed out of time. Despite these appearances, however, peasant villages have never existed in isolation, for peasants farm their land also in large-scale, complex societies. Villages survive and reproduce themselves by being connected to one another, both directly and by their mutual connections to cities and towns; urban elites play vital roles in village life and attain powerful significance within it.[21] Inequality and conflict, which characterize any complex society, necessarily implicate the village, so that villagers never move from day to day in simple, homogeneous harmony, modern romances to the contrary.[22] Diversity within a peasantry and conflict among various villagers define rural settings as much as do peasant connections to city and town. Any village attains its unique character as a little community by its participation in wider spheres of social order, exchange, and circulation. Its people work within an agrarian civilization, which, in turn, they bring to life. Aggregated peasant labor, indeed, fueled the economies, humanized the land, constituted the kingdoms, challenged the empires, and animated the religions that underlie the great bulk of human experience in Eurasian civilizations.[23]

A peasant's village is thus both intricately wrought by local inter-actions and extensively woven into wider worlds of human endeavor. Peasant history unfolds in its spatial complexity when we keep two analytic maps in mind. One centers on the village. The village sits at the center of concentric spheres of interaction and influence bearing on peasant life. Some factors that define a village setting lie close at hand, such as the land and the immediate neighbors. The provenance and movement of other, wider, influences are unseen by villagers: ideas, armies, and the demand for peasant produce. To imagine this realm of circulation and motion, we can map within those concentric spheres the central places connected to the village by routes of transportation and communication and by social networks of interaction and infor-mation. Transport and transaction costs help determine the reach, direction, and carrying capacity of routes; thus technology affects the development of central-place hierarchies. Social networks running along routes of movement and communication hold an agrarian society together; they form its connective tissue.[24] How networks engage vil-lages and what impact they have on village life are central historical questions that guide our inquiry into connections between what goes on in villages and in cities and towns.

Four types of social network shape the peasant's world: kinship, religion, state, and market interactions. Each network has its own rules, roles, and routines, accompanied by sets of symbols that attain coherence within a culture and give meaning to social action. These symbols enable the historian to speculate on the logic of social activity in village settings by sketching the contours of cultural complexity among peasants and in the process, distinguishing civilizations. What Henri Pirenne said of commerce clearly applies to all these four net-works in Eurasian agrarian civilizations during the millennium before 1900: they exist and are potent. The problem for the historian is to understand how they affect people and life in the countryside.[25]

Peasants participate constantly in each social network. Kinship net-works entail decisions about marriage, inheritance, and family alli-ances; kinship symbols constitute family identity in names, ethnic labels, and rules for appropriate marriages. State networks, founded on culturally legitimate coercive power, generate symbols to denote offices, rights, obligations, and authority, which attain meaning by being ranked in relation to one another; and among these symbols are local titles to property. Religious networks connect people to di-vinity and to other individuals within a community of believers; sym-bolic acts and adornments give people valued access to supernatural power and assets honored by fellow worshipers. The market and its symbol, money, create evaluations of equivalence among goods and services in manifold exchange relations. Though each of these networks is analytically distinct, they engage social participants simultaneously, and they affect one another. Kinship, after all, entails religious affiliation. Worship involves loyalty and authority. State officials impinge on family property rights and mediate property disputes. The state rests on its ability to protect families, religious institutions, and trade. The four networks are woven together so tightly that change in one necessarily involves the others; all pervade social order and processes of change in Eurasian peasant societies during the millennium after 900.

Yet networks manifest distinct capacities for social closure and inclusion. Kinship is most restrictive. Though kin circuits expand over time to include widening circles of real or potential kin, setting boundaries to exclude inappropriate marital partners remains a constant necessity within the symbolic and social structure of kinship, accomplished in Indian civilization through the idiom we invoke by the term "caste."[26] Religion, state, and market networks provide much more inclusive means to order exchange activity and to define human identities. Their vast expansions, embracing huge numbers of people and types of social transactions, constitute an obviously grand theme in the history of civilizations, hence of peasants. Aggregate human efforts to extend the reach of social networks have over centuries altered the contexts of peasant life in villages, though for the peasant the most compelling problems lie within immediate view. Land to farm, water for crops, food on the table, labor in the fields: all must be close at hand. But their acquisition entails peasant participation in all four networks that weave together the agrarian social system. Families look to see how the system around them is working to make decisions about how to live and work in the village, while far out on the horizon, beyond their view, events may be taking place that change drastically the context of their action, hence its outcomes and meanings.

To visualize this process in terms of an agrarian system that changes the context of village life, we need a second mental map of peasant society, one composed of regions. A regional map consists of many villages, each with its concentric circles, and each the core of peasant life. A region, ordered by its hierarchy of central places, would, fully developed, have at its center a major city. Smaller cities and towns, with smaller hinterlands, demarcate subregions. Villages constitute the vast majority but also the very smallest central places, tiny dots on the map. Whereas, on the village map, peasant history is the story of family farmers in communities, following routines transmitted over generations, working their land in networks of social interaction that form the connective tissue of their agrarian system, on the regional map, peasant history is the story of aggregate peasant activity in a region of that agrarian system composed of interconnected villages, towns, and cities. How over a thousand years peasants built the regions that would spatially order social change during the nineteenth century is a major theme in peasant history and in this book.

Neither the village nor the regional map alone is sufficient. Using the village map, we can study details at the core of peasant life, and deduce what village life is like more generally. Yet from this perspective, the fates seem to work, and unpredictability seems to originate, wholly outside the farming family's daily routine. Forces that peasants cannot see—migrations, population growth, and technological change; expanding states, religious networks, and market exchange—all appear to be exogenous factors impinging upon peasant activity. They penetrate the homeostatic village, often imposing their will by the actions of powerful people in the city. At one fleeting instant this picture of cause and effect might seem correct to scholar and peasant alike. But even over the relatively short term, it is partial and distorted, for those exogenous factors in any one village arise over time from interactions among cities, towns, and villages in a region. And regions themselves change shape and form in the process of interaction. Using the regional map instead, we gain a picture of spatial order in an agrarian system, but lose sight of the village as a product of human labor. We see in a region only the outer rings of interaction and influence that bear upon any one village. Our minds turn steadily toward major urban centers that express regional order as focal points for the social networks that hold the region together. Those tiny dots that are villages become useful for the scholar from this view only as archetypes or as data points in accounts of regional conditions in the smallest of central places, which are too small, numerous, and diverse to merit individual attention.

Each map alone thus diminishes the peasant community as an historic phenomenon and peasants as historical actors. Favored by anthropologists, the village map turns our mind away from local diversity in a region and from aggregate local activities that in the course of daily routine bring regions to life and thus shape village livelihoods throughout regions. Preferred by historians and economists, the regional map reduces the social core of peasant experience to an abstraction and treats peasants only as a mass. Juxtaposed, the two maps describe a spatial template with which to search out elements of peasant history that each alone would obscure, to pose new questions and put old ones in new light.

Together, the maps counter the assumption that the city exercises a timeless and natural dominance over the country. Urban centers, a defining feature of peasant society, often house the most powerful people in the peasant's known world. But whether such people have the power to direct village trends remains a subject for historical investigation and cannot be understood by simply dividing agrarian society into two sectors, urban and rural. Who could fault Fernand Braudel for comparing towns to electric transformers, except to ask in return why should not villages be seen as so many tiny generators? Braudel implies, rather, that villages compare better to light bulbs or electric motors, suggesting that the historian's task is to discover how far and to what effect urban electrical impulses reach out into the country.[27] This is indeed the question that underlies most research on the impact of British rule in India and of European imperialism generally. With these two maps in mind, however, our problem becomes one of tracing the rising curve of urban power during the creation of central-place hierarchies within regions, in the very long term. For this we need to look to the countryside not only for the effects or impact of urban initiative, but also for longer-term causes that involve aggregate peasant activity in world regions.

The two maps together also spotlight the peasant community as a historical creation whose characteristics need to be explained as much as those of a city, nation, or empire. Rather than viewing the village as an archetype of rural social order that can be abstracted into an image of "village society," and rather than treating the village as but one anonymous data point in an aggregate portrait of the regional past, we will look for the range of factors that shape village routine, the spatial distribution of those factors, the extent of their circulation, and their local combinations over time. Thus the social core of peasant life will appear in historical light as we compare villages in a region, so as to appreciate villages as little worlds of daily life that reflect and also generate regional order while they represent at the same time distinctive products of local peasant activity over generations. By considering villages to be products of conscious, meaningful social activity, we can see village social order and change as expressions of living peasant cultures.

This book considers the peasant millennium after 900, in the Tirunelveli region, from two temporal perspectives. The first treats epochs before 1801 in chronological sequence, in an effort to reconstruct as much as possible, at the present state of our knowledge, conditions and transformations during the medieval, post-medieval, and early modern periods. Chapter One argues that during medieval centuries, from roughly 900 to 1300, villagers built their political economy on social powers to control water for rice paddy cultivation, and built a system of agrarian order on shared devotion to South Indian gods. Chapter Two shows that massive change in agrarian conditions accompanied and followed the collapse of medieval South Indian kingdoms from 1300 to 1550, when migrations and frontier peasant settlement opened new parts of the region to agriculture; in this period peasants fought to control stretches of territory in units of extended kinship and localized state solidarity. These battles and the post-medieval agricultural expansion produced a new style of agrarian order, which became institutionalized during the early modern period from 1550 to 1800, when regional peasant life was woven together above all by tribute transactions between villages and royal authorities. The state replaced religion as the dominant social network in regional order and agrarian history. During medieval times, religious networks constituted the strongest threads in the agrarian system. Gods distributed peasants' most valued symbolic resources, and temple-centered devotion guided peasant efforts in kinship, state, and market networks. By early modern times, migrations had diversified the rural population; frontier cultivation had diversified agrarian communities; and technological change had elevated specialist warriors among diverse social groups competing to control agrarian resources. As a result, legitimate state coercion became dominant in the logic of regional agrarian order. Royal tribute demands and protection fostered trade and merchant power. Chapter Three concludes that in this context the British East India Company found ready allies and expanding opportunities for militaristic profiteering during eighteenth-century warfare, when peasant willingness to support an aspiring new regime with Englishmen at its head became the key to British success.

The last three chapters consider the nineteenth century: first, village activity within the colonial state; then peasant economic enterprise; and last, social conflicts that reconstructed customary rights to agrarian resources. Chapter Four shows that the new regime, like others before it, developed within political constraints set by key people in the countryside. The moral and political economy of colonialism developed from roots in villages, which established the rural base of Company Raj and fueled its growth into an Anglo-Indian empire in South India. Chapter Five argues that in this colonial context, the rapid expansion of agricultural commodity production that distinguishes the nineteenth century should be understood as a natural de-

13

velopment of very long-term trends in peasant social and cultural history. Accelerated by technological transfers from Europe, and shaped by English interests and power, peasant pursuits in the market, as in the state, altered the social balance of power in villages throughout the Tirunelveli region. Chapter Six argues that the very dramatic growth of the market as a social network of penetrating significance in peasant history during the nineteenth century resulted from efforts inside villages to alter production relations. In this last chapter we see that the market provided symbolic assets that assumed prominence in definitions of property and of ownership by peasants. By 1900, we can see that a regional peasant culture, which continued to value symbols of kinship, religion, and state as assets in the pursuit of a livelihood, had redefined the relative value of assets so as to give priority to the market in the critical matter of defining rights to agrarian resources.

The six chapters together describe a regional peasant culture that produced its own distinct style of agrarian capitalism, over a period that included a century during which British administrators headed the state. Dramatic changes after 1800 appear in this region to result more significantly from a very long-term process of local creativity and peasant learning, within an expanding world of interaction, than from exogenous shocks visited upon isolated villagers by the imperialist British during the industrial revolution. The story of this particular peasantry indicates that when historians bring peasant history in general into better focus, a new panoramic view of Eurasian history might emerge. The view we inherit today assumes that Europe became the vanguard civilization leading the way in social change during modern times. The conclusion to this book suggests another panoramic perspective: that the Eurasian continent became increasingly integrated by human endeavors which lowered transport and transaction costs assumes paramount importance, for it helps to explain why state and market networks increased their power to generate capital assets for people in all walks of life throughout the continent. By the eighteenth century, market networks had begun to surge into the cultural foreground by generating stores of capital eagerly sought by people in distinct cultural environments. Peasants and imperialists alike participated actively in producing Eurasian capitalism. But as in previous ages, imperialists seized the initiative in the process of capital accumulation; their dominance entailed the acceptance of their conception of history, so as to render the poor and weak marginal in the epic tale of modern transformations.

· 1 ·

SANCTIFIED PLACES

Medieval generations transformed South Indian village society by bringing nature under fuller control than ever before and by making places sacred, thus defining the agrarian landscape. What we know of Tamil society before medieval times comes mostly from poetry. Composed during some six centuries before A.D. 300, compiled thereafter, and preserved by the devoted recopying of palm-leaf manuscripts every few generations down to the turn of this century,[1] Old Tamil literature depicts a world of Tamil culture stretching from the Vengata Hills to Kanya Kumari, roughly the northern and southern limits of Tamil Nadu today. Old Tamil poets sang about traditions already ancient by the time of a mythical literary convocation, called a *sangam*, at Madurai, the capital of Pandya kings; South India's first historic period, 300 B.C. to A.D. 300, is called the Sangam period after that convocation. (Figure 1). Sangam poetry lovingly portrays diversity in both nature and society. Various types of people (*jati*) lived in five distinct natural realms (*tinai*), each realm characterized by its own way of life. The mountains, forests, seashore, arid tracts, and watery lowlands—each evoked for poets a specific set of peoples, gods, flora, fauna, and everyday social situations. Such natural and human diversity, with its attendant localism of social experience and identity, would typify South Indian culture during its medieval reformulation. Other key cultural elements described in Sangam literature would, centuries later, likewise come into play in the social construction of medieval South India. In Sangam poems, for example, lovers always meet each other perfectly matched and destined to marry, during their daily routine, in childhood, in their own communities; in this convention poets depict a persisting Tamil preference for arranged marriages between families in close physical and social proximity.[2] The poets also indicate that key people and places in the Sangam milieu manifested special powers. Wonderful but dangerous, wild animals, mountains, ferocious warriors, and beautiful women evoked both fright and thrill.[3] Centuries later, the medieval agrarian system would evolve when widening circles of Tamil kinsfolk learned to control that dangerous world by the twin powers of technological mastery of irrigation and the deities of the South Indian world. But this new social setting came into existence five hundred years after the world Sangam

15

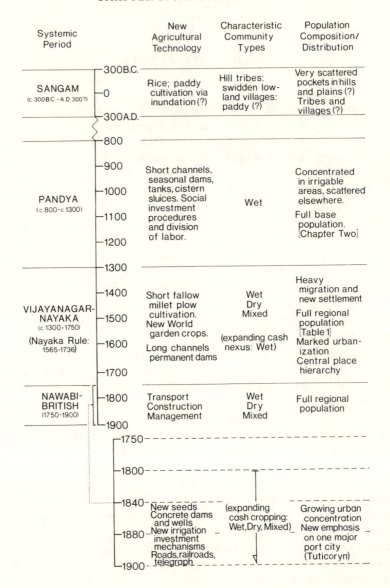

Systemic Period		New Agricultural Technology	Characteristic Community Types	Population Composition/ Distribution
SANGAM (c. 300 B.C. - A.D. 300?)	300 B.C. 0 300 A.D.	Rice; paddy cultivation via inundation (?)	Hill tribes: swidden low-land villages: paddy (?)	Very scattered pockets in hills and plains (?) Tribes and villages (?)
PANDYA (c. 800 - c. 1300)	800 900 1000 1100 1200	Short channels, seasonal dams, tanks, cistern sluices. Social investment procedures and division of labor.	Wet	Concentrated in irrigable areas, scattered elsewhere. Full base population. [Chapter Two]
VIJAYANAGAR- NAYAKA (c. 1300-1750) (Nayaka Rule: 1565-1736)	1300 1400 1500 1600 1700	Short fallow millet plow cultivation. New World garden crops. Long channels permanent dams	Wet Dry Mixed (expanding cash nexus: Wet)	Heavy migration and new settlement Full regional population [Table 1] Marked urban-ization Central place hierarchy
NAWABI- BRITISH (1750-1900)	1800 1900	Transport Construction Management	Wet Dry Mixed	Full regional population
	1750 1800 1840 1880 1900	New seeds Concrete dams and wells New irrigation investment mechanisms Roads, railroads, telegraph	(expanding cash cropping: Wet, Dry, Mixed)	Growing urban concentration New emphasis on one major port city (Tuticoryn)

poets knew had dissolved into disorder, under the impact of unknown external forces.

Migrations from the north into the Tamil country help to explain the collapse of the Sangam world and the rise of the medieval agrarian system after several centuries of turmoil that remain dark in the historical record. Tamil literature during the post-Sangam period indi-

Systemic Regions	Systemic Order Characteristics	System Defining Social Network	System Defining Civilization Context
Poetic regions, Nadus(?)	Kinship, tribal chiefs, village chiefs(?)	Kinship(?)	Dravidian
Mandalams [Map 3] Nadus [Map 9]	Expansive peasant community strong-holds among tribes Segmented, ritual stratification Vellala-Brahman alliance.	Religion	Indic
Chola-Pandya mandalams merge Tirunelveli region with central place hierarchy and transport grid [Map 4]	Tribes conquered and assimilated Segmented military and ritual hierarchy Warrior-Merchant-Vellala-Brahman alliance	State	Asian Land Empires European Seaborne Empires
British India, Madras Presidency, Tinnevelly District [Map 2]	Population disarmed Decreasingly seg-mented bureau-cratic and com-mercial system	Market	British Empire/ World System
Tinnevelly taluks organized around major market/ administrative towns [Map 5]	Political founding Ryotwari building Bureaucratic revision Mature system		

Figure 1 An Overview of Elements in Tirunelveli Peasant History before 1900

cates that religious ideas, personnel, and institutions moved from Gangetic North India into the far south. Two epics—one of which reflects Jain and the other Buddhist intellectual expansion—indicate that post-Sangam Tamil culture experienced widening spheres of social inter-

17

action and human circulation. The Buddhist epic depicts those spheres explicitly. Its heroine, on her journey toward perfection as a Buddhist nun, travels not only to Madurai and to other Sangam landmarks but also overseas; she hears tales about Buddha's home on the Ganges and about overseas kings.[4] The world seems to have expanded for Tamils, as new ideas, people, and surely technologies, too, entered the Tamil cultural scene; but little has survived to record these changes. Only as the medieval agrarian system comes into view, in its numerous inscriptions carved in stone and metal, do the implications of widening South Indian interaction with North India and elsewhere become clear.

Medieval South Indians record that their world consisted of large territories, called *mandalam*. Three of these housed kings bearing titles known to Sangam poets: Chera, Chola, and Pandya (Map 3). Medieval generations employed a range of tools to improve control over their environment, and their success made the centuries after 900 and before the early 1300s as important in South Indian as in Chinese and European history. How much of what medieval Tamils used to civilize their land came from outside and how much was indigenous, evolved from Sangam origins, remains highly controversial. Yet key points are certain. Radiating political alliances stabilized medieval core regions, within which irrigated agriculture provided the critical assets for social development; these regions centered on ancient core zones with Sangam traditions. The Sangam heritage thus helps to explain the significance of places and names in the cultural milieu of medieval Chera, Chola, and Pandya kings. Ancient Tamil ideas about powers inherent in particular places and people—including kings and poets—similarly help to explain how sanctified places and people became so potent in medieval Tamil minds. Yet, at the same time, key elements in medieval civilization arrived from outside the sphere of Sangam tradition. Tamil agricultural techniques certainly benefited from technological imports from North India and Sri Lanka. Religious imports likewise transformed Tamil culture. Tamils turned the watery lowlands depicted in Sangam verse into irrigated, paddy-growing centers of civilization, ordered according to Brahmanical ideology and around deity worship in temples. Social creativity in the Tamil country, in widening spheres of social interaction during medieval centuries, made the Tirunelveli region of the southern Pandya mandalam a realm Sangam poets would have marveled at.

AGRICULTURE

As the Sangam poets indicated, peninsular India is naturally diverse and replete with challenges to human ingenuity. Its mountain spine, the Western Ghat chain, divides South India into two tropical environments, one humid, the other semi-arid. When the southwest monsoon rushes inland off the Arabian Sea, from June to August, the Ghats force its winds skyward, and force the rains to fall mostly on the narrow western coast and on the mountains themselves. Some heavy showers do sneak through the Ghats to water eastern land, but most dark clouds that blow over the eastern expanse of the peninsula during the southwest monsoon are barren. In this rain shadow, Tamil Nadu receives the largest part of its meager rainfall during a seasonal cyclonic depression in the Bay of Bengal, from October to December, an event somewhat wishfully called the northeast monsoon.[5] West of the Ghats, therefore, South India is humid tropic, alive with green. To the east it is semi-arid, its natural flora hardy scrub, its land dusty red and brown. In this hot, dry South India of Tamil culture, people have built a civilization by working constantly to make the most of scarce water.

In Tamil Nadu, east of the Ghats, and in the far south, away from the northeast monsoon's most favored land, the Tirunelveli region is one of the very driest parts of the peninsula. North along the Tamil coastal plain, from Madras to Tanjavur, the land can expect more than forty inches of rain each year, whereas Tirunelveli averages under thirty. And here, according to that cruel fact of worldwide meteorology, where rain is most meager it is also most unpredictable.[6] But its location in the subcontinent does confer on the region some unique benefits. Here the peninsula narrows so that semi-arid and humid tropics lie in close proximity; they are divided by high jutting mountain peaks and are close to both the Arabian Sea and the Bay of Bengal. About 5,000 square miles in extent, the size of the U.S. state of Connecticut, Tirunelveli sits amidst a natural diversity of terrains that have from ancient times formed a lively arena for trade activity. A trade route in use from earliest antiquity connects the region by land northward through Madurai, and another connects it southward through Kanya Kumari to modern-day Kerala. The coast has always been open to the extensive trade of the Indian Ocean, and most importantly to the nearby island of Sri Lanka.

Bordered by both mountains and sea, Tirunelveli is also exceptionally diverse in conditions bearing upon agriculture (Map 6). Nearest the coast, less than twenty inches of rain nourish the sandy soil each year, and percolate quickly down into the water table. A bit farther west, toward the mountains, in the central part of the region, rainfall averages about thirty inches, and soils run from rich black loam and clay in the north to red clay and sand, to mostly red sand in the south. Along the base of the mountains, in the far west, a narrow stretch of

19

favored land receives southwest monsoon rains through the Shencottai Gap and some smaller gaps between the peaks.

With low rainfall, natural drainage plays a prominent role in defining agricultural conditions. In this, again, the influence of the Ghats stands out. Drainage routes in Tirunelveli not fed from the hills get very little water, so that river and stream beds, though they appear on maps, often sit bone dry for all but a few weeks each year. Many tiny streams do flow down the slopes of the Ghats eastward, and these pour water onto land at the foot of soaring hillsides. The Chittar, Pachaiyar, Nambiyar, Hanumathi, and streams in the upper Vaippar basin all bubble with life for several months near the Ghats, but dry out fast as they flow east. Among these only the Chittar and Pachaiyar carry water as far as twenty miles, to their rendezvous with the Tambraparni. The only perennial river in the region, the Tambraparni has its water source neither in the plains nor on hillsides, but high in the Ghats, in 250 square miles drenched by more than one hundred inches of rain every year. Tiny compared to the great perennial rivers of South India—the Krishna, Godavari, and Kaveri—the Tambraparni is for its size one of the most productive rivers in India. Dropping from peaks to plains in a series of crashing falls, it flows quietly along a nearly flat, shallow valley sixty miles to the Gulf of Manar, bearing plentiful water through a thirsty landscape.

Agricultural history in Tirunelveli is a tale of countless generations who carved from this dry land a thriving human habitat. Civilization here, as everywhere in the semi-arid south, has been created by hands that combine water, soil, seeds, and skill to make the most of precious rainfall. Technologically, two processes over the centuries formed the agrarian landscape we see today. On the one hand, people dug and shaped the earth to manipulate water, to put surface and subsoil moisture to work. Tamil people built their civilization around irrigation.[7] On the other hand, they adapted an enormous array of crops, seed varieties, and cropping techniques to exploit the potentials of different soils and variable water supplies. Their recorded history begins only after they learned to grow paddy. Their high cuisine even today depends upon irrigation for rice, its staple, as well as for chillies, vegetables, plantains, spices, betel, coconuts, and other delectables.[8] Irrigation has throughout Tamil history provided a proven means to raise land productivity. Not surprisingly, Tamils divide agriculture into two main categories, whose labels connote goodness and poverty, respectively. Irrigated, wet land is *nanjai*; and unirrigated, dry land is *punjai*. Each of these two categories of cultivation supports its own

20

staple grain—rice or millet—and in Tamil cultural tradition, one embodies the good life, the other meager subsistence.

In Tirunelveli, where microliths indicate prehistoric life in the sandy southeast dating back to perhaps the fourth millennium B.C.,[9] archaeological remains and literary evidence depict during the Sangam period an advanced nuclear area of paddy cultivation near the mouth of the Tambraparni. A very large number of megalithic burial stones from this period sit near Adichanallur, across the river from Srivaikuntam.[10] And Korkai, then on the coast of the tiny delta, was at that time a famed seaport, cited in both *The Periplus of the Erythraean Sea* and Ptolemy's *Geography*; it was the legendary first capital of Pandya kings.[11] Smaller nuclear areas existed up-river, too, and near Tenkasi.[12] No doubt the cradle of ancient Tamil culture lay on the coast, in paddy-growing lowlands; in Tirunelveli the most favored locale adjoined the Tambraparni delta. This small area received inundation from the river each season; it also benefited from sea trade, particularly in the pearls found on the seabed near Korkai, for which merchants sailed from Greece and Rome.

During medieval centuries, inscriptional evidence, upon which medieval South Indian history is based, reveals four major regions of development.[13] Only one, under Chera kings, rose in the humid tropics west of the Ghats. The other three spread across the semi-arid east, in what is today Tamil Nadu. In the far north, Pallavas ruled present-day Chengalpattu, in a realm then called Tondaimandalam (Maps 1 and 3). Pallava wealth flowed from huge irrigation tanks, called *eri*, man-made lakes behind earthen walls to store rain and runoff for use in paddy fields down slope. In what is now Tanjavur, powerful Chola dynasties built an empire that spread during later medieval times to embrace much of the peninsula to its south, including Tirunelveli. The Chola heartland, in the Kaveri delta, boasted a huge masonry river diversion dam, known as the Grand Anicut (*anaikkattu*). Over a thousand feet long, up to sixty feet thick, and eighteen feet high, the Grand Anicut pushed water from the river bed into channels that watered widespread paddy fields.[14] In the far south, centered in Madurai, the realm of the medieval Pandya kings drew its life from the waters of the Vaigai and Tambraparni rivers. Farmers in medieval Pandyamandalam used both water diversion and storage techniques; they built dams, channels, and tanks to make unpredictable natural runoff nourish paddy plants throughout the growing season.

Drainage control technology that was known at the latest by the ninth century was adapted, refined, and extended throughout Tirunelveli over the next millennium. The technology spread through the region by slow adaptive diffusion, as farmers exploited its potential for water control in an increasing array of milieus and locally advantageous combinations. There do not seem to have been dramatic technological revolutions, but very long-term trends made the landscape much more technically complex and productive in 1800 than it had been under the Pandya kings. New techniques for water control came into the region with migrants, who perhaps also brought new engineering skills and certainly helped to create the organizational capacity to build ever larger and more permanent works. Thus, as the region became more intensively farmed over the centuries, the range of irrigation technologies grew, and so did the range of production milieus into which irrigation could be creatively fitted. Throughout Tamil history, construction of irrigation works involved digging and building to train the flow of water; the techniques, materials, and productive outcomes shaped the land itself, but were at the same time shaped by the character of each setting. Building a wall at a right angle to the slope would dam drainage that, if not contained, would flow around or over the wall; devices to train that flow into other storage works through channels and masonry overflow outlets enabled dams and tanks to be built in a series along a drainage basin such as that of the Tambraparni River. Building with stone enabled larger, more permanent works to be constructed, and improved skills in using very flat drainage basins enabled water to be trained over greater distances, into connected expanses of paddy fields. But how much paddy could be produced with whatever supplies of cash, manpower, skill, and material always depended upon how much water was available.

Where water drained most copiously, that became a central spot in Tamil civilization, and in Tirunelveli this meant the Tambraparni River. Always the center of political order, the Tambraparni presents the greatest wealth of inscriptional and physical remains with which to reconstruct the pattern of technological development. Very little is known about the Sangam period, except what little can be gleaned from its poetry, but its irrigation seems surely to have depended upon natural flooding, with perhaps some small diversion work, so that paddy culture was concentrated near the delta and in pockets up-river, near the mountains, where seasonal floods were common and manageable with the simplest earthen works. Medieval Pandya communities flourished most notably not so much near the delta as up-river, in the vicinity of Ambasamudram, where the river carries a great quantity of water year-round in a shallow bed, and where numerous tributaries bring down spates of their own before joining the main stream. Later parts of this chapter will consider organizational dimensions of irrigation development during Pandya centuries in this area; there I cite inscriptional sources that also support the discussion, here, of technology.

Pandya-period irrigation appears to have rested upon both inundation and small diversion dams to push seasonal floods into fields and channels fairly close to the river. Most dams were probably temporary. Built each monsoon season on foundations of stone laid during the dry season, they would be raised in anticipation of seasonal flooding with tree trunks from nearby forests, a design that remained in use in parts of the river system until the twentieth century.[15] Though primitive when compared to later irrigation works, these dams represented a big advance over Sangam technology, for they could be utilized in many river settings, they demanded a knowledge of seasons and of spate cycles, and they required coordinated gang labor on a regular basis. The organized peasant communities of medieval Tirunelveli marshaled the skills, wealth, and labor for this purpose, under the authority and patronage of Pandya kings. The availability of wood from the nearby mountainsides and the many watercourses rushing down from the hills (each small, but gushing with usable water) would have given the up-river region its natural advantage as a locus for agricultural development under the Pandyas, given the constraints imposed upon farmers by the necessarily small scale of individual dams. Flooding threatened communities bunched close to the river, and the medieval center of Rajamangalam, adjacent to what is now Ambasamudram, was apparently washed away several times before being rebuilt (and renamed) some distance from the river, after 1300, when, as we see in the next chapter, technologies of water control appear to have improved markedly throughout the whole Tambraparni River basin.

POPULATION

Farming communities had by the ninth century built the skeleton of a settlement pattern that would fill out substantially during the medieval period. Core agricultural settlements, recorded in epigraphy, clustered along the length of the Tambraparni and the Chittar rivers, at the head of the Nambiyar, in spots near the mountains, and along a few routes of plains runoff, near the road to Madurai. By 1300, nearly every corner of the region had been settled to some extent, but the distribution of recorded villages, and the distribution of peasant microregions, called *nadu* (Map 9) strongly suggest that the north, and especially the northeast, was very sparsely populated.[16] Under

Pandya kings, peasants outside the riverine tract that was irrigated by small dams and by floods from mountain-fed streams eked out a meager subsistence, and were surrounded by vast expanses of uncultivated scrub; in contrast, settlements thrived and multiplied in places endowed with the best natural drainage, along the Tambraparni. In the Tambraparni valley, irrigated communities spread during centuries after 900. Here, in the watery lowland milieu that the Sangam poets would have recognized as the most prosperous and fully civilized, medieval efforts to control water supplies created a densely settled zone that encompassed more than half the total number of nadus, about 70 percent of all recorded settlements, and the vast majority of surviving inscriptional evidence. That Pandya civilization was built around irrigation is further indicated by mapping one of its core institutions, the *brahmadeya*. These Brahman settlements, at the heart of the Tamil agrarian system during the Pandyan era, were founded by land grants to learned, noncultivating elites, so they depended upon existing, substantial agricultural output. They dominate the surviving inscriptional corpus, for reasons that will become clear later in this chapter, and, for reasons obvious already, they were heavily concentrated in the Tambraparni River valley (Map 10).

A more distant reflection of agrarian settlement before 1300 emerges from nineteenth-century census data. About four of every ten Tirunelveli residents in 1881 belonged to castes with a definite history of migration, and most major migrations occurred after 1330, as we shall see in Chapter Two. Roughly speaking, the remaining 60 percent comprise the major castes of pre-1300 Tirunelveli, and, among these, five castes, about three-fifths of the "native caste" population in 1881, represent the castes most closely identified with agriculture in Pandya Tirunelveli—Vellalas, Brahmans, Pallas, Pariahs, and Vanniyas (Table 1). It is interesting, therefore, that the distribution of these five castes in the 1800s fits so closely the pattern of nadus in the fourteenth century. Brahmans as a whole were concentrated in the wet zone under British rule, as they had been under the Pandyas (Map 11). Vellalas who claimed strictly local origins in the census count of 1823, calling themselves "Pandya Vellalas," were residents primarily of the Tambraparni valley, but also of other, classically Pandya, irrigated spots near the Ghats (Map 12).[17] Even the more inclusive caste category of "Vellalas," tabulated in 1881, showed some concentration in the riverine wet zone (Map 13). The low castes that complemented Brahmans and Vellalas in the wet zone—Pallas, Pariahs, and Vanniyas—were distributed, in 1881, in a pattern roughly similar to Vellalas, though Pallas approximate the pattern most closely, and Pariahs and Vanniyas

Table 1 Tinnevelly District Castes, 1881 (listed by degree of spatial concentration)

Caste Group	Characteristic Occupations	% Population	History of Migration?	Index of Concentration	Zone of Concentration
Vaduga[a]	farmer	7.8	yes	45	dry north
Christian[b]	farmer/fisherman	8.3	yes (50%)	37	dry south
Vanniyan	oil presser	2.5	no	36	wet & mixed
Chetti[c]	merchant	1.4	yes	35	dry north
Muslim	merchant/ weaver	5.3	yes	31	wet
Balija	merchant	.8	yes	29	dry north
Kaikkolar[d]	weaver	2.6	yes (50%)	29	wet & mixed
Brahman	priest/landlord	3.5	yes (25%)	25	wet
Pariah	farmer/laborer	5.6	no	23	wet & mixed
Shanar	farmer	13.7	yes	19	dry south
Marava	farmer	9.1	yes	18	mixed north
Kusavar	potter	.6	no	15	mixed south
Vellala	farmer	8.2	no	14	wet
Palla	laborer	11.1	no	13	wet
Idaiyan	shepherd	5.3	no	13	mixed
Ambattan	barber	4.0	no	9	—
Vannan	washerman	1.2	no	9	—
Satani	temple servant	1.4	no	8	—
Kammalar	artisan	4.0	no	5	—
		96.4			

NOTE: Calculated from 1881 Census taluk tables, the index of concentration measures the degree to which a caste group is distributed differently from the whole district population. The minimum value is zero. See Chapter One, note 18.

[a] This includes Kshatriyas (.3%), Kammas (4.9%), Kambalattans (.8%), and Reddis (1.8%).

[b] Most Christians were either Shanars or Paravas.

[c] This includes five Chetti groups (Beri Chetti, Kasigar Chetti, Komati, Vellan Chetti, and "Chetti"). Many were migrants. All were distributed with the same degree of concentration, but in different areas. The index given here is that of the Vellan Chettis, which is representative.

[d] This includes eight individually enumerated weaving castes, the largest of which was the Tamil Kaikkolars (about 50%). The rest were Telugu or other immigrant castes.

SOURCES: *Census of India, 1881. Tinnevelly District Taluk Tables*, Madras, 1883; Edgar Thurston, *Castes and Tribes of Southern India*, Madras, 1909.

show secondary concentrations in northern and southern mixed-zone villages, respectively.[18] The social significance of these imperfectly overlapping caste distributions will emerge in some detail in subsequent chapters. Though it is very indirect evidence, this census data gives additional support for the conclusion that the Pandya era population lived chiefly in what I have labeled the wet zone. Thinly settled, the mixed and dry zones provided open frontiers for future settlers in search of farmland (Map 8).

KINGSHIP

The Tirunelveli region lay in southern Pandyamandalam (Map 3), whose capital city was that great Sangam landmark, Madurai, the ancient seat of Pandyan kings. The term "Pandyan" came to mean in regional culture the region itself, its kings, and by extension all competitors for the crown and other notables in the Pandyan realm. It is certain that families who became united during the medieval period under the jati or caste category of Vellala founded the Pandyan kingdom. They retained until recent times caste lore concerning their support for Pandyan royalty; and only they retained the title of "Pandyan" as part of their names.[19] There is also no doubt as to where these founding fathers lived. Most Pandyan inscriptions come from riverine irrigated villages. And most concern events involving temples, brahmadeya settlements, and war, for these were the major institutional means by which dominant peasants—Vellalas—built the medieval order in the Pandya country. They did so in a precarious and dangerous physical environment, where irrigation provided water for paddy crops only if the dams were built in a correct and timely fashion; even then they might fail under the force of floods. Peasants organized their control of the waters through village communities that lay surrounded by vast expanses swarming with actual or potential enemies. Inscriptions indicate that many groups on the land bore arms to protect themselves and threaten others: fishermen, tribals, and merchants alike.[20] This was a time when no single group could establish unchallenged military supremacy. Alliances were vital.

Pandyan political integration proceeded steadily after the seventh century, and was stabilized by the ninth. Dynasties at first probably comprised leaders of local alliances that pushed their power out from Madurai, which became the symbolic and military heart of the realm. To control the city became the necessary condition for sovereignty. Kings who could "sit on the throne" in Madurai could proclaim their ascendancy and extend their power from that base. When armies contested the city—as they did during the rise and fall of Chola dominance (920-1020 and 1090-1120) and during the Pandya demise after 1300—many self-proclaimed Pandyas issued proclamations from capitals elsewhere, but without firm claim to regional authority.[21] Even when he was seated on the throne, the king's power was always in question. He had central authority, but other lesser men had authority in small segments of the realm over which the king's superiority was always negotiable. Royal influence radiated from the capital through the many negotiated transactions that spun the web of the Pandya kingdom.

Internal and external boundaries fluctuated constantly, and defined shifting frontiers of influence among competitors. Externally, the Pandya realm overlapped with the Chera sphere to the south and west, and with the Chola domain to the north. Local chiefs shifted alliances on the frontiers as regional kings vied for local power, and war figured prominently in their activity, providing the major means for rulers to build their material power base. Inscriptions do not record a regular, peaceful system for collecting central state revenues and transmitting them to the capital. Booty and tribute gathered during military campaigns probably made up most of the king's income from land outside the immediate vicinity of the capital. A king thus had to intimidate local chiefs, and to be great had to expand his military reach. South of the Tambraparni, and near Tenkasi, Pandya armies constantly fought Cheras, who pushed around and through the Ghats. A few great Pandyas pushed northward into Chola country, but the Cholas had much more success lording over the Pandya realm during the twelfth century, after which the Pandyas rose again to challenge the Cholas up to the very gates of the Chola capital. The Cholas introduced armed garrisons in major Tambraparni River valley towns to protect their southern flank, a practice that Pandya kings retained after 1200, when they also initiated regular military tours in Tirunelveli to display their forces and to revive local allegiances.[22] Though later Pandya kings seem thus to have had much more organized military power than their early predecessors, they succumbed to invaders from the north and south—Cheras, Turks, and Vijayanagar armies—after 1300. From then on, Pandyas, even on the throne, were subordinated to higher powers, their realm incorporated in wider domains.[23]

Pandyan kings were the focal point of an elaborate redistributive system, wherein they received and dispersed material and symbolic resources through transactions that entailed ritual gift giving. By the ninth century, gift giving had replaced Vedic sacrifice as the most valued means to obtain religious merit, and had become the constitutive ritual of royal authority itself.[24] By gifts to temples and to Brahmans, men of means established their virtue and insured the prosperity of their realm, creating, at the same time, the moral basis of authority. Giving gifts also provided the ritual means to establish key political alliances. For example, one of the most common types of inscriptional records concerns gifts of taxes by Pandya kings to local temples and Brahman settlements. Because there is no record of such taxes ever having been paid to kings, it seems that local authorities would pay homage to the king by making such gifts in the king's name. Such a transaction would affirm the alliance between the local leader and the kings at Madurai, enhance the stature of both in local society, put resources into temple coffers, and constitute a ritual investment in local prosperity. Giving to god and to kings, then, also meant supporting a moral order that provided security for people on the land, both physically and spiritually. Part of the transaction would entail its recording and proclamation, with appropriate rituals, in a stone inscription that would praise the king by reciting his conquests. The whole transaction, of course, could either follow or forestall the local exercise of royal military might.

By such ritualized tribute payments, local leaders became members of the royal alliance network, received titles that indicated their superiority over local rivals, and gained new opportunities in the overall framework of royal transactions. One such local personality was Etti Sattan, whose name proclaims him a merchant,[25] and who is called in one inscription the leader of six places in Irunjolanadu ("land of the two Cholas"), a tank-irrigated nadu in the Vaippar drainage basin (No. 29, Map 9). Because of Etti Sattan's great munificence—he funded the construction of many tanks, both in his native locality and in the Tambraparni valley—the Pandya king bestowed upon him the title of Iruppaikkudi Kilavan ("leader of Iruppaikkudi," a village), and appointed him to a position of authority in the execution of a large grant to the great temple at Tiruchendur.[26] In addition to such grants, wars also provided opportunities for local men to move out into wider political arenas. For example, a family from Karavandapuram, near the Chittar, supplied several officers for early Pandya armies.[27]

Inscriptions indicate that many occasions to take part in royal transactions outside the locality presented themselves to local leaders. In fact, the bulk of the royal officer corps seems to have consisted of chiefs with powers rooted in specific localities. Lists of officers involved in various transactions reveal that most officers were identified with one specific place, as was Iruppaikkudi Kilavan; most are designated as *talaivan* (headman), *utaiyan* (possessor), *kilavan* (elder or leader), or *velan* (warrior) of such-and-such locality.[28] Of local chiefs named in inscriptions dated through the tenth century and published in *South Indian Inscriptions*, Volume IX,[29] all but one were identified with localities outside that in which the inscription was recorded;[30] they clearly held positions of authority based on local domains.[31] Royal enterprise widened local horizons. One inscription from Cheranma-hadevi, recorded during Chola domination, records an unusually complex grant in which twenty-three officers play parts; none of these officers was a local man, and nine came from the far-off Chola country; this illustrates the mobility of the elite that must have characterized all political frontiers of the day.[32]

But local chiefs were not merely royal camp followers. They made grants themselves outside their local domains to build their own alliances and replicate the royal redistributive system on a smaller scale. As they did so, they linked themselves to royal grants whenever possible. The Tambraparni valley logically attracted political attention, yet no chiefs that I have found in inscriptions hail from this core Pandyan area. Most inscriptions come from the wet zone of the Tirunelveli region, and the majority from the core area of Mullinadu (No. 11, Map 9) in the upper river valley, but we do not find chiefs with titles like utaiyan or kilavan resident in these parts. Instead, inscriptions record transactions involving chiefs and royal officers from outside the area with landowners and temples under the king's authority inside. Lists of royal officers become very lengthy under the Cholas, and seem to record the names of powerful men whose influence expanded under the Cholas and upon whom the grant's success depended.[33]

Kings and chiefs thus directed their disparate claims for tribute, their protective powers, and their ceremonial gifts toward the irrigated villages of the wet zone. Many inscriptions may, in fact, record the settlement of disputes over rival claims to status and wealth. The logic of domain pursued by all seems to have been inclusive and interpenetrating, so that many potentially conflicting claims could be legitimated and incorporated within a ritualized nexus that required protection of local landed elites and temples, on the one hand, and allegiance to the great kings, on the other. Kings needed ambitious and resourceful chiefs to extend royal power and to carry out gifts made on the royal behalf. Chiefs needed kings to legitimate their shares in the flow of tribute from productive, irrigated villages. Thus, though kings and chiefs competed, their domains merged into and depended upon one another. It is understandable, then, that a Chera king could make a grant of land just a few miles from a powerful Chola army; and that a headman in southern Tirunelveli could acknowledge the sovereignty of both the Chera and Pandya kings in one inscription, and of the Chola and Pandya kings in another, both in the same year.[34] This also helps explain why Tambraparni villages were throughout history very rarely subjected to pillage and plunder.

Transactions in state networks provided resources for investment in agriculture, especially in irrigation. In this respect, too, the Pandya state was marked by its localism. Pandya and Chola kings were apparently not directly involved in either extraction or investment outside their own core areas. The king's primary activity in his domain as a whole was to maintain the redistributive system on which depended his royal stature. But many leaders, each in his own core locality, acted as both extractors and investors. Outside the Tambraparni valley, single, locally dominant chiefs appear in inscriptions as patrons of irrigation. We have seen how Iruppaikkudi Kilavan invested in tanks. The head man of Vijayanarayanam himself paid for the repair of a local tank when it broke in thirty-two places during a storm, and then he endowed land to the village for continual upkeep of the tank. Similarly, leaders of Anmanadu and Karunilakkudi *nadalvan* put money into local tanks. The returns for such generosity are rarely specified, though one record shows that an investor stipulated as his reward a grant of tax-free land. But such transactions were not simple commercial investments. They cemented bonds of patron and client status that underpinned local political organization.[35]

Investments by kingly patrons in agricultural development often took the form of gifts to local institutions, particularly temples. For instance, one Puvan Paraiyan (a Pariah chief!) purchased land from the village assembly of Ilangokudi, in the Tambraparni valley, provided it with irrigation, and gave it to a temple, having renamed the land after himself. Similar transactions have been recorded in inscriptions from Attur, Mel Kadayam, and Pappakkudi.[36] By their protection and patronage of locality institutions, kings and chiefs established their own authority, put more resources into the hands of dominant landowning groups—their most essential allies—and helped develop irrigated agriculture, all at the same time.

TEMPLES

The centrality of deities and temples in medieval society derived from belief in the power of gods, in the efficacy of devotion, and in the value of honors bestowed by deities upon humans. Temples became focal points for social life and creativity as deities received gifts from pious donors. Material gifts supported ceremonies. Honors distributed in ceremonies denoted human worth in relation to divine beings and to people in society. In worship, people sought solutions to problems in health, marital, and other critical concerns; they simultaneously defined their position in the moral universe and their respectability among men. Leaders constituted their leadership in society by patronizing temple worship as well as Brahman learned men and priests.[37]

Gods thus became central points in redistributive systems: deities received material gifts and in turn passed out wealth, honor, and spiritual power. Inscriptions often show the spatial extent of a redistributive net around a temple, by showing the location of donations that supported temple ceremonies. Though some temples in the Tirunelveli region later attained wide renown, particularly the Shiva temple at Tiruchendur and the Vishnu temples at Srivaikuntam and Srivilliputtur (Map 10), Pandya-period temples characteristically only redistributed locally. The widest spread of a deity's umbrella of sacred influence apparently radiated out, late in the Pandya era, from the Srivilliputtur temple, said in one inscription to be the refuge (*abayam*) for six nadus in northern Tirunelveli.[38] Map 10 shows the major Tirunelveli temples before 1500; their transactional nets seem to have overlapped to cover the most densely inhabited parts of the region.

At all levels of the state system, to attain authority meant to fund temple worship. The 1961 *Census of India* gives dates of construction for major currently operative temples in Tamil Nadu; dates suggest that flurries of temple building occurred in Tirunelveli during high points of political competition, when leaders fought battles and donated to gods to establish their supremacy among rivals. Temples multiplied fastest, therefore, when the Pandyas were fighting off the Cholas, and then when Pandyas confronted the first influx of Vijayanagar power, that is, in the tenth, twelfth, and fourteenth centuries. The intervening years of dynastic stability were, of course, active times for endowing temples with material for daily worship and seasonal festivals, and for repairing and expanding temple buildings. But stability, ironically, seems to have slowed new temple construction.[39]

The story of the Sudikkodutta Nachiyar temple, in Srivilliputtur, illustrates the ups and downs of temple finance, and also the links that temples forged between kings and localities not only through patronage but also through the medium of popular religion. *Sudikkodutta Nachiyar* is an epithet for a Vaishnava devotional poet named Andal. The daughter of another poet-saint, Periya Alvar, Andal composed a famed work of *bhakti* (devotional) literature, the *Tiruppavai*. Her epithet means, literally, "the one who gave, after having worn it herself," and refers to a legend epitomizing Andal's love of god. She adored the Lord Paramaswami so completely, devoted herself to him so totally, that when she presented to him flowers that she had first worn herself, which normally would make flowers unfit for divine offering, he received the gift with joy because of her great love for him, embodied in her songs. Her legend continues that she wed Lord Paramaswami. On her death, her image was put by his in the temple, and it became the object of worship by devotees in turn. T.K.T. Viraraghavacharya, who has traced Andal's historic deification from a body of unpublished inscriptions, concludes that the temple in which Andal gave her gift must have been built by the early ninth century, that she herself loved the god and wrote her songs in the mid-tenth century, and that her image had been installed before 973, all during the reign of the Pandya kings and under their temple patronage.[40]

As a poet, Andal achieved fame throughout the Tamil land. The first commentary on her work appeared in 1170, and by 1274 her songs were sung in the great temple at Tirupati, far to the north in what is today the state of Andhra Pradesh. But as a goddess she remained only a local attraction. Viraraghavacharya argues that she became deified not because she was a famed Tamil poet-saint but rather because she became the patron-goddess of Srivilliputtur. Because her devotion won her the greatest of all rewards, her worshipers came to her to receive boons, to obtain access to divine grace. Gifts by royal patrons to support her worship thus can provide us with an index of how central royal donors thought Srivilliputtur, as a locality, to be. The Pandyas supported her temple as long as they had power. The Cholas, on the other hand, neglected her utterly, though they lavishly endowed temples in the core of their Tirunelveli domain, particularly temples in the upper Tambraparni heartland, Mullinadu. After 1200, when the Pandyas returned to power, inscriptions show that their numerous endowments revived daily ceremonies and annual festivities in honor of Sudikkodutta Nachiyar. In the 1200s, her fame began to spread. But with the fall of the Pandyas in the early 1300s, she received no new endowments again until 1453, by which time her worship had so declined that her temple and its Brahmans were destitute.[41]

Human hearts committed to gods made temples immensely potent focal points for personal emotion, artistic creativity, and social activity. Profoundly personalistic, even individualistic in its tone, the bhakti devotional religious movement in South India generated powerful attachments to sacred precincts. This made earthly spots holy. Localities took on meanings by their resident divine beings. Medieval religious trends produced a divine settlement pattern that became part of human central-place definition. Kamil Zvelibil has argued that this domestication of divine power "was probably the most popular element of the movement, and added much to its spread and attraction," a process that David Shulman depicts, in his study of Tamil temple myths, as the localization of transcendent divine powers.[42] As they directed their minds and their offerings toward sacred places, blessed by divine beings, people also forged a great variety of social bonds. Certainly the most dramatic of these were the ritualized links between levels of authority in the state, an ideological function effective because it was wedded to popular belief in peasant localities. Temples must also have forged a variety of horizontal bonds little noticed in the inscriptional record. Marriage alliances would have pivoted upon temples. Divine rituals also would have supported commercial contacts. Merchants seem normally to have endowed temples—with gifts of lamps, oil, sheep, and money—throughout the extent of their operations. Where trade organizations had stations, they made gifts to god "for the merit" of their members, presumably to establish a good local reputation. Individual merchants could also cement trade links by grants from one to a temple in the locality of another, because the second man could then contract to supply the goods required for the endowed temple ceremony.[43]

The integrative role of temples depended upon converting gifts into ritual goods and services, so the temple's economic role was basic to all others. Temples became institutional moneylenders, employers, bankers, landlords, consumers, local tax receivers, and centers of production and retail enterprise.[44] Such activities entailed many commercial transactions. In the simplest type, temple officers paid cash for oil to light lamps, or for supplies of flowers, ghee, cloth, and other items.[45] More important to temple finance, however, were deals between temples, officials, and local landowners. Two early inscriptions show how cash grants to temples by Pandya kings actually worked commercially. Cash grants to temples at Tiruchendur and Ambasamudram became loans from the temples to local assemblies of landowners, in named villages, who in return contracted to supply exact quantities of goods to the temples on a regular basis. Repayment was to be perpetual, stipulated as interest payments, so that the principal would never be repaid.[46] In addition to such contracts, temples regularly bought land,[47] loaned out cash for mortgages with possession,[48] and invested directly in irrigation and land reclamation by loaning out funds in return for a share of the increased crop production.[49] Larger and more complex contracts produced a number of intermediary roles for authorities who stood between landowners and the deity. In the Ambasamudram grant, the village assembly itself acted as the sole executor. But in the larger Tiruchendur grant, the king appointed three officers to insure that everyone adhered to the terms of the grant; one of these men was Iruppaikkudi Kilavan. In another cash grant, in Attur, temple priests contracted with temple managers to invest in local land: the priests would receive the profit of the investment and give the temple a fixed amount each year.[50]

Over time, such transactions could become staggeringly complicated. Though the full complexity of exchange relations rarely emerges within any one inscription, clearly what appear to have been simple grants must have many times been but single moments in a long series of deals. One example will suffice. In one village, a landowner leased land to several individuals, and temple servants stood as surety for the lease. A murder took place in the village. The tenants fled (we are not told why) and left the rent unpaid. The securitors then borrowed money from the temple to pay the rent, and the temple held the land until the loan could be repaid. When the tenants returned and liquidated their debt, temple managers refused to return the land unless all future taxes, except one, be paid into the temple treasury. The village assembly, to whom said taxes must have formerly gone, agreed to these conditions; it gave the land to the temple as *devadana*, "gift to god," recording the entire transactional chain in an unusually enlightening inscription.[51] Many gifts to god must have had histories of this kind.

VILLAGES

Because of their primacy as producers of goods and as local donors, village assemblies of landowners appear to have played a dominant role in temple management and finance under the Pandyas. Particularly important was the Brahman village assembly, called *sabha*, the institutional centerpiece of each brahmadeya village. Though temples did not invest their assets solely in Brahman villages, by any means, it seems that temples and brahmadeyas had close ties, because landowning Brahmans are highly overrepresented in the inscriptional record.[52] All but two major Pandya-era temples stood near flourishing brahmadeyas, and many inscriptions portray very detailed, day-to-day control by Brahman landed assemblies over temple affairs.[53] The sabha at Ambasamudram granted land for support of temple servants and managed local temple funds, for instance, and likewise the sabha at Vijayanarayanam invested temple funds itself.[54] When land was granted to the temple at Cheranmahadevi as a tax-free endowment, the sabha ordered the income so derived to be used for temple lamps.[55]

Even as temples forged wide links among kings, chiefs, and merchants, deities depended upon local landowners for material sustenance essential to maintaining redistributive power. In this agrarian system, where transport costs limited the movement of agricultural goods and services within tiny circuits that pivoted on village farms, all temples seem to have worked under the close scrutiny of people who dominated agricultural communities.

Villages in inscriptions are always said to be "in" or "of" a particular nadu. Burton Stein, in his path-breaking work on the medieval period, has called the nadu an ethnic microregion—"the fundamental building block of rural organization"[56]—which embodied the territorial claims of locally dominant peasants, that is, Vellalas. The institutional character of the nadu in the southern Pandya country remains in shadow, however. Though every locality recorded is situated in a nadu, and though many people called *nattar* ("people of the nadu") appear in inscriptions—perhaps members of a nadu assembly or simply important people in the nadu,[57] published inscriptions reveal that in only two of the region's thirty-two nadus did assemblies record actual convocations using customary formulae (*nadaka isainta nattom*, or *nattom*): "we (the assembled) people of the nadu." One sixteenth-century epigraph records a petition by the nattar of Tenkarainadu. And in the heartland of Sangam Tirunelveli, a medieval nadu organization clearly functioned in Kudanadu: it made grants of land, collected taxes, and conveyed royal orders from the twelfth through the fourteenth centuries.[58]

Though nadu assemblies may have functioned earlier and more widely than this evidence indicates, the most important institutional means for local resource control in the southern Pandya country seems rather to have been dominant-caste assemblies in single settlements or in circuits of villages. Historically, moreover, these seem to fit into a developmental sequence that reflects the progressive elaboration of community structures under the influence of wider Tamil and Indian cultural trends. At full elaboration, a stage already reached by 900, all the institutional forms I am about to describe existed side by side and in relation to one another. At this community level of agrarian order, trends in Tirunelveli seem to parallel those elsewhere along the Tamil coastal plain, even if, at the nadu level, trends differ in the far south.

The simplest and presumably earliest form of peasant organization, the *ur*, existed wherever people pursued settled agriculture; the ur encompassed one or several residential villages. In it could be found all production necessities: land, labor, service groups, and irrigation.[59] The elemental ur consisted of peasant cultivating families, but with the intensification of land use, extension of irrigation, and assimilation of new groups into the economy—at the bottom—labor became progressively detached from land control in many irrigated villages, a

process to be discussed more fully in Chapter Three. This differentiation in labor relations occurred only in irrigated villages, which produced diversity in the internal organization of Tirunelveli urs because
all were not irrigated.

Dominant peasants of the ur were entitled by terms that denote
"one in control"—*vellalar, velalar, karalar*—by which they announced
their power over the natural elements essential to agriculture, especially
water, and over their communities. These Vellalas appear to have built
collective community organizations even in very ancient times, especially where collective management of irrigation works became useful
in paddy cultivation.[60] Their assemblies, also called *ur*, continued to
operate even after the fuller elaboration of local institutional forms:
they gave money to temples, received money in return for goods,
allocated water rights, and sold lands to chiefs and to temples.[61]

By the ninth century, the ur landscape had become further complicated by the creation of brahmadeyas. Before 900, thirteen of these
Brahman settlements are recorded; by 1400, six dozen (Map 10).[62]
As gifts from kings, as centers of art and learning, and as nodes of
agricultural development, they were central institutions in medieval
Tamil society; yet before the thirteenth century, when royalty began
to celebrate their founding on a grand scale, few inscriptions record
the creation of a brahmadeya.[63] When most came into being, therefore,
the event itself was taken very much for granted. It was a routine part
of agrarian life, a regular activity like plowing the land, and equally
essential because it produced what Burton Stein has called the "Vellala-
Brahman alliance," the foundation for dominant-caste status for Brahmans and Vellalas alike in the Tamil country.[64]

Vellalas, from kings to peasants, supported brahmadeyas, and by
doing so raised themselves from a disparate set of locally dominant
peasants into a high-status category, a non-Brahman stratum above
all others. They thus patronized a cultural and social order that put
high value on the ritual powers of Brahmans, and, at the same time,
appropriated the symbolic resources of that order for themselves. Vellala patronage from temples and Brahman settlements proclaimed Vellalas to be prosperous and pious; and so it attracted allegiance from
other, similar groups in disparate localities. Devotion to gods and those
closest to gods became the ideological glue for the agrarian order;
and, because of this, Brahmans became locally rich and powerful. They
too worked actively, of course, to build this system of belief, devotion,
and deference. They incorporated peasant gods, such as Murugan, and
personalistic folk devotionalism into the Brahmanical system. They
taught, studied, wrote, recited, and officiated at ceremonies. Brahmans

thus created high culture in rural settings, brought honor to kings and dominant peasants alike, and confirmed the spirituality of temporal power.

Pandya Vellalas apparently sought eagerly the privilege of founding brahmadeyas. Procedures for doing so seem fairly simple. Appropriate land, bought from or donated by a prosperous ur, had to have irrigation sufficient to provide good crops for these Brahman, non-cultivating settlers. Established on such land, the Brahmans might also receive payments of grain for their upkeep to supplement their harvests, and they could also get help at troublesome points in the agricultural calendar, if necessary. Such payments would often have been formalized in terms of taxes, authorized by a king, chief, or local assembly.[65] With such support, the wealth and power of landed Brahmans spread throughout the political economy of irrigated agriculture, and, in time, permeated the entire wet zone.

By multiplication and strategic investments, some brahmadeya settlements developed into extremely elaborate and expansive institutions, what we might call "extended brahmadeyas." The best documented of these in Tirunelveli centered upon the sabha at Ambasamudram, called then Rajarajachaturvedimangalam, but let us call it simply Rajamangalam. At the center of agrarian life in western Mullinadu under the Cholas, when it attained prominence in the inscriptional record, it retained its stature at least down to the seventeenth century. Like other major brahmadeyas, Rajamangalam contained within its domain many subordinate urs and several subordinate brahmadeyas.[66] Stretching over about sixteen square miles, its triangular domain embraced villages within the area of the Tambraparni and several tributaries. Figure 2 illustrates the transactional web that supported extended brahmadeyas, as recorded in numerous inscriptions.

As already indicated, most of these transactions did not involve resource transfers outside localities, yet inscriptions indicate a very complex set of routine exchanges within local domains such as Rajamangalam. Most payments to kings and chiefs would have had more the character of tribute than of taxation: their irregular collection would have depended upon periodic demonstrations of military power from outside agricultural communities. A large set of inscriptional terms, however, refers to what can rightly be called local taxation: regular payments to a great variety of recognized authorities in implicit recognition of their worth and worthiness in agrarian life. These terms often denote obligations to exalted superiors: *irai*, for instance, meant "god," "king," and "obligation"; and *melvaram*, the most general term for land tax, still in use today, meant the superior or high share

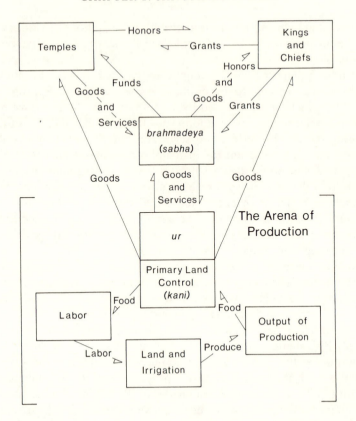

Figure 2   Transactions within an Extended Brahmadeya

of the harvest, as opposed to the cultivator's (literally "resident's") share, *kudivaram*. Terms often indicate, also, that landowners recognized obligations to authorities not only as a duty (*kadamai*), but as a duty upon which their landowning status itself depended (*kanik-kadan*). By contrast, many transactions seem more straightforwardly commercial in character, though contracts between individuals recorded in inscriptions depended upon the authority of kings, chiefs, temples, or local landowner assemblies.

Paid in cash or kind, transactional obligations over time generated a variety of rights and claims over land and its produce, a subject to which we return in subsequent chapters. One terminological issue deserves mention here, however, because it concerns the relation between landownership and exchange in the Pandya system. Members of ur and brahmadeya communities conducted transactions on the

38

basis of their recognized rights to land; rights, it appears, were effectively constituted by local recognition of and obligations to superior authorities. By paying their due, villagers obtained legitimate control over land and related resources, both goods and services, designated by the terms *kani* and *karanmai*. From the verb "to see," kani connotes close oversight over land and labor; in the course of time it came to mean "land," a measure of land, and ownership. Karanmai denotes control (*anmai*) over clouds, the rainy season, water for cultivation, and hence crops. Originally, in elemental ur communities, these terms may well have denoted primal powers over land and land use by cultivating peasants themselves. But with the progressive elaboration of local land relations and transactional ties, actual cultivation became conceptually distinct from kani and karanmai, so that many inscriptions record their transfer, as gift or contractual payment, to noncultivators—not only Brahmans but merchants, as well.[67]

New terms were not invented to designate the more varied and less primal types of land rights that came into being as the agrarian system evolved. Kani and karanmai thus came to designate both immediate control over land and harvest, exercised by members of shareholding communities, and established rights in the community harvest. Just what kinds of rights were the subject of transactions must be deduced from the context of inscriptional records, and were very often not stipulated in these records. Many inscriptions have thus been translated and discussed as though they involve transfers of primary land control, when in fact they involved rights to produce or to occupancy rights to land. One Pandya king, for example, made a so-called "land grant" to a temple at Cheranmahadevi, defined as kani over specific pieces of land. That this grant actually involved shares in the produce of that land was made clear for posterity only because the Vellalas refused to pay, and recorded their resolve in a separate inscription.[68]

Though this lack of clarity in terms so basic as those concerning land rights may seem odd to us, it makes sense in medieval Tamil terms, because all rights to land were mediated, in the last instance, through local landowning collectivities, for whom land, produce, labor, and water were conceived as a unified totality of resources. Given these facts of daily life, and given the assumed unity of religious, political, and commercial power, a great many people invested in and extracted from agricultural communities in Pandya Tirunelveli. Some simple examples of the sorts of transactions that are recorded inscriptionally will suggest the social dynamics of resource circulation and control by which individuals developed agriculture and pursued opportunity.

A chief might grant a temple the goods or cash he received regularly in return for services of patronage and protection from peasants in his ur; the temple worship, held in his name, would raise his stature locally. Or, instead, he might make the gift to the temple in the name of a king, perhaps at the king's insistence. In receiving the grant, temple servants could merely collect payments from the ur or from individual landowners; temple functionaries could sell the rights to collect those payments to a nearby sabha, in return for a cash payment or regular supplies of goods and services. If the chief had given the temple cash instead of a land grant, an enterprising intermediary—a Brahman from a local sabha, or a temple servant—might then contract with the temple for the required goods and services. Taking the money, the mediator could then buy rights to the produce from a given piece of land from a nearby ur or sabha. Whatever the type of payment he purchased thereby, the mediator would himself receive a lump sum, from which to meet his obligations to the temple and to garner some profit. Funding secure irrigation was always a good investment.

The importance of the sabha within this local exchange nexus stems from its apparently favored position as mediating agency for temple investments, and from its obvious related attractiveness as an object of pious patronage. By completing a number of deals over time—grants, loans, purchases, sales, and investments—a well-endowed sabha could build an extended local domain for its member families. Rajamangalam, doubly favored by excellent irrigation and royal patronage, carved out a little empire in Mullinadu under the Cholas and Pandyas. Nearby was stationed a large army and a widespread merchant guild, which brought protection, patronage, and commercial assets from far and wide into the hands of the sabha. Its temples received a great number of grants.[69] By such means, using their combined symbolic and material resources, Brahmans became under the Pandyas not only linchpins in the agrarian system as a whole, but powerful landowners in the communities where irrigated agriculture was practiced.

Had Sangam poets returned to their old haunts a thousand years after their day, they would not have been surprised to see the Tamil population clustered along routes of natural drainage in the watery lowlands. But much of the medieval Tamil world would have astounded them. Society had become much more complex. Tamil culture had changed. Farming communities controlled the water supply by forging alliances among dominant groups whose solidarity and superiority rested upon their cultural production of symbolic capital resources in religious ritual.[70] The honors created by temple worship

40

and by gifts to Brahmans composed a pool of resources whose control set the Vellala caste group above all other non-Brahmans, in relations of caste ranking that defined social strata nonexistent during Sangam times. The poets would have assumed that kings ruled the Pandya country from Madurai, but yet would have marveled at the temple ceremonies patronized by those kings and royal efforts to develop temple complexes and brahmadeyas. On these ceremonies, however, the power of Pandyan kings rested, for by ritual gift-giving the Pandyas cemented their authority in the irrigated communities that constituted the heart of the realm. In medieval centuries, peasant control of nature and family fortune thus rested above all on community order maintained by the shared participation of peasants and kings in religious networks, the strongest thread in the fabric of the medieval agrarian system.

· 2 ·

FARMING FRONTIERS

Migrations transformed human geography in peninsular India during two tumultuous centuries after 1300. The original migratory impetus appears to have thrust peasants and warriors out from medieval core agricultural zones—the Chera, Pandya, and Chola heartlands—during late medieval times. But migratory movements accelerated and expanded after 1300, when peninsular India became a southern frontier for farmers and warriors from the north, who had in turn been pushed out of their homelands during waves of southerly migration propelled by Turks from the Central Asian steppe, who established themselves in North India and triggered migratory conquests throughout the Indian subcontinent. A Turkic dynasty in Delhi sent an expedition south that reached Madurai in the 1300s and decapitated the regional political order in the Pandya country. Against this Muslim wave military men in the northern peninsula built a bastion at "The City of Victory," Vijayanagar, which became the capital of South India's largest indigenous empire in the fifteenth century. The capital of the Vijayanagar empire lay 700 miles north of the Tambraparni River, in the very center of the peninsula, and from it warriors and peasants moved south in search of land, adventure, and wealth under the banner of Vijayanagar emperors. Their movements and conquests set various Tamil groups into motion, in turn; their prowess subdued formerly nonagricultural people, who now dedicated themselves to farming and territorial control. As a result, on Vijayanagar's southernmost frontier peasants pushed their plows into land untilled during Pandyan times, in tracts north and south of the Tambraparni River. Warriors leading Vijayanagar forces set their power upon the Pandyan political domain. After two centuries of warrior and peasant effort, always in combination, a new regional order came into place in a region whose agricultural, social, and central place design had assumed the rudiments of the form we see today. The next chapter will consider that agrarian order. This one traces the work on the agricultural frontiers that underlay that early modern domain, at whose center lay the coercive power of militant kings.

WARRIORS AND PEASANTS

What caused it remains unclear, but a noticeable change in the agrarian system began during the last century or so of Pandyan rule, after the

expulsion of the imperial Cholas in 1190. The state in southern Pandyamandalam became increasingly centered upon the town of Tirunelveli, and on its major temple, the Nellaiyappa Koil. Though his
temple seems to date from the seventh century,[1] Nellaiyappa, like
Sudikkodutta Nachiyar, thrived under the latest and greatest Pandyan
kings. Tirunelveli became the southern Pandyan capital and the Nellaiyappa temple their ceremonial centerpiece in the south. Here they
recorded their conquests and announced their new brahmadeyas.[2]
Here they and their followers patronized god, so that four of every
five inscriptions in the temple date from the thirteenth and fourteenth
centuries.[3] The rise of Nellaiyappa parallels an apparent developmental surge in irrigated agriculture in the central Tambraparni valley,
touched on above, which continued under the Nayakas. Two of the
four dams that water the land around Tirunelveli were built after
1400, and a later grant mentions "Sundara Pandya's new channel,"
almost certainly the right-bank channel from the Marudur Anicut
(Map 18).[4] After 1200, investments in building the regional state were
concentrated in the central river valley, accelerating growth in irrigated
agriculture at the same time.

The rise of Tirunelveli town amid expanding irrigation occurred as
growing networks of social interaction in the region began to create
interlocal bonds among village peasant elites. Upon Nellaiyappa Koil
focused a transactional web that covered much of the southern Pandya
country. In the years between 1190 and 1320, fully half of all inscriptionally recorded arrangements for the regular transfer of supplies for
temple ceremonies tied Nellaiyappa to localities outside his own nadu,
Kilvembanadu.[5] Further indication that the temple had attained regional importance by the mid-fifteenth century is a meeting of the
Rajamangalam sabha on temple grounds, in 1477, to arrange funding
for a temple ceremony.[6] More direct evidence of interlocal elite connections during the 1300s comes from the fact that Vellalas "from
eighteen nadus" gathered to endow construction of the Visvanathisvaran Temple in Tenkasi; and "the Vellalas of the river valley" met
to expel *vellai nadans* from Tambraparni villages, a resolution discussed in more detail below.[7] Such signs of regional political integration perhaps reflect expanding networks of trade and marriage alliance,
which seem by the end of the thirteenth century to have made the
Pandyan heartland a markedly more integrated domain, focused upon
one central place.

Interlocal alliances were probably in part a response by the landed
elite to external shocks, themselves produced by expanding social
networks in South India as a whole, shocks that by the early 1300s
broke the Pandyan authority system completely apart. Chola conquest

had left its lasting legacy in a model of empire that emphasized provincial cities, huge royal temples, and garrison armies.[8] By 1300, migrant settlers had begun to arrive in droves, and their disruptive influence echoes in the resolution against the vellai nadan. More dramatic disruptions then came in quick succession. Chera armies conquered much of the Pandya country in 1310, during a protracted war of Pandyan succession; and, in 1333, a Turkic army under Malik Kafur ravaged Madurai. Though never in command of the countryside, the Sultanate of Madurai marked the end of Pandyan sovereignty over Pandyamandalam as a whole.[9] Henceforth the Pandyan elite could muster at best subregional control; and Pandyans retained kingship in Madurai only as a symbol in the hands of more powerful men. Like the Mughal emperor in Delhi, centuries later, under British East India Company protection, Pandyas at Madurai for two centuries after 1333 wielded symbols without the substance of power. Miniature Pandya dynasties sprang up in parts of the realm, the most successful at Tenkasi, where Tenkasi Pandyas patronized Visvanathisvaran and issued inscriptions into the 1500s.[10]

Soon after the founding of the Madurai Sultanate, in 1370, the Vijayanagar empire, South India's political response to expanding Muslim power from North India, exerted its might far south of its capital in the central peninsula, when Kumara Kampanna defeated the Madurai sultan, and Madurai became the southernmost outpost of the largest of all South Indian empires. But the Pandya country remained always under Vijayanagar a distant frontier, contested and remote. No emperor, no imperial general toured south of Madurai before the Madurai Nayakas established their effective independence from the empire in the mid-sixteenth century.[11] Though obscure and powerless Pandyas sat on the throne, to them nonetheless came immigrant chiefs from the north, riding under the banner of Vijayanagar—men like Ettappa Nayaka, whom we shall meet shortly—who came to receive Pandya legitimacy on their arrival in the south. Tirunelveli peasants lived under no single ruling authority during the Vijayanagar period. Immigrant Telugu and Marava bands carved out domains in the mixed and dry zones, outside core Pandya territory. Old Pandya elites struggled to control the wet zone, constantly confronting Chera armies from the south and west.[12]

Two centuries of rampant military competition after 1330 increased the regional power of specialized military men, who in turn forced change in the political pattern. Advances in military technology, starting with the later Cholas, must have played a part in the process. Cavalry now became critical in war. Horses, which do not breed well in the Tamil lowlands, had been imported by sea during later Chola times, and Malik Kafur's booty at Madurai included large numbers of horses and elephants.[13] After 1300, fort building and siege warfare set the tone of all major combat; by the 1500s, iron cannon became standard hardware.[14] The impact of new fighting technology deserves research in its own right. Yet even at a glance it seems that the military arts advanced significantly during the Vijayanagar centuries. Loose, temporary military alliances, characteristic of Pandyan warfare, became inadequate as the means of destruction became more sophisticated.[15] The cost of protection for nonmilitary folk increased, so that by the 1500s it was necessary and routine for old Pandyan elites to live protected by warriors (called *nayaka*), attached to Vijayanagar by their competitors, or both.

To establish their authority, warriors patronized temples and the Vellala-Brahman elite. Inscriptions reveal a related rise in warrior initiative in temple management after 1400, and a parallel decrease in brahmadeya transactions etched into temple walls.[16] It seems, then, that the relative importance in temple affairs of nonlocal, nonlanded elites rose dramatically under Vijayanagar.[17] Many inscriptions preserve, for example, appointments to temple office made by warriors, who may well have acted as arbiters in disputes over succession among temple servants.[18] Epigraphy indicates that chiefs dabbled in the appointment of lowly servants and dancing girls, but that their main efforts concerned key temple supervisory personnel, accountants and managers (*sthanikar*), who themselves seem to have become more influential in managing some of the larger temples.[19]

Military adventurers, especially nayakas riding under the Vijayanagar banner, established themselves over time as influential people in the agrarian domain of the Pandyan elite. They were protectors, patrons, and arbiters, whose power rested first on their military might, and—more essential in the long run—on their resourcefulness in their transactions with existing dominant elites in temples and local assemblies. One inscription, for instance, shows several nayakas at work assigning lands—apparently to settle a dispute—in several brahmadeyas in the river valley.[20] Two examples from the Pandyan heartland, Mullinadu, indicate the intimate role of this new elite corps in local affairs, and the diversity of that elite in their competitive context. In 1546, an agent of the Vijayanagar emperor appointed one man to write the accounts, arrange for the recitation of hymns, and supply garlands in a temple attached to Rajamangalam. Between 1506 and 1514, a Chera chief named Mutachai Kandan Keralan rebuilt the nearby temple at Melaseval and its brahmadeya, both ravaged by war. The Keralan then financed temple ceremonies, and appointed temple servants.[21]

As Vijayanagar power expanded and Pandyan power diminished, the goddess of Srivilliputtur, Andal, languished and her priests felt her suffering. They presented a petition, written in the words of the goddess herself, to Saluva Narasimha, a general of the emperor, crying out for his patronage. In this petition, the legend of Andal's marriage to the god became critical for temple finance; and it became prominent for the first time in temple inscriptions. For the Pandyan kings it had apparently sufficed that Andal be a sacred figure in Srivilliputtur, the most important town between Madurai and the Tambraparni on the Tenkasi road. But for a Vijayanagar general, her local status would have seemed inconsequential, so that her divine marriage would have been a major inducement for his patronage. This strategy apparently worked. Narasimha gave lavishly to support the temple, so that the wife of god could receive her due, so that the people could worship her joyfully and seek her beneficence, and so that the general's name would be glorified as the land prospered. He put the goddess "above all want and in positive affluence."[22] The stature of the general and of the goddess were raised at one stroke.

Warriors did not come alone into the Tirunelveli region. Massive peasant immigration changed the composition of the regional population, brought new techniques and productive powers to bear on agriculture, and established new domains for competition over territorial control. The centuries after the Pandya demise were not the first in which migration affected this region. Tamil Brahmans, at the very least, had been coming to settle here for many centuries; and an inward flow from west of the Ghats probably continued during the whole Pandya period. Nor did immigration stop in the 1500s. People kept coming from the region that was called Cheramandalam during medieval times, which became the native state of Travancore during the nineteenth century, and which provided countless Malayalam-speaking Tiruneveli immigrants over the centuries. The 1700s and 1800s brought new sorts of immigrants, prominently Muslims from the northern Tamil country, who settled in towns along the Tambraparni as weavers and traders.[23] But the centuries between 1300 and 1600 seem from all evidence to have been characterized more than any other period by mass migration and settlement. The three largest migrant peasant groups were Shanars, Maravas, and a group of Telugu-speaking jatis known in the far south as Vadugas (*vadugar* = northerner).

Shanars

Tending the palmyra palm is the ancient occupational specialty of the Shanars. A sturdy, unprepossessing palm, the palmyra provides fruit, drink, timber, leaves, and material for rope, baskets, mats, and myriad other uses. Its leaves are the traditional writing surface for Tamil manuscripts. This multipurpose tree thrives where most do not. Its huge ball of roots enable it to stand tall in shifting sand and to drink meager moisture from below; its scrawny foliage high atop its tall trunk rustles defiantly in the worst droughts. After planting, it takes about fifteen years for the tree to produce fruit and juice, the basis for country sugar, hence wine and spirits. A tree remains productive for up to fifty years, with virtually no tending except to harvest its products; this tending, however, means arduous climbing and hard labor high aloft. The palmyra thrives in sandy soils, where moisture lies at root level, and where, indeed, it has few competitors. Shanar settlements have thus over the centuries tended to concentrate in sandy tracts, and Shanar populations have, it appears, moved from established milieus of productive palmyra cultivation toward open ground in which to plant more trees. Because planting and cultivating the palmyra is an unusually extensive agricultural activity, Shanars move about more than most groups in the course of their work, over wide stretches of land, setting up thatched encampments as they go. Migration is thus inherent in Shanar work, and so is trade. It has been said that a deprived Shanar settlement could subsist entirely on the fruits of the palm; yet Shanars are also famed for their travels far and wide to exchange palmyra products.[24] As a matter of longstanding caste custom, therefore, Shanars are a peculiarly mobile cultivating jati, and their mobility has encouraged occupational diversification in response to new agricultural and commercial opportunities.

A missionary who worked among Christian Shanars in the nineteenth century, Robert Caldwell, speculated that they had come to the region in two migratory waves: one, of superior Shanars called Nadars, during the reign of the Pandyan kings; and a second, larger and later movement of low-status, tree-climbing Shanars, from southern Kerala, through what is now the Kanya Kumari District of Tamil Nadu. More recently, Robert Hardgrave, who studied modern Shanar caste politics, was unable to substantiate either of these waves and concluded, contrary to Caldwell, that the Shanars were indigenous to Tirunelveli.[25] Caldwell was undoubtedly closer to the truth. Though the legend of a first Nadar migration remains unsubstantiated, there is little doubt that the Shanars came from the south, as part of an ancient interaction between Tamil- and Malayalam-speaking people at the tip of the peninsula, and that their migration increased markedly after 1300.

In the fourteenth century appears the first inscriptional reference I have yet found concerning the Shanars, at a time when Chera military forces pushed into the collapsing Pandyan domain.[26] There is, moreover, an inscription from Kallidaikurichi, near Ambasamudram in the upper Tambraparni valley, that refers to a series of resolutions by "the Vellalas of the river valley"; the first resolution was dated 1379, wherein assembled Vellalas banned people they called vellai nadans from employment in Vellala villages, from free access to all Tamil villages, and from marriage to Tamil women. The inscription specifies that these nadans had previously been engaged as coolies, accountants, agents, and officials, so they were clearly an internally differentiated group. Their expulsion from Tamil villages and exclusion from marriage to Tamil women strongly suggest their non-Tamil origins.[27] Shanar immigration, moreover, continued into the nineteenth century, when Tinnevelly District officials noted Shanar arrivals from southern Travancore.[28] Seasonal migration to plant trees may well have developed into permanent settlement as palmyra palms matured to productivity. A comparison of the 1823 and 1881 census returns for southern Tirunelveli shows that Shanars increased from 3 to 20 percent of the population, which must indicate some migratory settlement during the intervening half-century.[29]

Shanars settled along two main routes. One, running north-northeast, took them into southern and southeastern Tirunelveli, and then along the sandy coast up into Ramanathapuram.[30] Another route pointed north, into the Tambraparni valley, and from there into the northern mixed and dry zones, where they settled in compact local concentrations. Six towns in northern Tirunelveli and adjacent terrain—today in Madurai and Ramanathapuram districts—became renowned as centers of Shanar commercial activity.[31] Though it is difficult to date the rise of these market towns, inscriptions from 1704 and 1710, recording the establishment of a brahmadeya and an agreement among merchants to support a festival in Sivakasi, suggest that the towns had achieved the status of market centers by at the latest the late seventeenth century.[32] By the early nineteenth century, two Tirunelveli towns, Sivakasi and Virudhunagar, were booming centers of Shanar commercial wealth. Shanars may well have continued to move north during the nineteenth century, as Hardgrave speculates, but the census figures suggest that they did so at a slower rate than from Travancore into the southern "palmyra forest."[33]

Thus the Shanars came to occupy three very different social milieus within which to seek their livelihood. In the sandy south, they themselves became the bulk of the population. Their settlements centered on the palmyra and on garden crops and hardy millets. They became skilled at digging wells into the high water table. They moved far from their villages to trade in country sugar and dried sea fish acquired from coastal villages. When they settled near the Tambraparni, however, or around tank-irrigated villages such as Vijayanarayanam and Sattankulam, they planted their trees where Brahmans and Vellalas were already established as locally dominant, so they had to pay these higher castes in goods, services, and subservience for access to land. In the mixed zone, both north and south of the Tambraparni, they found a more varied set of opportunities, including palmyra cultivation, gardens, and trade. One group of Shanars, near Kalakkad in the south, even became a minor military force, no doubt because, in the mixed zone, they were not the only new arrivals to come in search of land.[34]

Maravas

Renowned from Sangam times as fierce hunters, highway robbers, and soldiers, the Maravas hail from Ramanathapuram, just northeast of Tirunelveli. Slowly they converted to settled agriculturists over the centuries, but they never lost their attachment to martial skills and virtues; and, like the Kallars, even today they retain a caste tradition that stresses physical strength, power, rank, and honor. Most Maravas remained at least partly soldiers until the nineteenth century, and many managed to make a living until even more recently by selling protection (*kaval*) in localities throughout Tirunelveli. About the eighteenth century, a Marava historian has said, "The Maravas . . . used to carry a long stick and knife called a Pitchwa. This stick could be used to beat opponents and the Pitchwa fixed at the top of the stick could be used as a spear. These were the inseparable companions of the Maravas. When they heard the trumpet sound they would procede directly to their leaders' place from wherever they were. Those working in the fields would directly rush to the battlefields."[35]

Led by their chiefs, Maravas migrated into Tirunelveli with increasing regularity after 1300, and set up compact agro-military domains, fighting it out all the way. Their oral histories, recorded in the Mackenzie Manuscripts, retain the memory of their achievements. Zamindari estate records—many chiefs became zamindars in 1801—provide additional details. The ancestors of Marudappadevar, for example, abandoned their home "on account of troubles with the Muslims," and, on the way southwest, the chief and his followers "destroyed the Kallars of Visinganadu and the Kurumbars of Neccur, Kurumurai, and Tadagai," which latter places formed the core of a Marava domain, centered on the fort at Uttumalai.[36] Most such stories, of course, provide no dates. Yet they all revolve around military competition, battles with Muslims, Kallars, and Kurumbars (hunters); and all cite authoritative grants of territory from obscure later Pandyan kings. A few Marava chiefdoms may have been established before 1300, but those for which dates can be established arose afterward, such as those at Chokkampatti, Uttumalai, and Tirukkurungudi—all in the fifteenth century.[37]

The Maravas settled in concentrations near the Ghats, in the red-soiled northern mixed zone, especially between Rajapalayam and the Chittar River, an area with unique assets for them. The hills provided a fortress for retreat when rushing armies threatened defeat in the plains. There were pockets of irrigated land that could become sources of revenue for military protectors; there were also stretches of uncultivated land usable with tank and well irrigation, as well as for dry cultivation. Marava migrants thus skirted older areas of agrarian settlement, such as the Tenkasi vicinity, and spread, in time, quite evenly over the northern mixed zone, where they had become the subregionally dominant caste group by the sixteenth century.

But they also moved south and east from this primary zone of concentration to become specialists in the sale of protection both locally and subregionally. As military adventurers, Maravas were everywhere competitors for strictly local power in the centuries before 1801; they had most success in the southwest, where Arapangu Maravas established a protectorate over the great Vaishnava temple and sectarian center (*matam*) at Nanguneri.[38] The thoroughness with which Maravas in general dispersed throughout the region is attested by the census of 1823, which shows virtually no village outside the Vaduga-dominated tract without some resident Maravas.

The Maravas' position in the agrarian political economy differed according to location. Where they were thinly settled in areas of low productivity, they were poor agricultural servants selling protection for a fee. Where they could muster the power to protect something really big, as they did in Nanguneri, they became rich. But only two major Marava chiefs—Urkad and Singampatti—gained control of much good, irrigated land; these two became wealthy chiefs in a predominantly non-Marava area at the extreme western end of the Tambraparni valley. The bulk of the Marava population settled in a relatively poor agricultural tract of red soil and rain-fed tank irrigation in the northern mixed zone, where they concentrated on farming and on holding onto their dominance over nearly a quarter of the Tirunelveli region.

Vadugas

Rampant military competition in the northern peninsula pushed migrants, including Kannada- and Telugu-speakers, southward after

1300. After Kumara Kampanna's campaigns to extend the Vijayanagar empire's power in the far southern peninsula (he reached Madurai in the 1360s), the Tamil country presented a land of opportunity for adventurers from the north, who became, as we will see in the next chapter, a new force in the agrarian system. Though the impetus and leadership for migrant bands came from military men, migratory groups were diverse, and included merchants, farmers, priests, artisans, accountants, and administrators, the core of complete Telugu colonies in the Tamil country.[39] By the early 1400s this migrant wave reached Tirunelveli.

Ettappa Nayaka exemplifies the migrants. He received a title at the Vijayanagar court before departing his ancestral home near Chandragiri, which he left in 1423, according to his official historian, owing to "the disturbed state of the country." The band he led southward was as big as a good-sized town of the day, nearly fourteen hundred people: five kinsmen, two other nayakas, a village accountant, sixty-four bowmen, three hundred foot soldiers, and one thousand miscellaneous retainers. They reached Madurai in the same year. Assigned a territory by the Pandya king, Ettappa and his people subdued "refractory Kallars," carved out a base for themselves southeast of Madurai, and expanded from there over the next century and a half, always combining service to the Pandya king with conquest of local chiefs. Finally, in 1567, Ettappa's descendants moved their capital to the fortress they built at Ettaiyapuram in the Tirunelveli black soil tract, where like other Telugu chiefs of the day, Ettappa's heir seems to have benefited from, and perhaps partaken in, Visvanatha Nayaka's victorious assertion of Vijayanagar power in the Tirunelveli region in the later sixteenth century.[40]

Telugus concentrated almost exclusively in the black-soil tract, though some spread westward to settle closer to the hills. Telugus throughout the Tamil country display in their settlement patterns a distinct preference for black "cotton soil," perhaps, as Burton Stein has suggested, because they brought with them secrets previously unknown to Tamils for making it productive.[41] This is a real possibility, for the skill of Telugu farmers in making the most of the dry zone struck awe into many a British observer. Nonetheless, the distribution of the population on the arrival of Telugu migrant bands also encouraged this choice. Maravas had control of the only other part of the region relatively uninhabited in 1300. Unlike both the Maravas and the Shanars, once cohesive Telugu colonies had been established amidst vast expanses of land for future generations, there was little incentive for Telugus to move to other areas. Nine out of ten Vaduga cultivating caste members lived, in 1881, in the four northern taluks of Tirunelveli.

Though there was some greater dispersion of Telugu merchants—for example, Balijas—the only Telugu-speakers who shunned the dry zone were Brahmans, who settled in Tirunelveli in the same fashion as other immigrant Brahmans—Madvas, Gujeratis, Marathis, and Kannada-speakers—all favorite administrative agents in the expanding Vijayanagar imperial domain.[42] An oral account recorded in 1801 indicates that new immigrant warrior chiefs in Tirunelveli made special efforts to bring Brahmans from the northern peninsula into their new frontier settlements: "a great number of Brahmans of the different Naudus and Sects came from beyond the Godavari River and from the Eastern Provinces on the encouragement of the chiefs to civilize and populate their districts."[43] Non-Tamil Brahmans, in fact, formed nearly one-quarter of the total recorded Brahman population in Tirunelveli in 1823, the only year for which such data exists, and half of all Telugu Brahmans lived not in the black-soil tract but along the Tambraparni River.[44]

AGRICULTURE

Warriors and peasants built the basis of a regional geography of agriculture that would fill out during the centuries after 1500. Innovations were begun during the later Pandya centuries, when the central river valley surged ahead as the major area of irrigation development, taking the lead from the up-river nadus that surpassed all others in growth during earlier Pandya and Chola times. Growth in the central valley was clearly connected to the rising importance of Tirunelveli town, which became a regional headquarters under the last great Pandyas and, as we shall see, increased in political centrality thereafter. The Tambraparni runs deepest in what is still a very shallow valley near the western upswing of its mid-course northern curve. Here it is also fed by two considerable tributaries, the Chittar and Pachaiyar (Map 6). During the centuries after 1200, men of means patronized the construction of four permanent stone dams some distance apart in the riverbed, from Ariyanayakipuram in the west to Marudur just to the east of the mid-course bend in the river (Nos. 14 and 17 on Map 18). These stone anicuts must have required growing skills in design, handling of materials, and labor organization; in addition, from the sides of these post-medieval dams stretched long, winding channels, trained along a nearly flat valley to bring water to a series of tanks and thus to paddy fields plowed a great distance from the river itself. When complete, this network of dams, channels, tanks and fields defined a wide strip of irrigation that commanded nearly the full width of the valley, at mid-river about four miles across.

This post-medieval irrigation system was not built at one stroke, but rather in pieces, over many years; its major works were not guided by central planners or by self-conscious innovators. The system represents rather the slowly accumulating ability to command massive labor and capital to support large-scale building projects, and slowly improving engineering skills, brought together, it appears, under warrior patronage first under late Pandyas, then under Vijayanagar military men. An old tank, for example, could be fed with water from a new channel or dam to make its irrigation more secure and long-lived. What became an extensive, integrated system of water control was built one piece at a time by a host of individual patrons. This process of cumulative, interdependent building underlay the growth of irrigation, indeed, through the nineteenth century, when the Srivaikuntam Anicut, discussed in Chapter Five, was built to bolster water control in the eastern Tambraparni valley.

By the sixteenth century, when the Nayaka kings discussed in the next chapter established their southern headquarters at Tirunelveli town, the Tambraparni valley provided a continuous irrigation landscape stretching from mountains to sea, a ribbon of green whose development had, by the 1500s, continued for two thousand years. During Sangam times the core zone of irrigation development had been deltaic nadus, which depended on inundation. Medieval irrigation builders concentrated their work in the western, up-river nadus, the heart of the southern Pandyamandalam. Post-medieval warrior patronage concentrated instead in the mid-river valley, around the strategic capital city, at the intersection of the major north-south and east-west transport routes.[45]

Later Pandya and post-Pandya efforts to control drainage waters extended outward from the valley as well, north and south along the base of the Ghats, and eastward from the Ghats into the plains. The expansion of irrigation brought irrigators into less and less promising natural drainage areas. Villagers had built tanks in places poorly endowed with plains drainage during Pandya centuries. Etti Sattan, as we have seen, led one such locality. During post-Pandya centuries, however, countless tanks—in essence long, curved walls of earth and stone, built like outstretched arms to hold back water from seasonal rivulets—were built throughout the plains to capture the rain. In the best seasons they could support a good paddy crop; in the worst no crop at all; and in an average year, some crop, either of paddy or millet. Even in dry times tanks at the very least accelerated ground-water recharge, so they benefited wells dug below the tank wall. Tank building in post-Pandya centuries produced a region of little man-made lakes, each lake with its own local history and productive capacity; by the nineteenth century tanks in all shapes and sizes numbered about 3,000 and occupied every conceivable spot in the region.[46]

Irrigation, and the Tamil term nanjai, had acquired by 1500 a range of practical meanings in agriculture, because farmers applied skill in water control to various milieus, with distinct results in each. Where drainage was abundant, farming could concentrate on efforts to control more and more water to grow crops of all kinds. Where seasonal spates were short-lived and meager, farmers had to secure themselves against the possibility that water in the tank would not suffice to bring a water-intensive crop like paddy to maturity. This required the adaptation of many crops to cultivation under tank irrigation, and a practice developed called *nanjai-mel-punjai* ("dry crops on wet land") which became known in Anglo-Indian parlance in the nineteenth century as "nunjah-mel-punjah." Well-digging also became increasingly important in the mix of agricultural technologies as farmers pushed into the agricultural frontier after 1300. Wells must have been used in Pandya times, but are scarcely mentioned in inscriptions; their importance surely increased as farmers plowed more and more often land poorly endowed with drainage.

Extensive use of wells in agriculture must have entered the agricultural scene with migrants who came into the region during the centuries after 1300. Migrant caste groups most closely identified with well technology in the nineteenth century—Shanars and Vadugas—concentrated their activities in areas of poor drainage where wells remain to this day of greatest productive importance. These new farmers created a new style of intensive agriculture. Irrigation by wells is even today in the vernacular not normally put into the Tamil land-use category of nanjai, because wells, until the introduction of electric and petrol pumpsets after 1950, did not support fields of the characteristic nanjai crop, paddy. Lifting water by hand or with bulls strapped to a lift apparatus is so costly that agricultural wells were during our millennium used primarily to water the most valuable specialty crops—called "garden crops"—and to save field crops threatened by lack of moisture at the end of the growing season as the tank went dry. Unlike tanks and dams, which had to be built and operated by coordinated efforts among large numbers of people, wells could be dug and worked by a small group, and they have thus long tended to be assets owned by families or family partnerships. Wells provided drinking, bathing, and cleaning water outside localities endowed with copious natural drainage. Thus both for domestic and agricultural purposes, well digging was critical for farming families during post-Pandya agricultural expansion. On the frontier, farmers used wells, tanks, and dry crops to sustain new types of agricultural communities.[47]

To produce a livelihood on the frontiers of farming, villagers adapted and combined crops to the particular qualities of their agricultural settings. As generations carved and dug the earth to increase water supplies for people, animals, and crops, peasants also worked with genetic materials that could transform sunshine, moisture, and nutrients into food, clothing, and other human necessities. Communities in distinct agricultural settings became characterized over time by their particular blend of crops.

Soils, by their natural nutrients and water retention properties, perceptibly shaped cropping options. Map 6 simplifies the pattern of soil types and distributions, but highlights major features. The red soils that predominate in the west encourage runoff, and, when sandy, percolation as well, so they generate a relatively high and accessible water table and facilitate surface storage. When full of clay, however, as is often the case, especially between the Chittar and Vaippar basins, red soils bake like brick, so they make poor ground for field crops whenever surface moisture is low. Red soils tend more toward loam in the far north, nutrient-rich and moisture-retentive. In the north, red shades eastward into black loam, richest in nutrients and most retentive, able to retain every drop of moisture within easy access of plant roots. A natural buffer against famine, black loams discourage both runoff and percolation; they can support a crop to maturity even in drought, but they deprive the water table and discourage surface storage. In the northern black soil areas, the water table thus tends to be deep, so that wells are expensive and tanks rare. At the opposite extreme, in the southeast, the land is almost all sand, very poor in nutrients, and prone to rapid percolation and evapo-transpiration. These sandy soils, very weak ground indeed for field crops without irrigation, nonetheless produce a high water table, so that digging a well can mean here burrowing down a few feet in the sand; natural springs even bubble to the surface in a few spots.[48]

We cannot see the regional cropping pattern statistically until rather late in the nineteenth century,[49] but that pattern emerged slowly over the preceding millennium as communities developed their own specialized techniques in diverse natural settings. As does irrigation, crops by their distribution in the nineteenth century reveal a long process of experimentation and learning, during a peasantry's productive relation to their land. Farmers adopted genetic and water-control technologies that worked best in their specific natural settings. They thus produced in the natural mosaic that is the Tirunelveli region a patchwork of agrarian milieus. Technologically distinct areas became distinct in their diets, productive routines, agricultural techniques, and potentials for commercial development. With the exception of cotton, and perhaps chillies, both heavily affected by nineteenth-century commercialization (Chapter Five), crop distributions depicted in Map 7 appear to represent a pattern characteristic of the region by the sixteenth century. Under the Pandyas, as the preceding chapter indicates, the analogous map would have looked very much simpler; all the details of Map 7 did not come into existence until the 1800s.

As a general rule, farmers planted paddy wherever and whenever they had sufficient access to drainage water. Its greater caloric productivity per acre and high symbolic value as a dietary staple gave rice a paramount place in peasant productive decision making. Outside the Tambraparni valley and the Tenkasi vicinity, however, more than one paddy crop per year was extremely rare, and in many years, tanks on the plains fed by rain could not support a paddy crop to maturity. If the monsoon seemed not to be promising by planting time, applying the strategy of nanjai-mel-punjai, farmers would plant high-quality dry crops, usually *ragi* or *cholam*, under tank irrigation. If the season looked good, they could plant rice, so that where there were rain-fed tanks it became common for rice and millets to be planted alternately on the same field. Where drainage from the hills provided secure water supplies, rice prevailed. Nowhere could it prevail to the extent possible in the Tambraparni valley and upper Chittar basin, an unbroken stretch of actual or potential nanjai cultivation, the wet zone.[50]

Two-thirds of all paddy grown in nineteenth-century Tirunelveli grew in the wet zone, and almost all double-cropped paddy ripened in its fields. Nowhere but here did work in paddy fields and on irrigation so dominate daily life, and nowhere else did most of the population eat rice. Throughout the region, when a paddy crop could be raised it would be sown under the first showers of the northeast monsoon, and harvested three to four months later. This long season, from October to April, called *pisanam*, produced the bulk of the paddy grown in any agricultural year. When a second crop could be grown, it was planted as southwest monsoon rains ran down from the hills in June, and harvested in time to plant a pisanam crop. This second (*kar*) paddy crop depended almost wholly on Ghat drainage, so it was much smaller in size and scope, and highly prized. When harvesting

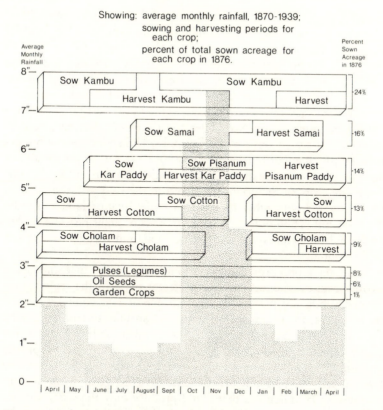

Showing: average monthly rainfall, 1870-1939;
sowing and harvesting periods for
each crop;
percent of total sown acreage for
each crop in 1876.

Figure 3 Tirunelveli Seasons and Crops, 1876

SOURCES: *Statistical Atlas of Madras Presidency for Fasli 1350 (1940/1)*, Madras,
1941; A. J. Stuart, A *Manual of the Tinnevelly District*, Madras, 1876, pp.
168-77.

and sowing seasons for these two crops overlapped, as they often did
in the wet zone, irrigation work and tending to paddy cultivation went
on virtually year-round, with only a brief slack time at the height of
the summer, in May (Figure 3).

Where paddy could not thrive, communities based their diets on
millets, and specific varieties became dominant according to soil and
moisture. Millets covered three-quarters of all land planted to foodgrains in the late nineteenth century—three times as much land as
paddy. In the region as a whole, *samai* and *kambu* were the most
popular millets, together accounting for 70 percent of all millet
acreage. But each dominated a distinct terrain. Kambu, the richer of

the two, drains the soils of nutrients, and flourished in the red- and black-loam area of the north. Kambu became so preferred as food for black-soil farmers that they grew cholam mostly for fodder, to strengthen the bulls that plowed deep the heavy earth. Kambu would normally be rotated with pulses, or planted on land left fallow for one year, unless the fields could be given heavy doses of manure, a practice that distinguished the most productive land of the best farmers. Sown during the monsoon, in November and December, kambu would be ready to harvest in three to four months. Unlike kambu, samai demands little of either nutrients or moisture and can be grown almost anywhere in the region at almost any time of the year. It thus became a favorite crop on the poorest red soils in the west and south, often intercultivated with other millets as a buffer against famine, should the rains fail. Though less popular, another drought-resistant millet, *varagu*, also produces well in wretched soil, and was grown in parts of the region.[51]

Nongrain crops provided important parts of the diet and many useful products. Concentrated in different parts of the region, they defined subtle distinctions in local cuisine and in commodities for trade. Pulses, for example, as legumes, contribute to soil fertility by their nitrogen-fixing action, and to human nutrition by their rich vegetable protein, calcium, and phosphorous. They can thrive on the poorest soil, and so were widely planted, and became prized on dry land adjacent to paddy fields. But they attained greatest dietary importance in communities that could produce only the worst quality millets, in the sandy south, where their cultivation became most widespread. Similarly, oil seeds were grown all over the region to provide cooking oil, soap, paint, varnish, and the stuff for oil seed cakes, used for fodder and manure. The two most widely grown oil seeds, prior to the spread of peanut planting in the twentieth century, were sesame and castor, both of which produced best in heavy red soil, and so became a specialty for peasants in northwest, where most oil was pressed for sale. By contrast, the kambu-eating black-soil farmers of the northeast specialized in coriander cultivation, which gave their staple diet a distinctive flavor.

Garden crops provided flavor, nutrition, stimulation, and profit, and their heavy demands for water and care made them available in greatest profusion, of course, in the wet zone. But as objects of well irrigation, they became specialties for enterprising peasants elsewhere. After the introduction of chillies in the sixteenth century, the Tamil cuisine began to attain its modern mix of spices. The concentration of chilli cultivation in the northeast suggests that the daily fare of black-soil farmers who cooked with coriander and ate kambu must have been heavily spiced with chillies. Plantain and tobacco gardening was concentrated, similarly, in the far northwest and in the southeast, respectively. The high water table in the southeast made this a place where wells and garden crops became critical assets in community life, for subsistence and for trade. In the sandiest and driest part of the region, the southeast, palmyra palms assumed special importance as well. Indeed, they became so numerous, so central to the survival of communities around shifting dunes, called *teri*, that official recorders called this the land of "the palmyra forest." It was, of course, a man-made forest, the product of long labor and a unique niche for peasant life.

The region's major commercial crop, cotton, covered up to 15 percent of all cultivated land by the late nineteenth century, a prominence that resulted from commercial trends after 1800. Long before then, however, cotton provided a basis for local and regional trade in cloth. A new, irrigable variety from Cambodia was introduced after 1900, but native cotton here had been bred to withstand severe drought. Short in staple, two varieties prevailed: one, probably older in this region, was planted on sandy soil; the other, which most likely came into Tirunelveli with migrant farmers after 1300, preferred heavy black loam. Though of about equal importance before 1800, the latter strain attained superior commercial status under British rule, and its cultivation boomed after 1840, in the land of what became called "black cotton soil," which grew three-quarters of all Tirunelveli cotton by the late nineteenth century.

Regional Design

During three centuries after 1300, generations laid down the region's modern pattern of central places, crops, and human settlement. Between the fall of the Madurai Pandyas to Malik Kafur in the early 1300s and the rise of Madurai Nayaka kings in the late 1500s, rampant military competition produced political chaos in Tirunelveli. No central authority provided a focal point for regional order, though symbolically Madurai and Pandya rulers remained in place and though Vijayanagar projected its imperial aura into the far south in the persons of its captains. By far the most important creative activity during this period was the building of diverse agricultural communities and the building of subregional agrarian domains around important towns in developing agricultural zones. The pattern produced in this period continues to develop today.

The medieval configuration of nadus vanished, replaced by a set of subregions defined as hinterlands of towns along routes of transportation and communication. Centers for worship, trade, defense, craftsmanship, and elite domesticity, major towns grew along major routes; Tirunelveli was the most centrally located and fully endowed, its population supported by expanding networks of dams, channels, and paddy fields. Smaller towns developed that would define subregions for state authority under the Nayakas and thereafter; in the nineteenth century, these towns became administrative headquarters for Tinnevelly District taluks (Map 5).

Sangam poets remind us that two productive milieus, neither devoted to field crop cultivation, were critical in regional life. To the west, Ghat mountain people brought wood, spices, and fruits to enrich life in the plains, and plains people looked to the hills for routes of passage to the humid tropics of modern-day Kerala, the region's most important overland trading partner throughout this millennium. To the east, the coastline supported port towns bustling with traders and coastal folk who harvested the sea, fishing in their catamarans (*kattumaram*) and diving for pearls. Life on the coast and in the hills developed as on thresholds between worlds, and depended for prosperity on trade with the plains.

Bracketed east and west by mountains and the sea, the plains became, as we have seen, a mosaic of local milieus along an agricultural continuum. Few if any viable communities could be entirely wet or dry, yet we can visualize a schematic continuum from the wettest to the driest types of communities that would, indeed, seem quite sensible to village residents themselves.[52] At one extreme, some communities commanded sufficient drainage to devote most of their land to rice, nourished by irrigation. On the other extreme, some depended entirely on rain to water their staple grains, millets. Dry crops were necessary and grown everywhere, however, and everywhere, too, some form of water control supplemented rainfall in agriculture.

Coherent agricultural zones developed because contiguous communities along the wet-dry continuum spread over stretches of land that became characterized by one village style of agricultural production. By the seventeenth century, when the region had attained its full human settlement pattern (discussed more fully below), the political economy and population centered on the wet zone, which curved from west to east from the Shencottai Gap down the Tambraparni valley (Map 8), sharply demarcated from the rest of the region in its agricultural and social constitution. North and south of this continuous nanjai domain, wet cultivation could nowhere expand for any distance. Pockets of irrigation at the base of the Ghats, and from tanks on the plain, were everywhere surrounded by tracts of millet and other dry crops. Though tanks dotted the entire region, they were much more likely to nourish paddy crops to maturity in the west, where more tanks had been built per square mile. Moving east from the hills in the north, the transition from a westerly zone of mixed wet-and-dry agriculture to a more easterly zone of predominantly dry cultivation was not abrupt in 1600, and is not today. The comparable boundary is even less pronounced in the south. But both boundaries, shown in Map 8, become clear when we compare zones to one another. Some of the very best local irrigation in Tirunelveli lies in the mixed zone, both north and south of the wet zone. No such pockets of excellent paddy land exist in the dry zone. In aggregate terms, a bit more than 10 percent of all cultivated land in the mixed zone benefited from some drainage irrigation in the nineteenth century, but less than 3 percent in the dry zone. The profusion of wells in the mixed zone and distinctive soil types made its cropping patterns in general more water-intensive than in the dry zone, a distinction much more pronounced in the north than in the south. In short, geographical zones exist juxtaposed to one another on the landscape, and distinctions between them seem logical in light of Tamil categories for agricultural analysis.

Each agricultural zone had its own style of life, for farming routines and material conditions dominated human experience. By the time the Nayakas ruled Madurai, irrigation water flowed most of the year through communities throughout the wet zone, and paddy fields stretched everywhere. Drainage watered every variety of garden crop. Over centuries, the soil had become alluvial in fields and tanks near the riverbed, and digging out silt from tanks to plow into fields enriched naturally poor soils, which, on high ground, outside the reach of irrigation, supported crops of oil seeds, pulses, and fodder grains. Palmyras dotted the land on every village fringe. Scrub that skirted the paddy fields provided some grazing for goats, cattle, and water buffalo. Natural vegetation on the sandy, rocky ground bordering the valley must have been scarce by 1600; it barely exists today. Paddy cultivation did produce low-quality straw in large quantities for cattle, however, and goats grazed on field stubble after every harvest, dropping manure as they moved along.

Over the crest of the Tambraparni valley, the narrow ribbon of green gave way to a parched red terrain. Outside the wet zone, the landscape everywhere was dry, often blown with dust, and a harsh place to live. In villages scattered over the land, millets were the prime foodgrains, and drought was always a threat. A bird's-eye view would reveal, in the mixed zone, pockets of bright green, more closely spaced closer to the Ghats, fewer and fewer to the east, normally supporting one paddy crop each year. Wells were many. They supported garden crops of all types, and could be pressed into service to save the rice harvest, with great labor by people and bulls to lift water with buckets. Many tanks would normally have nourished millets, not rice; and this nanjai-mel-punjai practice characterized farming wherever tanks could not be relied on to secure a paddy harvest. On land outside the circles of green around these little man-made lakes, hardy dry crops abounded. Throughout the mixed zone, dry fields would be most luxurious where the soil was rich loam, and much skimpier where clay or sand predominated. Many mixed-zone villages had neither good land for dry crops nor decent drainage for irrigation, and these were the most famine-prone of all in the region. That is why they depended so heavily on samai and varagu, coarse millets that fed poor people and stood between drought and famine. Wells watered tiny patches of garden crops, and provided drinking water. Palmyras thrived in the sand, and stretched over the land between settlements.

West of the 250-foot contour, villages were a long walk one from another, and to the east, much farther apart. Eastward, our bird's-eye view would reveal many fewer green patches, and the land would look on the whole brown and barren. At closer inspection, we would find scattered settlements of peasants growing many dry crops. In the north, kambu, cholam, and cotton covered most of the cultivated land, 85 percent by the 1870s. In the north the fields of the dry zone are black; they crack when dried out, and hold meager rainfall best when plowed deeply by the scrawny but hardy bulls. They become sticky, oozing mud during monsoon rains, and in this soil grow very few large trees, so that shade here is hard to find. Wells here, too, support garden crops and provide precious water for man and beast. Because of the richness of those black soils, droughts have been common, but famines have not. Diets were coarse and life was hard, but the work routine provided a stable subsistence, however meager. Those wells and black-soil fields would, moreover, become commercial assets of considerable value during the course of the nineteenth century.

Like the northern dry zone, the dry areas in the south presented a stiff challenge to skills of human survival. Here, however, the land was red, rolling sand. A tank here and there, dry most of the time, a natural spring, and, more commonly, a well dug into the sand would nourish a patch of green, with a village beside it, surrounded by scraggy fields of samai or varagu, some cotton, and—critical for nutrition— pulses. On and around the hot rolling hills of sand, between scattered settlements for miles and miles, palmyra palms stood firm, evenly spaced a dozen or so paces apart, unbending in the hot sun. Between them, here and there, one could see a little hut made of thatch, and perhaps a fire burning; people were at work, harvesting the palm, and cooking its juice into balls of brown sugar. Life was hard in the villages here, where garden plots were hedged by prickly thorns. But the people knew how to make a steady if meager living from the fruit of this land. And here, too, the nineteenth century would bring a commercial boom.

Each agricultural zone supported a distinct social milieu. Consider simply population density. When population statistics were first compiled comprehensively, in 1881, more than 750 people crowded into each square mile of the wet zone, and twice that many jostled between the low ridges of the central Tambraparni valley, where city, town, and villages had become virtually one sprawling maze of streets and houses crammed between paddy fields. By contrast, the dry zone sustained less than 250 people per hot and dusty square mile of land; towns stood out like islands in a dry seabed. Between these two extremes, the mixed zone was a mixture: pockets of high density fed by tanks were surrounded by stretches of dry land with scattered communities.[53]

More important for social life than population density, however, was the distinctive aggregation of caste groups in each agricultural zone. Kinship networks provided sustenance for families moving and settling on the land. Kin built marriage circles in caste groupings that sought security for their livelihood by forging alliances and stabilizing exchange relations. Agricultural zones thus over time became ethnic zones and zones for dominant caste alliances. Specific sets of castes became the social constituents of the production process in each technologically and naturally distinct agricultural milieu. The vision of the Sangam poets was vindicated. Available evidence enables us to reconstruct the outlines of the historical process involved.

As social groups, castes grew and spread over the centuries by innumerable family decisions, not only about reproduction, but about diet, marriage, residence, occupation, and religious practice, all of which involve the material and symbolic elements of caste. Kin networks expanded, fused, and split, as families built ties within established status categories and set up new groups that became the basis for new status distinctions. Marriage alliances built enduring jati clusters, while changing family fortunes pushed people, over generations, up and down in caste status. All this produced the caste map of nineteenth-century Tirunelveli, but little documentation. We can speculate, however, that families followed strategies designed to make the most of their material and symbolic resources, which would have varied in broad but discernible ways with their jati, so that, in the long run, their accumulated decisions resulted in a characteristic spatial distribution for each type of jati, recorded in census tables. Because we know the outcomes of their decisions, the range of resources available to each type of caste, and the competitive context of their decisions, we can begin to reconstruct the overall logic of caste settlement in the region.

That logic is most readily apparent for people in two sets of six relatively small and occupationally specialized castes, which together in 1881 comprised roughly one-third of the population (see Table 1). They demonstrate that one strategy can lead to very different settlement patterns and population distributions. One set consists of a half-dozen very low-status village service jatis that spread themselves over centuries according to the effective demand for their labor, that is, very evenly: everywhere they comprise a similar percentage of the local population. Washermen, barbers, shepherds, carpenters, blacksmiths, potters, and temple servants are in demand in every settled community. These jobs have always been performed by families with low stores of both material and symbolic resources, and not only by offspring of service families. Undoubtedly, downward mobility plus accretion from outside the caste system—for example of tribals—brought new entrants into these occupations.[54] These castes comprise, as do the much more numerous untouchable Pariah and Palla jatis, low-status categories into which many families would enter, over generations, and from which few would escape.

The other set of castes also consists of six specialized jatis, but these are of much higher status, though also small—some tiny, like a few of the service castes. These distributed themselves, too, according to the market for their services, using a strategy that would maximize their possibilities for livelihood. But they settled in the opposite configuration, that is, in dense local concentrations because they had specialized skills and hence interests in particular places. The Paravas, fishermen and traders, concentrated near the coast; most converted to Catholicism under Portuguese influence, and some became powerful trading magnates during the nineteenth century; especially at the port of Tuticoryn. The hunter population, of course, followed dwindling woods and game. Oil pressers and oil merchants concentrated where oil seeds grew best, in the red-soil tract. Muslims and weavers generally settled disproportionately in urban centers in the wet and mixed zones. Likewise, small merchant castes of all sorts concentrated, like their investments, in little trading domains centered on particular market towns. The Vellan Chettis, for instance, lived mostly in the eastern part of the black-soil tract, and Balijas in the west. Shanar, Parava, Chetti, and Muslim commercial operations radiated out from market towns where they predominated as traders.

In contrast to these small, specialized castes, a half-dozen jati groups who by their numbers and productive activity define the social geography of agrarian Tirunelveli, are large and occupationally diverse. Together they made up about two-thirds of the population in 1881: the Shanars (18 percent), Pallas and Pariahs (17 percent), Maravas (9 percent), Vaduga cultivators (Kammas, Reddis, and Kambalattans, 8 percent), Vellalas (8 percent), and Brahmans (4 percent).[55] The transactional ties within and between these jatis established the substantive social basis of agricultural development. Their settlement strategies, moreover, produced the spatial pattern of local caste resource control, because their growth, spread, and consolidation produced domains of caste dominance within agricultural zones. Again we can see that similar strategies generated diverse local outcomes.

Dominant caste domains emerged as powerful families created, over centuries, alliances based upon regular transactional ties, and obtained in the process predominant control of agricultural production.[56] A peasant family's ability to feed itself in drought and famine, and to muster every year the soil, credit, seeds, bullocks, plows, carts, manure, water, and labor to produce crops, depended upon a web of interfamily transactions within and between castes. Even when commercialized, these ties remained inherently multiplex, involving bonds of religion, caste, kinship, personal loyalty, authority, and deference. A dominant caste emerged as, through a stable set of alliances, it became endowed with sufficient material and symbolic resources to establish for itself a superior position in the total complex of transactions critical in agricultural production: that is, it became a jati of patrons more than of clients. The institutional means to build dominance are the subject of the next chapter, but here it is essential to indicate the historically complementary roles of caste status and caste concentration in the making of dominant-caste domains, hence the complementarity of material and symbolic assets.

High caste status is a symbolic resource; it is derived from a cultural ranking of humans by their proximity to the divine. Like transactions with the deity in a temple, exchanges between higher and lower human beings are necessarily asymmetrical; as in the temple, grosser material elements go up, and more refined symbolic elements go down. High status, in South India, therefore, became a valued means to gain material wealth. Brahmans, though small in number, became disproportionately rich and powerful as a landowning dominant caste in many of the richest irrigated villages in Tirunelveli, as throughout the Tamil lowlands. As we saw in the previous chapter, Vellalas developed as a high-status jati category precisely by patronizing Brahmans, by which they gained status and the means of dominance. No other non-Brahman caste has the traditional status of Vellalas, so the others had to rely for dominance much more upon concentrated populations. Organized thus, Maravas and Vadugas succeeded in keeping a large percentage of key agricultural transactions under their effective control. They never neglected to seek symbolic ascendancy, of course, by patronizing temples and Brahmans, but their dominant status did not extend, as did that of Brahmans and Vellalas, to areas outside their densely settled localities. Lower still, well below Maravas and Vadugas in caste status,[57] Shanars could not aspire to symbolic ascendancy. Their status obviated any possibility of an interjati alliance in which they might be on top. They dominated, therefore, only where they comprised the bulk of the population, where the majority of agricultural transactions could be retained within the jati itself, and where the highest among them, the Nadans, assumed the dominant caste role. At the lowest extreme of the ranking system, untouchable Pallas and Pariahs could at best hope for relative independence as peasant cultivators. When part of any interdependent jati alliance, they would always have had to make the trade-off between status and income that kept them permanent clients, always on the bottom.

Dominance thus always demands some degree of demographic concentration. The 1881 distribution of agricultural castes records the outcome of long-term processes by which dominant castes gained control of contiguous agricultural communities. Their dominance meant security for peasant families, a natural goal, buried among a host of factors affecting settlement decisions. Farmers would tend to clear land adjacent to their natal villages, and, in South India, to marry close by. Techniques of farming a particular type of land and planting certain crops would become received caste custom. Foodgrain preferences—such as an attachment to rice or millet[58]—and an aesthetic enjoyment of a certain landscape, its flora, and its fauna—all these might be reflected in caste rituals as well as in residential choices. The symbolic identification of a caste with a particular territory would, of course, deepen with time, as marriage networks became interwoven on the basis of status, power, and interests in land. As enduring family and caste ties produced both a tradition of territorial identity and an intercommunity structure of circulation and interdependence, intercaste relations, focused upon a dominant landowning caste, would become synonymous with agriculture itself throughout a dominant caste domain, and status in the caste would come to define status in its domain. The identity of social groups and land would interpenetrate.

Census data reflect four distinct domains of dominance in nineteenth-century Tirunelveli, each in one agricultural zone. The oldest dominant caste alliance, built during the Pandyan era, tied together Brahmans, Vellalas, and subordinant peasant jatis, principally Pallas and Pariahs. As the social basis for irrigated agriculture in Tirunelveli, the Vellala-Brahman dominant caste alliance established firm control of the wet zone, and of many localities in the mixed zone near the Ghats. Another, much later, dominant-caste domain had been built by Vadugas on the black soil of the northern dry zone. A third, much smaller and poorer, domain emerged from Shanar concentration in the southern dry zone. The wet and dry zones, therefore, had become by 1800 relatively stable both agriculturally and ethnically; and each had relatively uniform configurations of dominance and interdependence. By contrast, the mixed zone, an agricultural patchwork, became highly mixed ethnically. Sprinkled throughout were Vellala/Brahman-dominated irrigated communities. Maravas settled heavily in the north, but village census data from 1823 show their local concentrations to have been intersected and bracketed by concentrations of Vellalas, Shanars, Vadugas, and Pariahs (Map 17). Thus the zone comprised many minidomains of relative independence for non-Marava castes. A risky region agriculturally, unpredictable year to year, the mixed zone historically became a risky place to live politically, as well, because no clear-cut lines of caste subordination and superiority could be readily drawn within realms of community interaction. The emerging character of caste dominance in each agricultural zone would play a central role in Tirunelveli's political history.

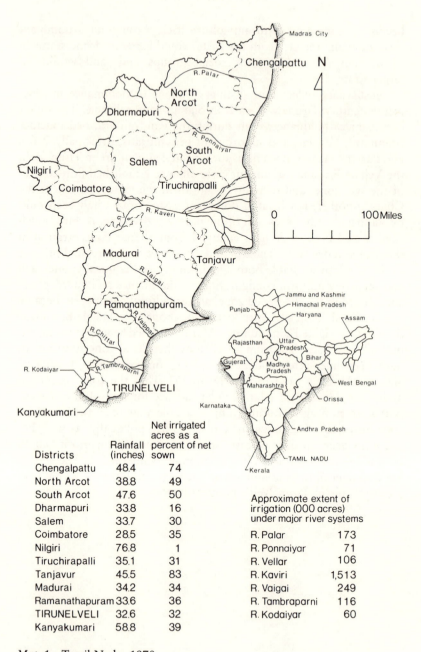

Districts	Rainfall (inches)	Net irrigated acres as a percent of net sown
Chengalpattu	48.4	74
North Arcot	38.8	49
South Arcot	47.6	50
Dharmapuri	33.8	16
Salem	33.7	30
Coimbatore	28.5	35
Nilgiri	76.8	1
Tiruchirapalli	35.1	31
Tanjavur	45.5	83
Madurai	34.2	34
Ramanathapuram	33.6	36
TIRUNELVELI	32.6	32
Kanyakumari	58.8	39

Approximate extent of irrigation (000 acres) under major river systems

R. Palar	173
R. Ponnaiyar	71
R. Vellar	106
R. Kaviri	1,513
R. Vaigai	249
R. Tambraparni	116
R. Kodaiyar	60

Map 1 Tamil Nadu, 1970

SOURCE: *Season and Crop Report, 1970/1*, Tamil Nadu Director of Statistics, Madras, 1973.

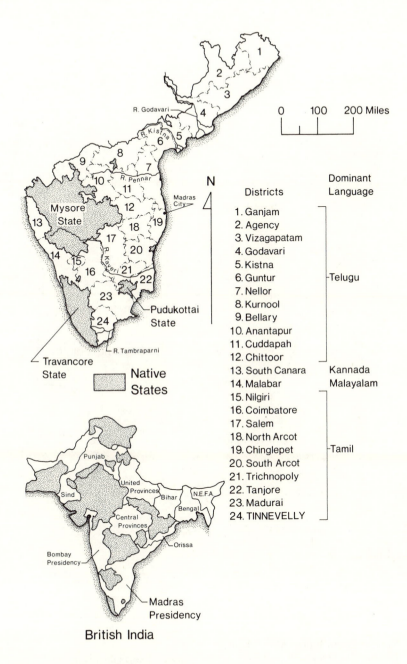

Districts	Dominant Language
1. Ganjam	
2. Agency	
3. Vizagapatam	
4. Godavari	
5. Kistna	
6. Guntur	Telugu
7. Nellor	
8. Kurnool	
9. Bellary	
10. Anantapur	
11. Cuddapah	
12. Chittoor	
13. South Canara	Kannada
14. Malabar	Malayalam
15. Nilgiri	
16. Coimbatore	
17. Salem	
18. North Arcot	
19. Chinglepet	
20. South Arcot	Tamil
21. Trichnopoly	
22. Tanjore	
23. Madurai	
24. TINNEVELLY	

Map 2 Madras Presidency, 1900

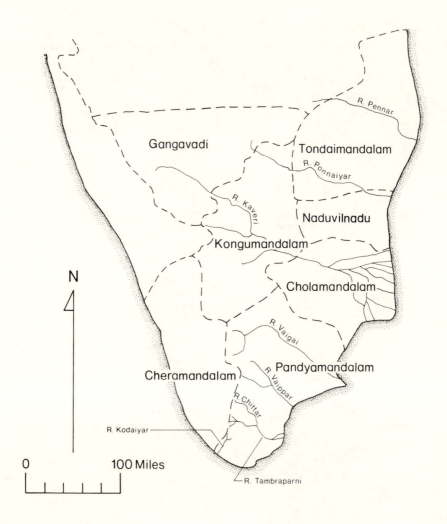

Map 3 South Indian Mandalams, c. 1000
SOURCE: Burton Stein, "Circulation and the Historical Geography of the Tamil
Country," *Journal of Asian Studies*, 37:1 (1977), 19.

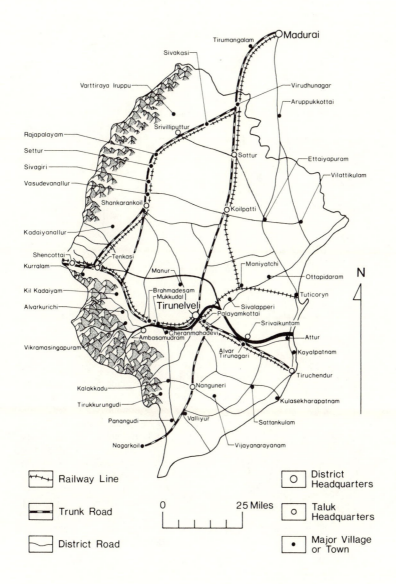

Map 4 Tirunelveli Central Places and Transportation, 1900

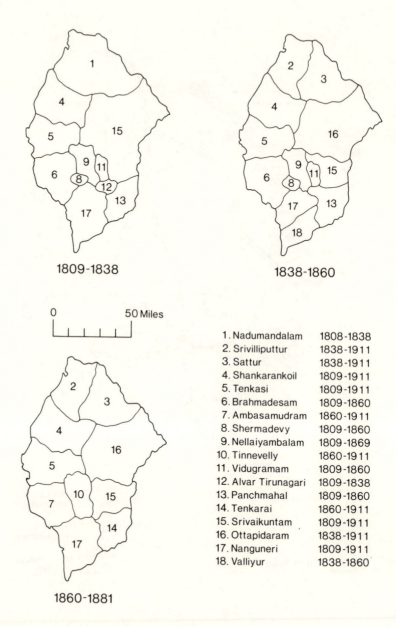

1809-1838

1838-1860

0   50 Miles

1. Nadumandalam	1808-1838
2. Srivilliputtur	1838-1911
3. Sattur	1838-1911
4. Shankarankoil	1809-1911
5. Tenkasi	1809-1911
6. Brahmadesam	1809-1860
7. Ambasamudram	1860-1911
8. Shermadevy	1809-1860
9. Nellaiyambalam	1809-1869
10. Tinnevelly	1860-1911
11. Vidugramam	1809-1860
12. Alvar Tirunagari	1809-1838
13. Panchmahal	1809-1860
14. Tenkarai	1860-1911
15. Srivaikuntam	1809-1911
16. Ottapidaram	1838-1911
17. Nanguneri	1809-1911
18. Valliyur	1838-1860

1860-1881

Map 5   Tinnevelly District Taluks, 1809-1911

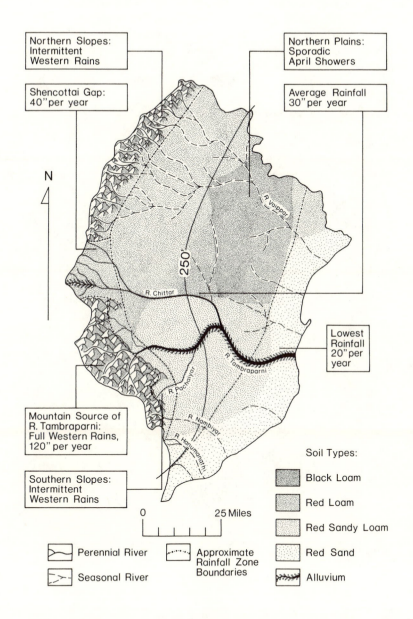

Northern Slopes:
Intermittent
Western Rains

Northern Plains:
Sporadic
April Showers

Shencottai Gap:
40"per year

Average Rainfall
30"per year

N

R. Vaippar

250'

R. Chittar

Lowest
Rainfall
20" per
year

R. Tambraparni

Mountain Source of
R. Tambraparni:
Full Western Rains,
120" per year

R. Pachayar

R. Nambiyar

R. Hanumanathi

Southern Slopes:
Intermittent
Western Rains

0   25 Miles

Soil Types:

Black Loam

Red Loam

Red Sandy Loam

Perennial River

Approximate
Rainfall Zone
Boundaries

Red Sand

Seasonal River

Alluvium

Map 6   Tirunelveli Rainfall, Soils, and Drainage

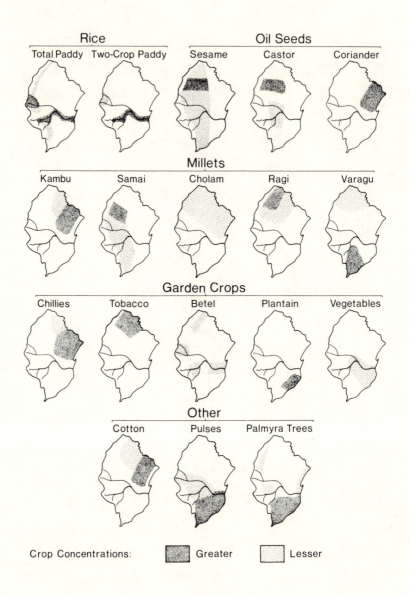

Rice
Total Paddy   Two-Crop Paddy

Oil Seeds
Sesame   Castor   Coriander

Millets
Kambu   Samai   Cholam   Ragi   Varagu

Garden Crops
Chillies   Tobacco   Betel   Plantain   Vegetables

Other
Cotton   Pulses   Palmyra Trees

Crop Concentrations: ▓ Greater   ☐ Lesser

Map 7   Tirunelveli Crop Concentrations, 1876
SOURCE: A. J. Stuart, A *Manual of the Tinnevelly District*, Madras, 1876, pp. 168-77.

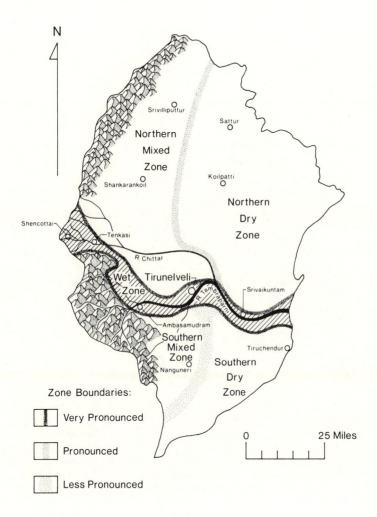

N

Srivilliputtur

Sattur

Northern
Mixed
Zone

Koilpatti

Shankarankoil

Northern
Dry
Zone

Shencottai

Tenkasi

R. Chittar

Wet
Zone

Tirunelveli

Srivaikuntam

R. Tambraparni

Ambasamudram

Southern
Mixed
Zone

Tiruchendur

Nanguneri

Southern
Dry
Zone

Zone Boundaries:

Very Pronounced

Pronounced

Less Pronounced

0   25 Miles

Map 8   Agricultural Zones in Tirunelveli

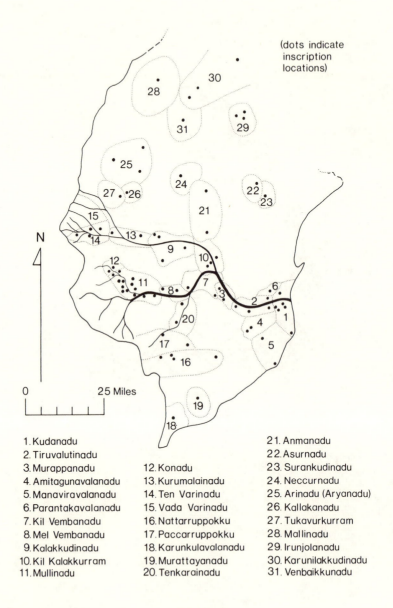

(dots indicate
inscription
locations)

N

0   25 Miles

1. Kudanadu
2. Tiruvalutinadu
3. Murappanadu
4. Amitagunavalanadu
5. Manaviravalanadu
6. Parantakavalanadu
7. Kil Vembanadu
8. Mel Vembanadu
9. Kalakkudinadu
10. Kil Kalakkurram
11. Mullinadu
12. Konadu
13. Kurumalainadu
14. Ten Varinadu
15. Vada Varinadu
16. Nattarruppokku
17. Paccarruppokku
18. Karunkulavalanadu
19. Murattayanadu
20. Tenkarainadu
21. Anmanadu
22. Asurnadu
23. Surankudinadu
24. Neccurnadu
25. Arinadu (Aryanadu)
26. Kallakanadu
27. Tukavurkurram
28. Mallinadu
29. Irunjolanadu
30. Karunilakkudinadu
31. Venbaikkunadu

Map 9   Nadus: Southern Pandyamandalam, c. 1000

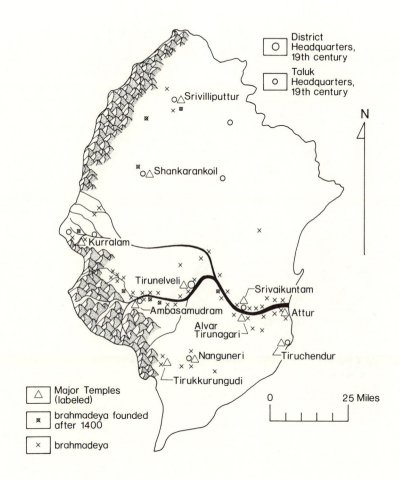

District
Headquarters,
19th century

Taluk
Headquarters,
19th century

N

Srivilliputtur

Shankarankoil

Kurralam

Tiruneveli

Srivaikuntam

Ambasamudram

Attur

Alvar
Tirunagari

Nanguneri

Tiruchendur

Tirukkurungudi

Major Temples
(labeled)

brahmadeya founded
after 1400

brahmadeya

0   25 Miles

Map 10   Tirunelveli Brahmadeyas and Major Temples, c. 1500

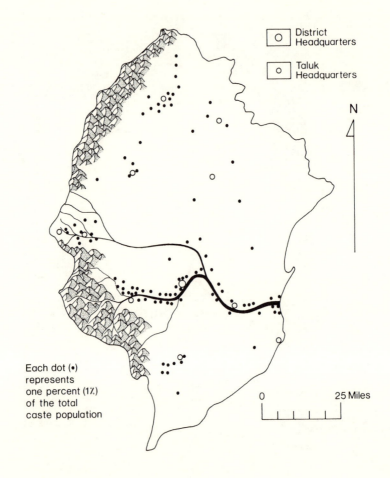

District
Headquarters

Taluk
Headquarters

N

Each dot (•)
represents
one percent (1%)
of the total
caste population

0   25 Miles

Map 11 Approximate Brahman Distribution, Tinnevelly District, 1881
SOURCE: *Census of India*, 1881, *Tinnevelly Taluk Tables* (TNA).

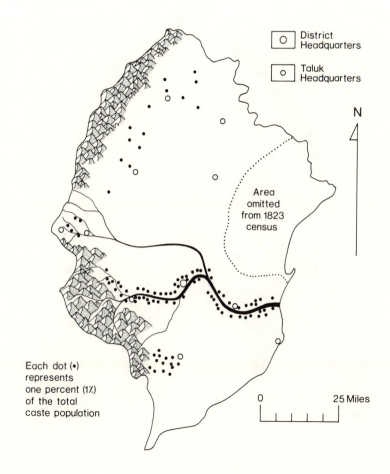

District
Headquarters

Taluk
Headquarters

N

Area
omitted
from 1823
census

Each dot (•)
represents
one percent (1%)
of the total
caste population

0   25 Miles

Map 12   "Pandya Vellala" Distribution, Tinnevelly District, 1823
SOURCE: "1823 Census."

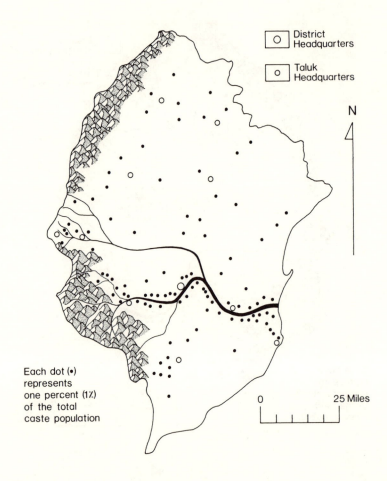

District
Headquarters

Taluk
Headquarters

N

Each dot (•)
represents
one percent (1%)
of the total
caste population

0   25 Miles

Map 13   Approximate "Vellala" Distribution, Tinnevelly District, 1881
Source: *Census of India*, 1881, *Tinnevelly Taluk Tables* (TNA).

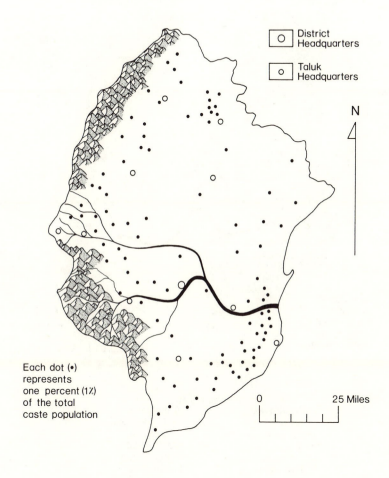

District
Headquarters

Taluk
Headquarters

N

Each dot (•)
represents
one percent (1%)
of the total
caste population

0   25 Miles

Map 14 Approximate Shanar Distribution, Tinnevelly District, 1881
SOURCE: *Census of India*, 1881, *Tinnevelly Taluk Tables* (TNA).

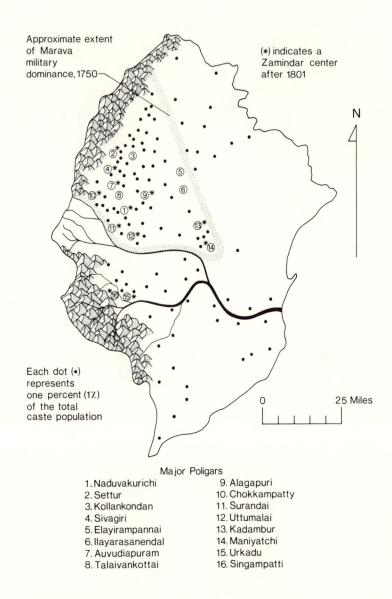

Approximate extent
of Marava
military
dominance, 1750

(∗) indicates a
Zamindar center
after 1801

N

Each dot (•)
represents
one percent (1%)
of the total
caste population

0   25 Miles

Major Poligars

1. Naduvakurichi
2. Settur
3. Kollankondan
4. Sivagiri
5. Elayirampannai
6. Ilayarasanendal
7. Auvudiapuram
8. Talaivankottai

9. Alagapuri
10. Chokkampatty
11. Surandai
12. Uttumalai
13. Kadambur
14. Maniyatchi
15. Urkadu
16. Singampatti

Map 15   Approximate Marava Distribution, Tinnevelly District, 1881,
Showing Major Poligars, 1801
Sources: *Census of India*, 1881, *Tinnevelly Taluk Tables* (TNA); H. R. Pate,
District Gazetteers, Tinnevelly District, Madras, 1917, pp. 274-75.

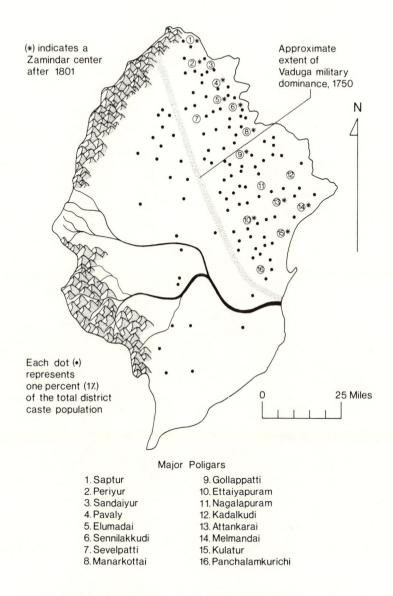

(∗) indicates a
Zamindar center
after 1801

Approximate
extent of
Vaduga military
dominance, 1750

N

Each dot (•)
represents
one percent (1%)
of the total district
caste population

0   25 Miles

Major Poligars

1. Saptur
2. Periyur
3. Sandaiyur
4. Pavaly
5. Elumadai
6. Sennilakkudi
7. Sevelpatti
8. Manarkottai

9. Gollappatti
10. Ettaiyapuram
11. Nagalapuram
12. Kadalkudi
13. Attankarai
14. Melmandai
15. Kulatur
16. Panchalamkurichi

Map 16 Approximate "Vaduga" Distribution, Tinnevelly District, 1881,
Showing Major Poligars, 1801
SOURCES: *Census of India*, 1881, *Tinnevelly Taluk Tables* (TNA); H. R. Pate,
District Gazetteer, Tinnevelly District, Madras, 1917, pp. 274-75.

Each dot (·) represents one percent (1%) of the total caste population

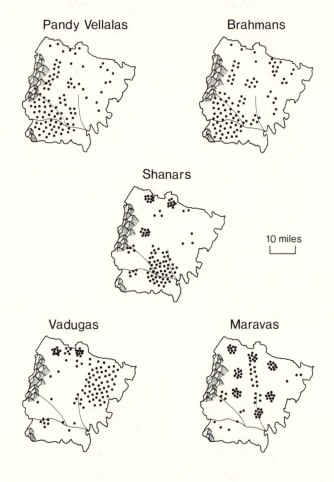

Map 17   Major Caste Distribution in the Northern Mixed Zone, 1823
NOTE: Map shows Tenkasi and Shankarankoil taluks.
SOURCE: "1823 Census."

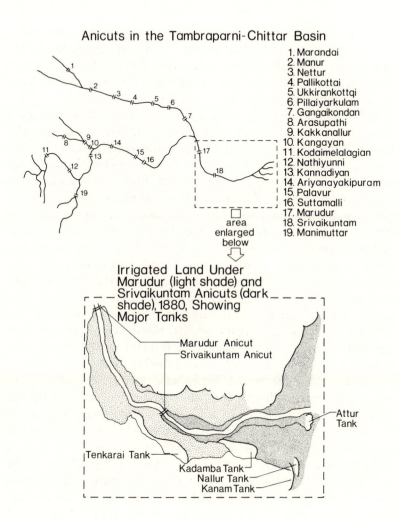

Anicuts in the Tambraparni-Chittar Basin

1. Marandai
2. Manur
3. Nettur
4. Pallikottai
5. Ukkirankottqi
6. Pillaiyarkulam
7. Gangaikondan
8. Arasupathi
9. Kakkanallur
10. Kangayan
11. Kodaimelalagian
12. Nathiyunni
13. Kannadiyan
14. Ariyanayakipuram
15. Palavur
16. Suttamalli
17. Marudur
18. Srivaikuntam
19. Manimuttar

area
enlarged
below

Irrigated Land Under Marudur (light shade) and Srivaikuntam Anicuts (dark shade), 1880, Showing Major Tanks

Marudur Anicut
Srivaikuntam Anicut

Attur Tank

Tenkarai Tank

Kadamba Tank
Nallur Tank
Kanam Tank

Map 18 Srivaikuntam Anicut in the Tambraparni River System

· 3 ·

TRIBUTARY STATE

Like the human landscape, transformed by labors on the frontier after 1300, the regional order that emerged in the late sixteenth century and matured thereafter would have seemed unfamiliar to a visitor from the medieval Pandya court. Nature had not changed. The monsoons continued to bestow their most luxurious bounty on the Tirunelveli wet zone, where Brahman and Vellala villages flourished, gods enjoyed devotion, and kings reaped honor. But like the farmers who plowed fields north and south of the Tambraparni River valley, the kings who ruled at Madurai were not of the Pandya fold. Pandya kings would have viewed the Nayaka dynasty, firmly entrenched in the capital city by 1600, as foreigners whose legitimacy as rulers derived not from ancient, indigenous roots, nor from the natural loyalties of Pandya peoples, but from sheer military force. The Nayakas themselves had no illusions about their ancestry. They had come from the Telugu-speaking lands north of the medieval Tamil mandalams, and, conquering under the umbrella of Vijayanagar imperial authority, had established their sovereignty at Madurai, putting an end in the process to the myth of Pandya royal authority that had survived the last effective Pandya king by two centuries. Nayaka charisma rose from the ritual supremacy of their capital and from their ability to patronize temples and Brahmans; this feature of the Nayaka state the Pandya kings would have recognized. But because the Nayaka realm was so much more socially diverse and politically complex than its Pandya predecessor in Tirunelveli, the new regional order rested squarely on the shoulders of military men. The army relied in turn on payments of tribute from royal subjects, especially peasants and traders who, being protected by Nayaka arms, generated increasing stores of wealth to support the warrior state. Regional order, defined and stabilized under the Pandya kings above all by ritual activity in religious networks, now became integrated anew by tributary transactions in state networks. Participating in this tributary state, the peasantry expanded its access to opportunities for market exchange, and, during the eighteenth century, made that series of critical decisions which founded British rule.

WARRIOR RULE

As the Vijayanagar empire collapsed, Nayaka armies reunited the Tirunelveli region through victories in a war that spanned the sixteenth century. The founder of the Nayaka dynasty, Visvanatha, commanded a Vijayanagar army that came south in 1529. He battled a shifting alliance of Pandyas and Maravas, which fought him to a standstill in 1543 after six months of inconclusive war, and beat his forces as late as 1547. On his death, in 1564, his son claimed independence from Vijayanagar, and, despite continued resistance, set up a stable Nayaka authority system by century's end, one that remained intact until 1736. Its capital was first at Madurai and later, as Nayaka power expanded, at Tiruchirapalli (Trichnopoly) further north, in the Chola country.[1]

The Nayakas consummated a process begun by the Cholas, merging Chola and Pandya mandalams. They also continued what the later Pandyas had begun, setting up a clear-cut hierarchy of urban centers to embody the relations of subordination in their new domain. These urban centers, moreover, reflect an increased urban concentration and lifestyle for the regional ruling elite, whose authority rose much higher above its local roots than did that of their Pandya predecessors. Nayakas raised Madurai to new heights of grandeur, tore down inadequate Pandya fortifications, erected new walls, and encased the city in stone. They added new walls and internal buildings to the royal temple of Sri Minakshi-Sundaresvara, in the heart of the city. Madurai was reborn, a transcendent political and ceremonial center that incorporated in its aura all lesser powers in the Nayaka realm.[2]

Endowed with the combined military might, ceremonial splendor, and political authority of Madurai, but on a lesser scale, Tirunelveli town became the southern provincial capital. Here stood the largest fort in the south, at Palayamkottai; the central temple, Nellaiyappa Koil; and the governor, known as the delavoy (literally, "commander"). Ariyanatha Mudaliar, a Vellala from Tondaimandalam, the first delavoy, rose through the Vijayanagar ranks to become a minister and general under his childhood friend Visvanatha Nayaka, with whom he rode south to command armies that subdued the Tirunelveli countryside.[3] The governorship became a perpetual patrimony in his family, and hence part of the family name, Medai Delavoy Mudaliar. In their mansion astride the Nellaiyappa Koil, in the heart of their capital, the Medai Delavoy Mudaliars became one of the richest and most powerful families in the region and remained so for centuries.

Under the delavoy's authority lay two distinct political realms, one in the old Pandya territories, and one in the subregions commanded by Telugu and Marava chiefs. In the first, a series of officers and official transactions linked the delavoy directly to the wealth and loyalty of irrigated communities. In the second, the Nayakas by necessity recognized numerous subregional chiefs as junior partners or "little kings" atop territorial segments of the Nayaka domain. Each little king received an appropriate title as the defender of one of seventy-two bastions of Madurai; each, based in his fortress town (*palayam*), was called a *palayakkaran*, or in Anglo-Indian usage, a poligar. The Nayaka system thus made use of a principle also at work in the contemporaneous Mughal empire, one that remained in effect into the twentieth century, wherein some lands were seen to be ruled directly by the crown—in Anglo-Indian terms sarcar or circar lands—and others were understood to be under the control of lesser royal authorities. But as we have seen, this principle also had an indigenous, Pandya legacy, for warrior chiefs had always been under Pandya kings more prominent outside the wet-zone political core of the realm than they were within it.

Ironically, though more complex than the Pandya system, the Nayaka state remains more unknown because of the relative dearth of inscriptions. We do know that it contained many more people and a greater diversity of communities than the Pandya state. To achieve order, the Nayakas developed many more specialized official positions and an elaborate state ceremonial language to articulate hierarchy among officers. One account, for instance, tells how the delavoy's son "was accustomed to go out every night in public procession around the town, seated in a lofty howdah, on the back of an elephant, clothed in rich, perfumed dress, covered with ornaments, with numerous lights, musicians, dancers, and other usual accompaniments of such spectacles," and how the Nayaka himself, worried that such display overstepped the boy's status, rode on horse all the way from Madurai to observe, and, in the end, to grant his approval.[4] Another story tells that the Medai Delavoy Mudaliar family gained its full name because the governor would receive poligars into his presence only when seated on a high platform (*medai*).[5] We can, then, imagine Nayakas atop a hierarchy of authority that stretched from Madurai to Tirunelveli, thence to subregional centers and to localities, whereas Pandyas had sat at the center of a vast set of more equal political relationships. The Nayaka system seems to have had less need for permanent stone records, which had served under the Pandyas to bridge infrequent exertions of royal authority. Now, as tribute flowed up and authority down the official hierarchy with more regularity, records of transactions became ephemeral, recorded only on palm leaves that turned to dust over the years. A new state order thus changed the character of historical records, as it had under early Pandya dynasties and would again after 1800.

Despite the dearth of records, it seems clear that a tension-ridden series of speculative revenue contracts channeled tribute from Tirunelveli localities to Tirunelveli town and to Madurai with some regularity after 1600. B. A. Saletore, in fact, argues that such a system had been in place in parts of South India by the thirteenth century. Its theory was simple, expressed in a passage from the *Sukraniti*: "Having determined the land revenue of a village, the king should receive it from one rich man in advance, or (receive a) guarantee (for its payment) . . . by monthly or periodic installments."[6] At each level of state hierarchy, political stature depended in principle and practice on one's ability to advance money up the hierarchy in anticipation of collection from below. Officials had not only to be rich, in relation to others in their sphere of influence, they had to maintain their stature by constant patronage and at least the possibility of coercion. The character of ties that bound together these layers of tribute differed markedly between circar and poligar domains.

Poligars ruled little kingdoms, which varied in size from the tiny Sennalkudi, Kollankondan, Urkadu, and Kadalkudi, to the vast Ettaiyapuram, Panchalamkottai, Sivagiri, and Chokkampatti (Maps 15 and 16).[7] Though larger ones contained a greater number of segments, and though Marava and Telugu domains may have been organized slightly differently, in general poligar domains were defined by territorial segments linked hierarchically by caste status and military rank. Marava sub-jatis and their component kinship branches (*kilai*) settled in compact areas, part of their strategy for defense and caste dominance. The 1823 census shows each sub-jati concentrated in a separate village in areas outside the Marava core domain in the northern mixed zone; and research on Marava settlement patterns done in this century shows that, in the Marava core domain, kilais are concentrated in the same way.[8] Within settlements, Marava families today rank themselves by their patrilineal proximity to one dominant chief. S. Kathirvel has shown this ranking system to have organized Marava protection services in the eighteenth century, when a chief in each village negotiated with clients for protection, collected payments, and dispersed the rewards to families under his command.[9] In core settlement areas, however, village kilais bunched together into localities of sub-jati dominance, and poligars grew up as rulers of land dominated by their own sub-jati. In 1823, twelve of twenty-one Marava poligar domains (then called zamindaris) were populated by only one sub-jati; in three others one sub-jati's numerical preponderance was overwhelming; and, in six others, though two (but no more) sub-jatis were more or less equal in size, that of the poligar most likely dominated as a result of conquest.[10]

Telugu jatis also concentrated themselves spatially. Sub-jati territories thus probably constituted segments of political order in their domains. Overlapping this caste polity, however, Telugus, and perhaps Maravas, too, set up a military and administrative apparatus that employed a number of castes, linking the poligar to each village in his realm. In Ettaiyapuram's domain, for instance, the poligar divided his territory among his kinsmen and other subsidiary chiefs, called *servaikkaran*, who owed military allegiance and tribute, and who demanded the same from village headmen under their control.[11] Needless to say, everyone accepted violence as a legitimate means to establish authority in poligar territory, and struggles by those below to resist demands from above were constant features of order itself. To the end of the seventeenth century, however, records do not indicate any major challenge directed against the topmost link to the chain of authority, that between poligars and the delavoy.

In circar territory, mostly the core Pandya nadus controlled locally by the Vellala-Brahman alliance, the Nayaka system depended on a different set of political relations. New military elites did not attempt to undermine old Pandya local leaders. On the contrary, Nayakas and their agents endowed temples and founded new brahmadeyas with unprecedented generosity.[12] Tribute collectors were subregional authorities with material and ritual resources under Nayaka protection and patronage. At first these were mostly military men, come to power in the Vijayanagar period; but after 1564 more and more they were Brahman immigrants, many Telugus, favored agents in the new regime, who received land grants in addition to official titles. Under them and beside them in irrigated localities, wealthy landowners constituted the final and critical link in the chain of Nayaka authority, and profited accordingly. At each level in the chain, of course, orderly transmission of tribute and honor could be backed up with force, if necessary, by troops at Palayamkottai. But routine authority rested upon officials' skill in generating for themselves local influence, by tying themselves into transactional webs in and around irrigated communities. They became patrons, protectors, and arbiters. Their names now adorn villages and irrigation works, to suggest their activity as investors in agriculture and water management. They appear in inscriptions most often as donors to temples. But they must have been active in local grain markets, too, for, as we will soon see, revenue collections "in kind" were in fact highly commercialized wherever paddy was grown. As commercial actors, officials were probably foci of saving and lending as an expanding cash nexus developed around irrigated communities during the Nayaka years.

By paying tribute, villagers and merchants obtained protection, their leaders attained stature as intermediaries, and they were left alone by state officials to manage internal affairs. The segmented character of the regional order thus remained intact even as the central power and wealth of state officers increased under the Nayaka regime. Like Poligars, Muslim merchants at Kayalpatnam were authorized to control their commercial domain in the port city in return for orderly tribute payments. Artisans, shepherds, fishermen, washermen, and other groups paid through their caste headmen.[13] Such payments entitled headmen to collect from members of their group. Local leaders thus had good reasons to accept and support the tribute system, and to placate Nayaka agents from Tirunelveli—even competing agents, whose rival claims might raise the cost of protection at times. European merchants were but another such group of tribute payers. Despite Portuguese conversions of Parava fishermen on the coast, and despite battles between Portuguese and Dutch merchants, these overseas foreigners did not attract animosity from the Nayakas, who were content to leave the coastal tract under the control of the merchants.[14] The Portuguese controlled, according to one account, "the entire civil and criminal jurisdiction of the fishery coast . . . and all the dues and taxes including the valuable revenue arising from the pearl fishery." Dutch and Portuguese warriors fought constantly on the coast during the mid-1600s, taking whole towns and villages from one another, without provoking Nayaka interference. Having won, the Dutch then proceeded to cement treaties of protective alliance; like the Portuguese before them, they covered their bets by paying for protection to whoever in the segmented Nayaka state system could help assure their safety.[15]

Thus the Nayaka regime was fertile ground for the growth of militant merchant power. Unfortunately, the structure of the regime did not generate records to document the rising volume of market exchange and commodity production that certainly occurred during the seventeenth- and early eighteenth-century sway of the Nayakas at Madurai. Long-term trends, however, indicate the process by which market networks rose to increasing prominence in peasant life before the mid-1700s. We have seen that waves of warrior and peasant migration after 1300 subdued tribes that commanded stretches of dry land between medieval agricultural cores in the Tamil country. Those tribes and their conquerors settled down to farming. They populated communities on the land between irrigated core zones, and dispersed techniques of dry farming and warfare throughout the peninsula. They thus increased the diversity of crops grown in regions like Tirunelveli and shortened the distances between communities that produced complementary products for exchange. Even as they established conditions for multiple circuits of local trade, their skills as warriors also increased the purchasing power of fighting men. Because they consolidated their control of territory with militant caste and kinship organization, their subsequent integration into a regional order demanded long years of warfare and a powerful Nayaka standing army, supported by allied poligar forces. To sustain this armed state apparatus required constant expenditure on ceremonial splendor and on military muscle. Revenue for these purposes came partly from plunder and occasional tribute, but more importantly from regular tribute payments that became tantamount to taxation on agriculture and trade. Collected by layers of intermediaries between localities and the capital, most of this taxation never reached Madurai, but stayed instead in local official hands to be spent on local and subregional state operations. As the state demanded more tribute, it protected trade and producers who generated more profits to tax. Population growth and burgeoning towns housing state officials, traders, and temples amid widening circuits of commerce lowered transaction and transport costs well below medieval levels.

The volume of sea trade also increased. First the Portuguese and then the Dutch, both established on the Tirunelveli coast and in nearby Sri Lanka, stimulated exports, brought precious metals, and acquired provisions for their own troops and ships.[16] Such coastal settlements of European traders dotted the whole of the Indian peninsula by the eighteenth century, and they clearly had their greatest effect on localities very near the sea, within a few days' bullock walk. Political disruption in the 1700s made this proximity even more important.[17] The Tirunelveli wet zone was in a favored position to benefit from the region's position at the tip of India, a critical juncture for Indian Ocean traders and a prize for competing European seaborne entrepreneurs.[18] Protected by the Nayakas, and with abundant water to grow the rice to feed towns, the wet zone and especially the Tambraparni bustled with opportunities for profit. Forest products traveled along the river valley to ports. Rice moved between villages and towns. Artisans congregated in major centers for weaving the cloth demanded by export merchants.[19] Here, craft producers could supply the demand from inland urban elites and European markets at the same time. Merchants, moneychangers, and moneylenders could facilitate state tribute payments and European financial needs. Commercial activity generated more wealth for the state to tax. As a result, a complex web of intersecting state and market interests developed during the seventeenth and early eighteenth centuries in the Tirunelveli wet zone. Centuries of migration, settlement, and peasant productive labor provided a base from which inland state and overseas market trends could after 1600 make market networks ever more significant for village livelihoods. State wealth depended on trade, and commercially active locals depended on state protection.

REVENUE TRANSACTIONS

The Nayaka state crumbled after 1740, forcing difficult decisions upon the peasantry and creating that environment from which emerged a British colonial regime. We shall turn to the colonial transition shortly, but to understand eighteenth-century events we must dissect the webs of state finance that contending powers fought to control after 1740. For though the Nayakas disappeared and their revenue system was distorted and racked by violent competition among contenders for regional authority, it nevertheless survived through the eighteenth century, when accounts compiled by East India Company officers reveal its working principles. From the top of the regional state to the bottom—from Madurai to Tirunelveli town to subregional centers to villages—state officials granted patronage, protection, and titles to office, passing down authority to arbitrate disputes and to exert legitimate force. Upward passed payments of tribute that expressed subordination and inclusion in the realm: payments in homage, service, goods, and cash. Each node in the transactional chain involved tense negotiations and at least potential conflict. Those below were better able to collect from producers and thus to transmit revenues upward in the chain of authority. Those above held higher state authority and more coercive power. Lower-level authorities, to maintain themselves in this system, had to protect their local powers from all threats, and higher officials did not have the means to bypass local leaders. Reflecting this political fact, investigations in circar villages concluded in 1789, 1802, and 1804, that village accountants routinely reduced their tax obligations by underreporting village cultivated acreage. No comprehensive survey of total cropped area had ever been accomplished in Tirunelveli before 1800.[20]

Segmented politically, the regional order was built of many tiny domains of revenue collection. By 1800, virtually every imaginable productive asset and social group was assessed for tax purposes. A list compiled in 1823 shows thirty standard taxes in addition to land tax, transit duties, protection fees, and levies on houses, streets, and fields.[21] Centuries of increase in the money supply accompanied diversification of coinage. In 1800, thirty-two types of silver and gold coins circulated in Tirunelveli. Clipped and debased to alter their value from place to place and time to time, they were minted as far afield as Surat, Porto-Novo, Tanjavur, Travancore, Arcot, and Madras. Grain and land measures also varied locally. Each circuit of villages could thus truly report to early nineteenth-century investigators its own traditions of revenue payment.[22]

But certain key principles unified the tributary revenue system. Most importantly, tax assessments were made in kind on field crops and converted into cash by standardized means that show widespread appreciation for the relative market value of crops. Irrigated land—nanjai (or nunjah, in Anglo-Indian parlance)—was assessed perhaps twenty times higher than dry land, punjai (or punjah).[23] Nanjai revenues were, moreover, collected using procedures that enabled officials to profit from price fluctuations in the paddy market. Low, even nominal, punjai revenues were collected from villagers only in cash, according to soil type, which provided a surrogate measure of land productivity. Garden land, watered by wells, was assessed at very high cash rates, reflecting the high value of garden produce and its perishability, which prohibited official commitment to its marketing.[24] The Tamil categories for land use thus took on new commercial meanings. Nanjai comprised irrigated land, whose characteristic crop was paddy; and, because of paddy's market value, nanjai also meant land assessed by state officials in kind, so that the state might profit from sales of its share of the crop, the melvaram. Punjai meant unirrigated land, which by definition grew dry crops, like millets; and, because of millets' low market value, punjai also meant land assessed at very low rates, in cash collected directly by village leaders and paid to state officials. Very high-value garden land paid suitably high cash rates, which became part of the meaning of garden land and of the wells that watered their valuable crops.

A second set of conventions distinguished poligar from circar land. Poligar land was mostly dry, and poligar territories were tightly organized, militant caste domains. Economically poor, they would surely have seemed to Nayaka officers politically impenetrable. Like all dry parts of the region, these lands would have produced some garden crops, salt, salt fish, palmyra products, cotton, cattle, oil seeds, and pulses, which generated some cash income for villagers. Small deposits of iron ore and small smelting works near the hills, basket weaving, carpentry, jewelry, pottery, and peddling—all generated petty profits. But poligars and their local followers fought hard over revenue from these sources. Since the kings at Madurai did, however, provide a focal point for order among poligars, tribute payments were essential, and these would most likely have been paid—first to poligars, then by poligars—in the form of ceremonial gifts, ritual homage, and above all military service instead of cash. This was one key rule of the regional regime under the Nayakas that did change dramatically after 1740, when cash was increasingly demanded from poligars, to the distress of many, as we shall see shortly.

Dry lands and poligar domains were thus for the Nayakas a critical military base but not a lucrative source of revenue. The state relied on revenue from irrigated villages. Early nineteenth-century records indicate the extent of that dependence. In 1820, about 20 percent of all Tirunelveli land—irrigated land—provided 85 percent of all state revenue from field crops. Most revenue from trade, crafts, and other sources would have also come from riverine locales, where urban occupations concentrated. At the same time, of course, much of the state's income would have been spent in these same irrigated milieus. As for poligar tribute, even after 1801, when it had increased dramatically over the 1700 level, poligar tribute, or peshcash, as it was called, contributed only one-sixth of the regional state revenue, though poligar lands held one-third of the Tirunelveli population and more than one-third of its land.[25]

The critical set of state financial transactions centered on paddy fields. Revenue officers made a thorough account of procedures in Settur village in 1796 (Table 2). The qanungo, a local revenue official, supervised the division of the grain heap on the threshing floor; he made deductions from the gross produce to pay village watchmen, overseers, laborers who had reaped and threshed the crop, plowmen, and workers who bailed water from the tank to nourish the crops when water ran low. In addition, he made a deduction for the village maniyam—village management fees—in turn divided among the landowners, village servants, and an unspecified group of maniyamdars, probably landholders who managed village external affairs. Finally, cultivators and government divided the remainder, the qanungo's fee being taken from the landowner's share. Government agents in turn charged for protection (kaval) and took one-quarter of the fees paid for labor supervision (*kankanam*), some of which they must have provided.

Table 2   The Division of the Crop at Settur Village, 1796

	% of Harvest
Cultivators' Share (kudivaram)	
½ net produce (after deductions)	36%
minus Qanungo's fees	−1%
plus share of village maniyam	4%
	39%
Government's Share (melvaram)	
½ net produce (after deductions)	36%
protection (kaval) fees	7%
¼ of supervision (kankanam) fees	.1%
½ of Qanungo's fees	.4%
	43.5%
Service Fees	
Qanungo	.4%
Labor Supervisors	.5%
Reapers and Threshers	4%
Plowmen	4%
Waterers (for bailing from tank)	.1%
Village Maniyamdars	6%
	15%
Total	97.5%

SOURCE: PBR,IOL, 19 March 1798, pp. 2175-90.

Where paddy crops were unpredictable because of poor irrigation, this on-the-spot division of the grain heap seems to have been standard practice. The procedure for settling the annual revenue account (ja-mabandy) was more complex when good irrigation, regular crops, and established grain markets prevailed, that is, in the wet zone. Here revenue assessment and collection by division of the crop, which East India Company men called "amani," began before the harvest, when calculations were made on palm-leaf manuscripts, as the crop ripened in the fields. Arriving on the spot at a sufficiently late date in the growing season, state agents estimated the gross produce in a village, and set an estimated melvaram, with contractual provisions for de-viations in the actual harvest. From this point on, procedures for kar and pisanam harvests differed. More valuable in the market, kar paddy, harvested from September to November, usually as a second crop, could not be assured in most years, and would be divided in the grain heap, as in the Settur model. The official received only grain as tax payment. For the pisanam crop, however, reaped from January to April throughout the mixed and wet zones, government agents would compute the estimated cash value of the melvaram, using an official local harvest price, known as the jamabandy price, for each village. The leading landowners would be responsible for paying the land revenue: on the principle contained in the *Sukraniti* and quoted above, they would advance three-fifths of the value of the melvaram grain in cash. They had also to provide some security for the remaining two-fifths of the melvaram as a condition for official permission to reap the crop. Threats to obstruct the harvest or to abscond with the grain became useful levers for revenue agents as the crop neared maturity. Then, having collected their due at harvest time in money and grain, government agents sold paddy throughout the coming months to generate the state's needed cash revenue. As for any grain merchant, security for stores of paddy against robbers and embezzling hired hands was always costly and troublesome.[26]

The paddy market thus transformed grain into government revenue. Speculating in the market became a key to official power at all levels of the state. Assured of grain to sell during the predictable rise in prices between May and November, agents with access to melvaram grain stores could use government grain for the personal profits they needed to remain viable intermediaries in the revenue system. Profits would be especially high when a poor kar followed a good pisanam season, which would accelerate rising prices after September. But any average year would provide ample income, as we can see reflected in paddy seasonal price trends.

There exist no minute price data before 1800, and no regional data in detail until the late nineteenth century, when information was gathered as part of administrative modernization discussed in the next chapter. Price levels would, of course, have been much higher during the decades after 1875, and local prices would have then become much more uniform than before the building of the railway. But monthly prices from 1875 to 1893, recorded in the *Statistical Atlas of Madras Presidency for F. 1350*, still reflected seasonal ups and downs characteristic of much earlier times, caused by the rhythm of the monsoon and of agricultural production through the year. Relative average prices, in short, from one season to the next, would not have changed their course of movement from the eighteenth to the late nineteenth century, though, as I will argue in Chapter Five, improvements in transport and in irrigation would probably have made late nineteenth-century relative seasonal prices more consistent over space and time. This said, the late nineteenth-century price data show that the chances for making more than a 5 percent return on sales of paddy bought at March-April prices reached a high of 80 percent in July and August. After that chances declined to 55 percent in November, because both wet and dry crop harvests would lower the value of pisanam crops in storage. Though bad kar conditions or dry-land drought could generate high profits from sales of stored grain, such profits would be a gamble on the monsoon, and losses from rodents, rot, and theft would increase over time. Consequently, in the eighteenth century, any paddy left in government stores as late as November or December might have to be sold at a loss, barring poor autumn weather.

With their hands on the grain store and their eyes on local prices, eighteenth-century local officials were key actors in the grain market, buying and selling grain on private and public accounts to boost their own and government income. In addition, of course, their grain had to feed soldiers stationed nearby (and resident permanently in the fort at Palayamkottai). Local agents were by no means disinterested bureaucrats. Even under the Nayakas, and certainly by the late 1700s, the distinction between "public" and "private" did exist, but more as a gray area for discretionary judgment than as a sharp line. State income depended upon local officials' ability to make advances in anticipation of land revenues, and to buy and sell melvaram grain in response to local prices. This was not a system that could be managed by bureaucrats from a distance, and attempts to work it bureaucratically did not work. In 1807, a British collector in Tirunelveli had to wait for approval from Madras to lower official selling prices after a bumper harvest in September and October; the month delay meant rotted grain in storage and lost revenue.[27]

In the net of transactions that produced state income, there was no clear division between private and public, or economic and political power. During the 1700s, and probably before, each officer at each level of state authority contracted what the British called "leases" with the officer above, paying in advance to be authorized to collect, in turn, from below. At the pinnacle of the system in Tirunelveli, the delavoy remained one of the richest and most powerful men in the region; his family owned fifty-two villages in the mid-nineteenth century, clearly the winnings of many generations' dealing in grain, land, and revenue contracts.[28]

Swarms of moneyed men worked the middle rungs of the revenue chain; they varied in wealth from renters of a few villages to bidders for whole subregions. The Company received twenty bids for the entire Tirunelveli revenue in 1790, indicating that others had risen to the delavoy's financial level.[29] Many subregional renters would have been grain merchants like Muttuswamy Nayaka, who operated in Tirunelveli town and became one of its largest wholesalers by his success as revenue contractor and securer.[30] At the base of the system were key families whose intimate control of the grain heap, village credit, and local know-how constituted the primary links in the revenue chain. These families had intimate knowledge of the harvest, melvaram accounts, jamabandy prices, market fluctuation, and official personnel. In fact, they did much local selling of melvaram grain.[31] The base of the state financial system was thus built inside agricultural communities, and this, more than any other level of the system, survived intact into the nineteenth century.

Villages

By working the land, building caste alliances, moving and settling in villages and towns, and making lasting arrangements to define order among unequals, the people who produced wealth from Tirunelveli soil had developed three major styles of community life by the later days of Nayaka rule. One community type characterized each agricultural zone in the plains, though the mixed zone did contain communities characteristic of the dry zone, and vice versa. Each community type, in turn, defined a local subculture that was spread throughout each agricultural zone. Thus for simplicity I will refer to wet, dry, and mixed communities as types that define local order in each zone, though in fact this convention simplifies the historical and geographical situation somewhat. By this simplification, we can more clearly follow events at the community level from the founding through the evolution of British rule.

The Dry Zone

Over the centuries during which communities in the parched terrain north and south of the Tambraparni developed, land was abundant and labor scarce. Little fixed capital was required for agriculture; the most important items were bullocks, plows, and wells. Survival risks were high, but anyone with family labor could find land to cultivate for at least a meager subsistence. Calories produced per acre could not be raised simply by adding more labor without additional water, but there was plenty of land over which the population could spread thinly over generations. Many dry zone peasant families belonged to castes for whom moving in search of land into Tirunelveli remains today a living oral tradition: Shanars, Maravas, and Vadugas, whose ancestors settled the dry frontier in pioneer communities. Their life depended on the skills of hardy peasant households, who sought to command within close reach all the essentials for existence. Interfamily cooperation within jatis generated occupationally diverse and locally dominant peasant castes. Shanars were cultivators, merchants, priests, and warriors. Maravas were farmers, fighters, hunters, and priests. Vaduga cultivators fought for their land, worked the soil, and served priestly functions, too.[32] A farming jati in the dry zone became self-sufficient by necessity.

With open space all around, no single caste could control access to land in the dry zone, where dominance depended on close control of labor power by means of kinship, caste, patronage, and coercion. Even dominant caste elites remained cultivators, and even the richest non-cultivating landowner would have poor peasant relatives close by. Because landowning, work in the fields, and dominance all went together, getting one's hands dirty in raising crops conferred relatively high status in the dry-zone cultural economy. Any caste could and would work the land. The 1823 census shows that despite its low population density, the dry zone's villages often had as many resident jatis as did villages in the wet zone; and most of these jatis would have tilled to survive. As a result, caste status did not become rigidly tied to specific roles in the production process, and did not play a dominant role in determining access to the means of production. The biggest landowner and the landless laborers in a village could be of the same caste.

By the same token, very low-caste families, such as untouchable Pallas and Pariahs, could in the dry zone set themselves up as relatively independent peasant households, giving their very low status in the regional caste system much less degraded social content here than in the wet zone. British officials noted this phenomenon in the nineteenth century, when they endeavored to induce all "laboring castes" to perform road work for wages, and discovered that dry-zone untouchables did not consider themselves mere laborers at others' command. Because they would not volunteer, and because they were not at the command of village high-caste families, Company officers had to use force to put them into road gangs, under the justification that all untouchable castes were of the same status, whatever their local circumstance.[33] (Such coercion was surely not unique to the nineteenth century, and perhaps was convenient during temple and tank construction over the centuries.)

Within dry-zone villages, inequality in control over productive resources seems to have arisen from several factors that could combine to create indomitable village magnates, or could conflict with one another to form competing factions led by powerful families with opposing sets of clients. Numerical size and physical vitality varied among families; fixed capital assets such as bulls, plows, and wells, would enable some families to live more independently than others, and perhaps to rise as local patrons.[34] One means to acquire such assets became ever more important: access to networks of trade and credit. In pursuit of wealth, moreover, some families were better connected than others, endowed with superior status in kin and caste networks. Among Shanars, the distinction between tree-climbing Shanars and landowning or merchant Nadars, and among Maravas, the importance for rank of lineal proximity to dominant chiefs represent two styles of ascribed inequality that could come to correspond substantially to material differences. The most critical factor, often combined with the least one of the other sources of local superiority, involved hereditary village offices, which remained the preserve of important families. These were the local legacy of state networks built under the Pandyas and subsequent rulers. These offices were especially important in the dry-zone community power structure: the headman (*nattanmaikkaran*), vested with highest authority (*anmai*); the accountant (*karnam*, or *kanakkuppillai*), who recorded state revenue obligations; and the watchman (*kavalkaran*), protector and enforcer. Headmen almost always came from the locally dominant peasant caste, and were the primary link between local and subregional authorities. They paid village taxes to their superiors and were thereby authorized to collect from villagers by whatever means they saw fit.[35] Outside the Vaduga-dominated northeast, accountants took the caste epithet "Pillai" as a rule, and may indeed have become an occupationally distinct jati, using this epithet that usually denotes Vellala status.[36] In either case, headmen and accountants commonly came from different castes, it appears; because both were powerful officers, this could provide the basis for factional feuds. Outside Telugu poligar domains, Maravas everywhere monopolized the position of watchman, and built thereby caste networks as specialists in protection. The powers of village officers, therefore, could in some instances be exerted in combination—most commonly, one imagines, when they faced together an outside threat; or could conflict with one another if, for instance, contending officers should compete for the same prize.

Officers commanded sizable grants of tax-free (*inam*) land to support their position in the community. That grants of land had been the preferred mode for compensating village officers in the dry zone before 1800 became clear to early nineteenth-century observers. By contrast, outside the dry zone, salaries for village officers in cash and/or kind were the rule, and most inam land was enjoyed by temples or Brahman families.[37] A register of all inam land compiled in the 1870s as part of a government effort to abolish all tax-free holdings reveals that even then dry-zone village officer landholding remained considerable. In a sample of 111 villages from that register, 44 headmen each held 22 acres, on average; 56 accountants held 17 acres; and 37 watchmen held 10 acres each—after decades of administrative effort to write such perquisites off the books.[38] This indicates how powerful these officers remained after 1800, a subject for further discussion in Chapter Four. Reflecting the scale of accountants' land wealth in the early 1800s, a British collector reported in 1817 that "they in some few cases cultivate it themselves, or with hired labourers, but by far the greatest portion of the land is cultivated for them by the cultivating inhabitants of the village."[39]

Dry-zone communities thus evolved in such a way that upon the brink of British rule there existed within them no structural correspondence between caste and class. Inequality operated within an environment in which it was difficult for any stratum to rise much above any other in village society. Ties that bound patrons to clients often included kinship and caste, and the few most powerful families in a community would be, more often than not, families with village office, relatively large landholdings, and some valuable fixed agricultural assets. These families would compose the inner core of the local power structure. At times united, when war between chiefs meant war between villages, families also engaged in local power struggles to do battle inside communities. Arms for battle were almost as important as arms for cultivation, and, in this rugged domain, survival demanded close cooperation among close kin, who depended upon one another. In villages more distant from one another than those in the wet zone, people in the dry zone nonetheless had ties that wove them into subregional realms: above all, ties of caste dominion. They lived in a hard world of stiff competition and locally tight sub-jati solidarity.

The Wet Zone

Irrigated land in the semi-arid south is scarce and highly prized; it exists only as a result of intense labor, embodied in walls and ditches of earth and stone, and expended in the drudgery of seasons in the paddy fields. Irrigation produces sufficient wealth to sustain not only people who labor standing in water but concentrations of people whose work comprises management and related tasks, as well as many who do no agricultural work at all. In the Tamil country, irrigated agriculture developed under the Vellala-Brahman alliance, through which high-caste landowners brought under their control land, labor, and water; established their status in the agrarian system as a whole; and developed technical skills to expand the irrigation economy, all at the same time. The local order of wet-zone life does not seem to have undergone major structural change after the fall of the Pandyas. New groups pursued their interests in communities without disrupting the working logic of land and labor relations.

It appears that irrigating peasant farmers pooled their resources within the ur assemblies from very early times. Certainly by the days of brahmadeya grants, it had become customary for any irrigated village to be owned by a group of family shareholders, each endowed with a portion (*pakam*) of the village's collective assets expressed as a fixed number of shares (*pangus*). Inscriptions record so many transactions between ur and brahmadeya assemblies that their internal organization must have been quite similar, for epigraphy would surely reflect any radical differences between them in the nature of rights to land. Nineteenth-century reports also stress that Vellala and Brahman landowning collectivities worked exactly the same way, except in matters of caste ritual custom.[40] We can thus suppose that landowning patterns looked the same in both, though we have inscriptional evidence primarily for brahmadeyas. Original brahmadeya grants (the only available ones date from the thirteenth to the seventeenth centuries) all present similar pictures.[41] In each, the land involved is described and its boundaries defined. This most often meant grouping several existing settlements; all the resources within the area are assigned to a set number of Brahmans in a fixed number of shares. The grant does not specify the land of any family or individual; land is for the group as a whole. It does not distinguish cultivated from uncultivated, irrigated from unirrigated land. It does not, as we saw in Chapter One, even distinguish payments in grain.

To own land thus meant to be a member of a family in a group of shareholders; and to own not soil itself but all the varied resources involved in one's family share. The land was not conceived as a clump of earth distinct from the social relations that made it productive, or indeed distinct from the trees and water and surrounding scrub that all fit together into the production process. Perhaps as a result, the most basic word for land in Tamil, *kani*, also means a particular measure of land (fixed in the 1800s at 1.32 acres), as well as any hereditary right whether to land, office, or other resource.[42] To illustrate the meanings of kani, service caste families in wet communities, possessed a right (kani) to a share (pangu) of the village harvest as payment for services in the village throughout the year. Family members would each also have a claim to a share (pangu) in family assets, showing that one set of related terms in Tamil can indicate analogous rights within different kinds of collectivity. Owning land within a community of farmers on irrigated land was understood to be analogous to membership within a family.

Under the aegis of Muslim authority in the Tamil country, after 1750, the Arabic term *miras* came into vogue as a translation for the Tamil term kani in the sense of "hereditary right." A court case from 1849, for instance, describes the miras or kani right enjoyed by the headmen among the Palla workers of Tentirupperi village: "fees received in grain or otherwise by the parties recognized as the heads of the Palla caste in compensation for services rendered by them in procuring labourers for repairs of irrigation and other purposes beneficial to government and to the village community in general."[43] A similar position of headman for service castes seems to have existed for washermen, barbers, and others who might be needed by high-caste patrons for emergency services at any time. Thus, among service as well as landowning castes, kani or miras indicates a right of resource control by virtue of group membership. But by far the most comprehensive and powerful of all kani or mirasi rights were those that embraced irrigated villages as wholes. Families who possessed (in Tamil, literally "controlled") shares in the village were *kaniyatchikkaran*; in the Anglo-Indian official lexicon they became known as mirasidars.

As in a family, how to define who would be inside and who outside the group within which shares were held became a key to community order. The ideal, most restrictive criterion for membership in a mirasidar collectivity would be direct lineal descent from an original shareholder. As late as the nineteenth century, some families claimed this status, and received in recognition special honors and favorable tax rates.[44] Yet even in the early Pandya period, complex resource transactions in the local economy required broader criteria for entitlement to community assets. Mortgages, sales, loans, and gifts of pangus were the transactional basis for brahmadeyas, royal income, temple finance, and irrigation development. The ritualized exchange relations that supported temple worship and Brahman communities—described in the previous chapter—effectively defined criteria for entitlement both wide enough to include all exchanges necessary to develop irrigation and narrow enough to keep paddy culture in the hands of a coherent caste alliance, the core Pandya elite.

By patronizing temples and Brahmans, Vellalas established themselves as a status group identifiable by regional dominance and ritual stature, so that ritual became the vehicle for alliances across kinship and territorial divisions. By shared participation in this ritual system, the Pandya peasant elite directed investments from royalty into irrigated communities, laid the basis for intervillage cooperation necessary for extensive development of irrigation, and set the criteria for pangu transactions outside the original village collectivity. All these were functionally significant elements in marshaling resources for irrigated agriculture, and the system worked extremely well. Intervillage cooperation (and, as we will see, conflict) would have been continual features of production routine, because drainage tied villages together over the lay of the land. Moreover, outsider investments in village agriculture were critical inputs at many points in the life cycle of tanks, channels, and dams, especially after floods or breaches in walls. Because expanding paddy culture meant trading in grain and speculating on future returns from investment in irrigation, communities had always to be open to exchange transactions in rights to land. The ritual complex established an institutional means whereby outsiders could obtain rights to village resources even as they venerated mirasidars.

Court records show that by the nineteenth century, it was possible for high castes other than Vellalas and Brahmans to own shares. Shareholding communities of more than one caste were not rare by then.[45] I have not found evidence to indicate that this mixing of castes among shareholders occurred before 1800; it might have. As a rule, restricting membership in mirasidar collectivities to people within the fold of the Vellala-Brahman alliance would have controlled productive exchange in these communities during the centuries before 1800. The ritual system that made this possible also enhanced mirasidar command of their work force, to which we turn shortly. Reinforced by symbols of caste status and ritual honor, this community order proved extremely effective, and spread wherever irrigation spread in the Tamil country; it dominated the whole of the wet zone and scattered throughout the mixed zone.

Within a mirasidar community, a pangu constituted a family's right to a collection of resources, and represented a mix of individual and collective control over productive assets. One share would consist of one set fraction of the community's total assets. It could include payments from nonshareholders who paid for access to village land; payments from cultivators of land in which the shareholders had invested; produce from bits of land farmed by the shareholder's family or by laborers; access to trees, grazing land, and woods; claims on the labor of village servants; and rights to water. A pangu also embodied responsibility: to provide a share of capital and/or labor for irrigation building or repair; to pay a share of the state revenue demand and other costs incurred by the village as a whole; and to work within the established traditions of a specific shareholding community. It seems that individuals could invest their own assets, raise the value of their shares, and manage some capital assets independently of the group—in addition, of course, to buying, selling, and mortgaging whole or divided shares. Such enterprise may lie behind the fivefold rise in the value of one pangu between 1773 and 1837.[46] At the same time, however, it is recorded that many communities rotated specific fields among shareholders from time to time, a practice that generated numerous court cases in the nineteenth century, but how generally this occurred before 1800 records do not say.[47] A variety of local customs to accommodate family with community needs must have prevailed. In any local arrangement, the complex of individual and group rights—including people inside and outside the shareholding group—would have been staggering. The first European ever to observe ownership at work in irrigated communities reported that all the various claims had been recorded in village accounts.[48] But registers notwithstanding, these communities were rife with opportunities for conflict among closely interconnected cultivating families.

Because water flows downhill, conflicts of interest would have flowed across boundaries between irrigated communities. Along the Tambraparni, channels flowed through fields in many villages. If one took too much water, those downstream might not get enough. If channels clogged with silt because of neglect in one village, villages downstream would be deprived of their just due. Even a small tank might serve more than one village; and tanks built in a series so that one overflowed into another would forge bonds of interdependence among their respective villages. If one tank broke it would release a flood to break the one below. A single tank in disrepair might affect one group of users of its water more than others, because uneven silting might clog one outlet more than another. Thus irrigation gives rise to many disputes over individual and small-group responsibility for collective and larger-group resources. If my fields do not get enough water, why should I pay as much for repairs as someone better supplied with irrigation? If you do not uphold your end of our collective bargain, why should I support your rights to water? Why should I pay for work on irrigation that will not benefit me directly at all? Within and between irrigation communities disputes would have been constant, heated, and in need of speedy, firm solution, so that paddy production could proceed and expand.

With conflict resolution a constant necessity, shareholders do not seem to have hesitated to take disputes outside their community for arbitration, and intercommunity squabbles naturally required an authority outside of but respected by many distinct shareholding assemblies. Officers of the state undoubtedly served this role. Temple managers, poligars, and sabhas with extended authority over extended brahmadeyas were also in positions to do so. Certainly mirasidars had no qualms about using the courts set up by the East India Company. Every kind of dispute imaginable—within families, castes, and shareholding communities, and between individuals and groups in separate villages—was rushed for resolution to the judges. In the six years from 1801 to 1806, the Zillah Court in Tirunelveli town heard 1,767 cases, almost all concerning property rights in mirasidar villages along the banks of the Tambraparni.[49] Thirty years later a collector reported that arbitration and adjudication were a continual burden for his staff and for the courts, because these villagers had no tradition of authoritative councils—panchayats—on account of their factional and conflict-ridden character.[50] Some sources of conflict were, of course, born of the nineteenth century, as we see in the next few chapters. But the need for authoritative decisions to resolve disputes within the production process was not: it was built into irrigated agriculture, and it became especially pronounced as a system of tanks and channels extended over time to involve many separate communities along the Tambraparni valley.

Power within communities centered on the most resourceful mirasidars, for though the villages were collective entities, they were anything but egalitarian. Most recorded brahmadeya grants distributed shares unevenly at the outset. In one grant a Brahman was given six shares, and another three shares, whereas thirty-six others were given one share each.[51] Family fortunes over generations aggravated initial inequalities; the village of Vasudevanallur was typical of recorded cases, where in 1849 two Brahmans, 4 percent of the shareholders, owned 25 percent of all shares, and nine Brahmans, 18 percent of all shareholders, owned fully 57 percent of the village.[52] Share distribution aside, the value of assets within shares would differ sharply, especially in the absence of a smoothly running system of land rotation among shares, and it is hard to envision rotation working so as to eliminate inequality. Fields farthest from the source of local irrigation were at a natural disadvantage, as were fields on high ground. In a collective situation, politics would also have played a powerful role in family fortunes. Individual families could usurp resources traditionally attached to shares, and then fight to keep them, either locally or by the favor of some higher authority. Again, a considerable number of court cases record such activity after 1800. But even before that, it seems that factions in villages were formed around families recognized as leaders in the community, who would have had many advantages in struggles occurring in that area between individual family and collective community assets. The heads of these families served, in the 1700s, as revenue contractors. In charge of village tax payments, they were dubbed "leading shareholders" or "head mirasidars" by early nineteenth-century East India Company administrators.[53]

Unlike the situation in the dry zone, village office did not become a base for power in the wet zone in the centuries before 1800. Remember that Pandya inscriptions do not record local chiefs resident in the wet zone but only in peripheral parts of the Pandya realm. There developed no tradition of wet-zone village headmen; their functions were served rather by leading mirasidars. Accountants and watchmen did not enjoy substantial tax-free landholdings; they relied rather on shares of the harvest from mirasidars, whose servants they were understood to be.[54] The state thus worked in and through village mirasidar bodies, whose power in the political economy of rice farming was supported from Pandya to British times. Furthermore, as the most highly educated, the highest in caste status, and the most socially mobile strata in the region as a whole, landed Brahmans and Vellalas became core personnel in subregional networks of state and market activity. Mirasidars became official revenue contractors and merchants; indeed, mirasidars were the government in the wet zone, not only at the village level; they and their caste stratum peers comprised the subregional ruling class.

Mirasidar wealth, education, and cultural refinement depended on freedom from work in the fields. Over centuries, landowning in wet communities became more and more detached from agricultural labor, and landed families could thus turn their minds toward more exalted achievement. Premedieval peasants had probably worked their own irrigated fields, but under the Pandyas this would have become increasingly rare. As the infrastructure of irrigated agricultural developed, fixed capital—in tanks, channels, dams, and fields—rose in value relative to labor.[55] Population growth and Pandya conquests generated numbers of cultivators excluded from rights to irrigated land; and more intense cultivation made work more continual, both in the fields and in irrigation building and repair. As Brahmans became the cultural model of elite behavior and style among dominant peasants, not putting one's hands in the mud would have become a mark of entitlement to elite stature. To own land in a village came to mean overseeing its productive use, forseeing its productive potential, and seeing that irrigation works were built, repaired, and managed properly. All of this meant supervising the labor of others. In light of these features of landowning among medieval paddy farmers, it is suggestive that the word for land and land right, kani, is derived from the verb "to see."

Exactly how Vellalas and Brahmans obtained client cultivators to labor for them remains unclear. Pandya wars with tribal chiefs probably procured workers from the defeated populations, because both major landless laborer castes—Pallas and Pariahs—boast even today distant martial traditions, and some families from these castes maintained themselves as independent cultivators outside the wet zone, as we have seen. One of the Mackenzie Manuscripts records an oral tradition in which the Pallas are said to be "mountain people" who settled in the plains.[56] This change of milieu might have been forced on them by wars with Pandya armies, although, on the other hand, primitive cultivators from the hills or plains might have voluntarily exchanged their precarious independence for better-fed subservient status in irrigated villages. The nutritional security of wet land has induced independent landowners to forfeit ownership for irrigation on their land; many such cases appear in the nineteenth century.[57] For those with only their labor to barter, client status might have seemed a tolerable price to pay for a position, however lowly, in the wet-zone economy. Deals of this sort would have been struck, no doubt, in conditions of dire necessity, during droughts and wars that hit hardest outside the wet zone. In command of water from the Ghats, Brahmans and Vellalas were in a strong position to establish themselves as non-laboring landed elites.

Laboring client cultivators, of course, entered the caste system at the very lowest stratum. They traded subsistence for untouchability in each generation. Their lowliness found expression in public behavior directed toward them—in temples, fields, housing locations, and on roads.[58] Labor itself became lowly in the cultural economy of irrigated agriculture. The physical lowness (*pallam*) of fields and channels (*pallakkal*) embodied the lowliness of fieldworkers, known as *pallakkudi*— low people—Pallas. Ritual pollution, associated with untouchable work, reinforced the desire of landowners to escape field labor, and at the same time limited the social and economic mobility of field hands, reinforcing their dependence on high-caste landowners. Probably long before the nineteenth century, and most certainly by then, Pallas performed almost all the most grueling work in paddy cultivation in Tirunelveli.

Labor organization reflected the variety of jobs that Pallas had to perform. Building and repairing irrigation works were gang jobs for men, who dug, hauled, and piled dirt and rock. Gangs would also have built roads, temples, and other buildings. Groups of a few men would plow, manure, and thresh, whereas groups of women planted, transplanted, weeded, harvested, and hauled to both threshing floor and storage. Men worked mostly with stone and earth, women with seed and grain. Small-group tasks could be done on a field-by-field basis, each mirasidar contracting for work individually. But at peak points in the production cycle, as during the weeks when kar harvest and pisanam sowing occurred simultaneously in a village, coordinated work would have been necessary. Finally, drying, storing, measuring, and carting grain were jobs for individual workers, which merged with domestic chores like sweeping, cleaning cattle stalls, and running errands for mirasidar households.

A variety of labor relations organized the performance of these varied jobs. Though the mix of mirasidar collective and individual labor management would have varied according to the distribution of land among shareholders and the degree of village cooperation, in general it seems that agricultural labor operations were organized through dyadic contracts between mirasidars, either as families or as a community, and various client laboring households. Some client cultivators would have had their own stock and sufficient labor to cultivate as sharecroppers. Some would have worked for a daily grain wage, paid seasonally or by the task. Some would have worked for only one household and other families for the village as a whole.[59] Gang labor, however, would be demanded by mirasidars of laboring caste groups as a whole. As we saw in the village of Tentirupperi, a Palla headman would be charged to raise work gangs when needed, and would receive special status by his position.[60] In some villages, the Palla headman might have organized the entire production process, working for one large absentee landowner or upon temple land, a situation that seems to underlie the seventeenth-century Tamil folk drama, *Mukkudal Pallu*, whose hero, as headman, seems to have had considerable skill and some social status.[61]

Over the centuries, a spectrum of bonds thus developed between landowners and cultivators. Tenancy was, of course, widespread. Vellalas and lower non-Brahman families often became tenants themselves, working land with their own or hired labor. Tenancy contracts before 1800 probably followed a pattern standard thereafter, when tenant obligations varied according to the quality of irrigation and the respective contributions to production costs of landlord and tenant. Sharecropping seems to have been most common on less well irrigated land; the share (*varam*) of the crop paid to the landowner would increase, the more adequate the water supply. This arrangement would spread the risk of a bad season, and reward the landowner for providing good irrigation, which he would be responsible to maintain. On the very best irrigated land, where sufficient water for paddy was certain, landowners could demand a fixed grain rent, called *pattam*, which also prevailed on temple lands and elsewhere when landowners did not supervise the division of the grain heap. Tenants of all kinds paid more when landowners supplied bulls, plows, manure, seed, or other items; or when they provided advances of grain for food.[62]

The poorer the tenant, therefore, the more he would rely upon mirasidar capital and food advances; and hence the more dependent his position. The very poorest clients, of whom the Pallas clearly composed the majority, could at best establish themselves as sharecroppers or as fixed-rent tenants. Without capital or crops by which to repay debts, they would have had to repay with family labor. With nothing to barter for food but their toil, many Palla families became perpetually bonded to mirasidar families or to whole mirasidar villages. Rights to the labor of Pallas became an asset like any other for shareholders, one that could be bought and sold, given as dowry, and attached to plots of land, an integral part of the soil.[63] When they observed this bondage, British observers called it slavery, though its origins and internal dynamics were quite different from the Mediterranean and trans-Atlantic slaveries that informed their use of the term.[64]

Thus the wet community evolved as a highly stratified social milieu where access to the means of production was thoroughly identified with caste status. In stark contrast with the dry zone, the wet zone was not a land of rustic warrior-peasants, but of two distinct peasant strata: one owned land but did not labor; the other labored without owning even, in many cases, rights to its own labor power. Here our standard notion of "peasant" does not seem to fit at all. Yet in its management and cultivation, the farm remained a family affair, albeit tied into a strong community order. Farms were small; they were worked with premodern technology; they were worked as a way of life, not as a business for profit. Farmers were, moreover, subject to taxation by ruling elites. Many peasant attributes thus apply to farmers within wet communities, though they comprised two strata, indeed two classes, defined objectively by relative access to the means of production, and subjectively by their caste identity. The elite stratum was a peasant elite, who lived on farms in farming communities, yet had become long before the 1700s refined, educated, and socially mobile. From these families came many of the region's most powerful, learned, and able people in the arts, literature, business, and government. Mirasidar high culture made the village itself the home of Tamil erudition and classical Sanskrit wisdom. These were peasants of a very special sort, perhaps unique in the degree to which they combined attributes normally assigned either to rustic family farmers or to urban elite intellectuals. They were country folk with wide horizons, who needed protection and arbitration from ruling authorities, and upon whom rulers in turn depended to establish the economic and ideological foundation for any stable regime.

The Mixed Zone

The contrast between wet and dry communities demonstrates that peasant living standards, wealth, political power, and social status came to depend not on caste status above all, as a conventional image of traditional India would suggest, but rather on family access to agricultural assets within a specific milieu. These assets included symbolic resources—caste status, temple honors, official titles, and cash— among which status was seemingly most predictive of material status, including as it did reference to one's kin group and appropriateness for honors and titles. Yet caste ranking did not predict family material stature across agricultural zones. Lower down the scale than Brahmans and Vellalas, Telugu and Marava peasant-warriors nevertheless commanded the dry zone and its resources; even Shanars held sway in stretches of the southeast. Lowest of all, the Pallas and Pariahs who farmed their own land in the north lived more independently than their wet-zone counterparts could ever have done. Comparing wet and dry communities, caste status by itself predicts peasant living conditions only where it became equated historically with the ownership of fixed capital, that is, in irrigated communities; here caste strata became so dominant politically because the wet zone provided the financial base for regional states, and rulers supported the Vellala-Brahman alliance. Within any community, families varied in stature within castes according to their control of capital valued in their specific milieu. To own a well in the wet zone meant little compared to what it would mean in a dry-zone village. Everywhere the value of land as capital depended on its water supply.

Vellalas and Brahmans became a formidable elite in the Tamil country because during the days of the Cholas and Pandyas they seized the land best supplied with drainage. After 1300, the states they built crumbled, but their capital retained and increased its value. They developed the social and material technology to extend and intensify paddy cultivation, protected and patronized by rulers whose realms depended on their water. Over time they commanded contiguous stretches of the infrastructure for irrigation in the northern coastal plains, in Tanjavur, and in Tirunelveli. From their extended networks of tanks, channels, dams, and fields, built bit by bit, one paddy crop at a time, grew the symbolic assets and social prestige of mirasidar elites.

That Brahman and Vellala elites would not have become such a prominent force in Tamil civilization without control of the Tamil country's best drainage becomes clear when we compare the position of wet and mixed-zone mirasidars in Tirunelveli. Though as descendants of the Pandya elite mirasidars attained elite status wherever they commanded drainage irrigation, their position relied on the quality of that irrigation. Accordingly, mirasidar stature remained over the centuries much less secure in the more isolated, less well watered irrigated villages of the mixed zone. The shifting fortunes of the goddess at Srivilliputtur, previously described, indicate the ups and downs of royal patronage for localities in this tract, especially when compared with the vast endowments enjoyed by the gods at Ambasamudram and Tirunelveli town. Following the demise of the Pandya dynasty, pockets of Pandya elite control and tank irrigation in the mixed zone were surrounded by dry-farming migrant peasant settlements. In search of land, water, and power came Maravas, Telugus, and Shanars, a new and threatening set of political interests to be reckoned with.

Evidence from nineteenth-century court cases and revenue records, discussed in Chapter Six, indicates that Vellala mirasidars tended to work land with their own hands more often in the mixed than in the wet zone; and in the mixed zone there were many nonmirasidar Vellalas who worked as tenants on Brahman mirasidar dry lands. Here, too, the relative productive power of dry and wet land was the reverse of that in the wet zone, not only because the soil was often better, especially in the north, but because the irrigation was often much worse. As a result, dry land surrounding irrigated villages became a much more important asset for mirasidar communities. On these dry lands, peasant households from various castes could set up dry-crop production, independent of any need for capital assets, that is, irrigation, under mirasidar control. Yet over these same dry lands mirasidars staked their claim, justified by their Pandya elite status and compelled by the value of this land as a potential source of income to supplement precarious irrigated agriculture. The fragmented character of mixed-zone irrigation meant that mirasidar kinsmen had nowhere to expand irrigation and hence to develop capital assets in agriculture. Instead they sought political domain over dry land, so as to gain thereby regular payments from dry cultivators established in the category of tenants. Thus the Tenkasi Pandyas, after the fall of Madurai, in the 1300s, rapidly established a bevy of new brahmadeyas, whose grants included payments from subordinate dry-land farmers.[65]

Faced with competition for dry land between Pandya elites and peasant farmers, the kings at Madurai, officials at Tirunelveli, and even poligars would have in principle favored mirasidars, especially Brahmans, by the cultural logic of kingship itself. Though kings large and small could not have actually enforced sanctions with much regularity, there did seem to emerge a lasting, if tension-ridden, custom, based on this principle, in many communities throughout the mixed zone. Dry-land farmers would pay a cash fee annually for the privilege of farming land within a mirasidar village domain. The fee, called swamibhogam, proclaims in its very name its justification: it means roughly "gift for the lord."[66] That this fee continued to be customary into the nineteenth century testifies to the fact that state authorities continued to patronize the Pandya elite in their dealings with the mixed zone. Mirasidars remained in place as preferred state agents and revenue intermediaries in circar lands through the eighteenth century.[67]

Poligar lands may well have been different. Maravas assumed strong positions throughout the mixed zone. Marava chiefs controlled some good wet land in places, and became forceful protectors, as well. In the north, Marava kaval chiefs and poligars seem to have respected the sanctity of mirasidar villages in general, even as they collected protection fees over the course of Nayaka rule. The fact that nineteenth-century records show no surviving custom of swamibhogam payments from Marava farmers to mirasidars may indicate either that Marava poligars never recognized mirasidar claims or that the custom went into disuse during political disruption after 1740.[68] Whatever the case, mixed-zone mirasidars from the north to the south were much more vulnerable to harsh political winds than their wet-zone counterparts, and winds blew hard after the fall of the Nayakas.

DECISIONS

Every second century after 800 brought trauma to people in Madurai city and forced critical decisions on people throughout the Tirunelveli region. Again in the eighteenth century, the capital broke open with war, as it had in the tenth, twelfth, fourteenth, and sixteenth centuries.

Again armies vied for the throne. When the Nayakas disappeared as the pinnacle of authority in the regional system of tributary payments, competition ensued that altered the rules of political negotiations throughout the countryside. The region broke into its constituent political regions, each the scene for distinct styles of conflict and accommodation that would gradually move villages at the tip of India into the embrace of British East India Company Raj.

Shocks to the Nayakas began in 1670, when troops from Mysore occupied northwestern Nayaka territory, far north of Madurai. Losses then followed in rapid succession: Maratha armies from the Deccan took Tanjavur, in 1674; the Marava Raja of Ramanathapuram declared his autonomy; and Dutch merchants recognized the raja's authority on the coast, with treaties and tribute, declaring him to be "the protector of Tuticorin and Kayalpatnam," and paying to him what had formerly been given to Madurai.[69] By 1694, the Mughal emperor, Aurangzeb, had conquered much of the peninsula and his governor, the nawab of Arcot, demanded tribute from the Nayakas, after which the nawab and others took turns conquering Madurai. The city changed hands at least ten times between 1732 and 1755, and four times in 1752 alone.

A petition of 1754 demonstrates the insecurity felt by political actors in this treacherous scene. Submitted to the British East India Company governor in Madras, it claims to represent the wishes of poligars at large, but is signed by only one, Nama Nayaka, and indicates that political transactions were at this time very far-flung in the Tamil country. Nama Nayaka requests Company help in the effort to reestablish a strong center of order at Madurai, where the Nayakas had lost battles to forces that he hoped would succumb to an army of allied English and nawabi soldiers. The poligar moans that he and his peers are "in a very bad circumstance having no ruler to command us," having "had no king for these twenty years past." He expresses their willingness "to pay tribute to the nawab according as it was customary" and promises that he would "endeavour to deserve his honour's favor." His motives are clear. Strong rulers at Madurai "will settle the country."[70] Disruption adversely affected many, including poligars, for it turned the terms of political negotiations in favor of the physically stronger contenders whose ambitions might be kept in check by a strong center. As it happened, troops under allied Company and nawabi command seized Madurai in 1755, and held it for the rest of the century; but, like the first Nayakas, they had to fight a shifting set of military alliances in the region for fifty years to accumulate sufficient power for settling the country.[71]

Disorder, however, also created opportunities, whose pursuit perhaps prolonged the transition to a new regime and certainly changed the rules of tribute payment in the countryside. Local Marava kaval chiefs began "acting like poligars" by collecting tribute from stretches of circar territory. Revenue agents used arms to press villagers for more of the grain heap. Poligars raided each others' land and took protection money from peasants and merchants wherever they could.[72] The price of protection rose, and early nineteenth-century inquiries indicate that people who needed protection paid dearly for it.[73] Oral accounts in the Mackenzie Manuscripts show that demands on poligars thrust deeper into their pockets. Company records show that the small and relatively weak poligar of Settur paid an annual mean peshcash of 1,554 strings of cash (chukrams) in the 1740s, but 2,524 chukrams in the 1770s, and 5,375 chukrams in the 1790s. Settur paid more frequently, too: in six years during the 1740s and in nine during the 1790s.[74] These payments went to captains of armies from Madurai, who collected what they could according to the force they could bring to bear. Madurai's revenue rose 50 percent above the 1744-1801 average during the regional command of Yusuf Khan, who toured Tirunelveli with a powerful army, and fell to a pittance during the height of poligar resistance to the Madurai regime.[75] Poligars in turn gathered in all they could, as did local revenue agents in circar land. After 1750, a variety of cesses that had not been collected before seem to have become routine: one a percentage commission charged by agents on the village revenue demand; another, called desakaval, a protection fee collected by poligars in circar territory, which was said to account for up to 40 percent of some poligar revenue.[76]

Competing warriors fought for the fruits of agricultural and commercial labor, and clearly siphoned off funds that might have been used in productive investment, such as irrigation building and repair; this diversion retarded growth in water control. But all was not chaos and decay. Temple building, it seems, surged ahead; new temple construction grew fastest precisely where poligar competition and resistance were most intense, in the northeastern domains of Ettaiyapuram and Panchalamkurichi poligars, and where kaval chiefs collided in the south. Warriors thus invested in temples to convert tribute into ritual honor. It is striking, therefore, that recorded temple construction did not increase in Marava poligar lands, perhaps because these Marava little kings were too impoverished and embattled for such investments, or perhaps because their handiwork did not survive.[77]

Some commercial investors also thrived. Because most fighting took place far from the Tambraparni, where Tirunelveli town, under the protection of Company and nawabi troops, was never seriously threatened, wet-zone paddy traders could seek high prices for their goods among hungry warriors.[78] The poligar of Panchalamkurichi contracted with boatmen and grain dealers near the Tambraparni delta to supply his troops, and merchants who supplied the Palayamkottai garrison made spectacular profits in collusion with local officials. Monied men with liquid assets to unload financed military competitors at all levels. The nawab sank in debt to Company employees. The delavoy owed huge sums to the Madras banker through whom he paid tribute to the nawab.[79] Moneylenders, called sowcars, paid poligar tribute and perhaps payrolls: "Most of the sowcars of the Southern Provinces have open accounts with the Poligars, and are in the habit of frequent dealings with them. For management of their concerns they have Gomastahs, etc. established in the Pollams to wait on the spot to receive the produce of different crops that may be assigned to the liquidation of their demands."[80]

Politically astute and well-connected people in positions to collect, transmit, store, and promise payments in cash and kind inserted themselves into profitable niches amid the turmoil. As the nawab's power grew after 1740, so did the number of Muslim names listed in accounts of revenue contractors, though the Medai delavoy continued as top regional contractor for many years and the East India Company itself assumed this position from 1783 to 1791. At the base of the tribute system, local contractors still came from the ranks of the established elite: they were mostly Vellalas, according to an account in 1793, when a list of major contractors in the region shows fourteen Vellalas, three Muslims, and one Chetti.[81]

The resolution of struggles over regional authority progressed in stages that probably parallel the trend two centuries before, during the sixteenth-century founding of the Nayaka dynasty. The armies of the new ruling power first seized control of the capital cities, Madurai and Tirunelveli. From this base they garnered the revenues of nearby irrigated villages, the most prosperous in the realm, and, in Tirunelveli, extended their protection over the whole of the invaluable wet zone. The strategic location of the central city, its temple, its fort, and its merchants served the forces of the nawab and the East India Company well, as it had the later Pandyas and the Nayakas. Revered, protected, and patronized by regional rulers for a thousand years, wet-zone agrarian interests looked to Tirunelveli and Madurai for support, and paid their tribute in return. They seem to have been won over to the new regime as early as the 1750s, disputes over the level of revenue exactions notwithstanding. For wet-zone elites, decisions did not revolve around a central moral question of loyalty to their king—or so it appears—but on questions of self-preservation and loyalty to a system of regional order that paid due respect to themselves.

Peasants and poligars outside the wet zone expressed entirely different interests and evaluations of the eighteenth-century situation in their political decisions to fight to defend or to expand their territorial and tribute-collecting power in the face of new claimants to regional authority. Village leaders and their chiefs struggled to form alliances that would better their position. As the Company brought superior force to bear, many poligars, like Ettaiyapuram, felt blows that propelled them toward an alliance with the Company and the nawab. Poligar support—gained chiefly with Company victories in the field, though Nama Nayaka's letter indicates that some supporters awaited Company commanders when they first arrived in Madurai—turned the military balance of power slowly toward the nawab and his Company protectors. By the late 1790s, only the poligar of Panchalamkurichi, Kattabomman Nayaka, kept his men in the field. After long and valiant years of war, Kattabomman's men finally succumbed to allied poligar, nawabi, and Company forces in 1801. Thus over the decades, critical decisions about who among competing claimants would merit payments of tribute from villagers in the region produced the foundations for a new regime.

· 4 ·

ANGLO-INDIAN EMPIRE

The Nayaka dynasty, having centralized political power more fully than any previous regime, collapsed in its maturity, unable to hold its capital against armies from the north. As before, the fall of Madurai triggered battles among contenders for regional power and among rival factions throughout the realm. The social costs of war mounted over decades. The 1790s brought a series of disasters: drought, famine, war, flood, and disease wracked the population. The last rebel succumbed in 1801. Military conditions for a new state structure had been established, once again, by bloody conquest, by shifting alliances, by accumulating peasant support, and by decisions simply to stop fighting, in that state of exhaustion which beats down resistance during prolonged periods of distress. Peace settled on the land. Villagers returned to farming. The work of building a new regional order could begin. Like the Nayakas, the new ruling elite, their troops in control of the old Pandya realm, set about consolidating their power; they did so within the largest domain of routine political relations of which Tirunelveli peasants had ever been part, the Madras Presidency.

The nineteenth century witnessed a slow but steady political centralization as urban elites expanded their power and urban centers became nodal points for professional administrative action in village affairs. That centralization progressed in three phases of imperial state building. Each phase had its particular significance for the peasantry; together they chart the creation of the modern political structure on which twentieth-century politicians built a nationalist superstructure in South India. First, the new regime settled into already functioning networks of state power and authority. Company officials, Indians and Englishmen alike, adjusted that system as much as possible to their own needs, while they adjusted their own expectations and goals in a constant process of negotiation. By doing so they created an Anglo-Indian language of official discourse, which had come into being by the early 1820s. Second, using that language, the new ruling elite developed a working ideology that systematized the terms of transactions between powerholders at various levels of state authority. The ryotwari system as it worked under the Company expressed the many tacit agreements about the underpinnings of Anglo-Indian political order in Madras Presidency. Third, within this ideological setting es-

101

tablished during three decades after 1820, state personnel imported industrial technologies, both material and organizational, during four decades of profound economic and imperial expansion from 1840 to 1880. The result was Queen Victoria's empire, built by self-conscious and self-interested efforts by Indians and Englishmen, village peasants, and urban elites.

COMMUNICATION

The Company came to power in order to enrich its treasury and to finance its trade with tax revenue. Its English officers came to know South India slowly and pragmatically—first in port cities, most importantly Madras, then in towns that came under Company authority with military victories. The first Company officer arrived in Tirunelveli in the 1790s, and revenue was his primary concern. He was a collector under the authority of the Board of Revenue in Madras, which served in turn under the Governor in Council. Initially, the collector was the only permanent English officer in administrative divisions of Madras Presidency, called collectorates, or districts. Judges, commercial residents, medical officers, and engineers would follow. At most, four or five Englishmen supervised government business in districts with populations in the hundreds of thousands and, by 1901, millions. English officers normally stayed in the district for a few years at most, many but a few months. Two very influential collectors, we will see, shaped district administration for one full decade each. Only these two were strong, activist experts in agrarian administration; the rest seem to have followed orders, reported dutifully to the capital, and carried on by established custom.

Under the district collector, a native officer corps performed most government work. The highest native officers administered subregions of a district, called taluks (Map 5), and were titled tahsildars; or they worked closely with the collector in district headquarters, where the seniormost native officer was the huzur sherishtadar. Beneath tahsildars, who held sway in taluks, village officers collected revenue and kept revenue records. Custom bestowed on native officers during the Company period considerable influence and power within their spheres of authority, and in a few years the collector could report that stable arrangements had been made to deliver the revenue from the Tinnevelly District to Madras. His success, as well as the stability of the revenue system for years to come, depended on the inclusion of existing local, subregional, and regional men of wealth and authority into the Company regime.[1]

To build the new state required a language of official communication, centered on revenue transactions. Few English officers would learn a South Indian language well. They instead transliterated revenue terms, official titles, and place names into English script and treated these as lexical items in their Anglo-Indian English jargon. Few villagers learned English, of course, so that the critical function of translation and interpretation, which enabled Englishmen to learn about their Tamil-speaking subjects and Tamils to learn what English officers needed to know, fell to literate native officers. These men learned, used, and shaped Anglo-Indian English to their own purposes, bringing to it words from many Indian languages, but most importantly terms from the Mughal legal and administrative lexicon. The language that evolved would have seemed utterly oriental in London. Correspondence during the Company period changed in form of expression as it passed from lower to higher levels of authority: communications to London were penned in standard English; district records that preserve and transmit local information are composed in a Tamilized Anglo-Indian English.[2] A handful of literate Tamils, especially those working close to collectors, learned English as fast as they could. Widening opportunities for English education, and hence for official employment, opened slowly but steadily, and more swiftly after 1840, by which time a select native officer corps had established mastery. These men produced the mountains of documents that recorded events in districts for historians and informed English official wisdom about the necessities of South Indian statecraft. Most native officials did not learn much English under the Company, though all officers outside the village did so increasingly after 1850. Anglo-Indian jargon introduced a set of terms, some with exact Tamil equivalents, some with near equivalents, and some entirely foreign, into the peasant's Tamil language during regular discourse with district and taluk officials.

By the 1820s, the Madras Presidency had become more linguistically complicated as its villages became part of one state. Language marked social stratum. A distinctively English style of Anglo-Indian speech unified the ruling elite and set them apart. A distinctively Indian style of English speech set powerful native officials apart from both underlings and superiors. Ordinary folk spoke South Indian tongues peppered with lexical items drawn from official jargon that were surely interpreted according to local conditions. Frustrating dialogues must thus have complicated the politics of administration among aspiring English and Indian officials, with constant translation required for what could have been a simple conversation for people speaking the same language. English dependence on native knowledge of English caused constant aggravation (this rings out loud and clear in Company records), fueled English suspicions of native officers, and spurred English resolve to train suitably English-educated Indian bureaucrats.

Englishmen devised the official lexicon for colonial discourse—they defined meanings shared by Englishmen in London, Calcutta, Madras, and districts—by formulating policy; policies codified the official language of Anglo-Indian governance. Two terms, utterly foreign to Tamil peasants, designated central policy concepts: zamindar and ryot. In 1801, Company officers applied in Madras districts the permanent settlement devised by Lord Cornwallis in Bengal, and confirmed poligars in possession of their land as zamindars, or landlords.[3] Henceforth, zamindars owned zamindari estates by virtue of annual tribute (peshcash) payments to government, payments fixed in perpetuity. Thus, shorn of an army and bound to the terms of the permanent settlement, men like the poligar of Ettaiyapuram became zamindars in 1801, and the political distinction between poligar and circar land, established under the Nayakas, survived in Anglo-Indian form. What policy to apply to circar land occupied Company minds in India and London until 1820, when the policy principles devised by Thomas Munro, who became governor in that year, gained official supremacy. Munro's principles—the ryotwari system—defined the state itself as supreme landlord, and individual peasants as landowners who obtained title by paying annual cash rent, or revenue assessments, to the government. The ryots, as peasants were called, received, in return for revenue payments, a pattah, an annual receipt that constituted title to land. Munro's plan called for rents to be set suitably low and fixed for a period of thirty years, to afford peasant farmers security from the arbitrary and mounting exactions from revenue intermediaries that he believed had damaged peasant property rights in the past.[4]

Munro's ryotwari policy set down definitions for key terms. It established an orthodoxy among personnel who construed justice and efficiency in colonial South India, and guided official thought and action forever more. But by itself it could not solve all communication problems that faced the Company regime. Transportation was slow. Overland dispatches to and from Madras and Tirunelveli town normally took more than a week to reach their destination, though the sea route was somewhat quicker. Linguistic and cultural barriers obstructed understanding. Transmitting orders from the presidency capital to villages in the districts and communicating information about revenue matters in return entailed multiple acts of translation and interpretation by actors on opposite sides of subtle cultural boundaries. The term ryot, for example, designated all peasants to Thomas Munro, but no district collector could work effectively without recognizing important distinctions among the peasantry, such as those that distinguished family farmers in the wet and dry zones of Tinnevelly District, or those that separated greater and lesser families in every village community. In the village itself, to be a peasant meant much more than to pay rent to the state; it entailed caste identity and customary relations of inequality that put each farmer in his place in local society but had no place in ryotwari theory. Likewise, zamindars remained little kings for their subjects; they retained the title of raja and held customary authority in ritual and caste structures that defined their territorial domains.[5] Native officers, too, did not see themselves strictly in the narrow bureaucratic terms defined by the new orthodoxy; nor did others on the Tamil side of the Anglo-Indian cultural divide see them so simplistically. The families that served in the regional officer corps after 1801 had done so for years before. Their personal powers hinged on their status in society and depended on their ability to accumulate wealth, dispense patronage, and wield influence in their spheres of action. They logically viewed state authority as being vested in themselves as persons, and, by extension, in their kinship groups and social strata. The same could be said of village officers, who worked in state and in other social networks simultaneously to build and to expand their own family resource base.

Working principles for orderly state finance under the Company and for progressive centralization developed in negotiations across cultural boundaries in which native officers were decisive. The very highest positions in the regional officer corps were filled by urban descendants of the Nayaka regional elite. Many were Brahmans, whose literate skills and rapid move toward English education enabled them to dominate the highest posts held by Indians well into the twentieth century.[6] Looking at the whole range of native officers in the taluk and district headquarters of Tinnevelly District, however, we find that Brahmans dominated only the very highest posts, and that overall official power remained concentrated in the Pandya Vellala-Brahman alliance.[7] In addition, a great many officers were landowners, and among these it is no surprise to find landed interests concentrated in the Tambraparni River valley. In 1851, about 60 percent of all native officers required to report their landholdings had either inherited or purchased land.[8] About one-third of this land had been acquired after obtaining office, which supports one collector's view: "The purchase of land is the first object of every public officer. As soon as he comes to office he looks around for an eligible spot of ground and the deep schemes that are laid to obtain it are not perhaps to be credited and

105

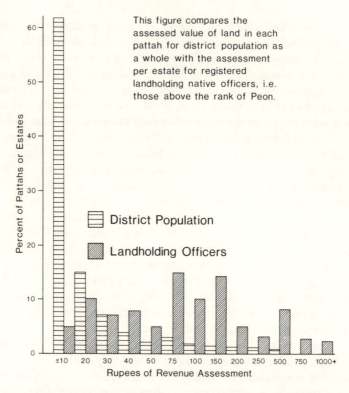

This figure compares the assessed value of land in each pattah for district population as a whole with the assessment per estate for registered landholding native officers, i.e. those above the rank of Peon.

Figure 4 Tinnevelly District Native Officers' Landholdings, 1850
SOURCES: PBR,TNA 3 July 1851, vol. 2291, pp. 9079-102; PBR,TNA, 4 December 1851, vol. 2309, pp. 16051-54.

until it is accomplished the individual is restless and uneasy."[9] Yet the majority of reported holdings, described as "patrimonial property," constituted a patrimony for landed officers of very substantial proportions. Total officer holdings averaged 39 acres, assessed at an average 75 rupees land revenue, compared to averages of 10 acres and 21 rupees for the general population. Figure 4 shows that landowning officers had relatively few petty holders among them. This reflects, in part, the high value of irrigated land along the Tambraparni, for about two-thirds of their holdings lay in Tambraparni taluks, and only 15 percent in the dry zone, compared to proportions of 30 and 48 percent, respectively, for the general population.[10]

The men who translated the terms of Munro's ryotwari policy into Tamil and interpreted rustic realities for English officials were thus

106

well equipped for the task. Their interest lay in the stability of the new regime and their concern was with their future in its expanding power. The personal powers that enabled native officers to perform their roles in the state were rooted, too, in their status as an established rural elite. From this advantaged position they could negotiate and communicate both upward in the chain of command with English officials and downward with village officers and peasants. When negotiating to put Company policy into practice in the countryside, they bridged cultural boundaries by sitting—in virtue of their interests and their culture—on both sides of the table.

IDEOLOGY

The overarching imperative for Englishmen was to centralize state power by channeling resources into the grasp of English officials in urban centers. Their efforts concentrated above all on tax information and revenue. Both native officers in town and village leaders in the countryside could benefit from this endeavor, which forged a lasting bond of mutual interest that set the new regime on firm footing from the outset. But central state power also threatened the personal domains of key people in town and country whose active participation in the state was essential. Segmentary domains of political power had thus to be breached and integrated to centralize control over information and taxation. For Englishmen the ideological basis of this project was captured in Utilitarian theory, which envisioned that prosperity and justice flowed naturally from government policies to secure private property rights and law and order, the goals of ryotwari.[11] Yet amid the cultural and political mosaic of colonial South India, the practical principles of government could not be founded on this basis alone. For from the Indian side came conceptions of justice and moral order, as well as perceptions of self-interest, that inserted themselves into the ideology of colonial statecraft from the outset. Events that produced institutional foundations for the collection of revenue in village Tirunelveli thus reveal Anglo-Indian colonial ideology in the making.

The theory of ryotwari dictated that every year each cultivator would pay directly into the treasury, through a chain of disinterested bureaucrats, cash taxes for family land. English advocates of ryotwari believed that it captured the essence of customary procedures in village South India, at the very least in villages dedicated to dry-crop farming;[12] they did not realize how much information, authority, and wealth involved in regional state finance before 1801 had been contained within local circuits of peasant life. A first step to centralize information was taken in 1801, when the collector ordered a survey of all cultivated land in Tinnevelly District. Completed in 1804, it recorded revenue dues from each village at that time, in one currency, the rupee, and aggregate cultivated land in each village, using customary measures for wet and dry land, respectively.[13] The survey lumped several, sometimes many, settlements together in "revenue villages," the first preserved list being that recorded in the 1823 census.[14] The details of the 1804 survey seem to have been kept in taluk offices until gathered together under Munro's orders in 1821, by which time the central authority in the region commanded an unprecedentedly full account of all dues from all farmland, itself a major accomplishment for the day. The surveys provoked animosity from village officers, who feared surveys as a threat to their autonomy and authority; a delegation presented their protest to the Board of Revenue in Madras.[15]

But early surveys constituted no such threat. They did not demarcate fields in villages. Nor did they assess individual landholdings. The power and authority to assess and collect stayed in the hands of the village officers. Even the best of the early surveys—several were conducted after 1801, culminating in the effort that produced the 1823 census—remained useless for assessment and collection by officers outside the village. In 1837, after sixteen years of annual ryotwari settlements, which began on a regular basis with Munro's governorship, half of all the dry fields in Tirunelveli were entirely unmarked and thus unidentifiable by nonvillagers. The so-called fields that were recorded on some early surveys could comprise up to seventy-three acres, many times more than could be farmed by one family. Who cultivated what land could thus only be ascertained by village officers.[16] District collectors and talukdars reported in annual accounts that a ryotwari settlement had been completed each year, but they in fact had no way to tell which peasant owned what land, how much it was assessed, or even if any particular peasant had paid, except from village officers. Not only was the first classification of soils assigned by the collector to be done "by the villagers themselves," but lands plowed up after 1804 were classified in the same way, under the eye of village officials.[17]

Dry-zone villages best approximated Munro's vision of peasant South India, but periodic checks by British officers always revealed that the revenue system looked very little like that which Munro prescribed. One inquiry showed that in Tinnevelly District the worst quality soils were recorded by accountants as most widely cultivated, whereas the best soils were left fallow by farmers year after year, a good ploy for reducing tax demand, but not good farming technique. Also revealed was the fact that twenty "extra collections," on top of land revenue, remained in force in dry villages, all the legacy of pre-1800 traditions, and most were paid to village officers for their own benefit.[18] In the 1820s, a collector bemoaned that there was "little left of the permanent classification and assessment" of soil types in the district.[19] And in 1827 Munro himself singled out Tinnevelly District for the excessive powers wielded by village accountants (curnams) in dry villages: "there are no detailed revenue accounts, or even abstracts . . . that can be depended upon. Too much is left to the curnams. They execute many of the duties which properly belong to the Collector and Tahsildars; they distribute the assessment; they assess the ryots as they please, entering their lands under . . . higher or lower rate."[20]

Village officers in dry villages—headmen and accountants—were simply not accountable; and, as we shall see, neither were village watchmen. Urban officials had very little sway over revenue transactions in the countryside except to enforce collections at a level set by custom and paid through customary channels, with customary loopholes and deals under the table. In negotiations between officers of the Company regime in town and country, before and after 1820, it was agreed that the position of village leaders would remain intact in return for revenue payments. Given limited opportunities for peasants to earn cash, existing officers, with their landholdings and traditional authority, stood the best chance of delivering revenue regularly. Tax-collecting authority in turn bolstered village leadership, both politically and economically. Until peasants could put their hands on the requisite cash and urban elites could control village revenue data—conditions that emerged only after mid-century—headmen and accountants remained unassailable in their transactions with urban officers.

Wet-zone Tinnevelly District did not resemble Munro's vision of village India at all. Yet here lay the state's prize tax mine. The best irrigated land in the region lay near the district's most important urban centers, including district headquarters, where high government officials engaged themselves in revenue operations and owned substantial acreage at the same time. Munro's policy, never designed to accommodate collective landholding traditions that were normal in areas that had once been medieval centers of Tamil civilization, clashed with custom and vested interests in villages at the heart of Company territory in Tinnevelly District.[21] The Company needed a steady flow of cash into the treasury, and policy makers resolved to detach government from its customarily deep involvement in paddy markets in order to prevent what they saw as corruption among profiteers in state service, and to increase thereby revenue receipts. But the customary system of dividing the harvest and realizing state revenues in paddy sales during the course of the fiscal year held many advantages for mirasidars. Not only did it put profit into the hands of mirasidar middlemen, it adjusted state tax demand to the two seasonal sources of variation in mirasidar agricultural income: yields and prices. The English plan to collect fixed money taxes, inflexible in the face of fluctuating yields and prices, and payable by each individual landowner, met implacable hostility in irrigated villages.

Urban officials followed two directives in negotiations with village mirasidars: to secure annual cash revenues at the lowest possible administrative cost, and, with that end in view, to accommodate mirasidars on matters that did not threaten the revenue. Mirasidars approached the bargaining table with two goals foremost in mind: to secure their income, and, for this purpose, to accommodate officials as much as necessary, for from officials they needed patronage for irrigation investments, protection for property rights, and other essential services. Negotiations between urban officers and village landowners built a working system for state finance on their ideological meeting ground, which posited support for local mirasidar interests, payments in cash for that support, and the necessity of negotiation itself.

Local experience before 1820 hardened resistance to Munro's plan. During one three-year and one ten-year period of revenue collection under village contracts (or leases, as they were called), collectors converted the average government grain assessment (melvaram) for each village into cash at a price reached by averaging official conversion (jamabandy) prices from 1801 to 1808. Starting in 1808, tahsildars demanded full payment for the cash amount thus calculated from each village contractor before giving official permission to harvest the year's crop.[22] Then prices fell. Soon thereafter, drought reduced yields during years of severe dearth, from 1811 to 1813. Government did not adjust conversion prices, intervene to stabilize market prices, or adjust melvaram demand to output. Revenue contractors who had signed lease agreements for whole villages defaulted on their obligations to government. Many villages reverted to the old (amani) system of dividing the grain heap, and collectors complained of corruption and embezzlement by local officers who sold consignments of government grain.[23] Neither collectors nor mirasidars were very happy when the new governor, Thomas Munro, commanded an even more radical movement to fixed cash revenue assessment, payable by each individual mirasidar, who would under his scheme face the same losses that had befallen lease revenue contractors.[24]

Mirasidars protested loudly. At Perunkulam, near Alvar Tirunagari, they refused to permit a ryotwari settlement in their village and repulsed efforts to conduct a survey. Petitions were sent from villages to Madras, explaining the grounds for such action: inflexible revenue demands in the face of fluctuating yields and prices threatened mirasidar income; revenue payments by individual mirasidars contravened collective landholding custom, therefore property rights the Company had vowed to protect. Identical complaints came from many mirasidar villages in other districts, most prominently from Tanjore.[25]

The Board of Revenue, under firm orders to introduce a ryotwari settlement, responded with a compromise to accommodate mirasidars to the fullest feasible extent.[26] The Board ordered collectors to "preserve the rights of mirasidars,"[27] and to introduce an assessment and collection scheme called olungu, named after a Tamil word meaning orderly but designed to be otherwise. The olungu system would allow conversion prices to fluctuate slightly each year in response to changing market prices, and would assess village farmland as a whole, not individual fields. The olungu system would nonetheless require mirasidars to pay cash every year. Their individual assessments would be set by first multiplying total reported village cultivated acreage by an estimated output per acre; second, taking this estimate of total village output to calculate government's share (melvaram); third, converting the melvaram into cash at average pre-1820 jamabandy prices; and last, dividing that village cash assessment among landowners.[28]

The new system thus left much of the old system intact. Customary estimates of output, old jamabandy prices, local ability to underreport cultivation, and collective village asessments remained in force. Leading mirasidars continued to be de facto village contractors: they paid cash security for the village revenue, collected melvaram grain, sold it on their own account, paid government village taxes, and gathered such profits as might accrue from this series of transactions.[29] Assessment rates continued to embody local tradition; this epitomized that commitment to protect mirasidar rights professed by the Board, which scolded one collector for even suggesting that the diversity of rates might be reduced to streamline revenue procedures.[30]

Cash assessments with little flexibility from year to year nonetheless threatened mirasidars faced with seasonal insecurities. Resistance to the new system shows mirasidars at work negotiating to bend it as much as possible to their interests and sense of fairness. Many mirasidars refused for years to sign binding agreements, called muchilkas,

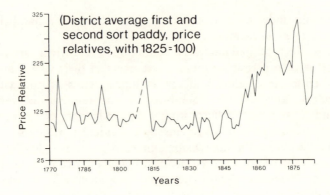

Figure 5 Tirunelveli Paddy Prices, 1771-1884
SOURCES: W. Robinson, *Minute on the Proposed Settlement of Tinnevelly*, Madras, 1868; Jamabandy Reports.

which committed villages to the terms of olungu revenue settlement. During the 1820s, collectors, under the Board's orders, allowed mirasidars to shift back and forth from the olungu system to the old (amani) system of dividing the grain heap, presumably in order to ease the transition and to convince mirasidars that the new system could secure their incomes as well as the old one. Under collectors' orders, tahsildars pushed to get muchilkas signed. To this end, tahsildars could refuse services, such as irrigation advances or arbitration, and they could deny tax remissions. Market trends did not cooperate, however. Prices fell during the 1820s (Figure 5) and mirasidars sought security by shifting back to the grain-heap division system, which in effect returned losses from lower market prices to the treasury. In 1827, after two years of very low prices, half of all irrigated land and "by far the greatest proportion of government revenue" were back under the old (amani) system. Embezzlement from government grain stores and worries about revenue losses from low prices gave collectors endless headaches.[31]

The Board made a bold move in 1830, by forbidding mirasidars henceforth to shift back to the old (amani) system once they had signed muchilkas. Negotiations became more intense, and reveal that different sorts of insecurity preoccupied mirasidars in differently irrigated localities as they approached the bargaining table. For villages west of district headquarters, in the upper Tambraparni valley, prices were the major concern. In 1830, when a good kar crop was about to be cut up-river, a poor crop down-river sent paddy prices soaring for a

112

few months. Mirasidars in favored villages rushed to sign muchilkas, thus putting more of their crop in their own hands to sell. They were not allowed to change their minds thereafter. A few villages that still resisted were subjected to more intense official supervision of mel-varam grain sales, which took away much of the charm in the old system; this, combined with higher prices for a few seasons, convinced even stubborn mirasidars in Cheranmahedevi to sign muchilkas. Un-derlying their agreements were not only favorable price trends but also a steady increase in cultivated acreage, and probably output per acre, over the levels assumed in revenue computations. We will return to these trends in the next chapter.[32]

We will also see in the next chapter that mirasidars east of district headquarters on the Tambraparni could not be as confident about either prices or productivity. Thus they resisted the new revenue scheme longer than mirasidars up-river, and negotiated to push olungu assessment rates below customary rates proposed by tahsildars. Floods, silting, and decayed irrigation under the Marudur dam eroded their chances for good kar harvests, the most lucrative in the mar-ketplace; the probability of good kar crops sank to about half that enjoyed by up-river farmers in some eastern Tambraparni villages.[33] Profits from grain sales by individual farmers thus provided little in-centive to convert to the new system. Half of all land irrigated in the two biggest taluks in the eastern half of the river valley remained under the grain-heap division system in 1835. Landowners sought official assurance that adequate provision would be made for tax remissions in the event of poor harvests. Grain assessments, they contended, were pitched too high, for their yields were declining—a claim verified much later when government financed the Srivaikuntam dam project (dis-cussed below) in large part to forestall otherwise necessary reductions in irrigated land tax rates.[34] Heated conflict pitted mirasidars against one tahsildar over the signing of muchilkas. Finally the collector in-tervened, granting a liberal remission procedure and agreeing to use a revenue survey of 1802 rather than a more recent one, probably because the old survey lowered the assumed paddy acreage on which assessments would be based. This finally convinced mirasidars to sign muchilkas.[35]

By resisting the olungu scheme, mirasidars in the eastern Tambra-parni River valley asserted a reasoned moral claim on the state either to lower effective revenue demand or to improve irrigation. This gov-ernment, like those before it, patronized irrigation primarily by putting funds into village hands—another theme for consideration below. It was thus logical for officials to accept mirasidar demands, which in effect left more funds in mirasidar hands to invest in irrigation. The collector implicitly recognized the legitimacy of mirasidar insistence on this score; perhaps the English began to realize that irrigation finance played an all-important role in cementing bonds between state and village in irrigated South India. What better incentive for villagers to pay more tax than to receive, in advance, improved irrigation? What better means to increase state revenue than to patronize work that would expand paddy cultivation? The moral economy of irrigated communities and of the regional state had been intertwined since Pandya times. Although official enthusiasm for direct government investment in irrigation would not prevail among Englishmen until the 1840s, under the influence of Sir Arthur Cotton, its inspiration might well have been derived from mirasidar efforts to remove impediments to olungu revenue settlements.

Mirasidars outside the Tambraparni valley would not have looked to regional state authority to improve their irrigation. Their tanks had always been built and repaired by local efforts. They could seek lenient tax procedures, however, to protect themselves from rapacious exactions during the frequent bad seasons, and they did so. They faced other insecurities, as well. We see in Chapter Six that they had trouble collecting swamibhogam rents from their dry-land tenants. Some faced threats to the very ownership of tenant land. Some faced other local legacies of eighteenth-century turmoil: Marava toughs reportedly carried away crops at will as late as the 1820s.[36] Bad seasons hit them much harder than they did Tambraparni mirasidars. Famine and epidemic destroyed crops and families during two wretched years, 1831-1833, especially in the southern mixed zone.

By 1831, all but a few mixed-zone mirasidars had signed muchilkas binding themselves to the olungu settlement, having reached by that time what must have seemed adequate provisions for remissions. But the assessment scheme proved still too inflexible to allow for dramatic crop shortfalls such as those during 1831-1833, which sapped not only current income but resources for investment in future productivity, and which were periodic in mixed-zone irrigated villages. Mirasidars and their tahsildars apparently created necessary flexibility in the system by negotiating under the table, out of the collector's view, a shift in land classification that lowered tax demand. Annual revenue accounts show a steady movement of land out of the irrigated, nunjah, category into the more mildly assessed nunjah-mel-punjah category—a movement never noticed by collectors in reports to the Board. Proportions of nunjah-mel-punjah land more than doubled during the 1830s and 1840s, primarily in the mixed zone.[37] This underhanded yet necessary procedure secured the revenue for tahsildars whose careers depended on reliability in revenue matters, without awkward remissions accounting that demanded minute justification; it allowed landowners to escape excessive tax rates on poorly irrigated land; and it depended on implicit acceptance by officials and villagers of the need to adjust state demand to local exigencies.

By the 1840s, the ideological underpinnings of the colonial state had been firmly established in the Tirunelveli region by more than forty years of hard bargaining that pitted state demands and English expectations against the power, interests, and convictions of village leaders. Imperial intellectuals at century's end would look back on the period of Company regime disparagingly. Muckraking tracts that exposed official corruption and oppression multiplied during the 1840s, as the Company's charter renewal approached, and revealed much in the workings of Company statecraft that offended forward-looking minds. But in this corner of the Company's domain we find, beneath contending claims and conflict over the terms of revenue settlement, a shared conviction by key actors in the drama that both peasant interests and state expansion had to be accommodated in the colonial political process. The moral economy of peasants expressed itself at the foundations of the colonial regime.[38]

TECHNOLOGY

This ideological framework remained intact, but changing technologies after 1840 weighted the odds of success in political negotiations in favor of aspiring urban bureaucrats. New techniques had come into Tirunelveli for centuries, with serious repercussions, but the arrival of the industrial revolution after 1840 wrought unprecedented change in the context of peasant life. New World crops, most importantly chillies and tobacco, had arrived on European ships. Guns and military techniques from abroad changed the face of war during the centuries before 1801, having come by land and sea. Paper and ink provided materials for permanent records that allowed English officers to amass mountains of documents for administrative purposes. Imported English organizational skills and the English language itself helped to integrate South Indian localities under the Company. But after the Company regime had planted itself firmly at the tip of India in the 1840s, a new era of government-sponsored technological transfer from Europe began. Key imports included hardware—railways and telegraph lines, and materials for modern seaports and dams, about which more will be said in the next chapter—but also ideas about efficient, bureaucratic management; scientific knowledge proved at least as effective as tools in reshaping peasant relations with the colonial state. Like chillies and tobacco, these new technological imports were quickly domesticated and rendered part of Tamil peasant culture.

The 1840s and 1850s marked a nineteenth-century watershed in South India: prices, seasons, government policy, international market conditions, and the intellectual climate registered important and interconnected shifts. This historic conjunction will emerge in increasing detail from now to the end of our story. Here the important point is that the official intellectual climate in Madras Presidency began to change dramatically in the 1840s. Cries for reform came from many directions. Unprecedentedly low prices from 1840 to 1843, the culmination of a downward trend through the 1830s, triggered complaints from landowners about oppressive taxes and revenue officers.[39] Faced with mounting demands from Calcutta, Madras hungered for revenue. Drastic reform seemed the only solution, and the Company's impending charter renewal in 1853 afforded the opportunity. Bold reports denouncing the Company multiplied; most proposed more central control and evenhanded, bureaucratic management, to achieve Munro's cherished ideals.[40] To the loyal chorus of Utilitarian and Evangelical criticism, an organization of native gentlemen in Madras even added their voice.[41]

The collector of Tinnevelly District, E. B. Thomas, waged a campaign in this context to renovate district administration. He submitted critiques of irrational and regressive tax assessments; worked out a plan for comprehensive survey and settlement, on scientific lines; proposed a new tax scheme; and implored the Board to allot more funds for works of public improvement, especially roads and irrigation.[42] Financially strapped, the Board had little interest in grand plans, though it authorized a pilot project to survey and reassess four villages, and though Arthur Cotton's influence in Madras did inject new interest among the Board in irrigation works.[43] But, more to the point, the Board ordered collectors to end all concessionary tax rates. The nunjah-mel-punjah land classification was struck off revenue accounts in 1841, though without much effect on land tax demand, for old rates seem to have stayed in effect as all nunjah-mel-punjah land was reclassified under either nunjah or punjah headings.[44] On other concessionary rates, Thomas retorted that these could not be discontinued, because they represented items of longstanding agreement between government and landowners, and as such were essential to order in the whole revenue system.[45] The Board insisted that at the very least tax-free inam land be erased from the books. The collector immediately

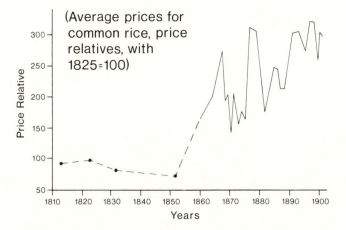

Figure 6 Madras Presidency Rice Prices, 1813-1901
NOTE: 1813, 1823, 1832, and 1853 prices are averages of the preceding four years.
SOURCE: Dharma Kumar, *Land and Caste in South India*, p. 91.

exempted all village-service inams—held by village officers—from the purview of this order; then he reviewed the status of a few other types of tax-free holdings each year on the death of their holders.[46] Dramatic change in the terms of revenue arrangements reached over years of hard bargaining would await the end of the Company regime, when economic conditions facing government and peasant alike had been altered by rapid inflation.

Prices skyrocketed after 1854, the first year on record in which prices in Tinnevelly District soared even as a very good season followed a bad one. District prices parallel the presidency trend (Figures 5 and 6). They flew up from the mid-1850s through the end of the century, though with sharp downturns in the sixties and eighties.[47] The immediate local impact was to increase assessment rates rapidly in irrigated villages under the olungu scheme, so that mirasidars now cried out for that which they had so long resisted: fixed cash land tax assessments. In 1859, a "lump sum" assessment on irrigated land was put into effect.[48] In the long term, the impact of the inflationary trend was to lower real land tax demand. In 1864, an owner of irrigated land sold one-third as much paddy as in 1825 to meet the average wet-land tax. Even during the slump of the 1870s, he would have had to sell only half as much of his paddy as in 1825 to satisfy the collector. For the state, inflation depressed its local buying power. Expressed in

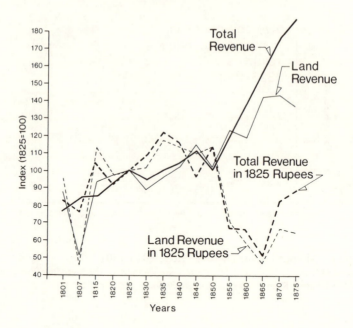

Figure 7 Tinnevelly District Revenue Collections, 1801-1875 (in actual and constant rupees)

NOTE: Calculations of constant rupee revenue are based on district paddy prices, as in Figure 5. Total revenue includes local funds after 1870.

SOURCE: A. J. Stuart, A *Manual of the Tinnevelly District*, Madras, 1876, pp. 182-83, 208.

constant rupees, state revenue fell to about half its 1850 level by 1865 (Figure 7).

Then the 1857 rebellion in North India shook the foundations of British rule, and the first priority of policy makers under the Crown became to fortify Queen Victoria's domain not only militarily but economically, as well. Projected costs outraced revenues. Pressure came to bear to increase state income in all parts of the empire.[49] As a first step, officers in Madras districts received orders to confiscate and sell at auction the land of taxpayers who fell into arrears. Tinnevelly District sales under "coercive process," as this procedure was called, increased by a factor of ten during each decade from the 1850s to 1880, from 30 to 3,000 to 30,000 rupees annually.[50] Even so, despite a planned complete revision of the land tax system, projected for completion during the 1870s, land taxation remained too inflexible a financial base for the state. Rates were fixed for thirty years and then could be raised only incrementally, given the politics of land revenue.

118

Old taxes of other kinds were increased: sea customs, salt taxes, stamp and forest taxes. New types of taxation and institutions for their administration were introduced. By 1885, local, district, and municipal funds, managed by boards of native dignitaries under the collector's control, accounted for 12 percent of all Madras Presidency revenues. By 1875, more was spent on local fund projects in Tinnevelly than for all ordinary administration; annual post office receipts leaped from 13,000 to 42,000 rupees between 1860 and 1875, and forest revenues rose from 13,000 to 21,000 rupees within three years after 1873. Such new revenue sources enabled the government's real income in the district to bounce back by the 1880s; brought about a relative decline in the importance of land taxes for state finance, which continued through the end of British rule and beyond; and fed the rapidly expanding infrastructure of Queen Victoria's Indian empire.[51]

As government wealth and power grew, its imperial edifice centralized rules of work so as to manage more efficiently all transactions among officers and between officers and citizens. Specialized departments multiplied in Madras, each with its own officers in the district, eroding the once omnicompetent authority of the Revenue Department and its collectors. Departments of survey and settlement, public works, forests, police, registration, and agriculture, and special agencies cast on the model of the Inam Commission evolved after 1860 to specialize in what had been functions of the collector's office staff. They became distinct bureaucratic entities and, like municipal and local boards, they commanded resources and authority to remake district administration along lines that characterize modern times. More specialized official work became more standardized throughout all Madras districts. What had been a variegated administrative landscape—composed of districts with their own peculiar traditions—disappeared forever, as departments devised set rules for official work in all districts, enshrined in the 1885 *Manual of the Administration of the Madras Presidency*.

To qualify as an officer of state would no longer demand detailed personal expertise in local administrative discourse and intricate political reality. Quite the contrary. Careers would henceforth be made by imbibing the ethos and discipline of an Anglo-Indian imperial bureaucracy, which demanded ever larger numbers of qualified native personnel. English education enabled officers to move far and wide; and professions that complemented administrative and judicial institutions—above all, the law—attracted suitably endowed native families. Improving networks of roads and railways, and growing numbers of schools in booming towns, facilitated mobility into urban professions. Though the number of natives appointed to posts above the rank of tahsildar grew after the Civil Service Act of 1861, the number of educated Indians qualified for such posts grew even faster. In Tinnevelly District, the number of schools receiving some state aid jumped from 273 in 1857 to 1,052 in 1876, and their pupils from under 7,000 to over 13,000. Tinnevelly students taking civil service exams numbered 135 in 1870 and 250 in 1876. In the whole of the presidency, 70,000 students wrote university entrance or higher exams during the twenty years ending in 1885.[52]

To bureaucratize agrarian administration demanded more than bureaucrats, however. Officers needed detailed information and uniform records by which to manage land taxes and disputes over land rights. Steps in that direction began in earnest in Tinnevelly in 1862, with the beginning of survey and settlement. Sixteen years to complete, it cost more than 75 lakh rupees, nearly 75 percent of the district's annual revenue at its completion in 1878. Survey and settlement involved five steps, each in its own way a major feat: boundary demarcation, survey, soil classification, assessment, and the recording of rights.[53] Together these provided the technical basis for a new style of state action in peasant communities.

Act 28 of 1860 empowered the Madras government to define and protect boundaries throughout the presidency. Teams of surveyors fanned out. They demarcated fields in each village, as indicated by cultivators and village officers. Surveyors drew boundaries on the ground, marking them with stones, and designated the limits of residential sites, forests, "uncultivated waste" land, and all other public land, including roads, tanks, and river beds. Having registered boundaries in accounts, Survey Department officers measured and mapped everything of government interest on the land, using standard English measures: acres and square miles.[54] These maps provided data for a comprehensive recording of rights—whose social content we shall consider in Chapter Six—printed in bound survey and settlement records. For the first time ever, all rights and tax obligations for each field in the district became public record, visible at a glance to any officer in headquarters.

Settlement officers then calculated tax assessments on each field. They classed lands according to productivity by conducting 179 crop-cutting experiments in 1865 and 256 more in 1868, and by comparing their results with local testimony.[55] Soils were thereby ranked into twenty-eight types and grouped into classes according to dominant soil type in each class. Fields were then grouped into tracts containing similar types of soils and assessed accordingly. Final assessment rates resulted when officers converted the estimated average gross yield for each soil type into money, using average district prices from 1843 to 1863; deducted from gross yield an estimate of cultivation costs; and reached a money value for half the remaining "net product," which became the standard assessment for each soil type. For particular tracts of land this standard assessment would be adjusted upward or downward to account for conditions bearing on farm profits, such as irrigation quality, topography, and proximity to markets, railway, or seaports.

Settlement officers in practice performed a politic sleight of hand. They did take all the steps described above, but also, in a more practical vein, translated customary assessments and cesses into a new bureaucratic jargon, making local adjustments as circumstances warranted. What appeared in settlement reports as scientific calculations of yield, production costs, and state rent on farmland were largely bogus—a fact revealed in an extended critical minute by a dissenting member of the Board of Revenue, W. Robinson, who concentrated specifically on the fallacious assumptions used to compute "net product."[56] As a result of politic and practical settlement procedures, land tax rates in Tinnevelly District changed very little. Rates on land in the wet zone rose only 0.4 percent after survey and settlement. The average assessment on all land declined 2 percent.[57] The most dramatic change in rates reflects real trends in productivity that would have been obvious to peasants and officials alike in their dialogue during settlement proceedings: relative rates on the best dry lands, which produced valuable crops, especially cotton, rose; whereas rates on poorly irrigated land, especially under rain-fed tanks, seem to have fallen. In the end, actual rates appear to have resulted more from calculations about rates justifiable to rate payers in particular local circumstances than from science, though scientific rent theory provided justification for the bureaucracy.

Survey and settlement procedures nonetheless altered forever the style of peasant interaction with the state, for they succeeded in their most important goal, to channel copious information, and thus power to define the terms of revenue transactions, into urban official hands. Officers in district headquarters would never again contemplate bizarre local weights and measures, never again travel to villages in order to find out who owed what tax and who owned what land. At their desks bureaucrats could study books of uniform records, which enabled qualified men to perform revenue and other duties of state anywhere in the presidency.

This movement of information into urban centers accompanied a movement in the same direction of people, commodities, and wealth that accelerated with cheapening transport and communication during the period of survey and settlement. After mid-century, we see an agrarian society animated by increasing mobility. In 1876, the number of people departing railway stations totaled more than one-fifth the entire Tinnevelly District population, and 25,000 workers left by sea for plantations in Ceylon, while 24,000 tons of freight left district railway stations.[58] Wider movements meant that specialized actors in both state and market networks needed information pertaining to wider spatial domains, and that their interests in particular places concerned particular subjects that had to be grasped in terms applicable throughout those domains. Thus the records of Queen Victoria's imperial domain contain comprehensive and uniform data on wages, prices, yields, and the like—they are a gold mine for modern economic historians—but little local color and almost no descriptive prose devoted to routine local affairs. Once again we find that dramatic change in the character of historians' raw material accompanied structural change in the agrarian system within which peasants work their land.

Consider simply the implications of comprehensive maps and registers of land ownership. Farmers in great numbers used offices of the Registration Department from the department's creation in the 1860s, especially to record mortgages.[59] Registration records, settlement records, and pattahs now became absolutely authoritative symbols of ownership: they defined for all to see precisely who owned what land and who held what land on mortgage. Any dispute could be officially put to rest by bureaucrat or judge by reference to documents on his desk. No knowledge of local custom or perusal of contradictory evidence would be required, and none would confuse the issue under official consideration. As we shall see in Chapter Six, before survey and settlment, all documentary evidence concerning ownership and tenancy had been suspect, which slowed court proceedings, increased court costs, and undermined judicial decrees. A technical means to lower costs and quicken state operations, survey and settlement enabled more people to use state offices, enabled officers to make more decisive moves into local affairs, and thus altered the course of conflicts and conflict resolution in town and country by bringing more information into government offices.

Among all the interventions into village society that nurtured the Anglo-Indian empire, dividing public from private land stands out as the most important. Though mountains and forests were not surveyed until the twentieth century, forests assigned to the public domain were demarcated and their extent recorded on maps. The Forest Department could then use this data to establish "reserved forests" during the

1870s, and to restrict access to forest resources under the department's control. This, of course, generated a landslide of court suits, particularly from zamindars whose claims to vast wooded tracts of mountain land suffered.[60] Defining public land in and around every village and town invaded localities even more deeply. For decades, government had claimed to own all land classified as "uncultivated waste," that is, land that could be cultivated but was not, or at least was not included among fields for which landowners paid land tax. But officers in cities had never held technical means to enforce government claims to "waste." They could not define exactly what belonged to whom, what land a particular pattah included, or even what lay in a specific village. Now government could actually sell rights to "waste" to raise cash for official projects such as the Srivaikuntam dam, which thus received 60,000 rupees.[61] Government control of public land provided means to protect public works once built, as well; for until the survey, landowners could lay claim to any uncultivated land by plowing it up, according to local customary and legal precedent. Farmers had thus frequently plowed their way into roads, irrigation channels, and irrigation tanks. Now city bureaucrats could nullify such a claim or make landowner pay the treasury to retain it.[62] "Waste" was now public in fact and in law.

Empire

Events at Ettaiyapuram reflect facets of local experience during the mid-nineteenth-century transition to industrial empire in South India. Jagavira Rama Kumara Ettappa Nayaka, thirty-sixth in his line, was descended from the powerful poligar who fought beside British troops to establish Company supremacy in Tinnevelly District. His ancestor had likewise fought alongside Visvanatha Nayaka to become one of the greatest of the little kings in the Nayaka realm. Jagavira inherited respect in the eyes of British authorities. His father and grandfather had been prominent among native gentlemen who patronized public works beginning in the 1840s. Jagavira himself was invited to meet the Prince of Wales at Tuticoryn, in 1877.[63] Although he was a minor at his father's death, Jagavira did not have his ancestral estate taken under the control of the government Court of Wards, which was routinely done in British India to protect the assets of young zamindars. The collector, R. K. Puckle, left the estate in the hands of the zamindar's manager, Ramaswamy Nayaka, "out of respect for the wishes" of Jagavira's mother.[64]

It had become customary in Tinnevelly District for collectors to exercise this option whenever they perceived no imminent danger of disarray in zamindari finance; and, before 1860, even when estates were taken under the court's wing, they were generally left to the zamindar's own managerial staff. Two exceptions stand out—the always bankrupt Sivagiri and ever-turbulent Chokkampatti estates—which demonstrates that where breach of the peace or failure to pay peshcash occurred, Company officers felt a pressing need to intervene in zamindari affairs. Otherwise, zamindars under the Company were left to their own devices. R. K. Puckle had faith in Ettaiyapuram, it seems. After a visit to the estate, in 1871, when Puckle found the zamindar's people had made little progress on reforms he had suggested, the collector nonetheless wrote to the court that no change in its control was required at that time.[65]

So well entrenched had the official tradition of respecting zamindari autonomy become that the estate manager, Ramaswamy, bristled at what he perceived a threat to his authority in the collector's inspection of 1871, because Puckle had perused estate records and interviewed estate servants without the manager's permission. Angered, Ramaswamy fired those servants and stopped progress altogether on Puckle's pet reforms. This was a serious mistake. Times had changed. Puckle's indulgence had clearly been born of respect for tradition, not of conviction. He immediately took the estate under the Court of Wards, appointed one Vengata Rao as manager, and proceeded in a few short years to overhaul the entire zamindari administration along ryotwari lines. When Jagavira came of age, he ascended to the head of an entirely revamped estate bureaucracy, with a full treasury and new managerial staff.

For Puckle, this was a typical piece of work. Having entered the Madras Civil Service in 1851, he became director of revenue settlement in 1859 and, having worked in Trichnopoly and Salem districts, headed the settlement in Tinnevelly District from 1866 to 1877, during which time he also served as collector. Possessing superior skill and energy in official politics, and with powerful friends in Madras, he personally made all the arrangements for finishing the Srivaikuntam dam project, quite a feat given the press of all his other duties. He was one of those who drove forward the change in government style during the decades of his service. Inspired by the most advanced ideas of the day and certain of his goals, he saw no limit to the good that government could do, and he envisioned Ettaiyapuram as a model for future zamindari reformation. His ambition seethes in the words he used to justify Ettaiyapuram's takeover by the Court of Wards:

The prospects of the zemin are very hopeless as things stand at present, and it would be a great pity to lose an opportunity that will never return again. . . . In the next four years we may survey the zemin, register the holdings, settle all disputes, abolish anomalies, repair irrigation works, make roads and almost double the revenue, while greatly improving the condition of the ryots.[66]

In the decades after 1860, urban officers of state invaded many domains of authority and resource control that they had previously touched but lightly. They almost always met resistance. To save forests from plunder and to tax forest assets more effectively, officials moved in to regulate access to wood and hillside, and in doing so trespassed on the claims of many zamindars, who took up the battle in courts of law, where some cases remained for a hundred years.[67] More covert resistance came from locals who could feel their bargaining power slip away. The terms of the contest moved steadily in favor of the Anglo-Indian bureaucracy, which used its increasingly potent technology to create an overarching system of political authority throughout the presidency, within which to exert influence on local affairs. Locals had no choice but to utilize that system, even to keep their local powers. By the survey and settlement, government obtained enough data to supersede village officers as final arbiters in disputes over local land rights; like Puckle's men in Ettaiyapuram, everywhere they went settlement officers arbitrated local disputes, some of which had obstructed progress on works of local improvement like roads and bridges.[68] Even as better transport built wider markets for local products and labor, central authority reached out to dissolve segmented political domains woven into agricultural life.

Economic and political integration progressed in tandem, at the tip of India as around the globe. They did not destroy but transformed the powers of key people in South Indian village communities. Channels of trade and authority that tied peasants securely into Queen Victoria's imperial system lessened local autonomy, widened village horizons, and brought new interests and notions to bear on community relations. Yet new waters flowed locally in old channels. In fact, just as the olungu scheme of revenue settlement had been designed to protect the mirasidar rights and income, R. K. Puckle sincerely sought to bolster young Jagavira's wealth and stature. The idea was not to end the zamindar's power, only to put it on firmer, more modern, footing, with more prosperous, contented subjects, and with, no doubt, sufficient cash in the treasury to pay all government dues. As a little king, a raja, the zamindar was perhaps diminished. His people might no longer feel that Ettappa Nayaka commanded their fate. But his lineage remained and remains today the richest and most powerful of its kind in the region.

Likewise, survey and settlement did deprive village officers of some levers they had formerly held to manipulate village affairs. Their tax-free land, for instance, became taxable. But they remained substantial landowners. And, as the bureaucracy widened and tightened its grip on agricultural resources, village officers remained, in the words of one report, "the keystone of the arch" of Madras administration.[69] Each new government initiative needed their cooperation to succeed, while still limited sanctions from the city left them plenty of room to maneuver on the fringes of authorized activity. Like zamindars, village headmen were no longer the little kings they might once have been, but they remained resourceful peasant leaders endowed with symbols of authority, superior economic assets, and powerful local allies; the leaders of dry-zone villages were still more than mere rustic bureaucrats. As in settlement procedures, the modernization of rural administration changed the jargon and veneer more than the substance of local power relations.

The creation of village bureaucracy in the wet zone similarly shuffled titles and duties among existing powerholders, the wealthy mirasidars. Men called "principal mirasidars" comprised some 10 percent of the recorded mirasidar population in the 1823 census, and as we have seen revenue transactions continued to rely upon their wealth and power through the 1850s. As more mirasidars received pattahs and collective order raveled apart in irrigated villages—a subject for the last chapter—collectors strove to establish official headmen where none existed ever before, although official wisdom in Madras held that headmen traditionally characterized all South Indian villages.[70] These mirasidar headmen initially received no pay, and had little new power as a result of their office, so recruitment lagged. Influential shareholders generally refused the job as demeaning, and then it would be snatched up by some lesser man, who might see "opportunities of indirectly procuring . . . remuneration."[71] In some villages this engendered factional feuds when one group refused to recognize a headman from another faction, so that more than one headman had to be appointed.[72] But by the end of survey and settlement, in 1878, new standard practice had evolved with respect to the function of headman in mirasidar villages. Leading landowners became headmen, sometimes for several villages; many employed educated specialists familiar with legal codes and bureaucratic procedures. Not content to leave their interests in the hands of the headman, however, mirasidars often hired their own legal counsel to represent them in official dealings. Puckle wrote that because mirasidar headmen

> are generally principal landholders and often resident at a distance from the villages in which they hold office, they keep private Gomastahs, Seti Maniyams as they are called, to perform the chief part of their duties. There is moreover usually a Kudi Maniyam or representative of the people, who watches their client's interests and conducts the business of the village generally.[73]

Many of those mirasidars, "resident at a distance from the villages in which they hold office," might have moved into the widening world of opportunity created by the growth of government and urban employment. Like Vengata Rao, a considerable landowner himself in a village near district headquarters, who became naib sherishtadar and then the deputy collector who managed Ettaipuram zamindari for the Court of Wards, many young men from the mirasidar fold looked out into that widening world with high hopes.[74] They flocked to schools, wrote exams, and staffed government posts that opened up to them. They taught school, tutored hopeful youngsters, studied professions, started businesses, and otherwise built futures in the city based on inherited assets in wet-zone villages. Brahmans like Vengata Rao achieved success out of all proportion to their numbers and their landed wealth. Yet, to judge by mid-nineteenth century evidence on the caste composition of the officer corps, high caste non-Brahmans, especially Vellalas with roots on the banks of the Tambraparni, entered competition for elite jobs in hot pursuit. Assets in trade would have become increasingly fertile ground upon which to build a career in town, enabling families from an array of castes, even those not among the regional landed elite, to move in the same direction. The official and professional class of urban Indians expanded steadily after 1860, filled by families with agricultural and commercial moorings. The imperial bureaucracy swarmed with their sons.

Even as the empire dissolved many of the once local segments in the regional state, and drew many of the once locally bounded agrarian elite families into state service, it left many little segmentary domains intact in the countryside. Some locals could not be brought by carrot or stick into the imperial mainstream. They inhabited little worlds depicted by officials with contempt and frustration—worlds of violence, corruption, and crime, as they saw it. There remained dark shadows across the shiny edifice of Queen Victoria's empire.

Maravas, particularly, attained renown as underworld elements.[75] Marava zamindars, especially Sivagiri and Chokkampatti, proved troublesome for officialdom. They broke laws of civil society, fell into arrears, resisted efforts by the Court of Wards to manage their estates, and fought the government every step of the way over control over hillside forests. But more vexatious by far were Marava kaval chiefs and village watchmen, who until the last days of the empire provided essential police services outside of central government control. Crime and criminal investigations remained very much a local affair in their hands. Even one district judge joined the general population by paying for private Marava protection services; and a series of investigations revealed that any attempt to take control of rural police work away from local Marava leaders would prove much too expensive and potentially disruptive.[76] Although the Madras constabulary, established in the 1860s, consisted of non-Marava constables, all posted in town, private subscriptions with Maravas would secure life and property for villagers and many townsfolk alike in Tinnevelly District through the end of British rule.[77] Again we find the regime bending to the necessities of rural political economy, justifying itself by reference to costs and to the need for stability.

In the late nineteenth-century imperial setting, political men initiated a discourse with government that would grow into nationalism, South Indian style.[78] Like this one, each of the next two chapters will at the end touch on features of early nationalism that arose from nineteenth-century trends in the Tamil countryside. Here the salient point is that the men who first articulated their demands in the provincial political arena—many of them idealists, to be sure—sought in part to secure a voice in the imperial administrative system analogous to that which their fathers and grandfathers had enjoyed in settings such as Tinnevelly District from the founding of the Anglo-Indian regime. Political activity did not derive from popular protest over government attacks on living standards. Politicians came predominantly from backgrounds in towns and wealthy rural settings such as the Tambraparni River valley; they represented the most successful and mobile sectors of the native population; and their grievances centered on competition for advancement and on limits to advancement built into government policy. Articulate political leaders sought to improve their own and their constituents' wellbeing by petitioning and protesting government. The bases for nationalism were laid in South India in an evolving Anglo-Indian ideological idiom that wedded British and Indian interests at the pinnacle of society, and at the same time provided for oppositions and disagreements within the political elite. The working ideology of the regime thus manifests considerable continuity from its inception through the early decades of the twentieth century.[79]

Out in the village, farmers had little reason to protest government policy except as individuals seeking redress for particular wrongs. The colonial regime had been built from the beginning by active decisions on the part of key rural personnel. Its ideological underpinnings had been laid in considerable part in negotiations between powerful villagers and officials in town. Government wealth and power grew over the decades, but unlike many colonial situations, this one did not find Englishmen bettering their own lot in visible opposition to Indian economic interests in the countryside. Englishmen did indeed penetrate market networks, as we shall see in the next chapter; they did indeed channel more and more power and wealth into their own hands; but they did so as the total range of economic opportunities expanded for the most important people in Tinnevelly District, and they succeeded within a set of institutional arrangements that accommodated those people's interests and ideals.

In most villages, therefore, most farmers could pursue their livelihood without running up against limits imposed by government. A great deal of what government did in the village worked to the benefit of commercially active and politically well-placed villagers. Where government interests collided with village elites, officials managed some form of accommodation, either openly, as in the case of headmen, or otherwise, as in the case of Marava watchmen, citing ideologically and financially sound rationale. In the final analysis, the stability and continuous evolution of this colonial regime depended on a context within which a greedy government and growing rural population could both seek their goals without running into one another: it required general economic expansion, which provided favorable conditions for Anglo-Indian empire in southernmost India until the late decades of the nineteenth century.

· 5 ·

COMMODITY PRODUCTION

Nineteenth-century industrialization made much of the world Europe's agricultural hinterland. Industry escalated European demand for peasant crops, among which cotton assumed overwhelming importance as a raw material for English cloth manufacture. Industry also dramatically reduced the cost of bulk transport, thus that of supplying English mills with overseas cotton and of supplying the world with English factory products. At the same time, industrial technologies enabled Europeans to expand and tighten their political power in strategic corners of the world economy, thus to secure markets and improve their terms of trade.[1]

Peasants and merchants in South India participated avidly in the worldwide upsurge in agricultural commodity production that accompanied European industrialization. They did so in an Anglo-Indian imperial setting, and therefore under the influence of Europe's leading industrial power. The Tirunelveli region held particular importance in South India, because it produced high-quality cotton that fetched high prices first in the Company's remittance trade, and then in English agency house trade with English and other European manufacturers of cotton cloth. In addition, government efforts under Company and Crown to lower transport and communication costs, with both military security and commercial development in view, cheapened commodity exchange among the diverse agricultural communities that composed the Tirunelveli region. As a result, rapidly expanding peasant cultivation of cotton for export converged in its effects on the region's economy with steadily increasing production of all variety of peasant commodity crops. A traditionally active region of peasant and merchant enterprise thus rapidly became even more active during the nineteenth century, with important social and political consequences. Expanding peasant commodity production in the Tirunelveli region's diverse agricultural and social environment slowly but steadily shifted the social distribution of economic power, and stimulated social conflicts that would, by century's end, animate early nationalist politics.

TRADITION

Previous chapters depict a region alive with opportunities for trade and energized by efforts to produce commodities. Medieval agriculture, crafts, and trade concentrated in the Tirunelveli wet zone and in the precincts of brahmadeya communities and temples. Medieval merchant organizations built outposts along the Tambraparni for long-distance trade. Pearls in the seabed attracted overseas merchants. Yet, as we have seen, most exchanges in peasant products occurred within small circuits of trade surrounding irrigated communities. Under the later Pandyas, a settlement of Arab merchants oriented toward the Indian Ocean trade was established at the small port of Kayalpatnam,[2] and the contemporary expansion of transactions recorded in inscriptions around the Nellaiyappa temple also indicates an expansion of trade connections during late medieval times. But the creation of the commercial environment that survived to the beginning of the nineteenth century would await the arrival of peasants and warriors who opened the region's internal farming frontiers during Vijayanagar times, from the fourteenth to sixteenth centuries. By the time that the Madurai Nayakas sat on the throne, bases for subsequent commercial development were in place. Peasant commodity crop production, in the context of the Nayaka tributary state, proceeded throughout the seventeenth and eighteenth centuries.

From the founding of the Nayaka dynasty to 1800, towns grew along major routes of transport and diverse peasant communities were integrated within a regional trade system. Elite consumption, based on profits from trade and from tribute, stimulated urban concentrations of artisans, especially weavers, in towns that benefited from locally substantial water supplies and paddy crops. Overseas demand had the same effect. First the Portuguese and then the Dutch purchased wet-zone products. They paid with precious metals, European products, and items obtained in their trade along the Indian coast and elsewhere in the trading world of the Indian Ocean, especially Sri Lanka. In the Tirunelveli wet zone, town-based weavers of cotton cloth obtained their cotton from cotton-growing villages near the river valley, both north and south. European contracts for exports encouraged inland traders to make advances for export supplies. Nayaka tribute demands produced similar interconnected forward contracts for products, cash, and credit; the limits of these networks defined small commercial hinterlands around towns throughout the Tirunelveli region, and these hinterlands became the foundations for taluks.

The 1823 census and a variety of documents that survey commercial activity depict the region's economic geography in the early nineteenth century. The census records two dozen major market towns in the Tinnevelly District at major road junctions and three major seaports: Tuticoryn, Kayalpatnam, and Kulasekharapatnam. A dozen large temples held annual fairs with large congregations of merchants and petty traders. There were thirty-five weekly markets and twice that many small temple festivals with commercial components.[3] Experience and descriptions of such periodic gatherings led Thomas Munro to report, quite astutely, in his presentation to Parliament in 1812 that, in India, "religion and trade are sister arts: the one is seldom found in any large assembly without the society of the other."[4] Six fortified market centers, called *pettai*, protected trade during eighteenth-century war years. More than sixty towns held considerable numbers of permanent shops and artisan workplaces. All but a few villages had several permanent trading establishments of one kind or another. Every community on record supported annual festivals and fairs, and all had some resident noncultivators who depended for their livelihood upon some form of commerce.[5]

There were three levels of trade activity: local, regional, and long-distance. Local trade engaged petty peddlers and hawkers, who trav-

Table 3 Items of Local Trade in Turenelveli, c. 1820

Food Supplies	Materials and Products
grains (paddy, rice, kambu, cholam, ragi)	cotton
oils and oilseeds	cotton thread and cloth
spices	dyes
milk products (ghee)	wood
palmyra products	timber
jaggery	beams
jaggery candy	firewood
palmyra fruit	carts
toddy	tools
arrack	palmyra products
garden produce	beams
tobacco	leaves
vegetables (chillies, onions)	mats
plantains	baskets
dried vegetables	coir and coir products (brushes)
salt fish	gunny
salt	lime
	bricks
	silver
	iron ore, crude iron, iron products
	stones
	bullocks
	grass, fodder, manure

eled from village to village and from village to town carrying small loads on their heads, getting goods and cash in exchange for their wares, moving to the rhythm of the monsoon. They would appear in dusty groups, haggling and straggling along with their ragged baskets, at weekly markets, at fairs and festivals, and, without fail, on the threshing floor at harvest time. They carried all the little necessities of country life from jewelry to nails, from thread to spices, pins, and salt fish (Table 3). They also carried items from localities in different parts of the Tirunelveli region, which they obtained through circuits of regional trade between agricultural zones (Figure 8).

Trade between zones in the plains, and between the plains and both the hills and the seacoast, centered on towns near the hills, on the coast, and in the wet zone. These towns, with substantial traders, acquired and dispersed goods through exchange networks in their

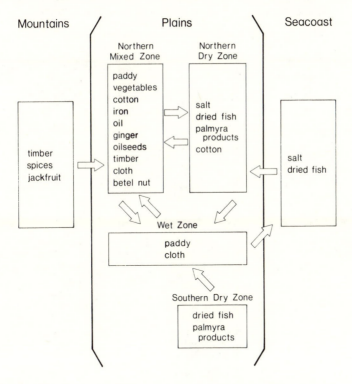

Figure 8 Major Commodities in Trade between Agricultural Zones, c. 1820

SOURCE: "Report on Inland Customs," PBR,TNA, 26 October 1837, vol. 1553, pp. 13571-91.

small hinterlands. The most important towns were Srivilliputtur, Virudhunagar, Tenkasi, Ambasamudram, Tirunelveli, Srivaikuntam, Tiruchendur, and Nanguneri (Map 4); in these towns, during the eighteenth century, regional governments set up inland customs stations that survived to 1833. The seaports, Tirunelveli town, and a few towns near gaps in the mountains evolved into export and import centers for trade networks that stretched outside the region. By land, the region's best long-distance trading partners were territories west of the Ghats and due north. By sea, the island of Sri Lanka and ports of call dotting the peninsular coast provided imports and received exports. By bullock and ship, tobacco, cotton dies, cloth, paddy, jaggery, animal hides, and pearls traveled far from the region into channels of long-distance trade (Figure 9).[6]

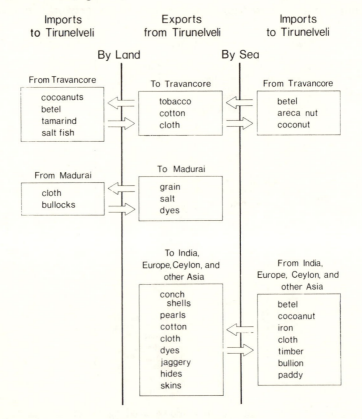

Figure 9 Long-Distance Trade Flows, c. 1820
SOURCE: Madras Presidency, Revenue Department, "Report on the External and Internal Commerce of Madras Presidency," 1820-1830.

Peace enabled the region to regain and surpass its traditional commercial vitality without delay in 1801. There was considerable room for improvement. Centuries of commercial development had not erased many serious obstacles to commercial expansion, and circuits of commodity exchange remained on the whole tightly circumscribed. Early nineteenth-century collectors complained bitterly of the limited extent of paddy markets, which made provisioning even district headquarters difficult and expensive. Such limited markets, which in the dry zone had been disrupted by warfare, made it difficult for taxpayers to realize the revenue demand in cash. Violent ups and downs in paddy prices along the Tambraparni, over small distances and during short periods of time, indicate the difficulties encountered in moving paddy from one part of the valley to another when the first price and market data were collected in the 1820s. After the eighteenth-century wars were finished, the most serious obstacles to trade lay on the land itself. Irrigation works, paddy fields, rivers and streams, and monsoon floods blocked the flow of goods; bullocks carrying loads on their backs had to descend into water constantly in order to move from one part of the most productive agricultural zone of the region to another, because there were no bridges whatever. Outside the wet zone, though dry land made transport easier, the monsoons turned the region's most productive black soil into a vast and deep muddy quagmire impassable for many weeks at a time. It is little wonder that British observers unanimously cited roads and bridges as the most important public improvement for commercial development.

EXPANSION

Peace itself lowered transport and transactions costs. Very little was done by the government to improve roads and bridges before the 1840s, but nonetheless inland customs receipts indicate a quickening of regional trade between agricultural zones after 1820. During the twenty years from 1818 to 1838, government invested a mere 15,663 rupees on roads and bridges, when more than twice that amount was required to build a single substantial travelers' resting place, called a choultry. Private donors, indeed, subscribed nearly that much, 15,000 rupees, to build just one bridge at Brahmadesam in 1838.[7]

Government began to invest in transportation during the years of reform following 1840, and its funds were put to good use, stimulating numerous private contributions. The first official act to signal a new era came in 1840, when one of the district's top native officials, the naib sherishtadar, a Vellala mirasidar named Sulechanam Mudaliar, personally donated 40,000 rupees to build a bridge across the Tambraparni connecting Tirunelveli and Palayamkottai.[8] Henceforth, public and private funds flowed much more freely to improve the region's transportation. Choultries were favorite objects of private patronage. Of the eighty-three under government protection in 1876, fifty had been built before 1801, only six in the next forty years, and twenty-six after 1840.[9] Even after the construction of railway lines through the district in the 1870s, road construction continued to attract funding during survey and settlement operations and under the aegis of local funds, which after 1866 collected more than 100,000 rupees each year to be spent on local roads.[10] The biggest road-building projects were completed before mid-century, when the trunk road was built linking Tinnevelly and Madras, and the cotton road was built to link the Tinnevelly District cotton-growing tract with the port of Tuticoryn. Both roads were very substantial projects that involved not only bridge construction but also building up the roadbed with quarried stone and tons of dirt, to raise and drain the roadway above ground level throughout the length of the black-soil tract. To fund the cotton road, government invested the several lakh rupees that accrued to the treasury when government withdrew from direct control of temple funds. Building the cotton road employed as many as 30,000 workers annually during the late 1840s—when one government engineer demonstrated the need for a raised roadway by sinking up to his horse's ribs in oozing mud at a cotton-road construction site.[11]

Roadwork lowered transport costs considerably, even before the building of the railway in the 1870s. Considering a seventy-mile stretch of road from Madras City to Wallajahnagar, in Chinglepet District, the Public Works Commission calculated that transport costs per ton per mile declined from over 17 rupees to about 5 during the thirty years from 1821 to 1851,[12] and similar reductions must have occurred on the seventy miles of cotton road from Srivilliputtur through Sattur and Ettaiyapuram to Tuticoryn in the Tinnevelly District, as well as on the ninety miles of trunk road from Madurai to Tirunelveli town. The railway, of course, lowered transport costs still further in the 1870s, by which time built-up roads through the cotton-growing tract and roads and bridges through the Tambraparni valley carried huge quantities of produce for the market. Railways carried 25,000 tons of goods through district rail stations in 1876,[13] but ten years before that a collector estimated that ten times that tonnage—250,000 tons— moved along the trunk road between Madurai and Tirunelveli town, and this was not even the busiest road in the Tinnevelly District. That distinction went to the road running southeast from district headquarters through Palayamkottai to Tiruchendur; it carried tons of paddy and other goods for consumption and export, as well as thousands of pilgrims to and from the great temple at Tiruchendur.[14] Bridges across riverbeds meant that traffic could move all year without descending into the muddy and treacherous bottom, risking broken legs and damaged loads. Roadbeds enabled bullock carts to supplant bullocks' backs as the standard carrier for overland cargo. Two bulls could carry about ten times more in a cart than on their backs, and the cargo did not have to be unloaded every night of a long journey.[15] The network of roads and numerous middle-sized market towns of the Tinnevelly District thus threaded village producers into a regional trade system as transport costs declined, enabling more families to seek cash incomes from their farms and their labor.

Map 7 demonstrates that villagers everywhere had some farm produce to sell. The wet zone concentrated on paddy. Oil seeds grew in abundance in mixed and dry zones, and could be shipped without spoilage and stored for sale in town. Garden crops—chillies, tobacco, betel, plantain, and vegetables—in addition to pulses and palmyra products provided valuable loads for bullock carts to carry from one part of the region to another. All these traditional commodities of regional trade between agricultural zones circulated more widely and in greater quantities as roads improved. But by far the most dramatic increase in commodity production resulted from skyrocketing demand for raw cotton from industrial Britain.

Somehow a small parcel of fine white cotton from Tinnevelly District reached Canton in 1803. It fetched "two or three more tales per pecul than Surat or Bengal cotton" for the English East India Company merchants who sold it there, so that henceforth "tinnies" cotton became a Company staple in the China trade.[16] By 1807, the collector reported that cotton grown for the China market had become "very popular in recent years," and that Virudhunagar had become the foremost cotton mart in the black-soil cotton tract in the northern dry zone.[17] The collector commanded a good view of the cotton export trade because Company merchants bought their cotton using the district treasury as a bank from which to pay native merchants in inland cotton marts like Virudhunagar and Sattur. For some time, Company officials recoiled from policies to encourage cotton exports lest they drive up the cost of Company cotton cloth exports.[18] But by 1811 the Company's commercial resident began to complain about dirty and unreliable supplies of tinnies cotton. Soon after, the Board of Revenue asked collectors to suggest means to increase and stabilize the supply of export cotton.[19] Little could be done except to increase the flow of Company funds into forward contracts. In 1818, the collector reported that heavy demand drew every available ounce of raw cotton into the export market; and, to a Board inquiry as to whether additional incentives (such as lower land tax rates) might stimulate more cultivation for export, he replied that "It is want of hands, not of any premium for the cultivation of cotton, that prevents extension of it, where the soil is favorable." Cotton, a traditional crop for trade between agricultural zones but never exported overseas before 1801, generated nearly half of the district's export earnings in 1820.[20]

The growth of cotton and general commodity crop production accelerated during the four decades after 1835. Table 4 shows that in the decades from 1835 to 1875 there were no disastrous strings of several years when drought, dearth, malnutrition, and infectious disease would make the population highly susceptible to premature death, such as punctuated the 1790s, 1810s, 1830s, 1870s, and 1890s. Consequently, population grew faster than in any other intercensal period of the nineteenth century. In addition, investments in road and bridge building lowered transport costs more rapidly than during any period of comparable length in history. At the same time, export demand for Tinnies cotton soared. British industrial demand for raw cotton increased an average of 38 percent every five years from 1820 to 1850; every five years, during this thirty-year period, English mills consumed on average 43,000 tons more clean cotton, pressed and baled for shipment overseas, than in the previous five years. This means that

Table 4 Population Growth, 1801-1901

Census Date	Tinnevelly District Total Population (thousands)	% Population Increase	Instances of Severe Famine
1801	572		late 1790s
1821	741	30%	1811-1813
1841	951	28%	1831-1833
1861	1,370	44%	none
1881	1,699	24%	1876-1878
1901	2,060	21%	1898-1899

NOTE: The years from 1835 to 1876 witnessed no season severe enough to be described by observers as years of dreadful hardship. The official designation of "famine year" was not applied in Madras Presidency until 1876.

SOURCES: A. J. Stuart, *Manual*, Appendix 1, p. 1; TCR,TNA, Vol. 7977 (1849), p. 7; Dharma Kumar, *Land and Caste*, pp. 120-21; *1823 Census*; Jamabandy Reports.

worldwide, every five years, roughly 120,000 tons more raw cotton in the field ripened to be picked, sorted, cleaned, pressed, baled, and shipped overseas to meet British demand alone.[21] The American South provided most of the requisite cotton supply, but by the 1850s, India produced nearly one-fifth. The American Civil War increased India's share for the whole of the 1860s to 46 percent, and even in the 1870s, when America's share bounced back to 54 percent, India supplied 25 percent of the cotton consumed by English industry.[22]

Growing demand for cotton revolutionized the Indian export trade after 1835. Tirunelveli, which boasted both high-quality soil for cotton cultivation and thriving centers of cotton cloth weaving, shifted rapidly from export handicraft manufacture of cotton cloth to export peasant cultivation of raw cotton, cleaned in market towns, and shipped out from the ports of Madras and Tuticoryn. Cotton cloth exports by sea from Madras fell from 53 percent of all exports, by value, in 1820, to 29 percent in 1840, and to only 11 percent in 1850.[23] Overland exports of cotton cloth from Tinnevelly District increased after 1830, going mostly to Indian native states, Travancore and Mysore; but total Tinnevelly cloth exports declined from ten lakh rupees in the five years after 1830 to less than three lakh rupees during the five years after 1845.[24] Meanwhile, overseas export tonnage of raw cotton doubled twice from 1825 to 1845 and doubled twice again during the next thirty years, to about 13,000 tons annually in the 1870s. Steamships carried ever larger loads out of Tinnevelly ports, especially Tuticoryn, which was being modernized to handle bigger ships while the cotton road was being built. Freight tonnage per ship tripled from 1840 to 1875, from an average of 50 to over 176. The cash value of cotton exports rose eightfold during the half-century after 1830, from less than eight to more than sixty-four lakh rupees annually.[25]

Merchants initially financed cotton exports by using funds provided by the district land revenue system, but after the abolition of the East India Company as a trade organization in 1833, private export firms, called agency houses, had to import cash into Tinnevelly District to pay for cotton exports. During the 1820s, the district generated an average annual export surplus approaching sixteen lakh rupees. This the Company used to remit revenues to Madras, Calcutta, and London. But exports outpaced revenue receipts. Cotton exports alone were valued at 30 percent of government revenue in the 1830s and soared to 150 percent in the 1870s, having peaked at 400 percent during the American Civil War.[26] Imports did not begin to cover the cost of exports. Import values climbed slowly from 10 percent of exports in 1830 to 44 percent in 1850, to 60 percent in 1860. By the 1870s, imports were valued at two-thirds the value of exports, a proportion that characterized the last decades of the century.[27] Exporters, using the district treasury as a central bank, could pay into the treasury in Madras or London, and in turn draw upon the treasury in Tinnevelly for funds with which to engage in contracts to purchase native cotton. Land revenue receipts thus paid peasants for their cotton. But this mechanism did not provide sufficient funds for cotton exports to expand as rapidly as they did during the decades after 1835. Supplies of cash in the treasury and in the countryside did not suffice to finance expanding exports, and neither did merchandise imports; the Company and then agency house merchants imported an average of 122,500 rupees in silver annually into Tinnevelly District from 1835 to 1850, during a period of net silver exports from Madras Presidency as a whole.[28] Government, in effect, used the rich land revenues from the wet zone to finance cotton exports, and in addition merchants brought in piles of coin to contract for cotton supplies from inland native merchants. This new flood of cash poured especially into dry-zone villages endowed with black cotton soil, as cartloads of cotton rolled out of villages toward the port of Tuticoryn.

Towns bustled and grew. Taluk headquarter towns, with their courts, administrative offices, treasuries, and post offices, became headquarters for merchant houses dealing in products for regional and overseas markets. The district's twenty-four major market towns lay at major road junctions (Map 4), and benefited quickly from declining transport costs by road and then rail. Town population figures are not available until 1881, after which rapid growth surely reflects an earlier trend that continued to bring more and more people to live and work in town after 1835. These twenty-four towns grew an average of 53 percent during the years 1881-1901, when total district population grew only 21 percent (Table 4). Towns in the cotton-growing north, marketing centers at railway junctions where cotton exporters also located ginning facilities, grew three times faster than the average rate for the twenty-four towns. District headquarters, fed by the growth of government income and employment, grew 92 percent, when we consider Tinnevelly and Palayamkottai as one urban complex. The port of Tuticoryn grew 72 percent, and by the last quarter of the century cotton exports from Tuticoryn surpassed those from the port of Madras. Urban growth during the last quarter of the nineteenth century, indeed, surpassed the rate of growth during the first two decades of the twentieth century, when overall growth slowed down to 14 percent, though the relative rapidity of population growth in cotton towns, district headquarters, and Tuticoryn continued.

To be sure, the commercial boom does not explain all this population growth in the towns. Two famines, in 1877 and 1898, just before census counts, forced poor peasants into town to search for work and food. Toward the century's end, slowing rates of growth in irrigated agriculture, to which we also turn below, would have sent the sons of landowners and laborers alike to town, the poor for work and the rich for education, government employment, and business. But decades of strong commercial expansion throughout the region fueled the growth of towns, and growing towns generated demand for agricultural products. Cotton towns in the north became heavy consumers of rice from the wet zone; rice arrived after 1874 in bulk loads on the railway, brought by major grain dealers who were also active in cotton markets.[29] Garden crops that could be dried for long hauls and storage also found wider town markets. Palmyra products and salt fish did the same. Cotton towns on the railway, the port of Tuticoryn, and district headquarters in the central river valley transmitted most of the urban demand for goods and services. More and more, peasant farmers produced commodities for towns and for local, regional, and overseas markets. As a result, a great number of farmers had cash to invest in the productivity of their land.

Investment

Increasing productivity depended on farmers investing proceeds from one agricultural season in the next. Commodity markets provided peasants with cash for investment, but the investment climate varied over space and time, constrained by three major factors: seasonal fluctuations in prices and yields, government tax policy, and government patronage for irrigation. All three factors combined to create a much more favorable investment climate after 1835 than before, and the twenty-five years before the 1877 famine were the most favorable of the whole century. When seasons blessed crops with timely rain, when prices for products rose, when government tax demand fell relative to peasant farm income, and when government supported irrigation projects, investment conditions became most favorable. For many villagers, however, especially those in the mixed zone with neither good irrigation nor good soil, seasonal scarcity, high tax rates, and low government patronage for irrigation made productive investments difficult. Disadvantaged farmers did not reap profits from crop sales sufficient to invest in more farm output and better living conditions.

Land taxation made its major impact during the decades before

141

1854. All observers agree that it pressed most heavily on the poorest land and the poorest villages, and laid the least real burden on the rich. The very best black-soil and irrigated land were assessed at low rates relative to their income-producing power. High tax rates on precarious tank-irrigated land prevented repairs from being done, in many cases, because rebuilding a broken tank or repairing a damaged tank embankment would trigger exorbitant tax rate hikes. E. B. Thomas, collector during the 1840s, argued repeatedly that in addition to stifling investments in tanks, tax rates discouraged farmers from digging wells. R. K. Puckle, collector in the 1870s, followed the same line of attack when he argued that high tax rates on all double-cropped lands prevented farmers from sowing a second crop unless absolutely sure of a good paddy yield to support enhanced revenue payments, though they might well be able to produce a good crop of cholam or ragi.[30] Tax procedures thus combined with early assessments to discourage some productive investments, most severely, it seems certain, in areas that depended on small-tank irrigation and poor dry soils, most common in the mixed zone.

Commercial expansion after 1840 and inflation after 1850 decreased the real tax burden on all land, and during the 1840s government also began to patronize irrigation work. An enthusiastic Englishman proclaimed in 1843 that "as long as one drop of water is allowed to run waste into the sea, we must take blame unto ourselves for not exerting our best efforts to obviate the evils of poverty or the dreadful effects of famine."[31] State outlays from the treasury for irrigation tripled from 1835 to 1875, though inflation eroded the purchasing power of those expenditures (Figure 10), and for the years 1868-1874 most of the increase went into one irrigation project, the new dam and channels at Srivaikuntam. Until 1868, almost all government funding supported what were called "repairs." Collectors and tahsildars parceled out funds to contractors to shore up a tank wall, rebuild a broken channel, or patch a crumbling dam.[32]

Repair work was done by interested local parties who were responsible for its quality, who themselves donated assets to the project, and who also reaped much of the benefit. Such work, therefore, like rural governance in irrigated villages, was done by mirasidars, especially by the most well-to-do shareholders. The very first government outlay set the pattern. The collector discovered that in 1807 the Marudur dam (Map 18), which fed sixty miles of channels and two dozen tanks in the eastern Tambraparni valley, was crumbling. Some thousand feet long and a foot thick at its crest, built of rough-hewn stone, its complete renovation would have disrupted irrigation and crippled land revenue in a large portion of the wet zone. Rebuilding would

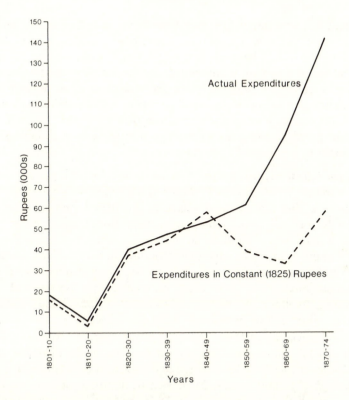

Figure 10 Tinnevelly District Government Irrigation Expenditure, 1801-1874 (in actual and constant rupees)

NOTE: 1856 and 1873 data not available. 1801-1830 expenditures include all public works.

SOURCES: A. J. Stuart, *Manual*, p. 140; *Public Works Commission Report*, Madras, 1852, Appendix Q; TCR,TCO, "To Board, 1858," Letter No. 201, n.p.; *Reports on the Administration of Madras Presidency* for 1858/9-1872/3; *Public Works Commission Report*, Madras, 1869, "Reply by Tinnevelly Collector to Questions on Kudimaramat."

have cost, in addition, much more than the collector could spend, so he called in the government engineer, who laid out plans and a budget. Approved by the Board of Revenue, repairs began with funds from the treasury.[33] A later collector described this "system of perpetual patching," in 1830, in the following words:

The persons employed in these works are almost exclusively the Pullers, the slaves of the Meerassidars. The consequence is that Maramut Works are carried on by making advances to the Meerassidars, who pay their slaves at whatever rate they please, and always contrive to appropriate a part of the money allowed to their own use. The execution of repairs has thus come to be considered a source of annual income for the Meerassidars, and it is therefore in their interest to execute them in as slovenly a manner as possible with a view to further outlay within a short period and so long as the cultivation of the current year is not endangered by the delay to contrive that something should still remain to be finished in the next year.[34]

Government irrigation work depended, therefore, on private assets and initiative from mirasidars. Much work began with complaints in petitions saying that decayed irrigation threatened the land revenue. Officials normally took binding agreements from landowners to cultivate a fixed area of land for so many years after state-funded work was complete, to repay government outlays in taxes. Many treasury outlays thus amounted to loans. Any major project also required many private investments in feeder channels, maintenance, repair, field construction, leveling, and the like, always left in local hands. Finally, private contributions in cash and kind often became critical components in official calculations about irrigation work. Records overflow with official notice that treasury outlays essentially provided seed money to attract local investors. Landowners in Sivalapperi, for example, gave 10,000 rupees, 25 percent of the total estimate, toward the repair of their tank, which, in 1868, had sat broken and useless for three-quarters of a century.[35] Not only countless small projects, for which settlement officers, for instance, gathered up funds in the course of their other duties, but even the very largest project, at Srivaikuntam, depended on local contributions. Landowners whose land would benefit from the Srivaikuntam dam and channels gave cash, donated material and labor, and even completed part of the work at their own expense, to save government money and to speed up the project. In addition, of course, mirasidars contracted to get work done and to deliver materials under government commission.[36]

Planned by one Captain Horsley, a contemporary of E. B. Thomas and protégé of Arthur Cotton, the Srivaikuntam dam project reached the design state in the early 1850s. It was delayed by the 1857 rebellion because it relied upon imperial funds, but started moving again in the late 1860s under the leadership of collector Puckle, whose influence, energy, and skill got the job done within five years. Puckle negotiated personally with mirasidars, got their commitments, worked out details with engineers, and lobbied for funds in Madras. Though small by all-Indian standards, it was the largest nineteenth-century work in Tirunelveli, and became a model of success. Because the dam and two new channels delivered water to an already existing set of channels, tanks, and fields, farmers soon achieved the officially projected 32,000 acres of new cultivation.[37]

The project typified Madras efforts to improve irrigation under the Crown. Government largess gravitated toward very large works. By the time of Indian independence, in 1947, Madras Presidency government had spent 70 percent of its total outlay for irrigation building on twenty-four major projects, which together affected almost half of all irrigated land in the province; each watered about 162,000 acres of land. The government possessed neither the funds nor the executive capacity to do much work on the tens of thousands of tanks that irrigated the other half of Madras wet lands.[38] Officials thus concentrated time, effort, and money on work over which they could retain most control, which promised high yields in higher land revenue, and which thus stimulated maximum new private investment. In the quasi-commercial accounts of government irrigation work, small tank repairs and rebuilding had none of these advantages. Under British rule, small and scattered drainage irrigation works never received government funding in proportion to their significance in agriculture.[39]

During the nineteenth century, manpower and budget constraints channeled Tinnevelly treasury outlays mostly into the wet zone. Of three thousand tanks counted in the district in 1850, eighty-three percent were listed as "government repaired,"[40] but this in reality meant they had received some money by official reckoning, and, in some cases, had received attention from government engineers. The corps of public works officers in 1850 numbered fewer than seventy-five men, including one European engineer and eight trained Vellala supervisors, called maistries.[41] These men could not inspect every tank, let alone prepare estimates and superintend work in scattered localities. Yet forty-one dams on the Chittar and Tambraparni rivers (including temporary dams not shown in Map 18), together irrigated 80 percent of all double-cropped paddy land and half of all single-cropped paddy in the region; these naturally attracted government attention. Presidency guidelines also directed decisions toward irrigation work that promised the best financial returns to government. That work was concentrated along the Tambraparni valley, where private investors lived, well-endowed; where late eighteenth-century warfare left disrepair in its wake; where government reaped most of its tax revenue; and where influential mirasidars had personal interests in the work.[42]

The investment climate did not favor farmers who depended on small tanks outside the wet zone. Regressive taxes pressed on their meager incomes. Seasonal ups and downs meant that gains from one good year would often have to be eaten rather than invested in the next year. Merchants did not find important sources of supply in such villages. Government patronage for irrigation was meager. In addition, many of the locally rich landowners, upon whom irrigation had depended for centuries, were less capable than before of making investments in repair and construction when it was necessary. Zamindars, mirasidar assemblies, temples, and revenue contractors had provided capital during centuries before 1800. Under British rule their capacities to invest, especially in poor tank-irrigated villages, seem to have declined, in part for financial reasons (among which tax rates stand out), but also for political and legal reasons. Among these latter, the development of private property rights and the dissolution of landowning collectivities—subjects of the next chapter—are important, because they destroyed the investment capacity of mirasidar assemblies altogether. Landowners watched as social institutions that had facilitated tank repairs for centuries crumbled. Government did not step in to assume the investment functions that had been part of the segmented political authority structure in centuries before 1800. We cannot quantify the decline in total investments in tanks. But clearly conditions were not favorable for investments in the productivity of small, isolated irrigation tanks.

One British officer, A. T. Arundel, understood the dynamics of decay in tank irrigation. Because the Tambraparni flows full most every year, he reported, despite floods, silting, breaches, and deterioration, farmers who use its water always have an incentive to get repairs done immediately, and investors abound with ready cash for the job. Constant use renders complete reconstruction, however, impractical, as in the case of the Marudur dam, so riverine irrigation always needs repair. Patched perpetually, it worked, always crying out for improvement. A small tank, by contrast, when fed by monsoon rains alone, might receive enough water for a paddy crop only one year in three; even in perfect condition it might not be able to irrigate one acre. Sufficient water to test its strength might arrive only one year in ten, so that defects and decay might go undetected until a flood broke the tank wall. Damage would then require a relatively large investment, yet given its insecurity and isolation, the tank might not attract investors for the task.[43]

The best endowed villages along the Tambraparni were in the strongest position in every way to attract investors. The tank at Adaichani, near Brahmadesam, in the western valley, steadily increased its irrigated acreage before 1850, with the help of regular private and government investment.[44] When the Kadamba tank, across the river from Srivaikuntam, broke under floods in 1796, however, though officials made some effort, neither the tank nor its feeder channels were repaired for many years because of a decay in water supplies from the Marudur dam that made investment in the eastern valley a bad risk. It was to reverse this situation that Horsley planned the Srivaikuntam dam project. It worked. But investors outside the valley had less good fortune—for instance, the landowners at Sivalapperi, mentioned above, who raised 10,000 rupees to repair their tank. This tank, too, broke in the 1796 floods, and several attempts to put together a consortium of investors failed before R. K. Puckle himself entered the scene. He backed a project at Sivalapperi that would have consumed but a tiny fraction of the funds being pumped into the Srivaikuntam dam construction. But the plan failed, and the tank lay broken and useless until after Indian independence.[45]

We will see in the next chapter that mirasidar village unity was being undermined by nineteenth-century trends, and in the mixed zone, crumbling tanks might have been both cause and effect of problems faced by mirasidar collectivities. Such seems to be the case in Manur, a tank village between the Chittar and Tambraparni, and home to one of Tamil Nadu's first recorded brahmadeyas, where the long feeder channel to the tank from the Chittar silted up and thus brought less and less water to Manur paddy fields. Less paddy land produced less to invest in repairs. Despite some government help, the civil engineer pronounced in 1847 that this tank would never regain its former capacity.[46] Seed money for such cases remained hard to come by until the end of British rule.

Roads and railways constituted government investment in areas without irrigation. In the process of increasing productivity, peasants did the rest. Cotton acreage grew rapidly, as we see below, and its proceeds seem to have financed feverish efforts by peasants to tap the water table. Digging a well would provide water for garden crops as well as for man and beast. Statistics on agricultural wells show the most rapid increase in the cotton-exporting north: recorded wells more than doubled there between 1823 and 1850, compared to a much more modest increase of 11 percent in the whole Tinnevelly District and an actual drop in both the Tambraparni valley and southern taluks.[47] Boom years for cotton exports during the American Civil War witnessed rapid strides in well digging. In the 1860s, they multiplied at more than triple the pace of the 1850s. A sample of 357 villages in six taluks reveals that about half of all recorded wells in

1876 had been dug during the previous twenty years; and these recently dug wells were most prominent in the cotton-growing north, where, for example, they constituted 80 percent of recorded wells in Otta-pidarum taluk, compared to 28 percent in Ambasamudram and 21 percent in Nanguneri taluks.[48] The post-1850 surge in well digging reduced the ratio of dry acreage to well-watered land for the first time in the century. Twenty-five acres of dry land had been sown for each well in Srivilliputtur and Sattur taluks in 1850; that figure dropped to seventeen acres in 1875.[49] The slump in well digging after 1870 (Table 5) surely indicates the lasting effects of the 1877 famine, which was less severe in Tinnevelly District than many other parts of South India, but nonetheless wiped out the savings of many families, who required some time to recover and resume agricultural expansion.

Cotton farming produced another asset, in addition to cash income, that could be invested—cotton seeds, which provided superb fodder for bulls and cows. The population of bulls thus increased much more rapidly than the human population in cotton-growing tracts. There were twenty-eight bulls for every one hundred people in Sattur and Srivilliputtur taluks in 1823, and forty-two in 1876.[50] More bulls meant more power to pull carts and raise water from wells, which

Table 5 Agricultural Wells, 1823-1900

Years	Number of Wells (000s)	Mean Acres Dry Cultivation (000s)	Mean Dry Cultivated Acres per Well
(1823)	(17)	(437)	(26)
1850	19	540	28
1860	22	620	28
1870	34	840	25
1880	34	800	24
1890	35	830	24
1900	40	840	21

NOTE: The 1823 figure includes nonagricultural wells.

SOURCES: *1823 Census*; PBR,TNA, Vol. 2039, pp. 16081-89; PBR, 28 August 1863, p. 5029; Jamabandy Reports F. 1276, F. 1281; PBR, Revenue Settlement, 23 March 1893, No. 113A; *Statistical Atlas of the Madras Presidency for F. 1300; Annual Report on the Administration of Madras Presidency*, 1862/3; PBR, Revenue Settlement, 28 February 1903, No. 67, p. 64; G.O. Revenue, No. 304, 31 January 1908, Appendix No. 11, pp. 82-83.

decreased transport costs and the cost of garden-crop farming. More cows meant more milk products to consume and sell. Cotton towns on the trunk road from Madurai became scenes for lively cattle fairs to which dealers brought hardy bovine stock bred in the Coimbatore District.[51] With more cash to spend for superior stock, and more high-quality fodder to feed the bovine population, peasants built a robust and growing population of work animals and milk cows that supported expanding agricultural production in the dry zone.

PRODUCTIVITY

The investment climate improved steadily after 1835 and remained favorable until the 1877 famine. Wet- and dry-zone producers of paddy and cotton were clearly in the most advantageous positions. Garden producers and growers of domestic commodity crops like oil seeds, palmyras, and pulses also reaped advantages that could stimulate increased land productivity. These three sets of peasant producers, all working within expanding circuits of commodity crop marketing, made the nineteenth century a period of overall growth in agriculture. And the relatively good monsoon seasons for forty years after 1835 converged with trends in government policy and export markets to make this period one of exceptional growth. Momentum gained before the 1877 famine slowed somewhat thereafter, when statistics reveal rather sluggish growth, in irrigated agriculture in particular, and when, as we have seen, rapidly growing town populations expanded even as overall population growth in the region slowed considerably. Looking at the century as a whole, we see gradual growth, poorly documented, before 1835; rapid growth for the next forty years; and then continued but slow growth after 1875.

Seasonal fluctuations amid an overall growth trend stand out in all statistical series pertaining to agriculture, the most important of which are abstracted in Tables 6-10.[52] Total cultivated acreage expanded at a rate exceeding 1 percent per year from 1825 through 1886, when cultivated land per capita remained fairly constant.[53] Dry cultivation shows most dramatically the effects of seasonal rainfall variations on the extent of sown acreage, which expanded in fits and starts. Irrigated agriculture shows less variation in sown acreage from season to season; and the fact that rates of variation decline over the century shows clearly that investments in irrigation improved overall water control in the region (Table 6). Price variations also caused variations in sown acreage, as shown by cotton statistics (Table 7). Cotton acreage expanded more rapidly than any other category, but it also fluctuated

149

Table 6 Total Cultivation, 1825-1886

Years	Total Cultivated Acreage					Total Dry Cultivation					Total Irrigated Acreage				
	Mean	V	G	(R)	PC	Mean	V	G	(R)	PC	Mean	V	G	(R)	PC
1825-1837:	607	11%	1.6%	(.6)	.71	449	13%	1.3%	(.4)	.53	126	9%	.7%	(.3)	.15
1843-1854:	740	3%	.4%	(.5)	.58	547	3%	.3%	(.3)	.43	177	11%	.7%	(.3)	.14
1858-1876:	980	11%	1.5%	(.7)	.58	764	14%	1.7%	(.7)	.45	216	7%	.5%	(.4)	.13
1877-1886:	1,078	3%	.5%	(.5)	.63	822	4%	.5%	(.4)	.48	257	4%	.6%	(.5)	.15

NOTE: *Mean* = mean cultivated acres (000s)

  V = variation (standard deviation as *percent of* mean)

  G = annual growth rate (slope of regression line as *percent of* mean)

  (R) = correlation (Pearson's R) (showing the fit of the trend to the actual cultivation data)

  PC = per capita cultivated acreage (using nearest census data to the end of each period).

SOURCE: Jamabandy Reports.

Table 7 Cotton Acreage, 1829-1886

Years	Mean	V	G	(R)	PC
1829-1848:	106	20%	2.4%	(.8)	.11
1852-1875:	208	31%	3.5%	(.8)	.12
1876-1886:	303	16%	4.3%	(.9)	.18

NOTE: *Mean* = mean cultivated acres (000s)
$\quad\quad$ V = variation
$\quad\quad$ G = annual growth rate
$\quad$ (R) = correlation
$\quad$ PC = per capita cultivated acreage

SOURCE: Jamabandy Reports.

more dramatically than any other dry crop in sown acreage because peasants watched the market as well as the skies. Forward contracts by merchants during boom cotton export periods pushed up cotton acreage, and supplies of cash to extend cotton acreage dried up when the export market slumped.

Seasonal cycles stand out clearly in statistics for the years around famine periods in the 1830s and 1870s. Rapidly contracting and expanding dry-crop acreage in the 1830s before, during, and after the famine years appear statistically in high rates of variability for sown acreage during the period 1825-1837 (Table 6). After 1843, collectors report relatively good seasons with more generous and timely rains, so that during the period 1843-1854 farmers could plant dry crops on their land to a more constant extent, and acreage variability declined. In addition, statistics show that drought years and years of expansion in agriculture witnessed a shift in planting strategies. We saw in the previous chapter that bad seasons in the 1830s forced farmers to seek lower tax rates in the mixed zone by moving their land out of the nunjah into the more lightly assessed nunjah-mel-punjah revenue category. Tables 6 and 10 show that this move had its agricultural justification, for expanding dry cultivation during the 1830s must have resulted as farmers of land under barren tanks sowed their fields with millets (Table 6); and irrigated acreage outside the Tambraparni valley declined because tanks could not support paddy crops to maturity (Table 10). During the better seasons after 1843, dry-crop sown acreage expanded more slowly than during bad years before 1837, because even though good rains enabled new land to be

Table 8 Irrigated and Dry Cultivation, Growth by Taluk Groups, 1825-1854

Taluk Groups	1825-1837						1843-1854					
	Dry			Irrigated			Dry			Irrigated		
	%	G	(R)	%	G	(R)	%	G	(R)	%	G	(R)
Tambraparni Valley												
upper	45	.2%	(.4)	49	1.6	(.5)	49	.2%	(.2)	51	1.5%	(.9)
lower	74	-.2%	(.0)	21	.9	(.4)	49	-.9%	(.5)	51	0	(.0)
Tenkasi taluk	55	1.8%	(.3)	31	-.9	(.4)	65	1.3%	(.4)	32	.4%	(.2)
Northern taluks	88	1.8%	(.4)	9	-1.7	(.3)	91	1.0%	(.5)	9	.7%	(.3)
Southern taluks	80	-.1%	(.2)	13	0	(.2)	67	-2.3%	(.5)	33	.3%	(.1)

NOTES: The "upper valley" consists of those taluks watered by anicuts above Marudur.
% = percent cultivation type to total cultivation
G = annual growth rate
(R) = correlation
SOURCE: Jamabandy Reports.

Table 9 Types of Irrigated Cultivation, Growth by Taluk Groups, 1843-1854

Taluk Group	One Crop			Two Crops			Cultivation Category Kar			Pisanam			Rain-fed Tanks		
	%	G	(R)	%	G	(R)	%	G	(R)	%	G	(R)	%	G	(R)
Tambraparni Valley															
upper	67	1.1%	(.7)	36	1.7%	(.8)	35	2.9%	(.8)	65	2.0%	(.9)	8	4.5%	(.5)
lower	71	−.1%	(.2)	36	1.0%	(.3)	30	.6%	(.2)	68	1.4%	(.8)	9	2.5%	(.4)
Tenkasi taluk	89	−.4%	(.2)	15	6.6%	(.7)	23	3.7%	(.6)	77	2.3%	(.7)	2	−1.4%	(.2)
Northern taluks	84	.2%	(.3)	11	1.2%	(0)	11	4.9%	(0)	89	2.0%	(.4)	62	2.4%	(.3)
Southern taluks	94	.4%	(.1)	24	1.6%	(.1)	22	4.4%	(.2)	78	3.1%	(.5)	25	2.4%	(.3)

NOTES: The "upper valley" consists of taluks watered by anicuts above Marudur.
% = percent cultivation category to total irrigated cultivation
G = annual growth rate
(R) = correlation
SOURCE: Jamabandy Reports.

Table 10 Irrigated Acreage, 1825-1886

Years	Tambraparni Valley		All Other		District Total	
1825-1837:	1.5%	(.5)	−.8%	(.3)	.7%	(.3)
1843-1854:	1.2%	(.7)	.6%	(.1)	.7%	(.3)
1858-1876:	1.0%	(.5)	.2%	(.2)	.5%	(.4)
1877-1886:	.5%	(.4)	.9%	(.5)	.6%	(.5)

NOTES: 1825-1854 data represent taluk trends.
G   = annual growth rate
(R) = correlation
SOURCE: Jamabandy Reports.

sown to dry crops, both millets and cotton, land under tanks that had by necessity been sown with millets during bad years could now be planted with paddy. This general improvement in irrigated agriculture is depicted in Table 8, and Table 9 shows that much of the new irrigated acreage during the period 1843-1854 was land irrigated by rain-fed tanks, that is, by tanks not supplied by mountain rivers or streams. The rains, therefore, became more bountiful during the 1840s. For twenty years after 1857, however, statistics show a zero growth rate in rain-fed tank-irrigated acreage.[54] Dry cropping and wet-zone irrigated acreage expanded steadily, but tanks did not improve their ability to support paddy crops to maturity, and indeed many tanks seem to have decayed over the years. In the face of lean seasons, tank irrigators throughout the mixed zone appear to have relied more and more heavily on planting millets; and the productivity of dry lands seems to have increased in relation to irrigated land. This change is reflected in patterns of revenue assessment during survey and settlement operations in the 1870s, when the single most important change in tax rates was an increase in dry-land rates, especially on the best black soils, relative to wet-land rates, especially on the worst irrigated land.[55] We will see that this trend in the mixed zone parallels a trend in village power relations, because dry-farming peasants became more assertive in pursuit of property rights as wet-farming mirasidar communities faced declining agricultural security.

Growth in irrigated agriculture demanded copious natural water supplies, which farmers could harness to produce more paddy by building irrigation works and working fields more intensively. Conditions for steady growth existed only in the wet zone, and most emphatically in the upper reaches of the Tambraparni. While irrigated acreage sputtered and fluctuated elsewhere, investors public and private pushed Tambraparni acreage upward at a rate of more than 1 percent per year (Table 10). Investors to the east had little success before the building of the Srivaikuntam dam because the Marudur dam was crumbling and its main channels were choked with silt. Irrigated acreage in eastern valley taluks remained virtually constant before 1858. Poor kar crops reduced investment incentives; declining kar acreage indicates declining overall productivity for the period before 1860 east of district headquarters.[56] The new anicut changed conditions at one stroke. Whereas double-cropped acreage under Tenkari and Kadamba tanks (Map 18) stood at 70 percent of single-cropped acreage in 1849, double-cropped acreage doubled as soon as the Srivaikuntam anicut was built, and soared to 90 percent of single-cropped acreage in 1875.[57]

Increased land productivity under irrigation derived both from putting new land under irrigation and from working old wet land more frequently. Throughout the length and breadth of the Tambraparni valley, new land to irrigate had become hard to find by the beginning of the century, so that increases in productivity depended on more intensive use of water and labor to grow more on each acre. To grow a second crop, and even a third, became the mirasidars' goal, and was especially important in light of the higher prices fetched by kar paddy in the marketplace. This strategy, of course, relied on village access to river water throughout the year, which investments in irrigation, funded by paddy profits, made possible. Multicrop farms also needed more field labor, and, as we see in the next chapter, mirasidars became keen to remove the obstacles that hindered labor movements and increased labor costs.

Intensification and extension proceeded apace throughout the nineteenth century, but slowed markedly toward century's end, indicating that farmers faced diminishing returns even in the region's richest irrigated terrain. Under the Adaichani tank, mentioned above, kar cropping expanded four times faster than pisanam, even before 1850.[58] Double-cropping expanded faster than single cropping in the whole river valley, very much faster during 1843-1854. By the 1880s it seems that farmers on the Tambraparni had reached limits imposed by their irrigation technologies, though in that decade a series of good rains enabled rain-fed tanks to expand wet cultivation (Table 10). A study conducted just before World War I showed that irrigation in the western Tambraparni valley had increased cultivated acreage 20 percent during the last quarter of the nineteenth century, when agriculture began to stagnate.[59] Of all Tambraparni irrigated land, 94 percent was double-cropped by 1917. Total irrigated acreage under river channels in the Tirunelveli region hovered around 50,000 acres from 1900 to 1975. By 1917, even the Srivaikuntam dam project seemed disappointing, because its immediate success did not lead to continued expansion of command area or cultivated acreage.[60] Undoubtedly, diminishing returns on the farm led increasing numbers of mirasidar youngsters to seek their fortune in town, where professions, trade, and government provided expanding career opportunities. Sluggish growth in field labor employment must have pushed many landless laboring Palla families into the labor market as well, where they looked for work not only in town but overseas on plantations in Sri Lanka and Malaysia.[61]

SOCIETY

In the nineteenth-century Tirunelveli region we find an agrarian society steadily expanding its productive capacities and commercial activities. Farmers in each generation produced more per acre and probably per capita. Their pursuit of widening market opportunities clearly increased the cash income per capita available in agricultural communities. They accomplished this growth using old farm technology.[62] What technological change did occur came from imported materials and techniques that lowered transport, transaction, and communication costs; in addition, concrete and iron did become increasingly common in dam construction. On the farm, traditional tools and techniques continued to serve peasants well. Water control improved, providing more security and more stable output under irrigation. Well-known skills and routines enabled farmers to extend and intensify production. Already established market towns, merchants, commercial networks, and forms of labor organization accomplished economic growth in village social settings.

Growth had subtle but serious social consequences; their economic dimensions merit consideration here, before we turn to attendant social conflict in the next chapter. Everywhere in the region, population densities grew and more people moved to live in cities and towns. Commercial development altered the spatial and social distribution of economic opportunity and wealth; it altered the terms of land and labor relations. Most important, perhaps, agricultural zones, and hence whole subregions, experienced growth quite differently from one another.

The mixed zone as a whole benefited least from improving economic conditions. Tanks that decayed during the eighteenth-century wars do not seem to have improved very much in their ability to sustain paddy crops after 1800. Where tank builders had pushed over centuries into less promising natural settings, tanks continued to provide a precarious supplement to dry farming, so that mirasidars who staked their claim to rural elite status on rain-fed tanks were in a tenuous position. In much of the mixed zone, in addition, dry land could not support valuable crops other than oil seeds and pulses, though in the north, land around Srivilliputtur did boast good black cotton soil. Droughts and famines hit the mixed zone very hard. Many Maravas suffered serious economic problems under these circumstances. There is little doubt that the surge in town populations that doubled the size of mixed-zone towns during the last decades of the century resulted in considerable part from moves by villagers, many of them Maravas, to find urban employment.

But the mixed zone did have some success stories. Certainly the biggest gainers in both the north and south were peasants endowed with good dry land, wells, and access to town markets. Among economic winners, the Shanars hold special importance, for their success produced dramatic changes in their relative economic standing, of a sort that did not accrue to any other caste group. Shanars became renowned for skill in expanding palmyra tree cultivation, digging wells for garden production, and marketing their produce in towns through networks of caste-organized commercial exchange. Especially in the north, in the black- and red-soil tract, Shanars excelled in both agriculture and trade. Shanar merchant houses dominated cotton marketing in several northern towns, most importantly Virudhunagar. Petty Shanar traders apparently forged a link between big town merchants and village producers, so that caste and kin ties among Shanars provided social conduits for the forward contracts that supplied towns with both cotton and domestic commodities. The rising fortunes of Shanars amid Marava populations in economic doldrums, and the rising fortunes of dry-land peasants in general amid economically stagnant or declining mirasidar villages, caused persistent social conflict from early in the century to the very end.

Like the towns in the mixed zone that housed merchants in search of profit and laborers in search of work, towns in the wet zone grew because of opportunities there for both rich and poor. But unlike towns anywhere else, wet-zone towns grew surrounded by luxurious paddy fields. Urban and irrigation economies remained, as they had been for centuries, closely intertwined: village mirasidar elites dominated towns; and village land, labor, and grain markets underpinned urban growth.

Conditions in and around Ambasamudram, a taluk headquarters town in the western river valley and the site of the old sabha of Rajamangalam, are illustrative of conditions in the wet zone. The town doubled in size during the twenty years before 1901, and then grew more slowly to reach 14,000 by 1911.[63] Landowners relied increasingly on tenants to farm their land, so that they could concentrate on urban careers in the professions, education, government, and commerce. A study conducted in 1911 showed that 60 percent of all river-irrigated land in the vicinity of Ambasamudram was worked by tenants, and that 90 percent of all rental income was collected in kind. Paddy payments in hand, landowners could feed their families and sell their paddy to support educational advancement and urban careers not only in Ambasamudram but also in larger urban centers such as Tirunelveli town, Madurai, and Madras. Tenants, for their part, sought other sources of income to supplement their share of the paddy crop: half of the 73 percent of Ambasamudram-area tenants with other sources of income, in 1911, worked as laborers, a quarter as small landowners, and a quarter as artisans. Most tenants, moreover, retained their tenant status for many generations.[64] Finding good, reliable tenants became a problem for landowners, who complained in 1908 that revised revenue assessments should take into account insecurities resulting from a paucity of trustworthy tenants in the Tambraparni valley.[65]

To maintain their grip on village land and on paddy payments for labor services remained essential for both elites and manual workers in town, because real income declined during the last decades of the century in Tinnevelly District, a trend that would have hit hardest those people who depended on cash income. This unhappy development, which did not characterize all Madras districts, must have resulted at least in part from diminishing returns in irrigated agriculture.[66] Though irrigated agriculture had benefited handsomely from improved investment conditions during the nineteenth century; though mirasidars had sunk their profits into more extensive and intensive paddy production; and though output had stabilized with improved irrigation, producing more with Tambraparni waters became increasingly costly and difficult toward the century's end. A thousand years of steady growth—punctuated by periods of distress and recovery—was reaching limits imposed by traditional technologies. Growth slowed and with it labor demand, while food prices rose in relation to wages. Landowners, tenants, and landless laborers alike had to seek their fortunes in town. Private investors looked for profits in business. Many invested in human capital by buying their sons an English education.[67] Government looked for large works of public improvement outside Tinnevelly District.[68] The overall pace of investment in fixed agricultural capital decelerated.

Social change in the wet zone did not involve any major shift in the social distribution of economic power, as it did in the mixed zone. The mirasidar landed elite retained its status, and the landless social stratum, composed mostly of Pallas, remained squarely on the bottom of the social hierarchy. In town, however, mirasidars, even as they moved into government service and professional and business careers, did face challenges to their domination of society from rising commercially active groups, which included Shanars. But more importantly, the Vellala-Brahman alliance, largely intact for a millennium, faced challenges from within as individual families sought their fortunes in the land and labor markets. On the one hand, well-endowed landowner families sought to widen market opportunities for themselves, which led them to espouse policies that would free the movement of labor and lower the cost of labor market activity. On the other hand, mirasidars sought to retain advantages that accrued to themselves in virtue of their social standing. Thus members of the old wet-zone elite were pitted against one another. By the early years of the twentieth century, their internal oppositions would find an ideological expression in Non-Brahmanism, which would dominate early nationalist politics in Madras Presidency.

The dry-zone agrarian economy experienced the most dramatic transformation of all during the nineteenth century. Wealth to be reaped from military action declined to virtually zero, and the wealth to be gained from market activity rose faster than any resident of this rugged peasant milieu could have imagined when the East India Company came to power. New transport technology transformed small, defensive commercial towns into expanding centers of cotton trade and processing at major railway and road junctions. Major protagonists in the cotton economy rose to social prominence. The dry zone, once barren land important to agrarian society only because it lay between irrigated core agricultural milieus—for centuries an area of fierce struggles over land control and tribute—became the scene of an economic boom that would last through the end of the century and beyond, as its towns continued to grow rapidly and to attract workers and investors in trade and small-scale industry.

In the dry zone we see more than anywhere else a dramatic personal confrontation between South Indian peasants and businessmen, on the one hand, and European capitalists of the industrial age, on the other. South Indian commercial expertise and peasant experience in cotton cultivation and marketing enabled cotton exports to grow enormously. But as the trade grew, English businessmen pursuing more power compelled structural change in the political economy of the cotton export trade.

Clearly village officers, endowed with substantial landownings and revenue authority, provided the primary link in the chain of transactions that sent tinnies cotton overseas. Because the Company initially financed exports with funds from land taxation, village officers could use their grip on village taxes to fund early cotton production for export in dry-zone villages. They would have received advances, initially in the form of loans of land revenue funds, and delivered cotton grown in their villages to a native merchant in a cotton mart such as Virudhunagar. From there the cotton would move, having been cleaned in town, to the port of Tuticoryn for export on the Company's account. As the volume of exports increased, revenues from dry-zone land taxation would have become insufficient to finance cotton exports, so that during the twenties and thirties the export trade would have required the transfer of land revenues from the wet zone into the dry zone.

With the construction of the cotton road in the 1840s, exports climbed and English agency houses assumed increasing importance in the cotton trade. To finance the trade, exporters had to import coin into Tinnevelly District and pay native merchants in advance for cotton to export. During the 1830s and 1840s, these forward contracts for export cotton generated numerous conflicts between English agency house representatives and native merchants; because of government involvement, conflicts made their way into government records. The English need for Indian cotton triggered efforts by Company officials and by Parliament to lower the cost and improve the quality of raw cotton supplies.[69] Improvements to the port and town of Tuticoryn enabled agency houses to move their base of operations in the tinnies trade to Tuticoryn from Madras. Bright tinnies cotton could henceforth seek its own markets in the world cotton trade, and exports from Tuticoryn equaled those from Madras by the 1870s, when the railway was built. To illustrate the quite distinct and diverse markets for tinnies cotton: in 1875, 82 percent of cotton shipped from the port of Madras went to London, but only 54 percent of Tinnies exports from Tuticoryn went to London: 10 percent went to Austria, 5 percent to Holland, 19 percent to Italy, and 11 percent to Hong Kong.[70] The cotton road, railway, and port improvements—all funded by the government—enabled English agency houses to establish better control of the cotton grown by dry-zone peasants.

That agency house control had remained unsatisfactory between the 1840s and 1870s is amply documented, for merchants complain bitterly that native middlemen dirtied the cotton brought to the port and adulterated bales to extract higher profits. Government brought an American expert, Thomas James Finnie, to convince Tinnevelly District cotton growers to plant long-staple American cotton and to adopt the cotton gin for cleaning raw cotton, in the hope that these technical innovations would improve the quality of export cotton and hence export profits. Finnie reported to his employers, however, that growers preferred native cotton for one very good reason: it resisted drought and produced well with little rainfall. He also reported that the cotton gin cost too much to operate and thus could be profitable only for very large cotton dealers; for the great number of small dealers who brought tinnies cotton to port, the native device, a small hand tool called a churka, very efficient in the hands of elderly women in the village, was better suited to their needs. Finally, Finnie reported that the reason agency house exporters did not receive cleaner cotton was that they did not pay cotton dealers in proportion to the cleanliness of cotton delivered to the port; agency houses would have to pay more if they wanted native dealers to fulfill forward contracts with clean and unadulterated cotton.[71]

Unhappy at Finnie's conclusions, English merchants had to wait for the railway to be built to improve their control of the export market.[72] In the 1870s, agency houses were for the first time able to set up their own trading stations inland at railway junctions, where they received all cotton from the hinterland destined for export. Thus they could stipulate that all export cotton had to be cleaned by agency house gins.[73] The railway thus not only decreased transport costs but, like the cotton road before, altered the spatial structure of the cotton trade itself. The cotton road had stimulated the growth of towns along the road and thus of the native merchant houses established in those towns, above all Shanar and Vaduga houses. These merchants expanded their operations and engaged an ever-increasing number of middlemen in their own forward contracts with farmers during the boom years of the 1850s and 1860s. In the 1870s, when agency houses set up their stations with ginning machinery at railway junctions, native merchants in towns along the railway were well positioned to expand their own operations. Merchants in smaller towns not on the railway line saw their operations shrink. Merchants in Sattur, Virudhunagar, and Koilpatti benefited; they became dealers in cotton seed, cotton, and grain;

and they established close working relations with agency house operatives and expanded wholesale businesses, as their less substantial caste brethren flocked to town to set up retail businesses and supply cotton and other products from surrounding villages.[74]

Merchant and farming families became prominent social and political actors in cotton areas and maintained their positions through the century and beyond because of widespreading commercial ties to growers and petty traders in dry-zone villages. Improving transport and booming towns gave more and more peasants in the village access to produce markets. Surely village officers must have been able to build on their early advantages to reap disproportionately large returns from commercial development, at least through the 1860s. Numerous reports indicate that substantial peasant families dominated village cotton markets; they owned carts and bulls and land that produced profits with which to sink wells and build imposing houses. Even today, villages in the dry-zone cotton tracts boast two-story homes that loom large on village streets and constitute the legacy of early commercialization among a peasantry differentiated by caste, lineage, and political status.[75] But as the population grew, as cotton exports expanded, and as access to markets became cheaper, village monopolies and monopsonies by such peasant strong men became more difficult to maintain. Studies of cotton marketing in the twentieth century indicate that a great many dealers, moneylenders, cartmen, and middlemen competed in villages around cotton towns.[76] The growing number of bulls, carts, and wells suggest that an increasing proportion of peasant producers could profit as individual families from market activity. By the end of the nineteenth century, when the powers of village officers had been hedged in by survey and settlement, when cash income provided peasant families with means to pay their own land revenue, and when opportunities for trade and work in town provided income independent of landowning, the social dominance of village officers, having been based for centuries on a segmented agrarian system, must have declined quite substantially from a high point during the eighteenth-century wars.

Company military power ended the heyday of militant little kings in the dry zone. Imperial technologies opened an era of expanding commercial wealth and power. Peasants with assets in land, with family labor, and with caste connections to merchants in town pursued opportunities that triggered the growth of commercialized peasant agriculture. In major towns, established merchant castes became powers to contend with. In the villages, commercially active dominant peasant castes, above all Vaduga jatis, transformed old military domains into thriving domains of commercial agriculture, while formerly subordinate families moved out into new realms of opportunity in the countryside. Some former little kings, now zamindars, like Ettaiyapuram, moved into the cotton economy from a base of operations along the cotton road, and in an estate that included a railway station. But as the empire moved in to reshape his administration, the cotton economy brought merchants and commercial activity into increasing prominence in the political economy of his domain and others like it. His family remained rich, but less so in comparison to commercial groups of lower traditional stature. Meanwhile, many zamindars and erstwhile little kings became impoverished compared to upstart agrarian capitalists. The relative decline of military men in the countryside would be but one of the subtle shifts in social relations that would trigger strife in village life during the rise of commodity production in the Tirunelveli region.

· 6 ·

CHANGING TRADITION

In their everyday lives, country people did not see the vast expansion of Anglo-Indian imperial power and agricultural commodity production. But surely, over the years, the elderly would have complained that things were not the way they used to be. Aged mirasidars would have grumbled that they had lost inherited privilege: now neither government nor peers honored old ways of collective order in mirasidar villages. High-caste patriarchs must have complained that they no longer received the deference enjoyed by their grandfathers; now social upstarts openly flaunted ancient rites of respect. Elderly agricultural laborers and village servants, for their part, would have grieved over their loss of rights to serve particular village families in every generation and to share in the village harvest in customary proportions; now their fate hinged on a fickle job market. The passing of village tradition would vex many, both inside and outside villages, and many would blame the British. But most customs that were transformed or that atrophied did so from local initiative, and not without resistance and conflict, some of it documented. Recorded social conflicts over rights in society, pitting defenders of the old ways against champions of change, provide keys by means of which to explore cause and effect in countless little transformations that, in the final analysis, comprise the social impact of capitalism and imperialism in nineteenth-century Tirunelveli.

Disputes about rights in rural society pervade peasant history, and we have touched upon many that in fact changed tradition very considerably during the centuries before 1800. Pandya-period warfare and many inscriptions reflect struggles by peasants and warriors to fix rights to land, labor, and tribute. Post-Pandya migration, conquest, and frontier settlement brought new contenders for wealth and power into the region; the most important of these contenders received honors at royal courts to validate their rights to local dominion. Under the Nayakas, warriors built a tributary state that generated new rights based on the ability to pay cash to state agents; in this context, financial middlemen between the peasant producers and the kings established rights to tribute and to land. Eighteenth-century war again reflects rampant conflict motivated by local action to protect and extend rights to village assets. Indeed, as we have seen, contrary responses by wet-

164

and dry-zone landed elites to eighteenth-century turmoil help to explain the course of events after 1750, and only make sense in light of their respective strategies for securing rights.

In 1801, many conflicts over rights engendered by eighteenth-century conditions remained unresolved. Englishmen then injected their own interests and conceptions of right into the agrarian system. Subsequently, during decades of growing state power and commercialism, villagers themselves changed their assumptions about property rights as they changed the rural distribution of rights to village land. After mid-century, as the urban population expanded with the concentration of state and market activity, conflicts over rights to urban space and to the public domain reflected a redefinition of caste relations to state authority. From the beginning to the end of the century, we can see subtle shifts in social power manifested in conflicts between groups over rights; and in the process of conflict and conflict resolution, we can see that this regional peasant culture changed its prescriptive and descriptive ideas about who had what rights in society.

CUSTOM

Two Tamil terms express principles of property right: *pangu* and *pattam*. Pangu means "share." Rights founded on the pangu principle accrue to members of a group, as in the paradigmatic case of family property. Pattam means "title." Rights founded on the pattam principle accrue to a person as the recipient of a title from higher authority, be it king or god or both.

We have seen that people in the Tirunelveli region applied these principles to build dominant caste domains. Medieval people extended the pangu principle to embrace whole irrigated villages, where Brahman and Vellala families shared village assets under the terms of grants from Pandya kings. During post-Pandya centuries, royal grants to Marava and Vaduga warriors designated territories on the agricultural frontier as domains for the little kings who became poligars, and who in turn granted land to their subordinates. Marava and Vaduga kinsmen certainly also applied the pangu principle to parcel out booty and land among members of lineage segments.[1] Thus competition among groups bounded by circuits of endogamy within caste, during centuries of political competition under Madurai kings, produced sets of rights to land, granted by royalty and held by families within dominant castes. Dominant-caste titles became synonymous with family rights to land and expressed proprietary status, legitimated by pangu and pattam principles. Oral accounts preserved in the Mackenzie Manuscripts record folk traditions that explain the course of property relations by reference to royal grants and caste status in the region.[2] Dominant castes expressed royal entitlement and dominance in their own caste names.

One constant set of cultural principles and symbols of entitlement, which hinged on the powers of kings and deities and on the bounded solidarities of kinship and caste, generated change over the centuries in the regional system of property rights. The first big change, after the original establishment of these principles in agrarian culture under medieval Pandyas, occurred during centuries of migrant settlement and warrior competition after 1300, when militant peasants established territorial control in what had been the dry periphery of Pandya rural domains, and when warrior overlords inserted their authority into the communities of the irrigated heartlands of Pandyamandalam. Militant migrants created domains of property right under the authority of intermediary royal figures who became much more prominent after 1500 than they had ever been under the Pandyas. Warrior overlords, who arrived on the scene during the Vijayanagar centuries, established themselves as protectors and patrons of brahmadeyas, temples, and irrigated communities in general, usurping authority previously held by local sharehold communities, above all, by sabhas of extended brahmadeyas like Rajamangalam.[3]

The second big change began under the Nayakas and continued through the seventeenth and eighteenth centuries: financial transactions that provided state revenues became increasingly prominent in definitions of property right. Payments in cash and in kind had surely solidified claims to property according to the pattam principle under medieval Pandya kings, most certainly within local circuits of dominant caste authority. But after 1600 not only did commercial capital provide essential tax revenues but individuals in the region established rights to land based on their ability to pay land revenue, and revenue collecting created ritual contexts within which people could compete for and solidify property rights.

By the turn of the nineteenth century, the regional system of rights to property included a great diversity of claims legitimated according to pangu and pattam principles, rights not only to land but to labor and to shares of the harvest and land revenue. Claims to rights often came into conflict. To establish any person's position in the property system, an observer would have to locate the person in a group whose collective set of rights could be located in relation to other groups and traced back to a ritual moment of entitlement. This process of locating and tracing was for participants in the property system a cultural necessity, accomplished orally in the lore that village elders passed on to their children. Locating individuals in bounded groups and in relation to higher authorities was also accomplished in rituals that constituted and expressed hierarchy among castes and rank among title-holders. Conflicts over rights, therefore, characteristically involved conflict among groups in competitive interaction with higher authorities, and rituals could, as a result, become occasions for heated competition. Precedence of place in group transactions with state authorities defined superior and inferior group and individual positions in hierarchies of property right. Caste boundaries, rituals of ranking, and state grants of entitlement were cultural implements for the social reproduction of rights.[4]

Locally, particular configurations of order and conflict in regional property custom characterized each agricultural zone. In the wet zone, an institutionalized structure of shareholding embraced whole irrigated communities and pervaded village life. Brahman and Vellala mirasidars owned whole villages, and together owned the whole of the wet zone. A mirasidar collectivity traced its entitlement back to Pandya kings and recreated itself each season in the routines of irrigated agriculture. Village laborers shared among themselves a portion of the village harvest; for everyone, caste status marked clear social strata within which families shared assets under the authority of mirasidar village shareholders. Custom did not dictate equality among families in each stratum, nor did it specify the exact value or content of each share, only that title to shares be construed within the appropriate stratum for each family: Brahmans and Vellalas ruled whole villages and shared the full range of assets; Pallas and Pariahs shared in the harvest and in the provision of labor services. Specific styles of life and forms of work symbolized a family's position in the system. So did styles of dress, speech, and residence. Brahmans avoided work in the fields, it appears, absolutely. Vellalas avoided manual labor whenever possible, though they might cultivate the land themselves or with Palla laborers as tenants to Brahmans. Pallas and Pariahs worked in the mud in paddy fields and lived in separate, polluted, neighborhoods. Caste status and rituals of avoidance and hierarchy constituted property rights, it could truly be said, by the terms of the original royal charter. Conflict, it appears on the basis of nineteenth-century evidence, concerned above all the rights of village mirasidars, in relation to which all other rights were defined.

A different tradition characterized the dry zone. Peasants traced their title to land to Pandya kings through the persons of dominant caste warrior chiefs whose ancestors marched with followers into the agricultural frontier after 1300. Titles passed through lineages and dominant subcastes down to peasants who worked their land primarily with their own family labor. Shareholding seems to have pertained only to territorial control parceled out among the followers of chiefs.[5] Much of the conflict during the centuries before 1800 seems to have involved competition to extend such territorial control and thus the scale of assets available to warrior-peasant alliances. Secure title to land for the peasant thus involved, historically, fighting with kinsmen and obtaining authorization by expressions of loyalty to superiors in warfare. Inside villages, family bonds seem to have mustered the productive assets necessary for agriculture. Dominant caste families, from the richest to the poorest, normally worked their own land with their own hands. Family alliances might be brought to bear to dig a well and share its water.[6] Lineage and caste factions lined up to define the village power structure, but do not seem to have systematized shareholding in village agricultural production. There was no village grain heap to be divided among strata of village workers and landowners. There was no gang labor to be organized and no village irrigation to maintain. Farming families traced their rights to land back through their chiefs to frontier conquerors. Families maintained their rights to farmland by working their own land and defending the territory dominated by their dominant caste alliance.

In the mixed zone, contrary wet and dry traditions confronted one another. Mirasidar sharehold villages saw themselves surrounded by warrior-peasants after 1300. At their border, mirasidars and peasants staked claims to the same land. Mirasidars could cite entitlement conferred by Pandya kings. Peasants could cite grants of dominion by Pandya kings to their chiefs. In such situations, history and culture supported the mirasidars, whose claim rested on prior settlement, superior caste status, and periodic support by regional rulers. Brahmans in particular would have been viewed by warrior-peasant leaders as a rural elite whose status had to be protected to bolster royal authority and the stature of little kings. Maravas would have felt this cultural imperative, as had Vellalas before them. Efforts on the royal behalf, such as by Vijayanagar commanders to support the temple of Sudikkodutta Nachiyar at Srivilliputtur,[7] would have reinforced mirasidar charter rights in the mixed zone. Leading mirasidars transmitted the bulk of circar land revenue to regional rulers through the eighteenth century, indicating the continuity in their status as owners of all land surrounding tank-irrigated villagers. The open character of village boundaries, evident in inscriptions that portray extended brahmadeyas such as Rajamangalam,[8] enabled mirasidars to claim and hold rights to land throughout the mixed zoned cultivated by independent peasant farmers, including Palla, Marava, and Shanar families who resided in hamlets at some distance from the core mirasidar settlement. For peasant farmers, rights to land rested upon authorization from mirasidars. Peasant property rights were defined and maintained through rituals that expressed the incorporation of hamlets into the mirasidar domain and the inferiority of peasant families in relation to mirasidars. In some instances, mirasidars extracted labor services, as we will see. But more generally peasants paid the cash fee called swamibhogam; it confirmed tenant occupancy rights, supplied mirasidars with needed income, and marked mirasidar superiority. Customary conflict over property rights in the mixed zone occurred not only within mirasidar collectivities and among expansive peasant warrior-peasants, but also at their common border, where mirasidar and peasant rights to the dry land clashed head on.

Customary determination of wet and dry property rights differed in their definition of land and in their genealogy of right, but rested on the same cultural principles. In a wet village, a bounded group of high-caste shareholders defined an elite stratum whose superior rights subsumed all others in the village and whose control over property extended to all village assets, including labor. In dry villages, individual families of dominant castes used their own labor to cultivate land that was not construed to be a unit within a collectively owned village. Mirasidars traced their title directly to royal charters and to traditions of Pandya hegemony. Dry-farming peasants traced theirs to warrior chiefs and to generations of labor that made the land productive and made the land their own. Yet both customary configurations of right depended on dominant-caste control of villages, supported by royal authority and maintained by caste alliances. For mirasidars and dry-farming peasants alike, land control derived from transactions and shared interests between themselves and rulers; this cultural principle remained in force but caused considerable conflict between landowners and state officials under the Anglo-Indian regime that came to power in 1801. Property rights also depended on the maintenance of group boundaries and relations of hierarchy among groups in agrarian society, which kept low-caste families in their place. Among these lowly folk were Shanars, who lived in their own separate hamlets, many on the outskirts of dominant caste villages; and, lower still, Pallas and Pariahs, who lived primarily on streets within mirasidar villages but set apart, at a distance, to express their extreme lowliness and exclusion from high-caste residential space. Maintaining caste boundaries and rituals of rank that defined low-caste subordinate proprietary status underpinned property rights throughout society; their maintenance would become problematic during the nineteenth century.

LAW

English Company officials debated for thirty years principles of property law for the Madras Presidency. Three intellectual and political factions contended. One championed a permanent settlement like that which granted ownership to zamindars in the Company's Bengal territory in 1793. A second argued that in South India villages, not zamindars, owned the land, and so proposed a system of revenue collection and property law to support collective village ownership. A third argued that in South Indian villages, the peasant, or ryot, owned the land, though peasant property rights had been undermined by centuries of war and oppression. After 1801, when the Company granted zamindar rights to former poligars, proponents of a permanent settlement lost ground; debate then centered on whether to apply village lease or ryotwari principles in circar land revenue procedures. In retrospect, ryotwari better fit dry and leases wet villages. But principles were at stake, and by 1820, Thomas Munro, the champion of ryotwari, had won the day.[9]

Munro's constitutional principles were radical even by European standards in his day. They seem aptly suited to a new state headed by a militant trading company from the most advanced commercial and industrial nation in Europe, which after Waterloo commanded military power second to none. Munro's scheme laid legal ground for radical division of property rights into distinct public and private domains and thus for dramatic growth in the state proprietary power and revenue. Ryotwari vested property rights to land outside the public domain in individuals, whose title derived directly and only from state authorization. Ryotwari defined legitimate objects of private property to be those that could be bought and sold, and protecting those private property rights would be one of the new regime's major policy commitments. The land tax system had to be built to guarantee individual property rights and the rights of the state as their protector. Annual land tax receipts, called pattahs, in 1820 assumed the legal stature of deeds, and revenue administration would henceforth apply ryotwari principles to set the terms and define—at least for itself—the nature of property rights, public and private, throughout agrarian society.

Munro and his allies knew the radical implications of their ryotwari scheme, if not its practical effects on village society. They envisioned that the system would set individuals free from legal constraints on market participation, removing impediments imposed under previous regimes by rapacious revenue renters and middlemen. By eliminating speculative revenue contractors and local renters from the chain of transactions that brought revenue from villages into the treasury, and by cutting through tangled webs of local collective property custom, the system held promise for increasing state property ownership and revenue receipts. Though English Company officers recognized that former South Indian rulers had assigned many-layered rights and property privileges to their subjects, ryotwari in principle viewed many of the resulting rights with pointed skepticism. Tax-free inam lands and mirasidar collective rights would merit especially critical scrutiny, and, in theory, they had no basis in law except when supported by documents showing grants by previous rulers. Always suspect, these rights could be challenged when state authority perceived a compelling interest to do so, which it did after 1840. The legal basis for aggressive state action in private property matters lay in Munro's ryotwari theory.

In practice, however, the ryotwari system did not force property customs into line with its theory any more than it did revenue procedures; rather, ryotwari principles provided a conceptual framework for decisions by officials in the presidency capital, in district headquarters, and, with time, in the countryside. Their decisions assumed significance for villagers because landowners defined rights to landed property in transactions with state authorities who worked in two chains of command, under the Revenue Department and the Judicial Department. Revenue officers—village headmen, tahsildars, and collectors—issued pattahs and exercised magisterial authority. The lowest effective judicial officers, whose decisions could be appealed, were district munsifs, three of whom sat in Tinnevelly District at midcentury. Litigants flocked to their courts with cases of all kinds, including a huge array of property disputes.[10] Above district munsifs rose the mufti sadr amin, the principal sadr amin, and judges at the Zillah or District Court. Only extremely rich litigants could appeal cases outside the district to the Sadr Adalat, which in 1862 became the presidency High Court in Madras, or to the Privy Council in London. An account from 1847 shows that thirty-seven litigants each spent an average of five lakh rupees on cases before the Sadr Adalat, an astronomical sum equal to one-fifth the total Tinnevelly District revenue at the time. Most property disputes concerned small parcels of land, and an original suit before the district munsif or sadr amin would cost about fifteen rupees. A very complex case, finally decided at Zillah Court after several years and numerous appeals, would cost appellants and respondents, in the 1840s, about four hundred rupees each.[11] Magistrates heard all cases free of charge, in the eyes of the law.

The Revenue and Judicial departments intertwined. A great many court cases began by appeals of revenue decisions, so that the Revenue Department helped to build case law by pursuing its policies. Revenue officers gave testimony regarded as trustworthy by most judges, and dispensed pattahs that constituted title to land. Only judges could decide who legally owned a piece of property, but judges could not issue pattahs. Revenue officials enforced judicial decrees, and so could undermine undesirable decisions by judges. Judges, for their part, though they relied on revenue activities, decided the content of laws to which revenue officials were accountable.

Departmental interdependence bred conflict. William Strange, a vocal mid-century critic of Madras judicial practice, cited with approval the words of a Calcutta columnist who bemoaned that "nothing was more difficult than to get a decision in favor of government."[12] Conflict derived from distinct departmental mandates. Grounded in both ryotwari theory and in Utilitarian ideas, the Revenue Department sought above all to secure state income, whereas the Judicial Department strove to decide who had rights to what, even when a case embroiled the government. In their affairs at court, therefore, revenue officials had clear objectives and were often caught in conflicts of interest that judges could never completely counteract in their pursuit of impartiality. Yet revenue officials could not succeed by acting above the law, and acting within the law often meant running into judges who might support the counterclaims of private citizens in those rustic judicial proceedings that Strange described as "humble imitations of Westminster Hall."[13]

Litigants flocked to court, and the means Indians brought to bear to win cases often provoked English ire. Critics called Anglo-Indian courts "hotbeds of corruption" and of "chicanery," mockeries of justice.[14] Yet in court questions of right were posed and conflicts resolved among contestants with sufficient means to make cases before the bench, and such citizens abounded, especially in and around mirasidar villages, near taluk and district headquarter towns. The Tinnevelly Zillah Court heard 1,700 cases annually during its first six years of existence, from 1801 to 1806; and seven courts in the district heard more than 2,500 cases annually at mid-century, each case involving as many as several dozen contestants on opposite sides.[15] By mid-century, few villages in the wet and mixed zones remained untouched by court decisions.

The law impinged upon property custom by rationalizing the state's pursuit of revenue and by instituting means to settle disputes among citizens. For its part, Revenue sought to establish its rights and to circumscribe opposing rights. Though revenue officials issued pattahs and enforced the laws, they had anything but a free hand to alter village property custom. They needed to collect steady revenues, which would suffer if policies met much resistance. They relied on powerful landowners whose rights and interests had to be protected. In addition, however radical Munro's theory, the British conceived their government to be just; they disdained overt usurpations and inconsistencies. Anglo-Indian principles of justice smiled particularly on the pattam principle of customary property right, and judges recognized, up to certain limits, the force of customary law in India as in Britain, even in some instances when it contravened the interests of the state, as William Strange complained. Political economy forged a bond of intersecting self-interest between landowners and state officials. The notion that property rights derive from state entitlement, granted in ceremonial situations charged with ritual meanings, forged a cultural link between contestants on all sides of property disputes, British and Indian alike. Judicial and revenue officers presided at dramatic events that established—even constituted—rights.

Collectors led the battle to establish state proprietary right, wielding whatever tools they commanded to enforce revenue claims. Fickle before 1820, they gave out rights in one year sometimes denied in the next. In one case, government sold a village at auction and informed the buyer later that his subsequent sale of the village had become illegal because he was no longer considered its owner under the terms of ryotwari.[16] After 1820, Munro's new system provided clear guidelines. The state was to be considered the ultimate landlord unless its rights could be shown to have been granted to villagers by previous rulers. On this basis, revenue officials moved to block sales of land that would create landlord rights between the state and its ryots. Mirasidar property posed a problem, for it clearly rested on grants from previous rulers and entailed landlord rights to tenant land. To adjust for these recognized facts, revenue officials created the legal notion of a "mirasi village," in which landlords enjoyed free rights to buy and sell land, for example, to liquidate a mortgage obligation. Collectors did not recognize this right for "non-mirasi" villages, so that farmers flocked to have their villages registered as "mirasi" in revenue accounts. Only thirty-eight "non-mirasi" villages remained in circar territory in Tinnevelly District in 1817, and this legal classification of villages remained on the books until the 1860s.[17]

Collectors defended state proprietary claims jealously in court. One refused to grant a pattah to a man who had taken one whole village into his possession by a mortgage agreement with three other men. When the collector learned that this was a "non-mirasi" village he sued to block its transfer into the mortgager's ownership. The collector could not ascertain who in fact owned the village: 22 shareholders were listed in village accounts, whereas 136 pattahs had been issued each year from 1825 to 1836. But the collector could fight in court to deny the pattah to one man; and after years before the bench, often at his own expense, the collector won his case, all in an effort to protect the state's landlord status.[18] Another collector fumed that investors in irrigation had established for themselves landlord rights to land in the Chokkampatti estate, which was illegal because those rights belonged to government, which had taken the estate under the Court of Wards.[19] Such battles did not alter dramatically the terms of property transactions in villages; in the great majority of villages, listed as "mirasi," the Revenue Department tied its own hands by recognizing previous grants of land by kings to villagers. Collectors fought for a principle: government had its own proprietary right, distinct from and superior to citizens'.

Limited means to alter customary rights vexed the collectors. Patrimonial rights persisted even in revenue administration itself. Village headmen inherited their positions and were hard to displace. Marava village watchmen retained rights to protection fees despite official displeasure. A variety of local officials in effect owned annual cash perquisites, mostly paid by landowners, which a study in 1826 showed to approach 10 percent of all government dues.[20] Some perquisites were subsumed under the official heading of "moturpha" taxes and collected with the land revenue until the 1860s,[21] but the remainder—an array of customary payments to local dignitaries for access to their presence and protection—were banished under law to that large nether world of "corruption" and "bribery." Many illegal rights to property thus survived; the Revenue Department had not the means to make them disappear; it could only refuse to enforce rights deemed illegitimate. But even this feeble effort had its effect, making such rights more tenuous, giving those who resisted some leverage.

One customary form of property, though illegal, enriched the state and the Revenue Department in particular, as well as mirasidars. Abolished in 1843, agrestic servitude could never again receive official sanction. Mirasidar rights to the persons of Palla laborers continued nonetheless; it had never required state enforcement. Revenue also depended on mirasidar rights to command Pallas when irrigation works needed repair, as we have seen. When roads needed to be built, public works officers justified their coercion of Pallas by citing a public right to Palla manpower, a right which they extrapolated from the village to the government.[22]

Low-cost Palla labor subsidized public works, and court decisions concurred with mirasidar litigants who argued that traditional rights enjoyed by Pallas in compensation for servitude should be deligitimated. This would have the effect of lowering labor costs. After 1820, judges denied Palla claims to security of income and employment in mirasidar villages; this decision would have had the effect of freeing worker movement and increasing worker competition in the labor market. Before 1820, judges upheld claims by laborers and service castes to fixed shares of the village harvest, in return for guaranteed village employment.[23] But soon thereafter such service mirasi proprietary claims lost all legal recognition.[24] One judge opined that these traditions violated principles of free exchange.[25] Another argued that labor contracts, like all others, must be documented to prove the rights enjoyed by parties on both sides, whereas in service mirasi cases the truth of the contract lay utterly obscured by conflicting claims of contending parties.[26] As a result, mirasidars enjoyed both bonded labor and legal freedom from claims by laborers to a share of the village grain heap.

The courts could not make labor free to move and seek the market value of its service. Yet the principles of ryotwari encouraged judges to make decisions that pushed the legal terms of property transactions toward those of the free market, where land and labor were commodities. In the same way, ryotwari encouraged Revenue officials, however constrained they might be, to expand the public domain.

LAND

Legal and executive initiatives to expand the public domain became a major force for change in village property custom. Revenue efforts followed the dictates of the treasury and centered on mirasidar villages. Very little was done until the 1840s, but then state hunger for revenue fixed official minds on that land which the state legally owned yet which mirasidars continued to possess under the heading of "uncultivated waste." Although the collector of Chinglepet District, an expert on mirasidar matters and a major proponent of the village lease system, had declared in 1817 that mirasidars owned all land in their villages, Thomas Munro countered that government "possesses . . . the absolute right of disposing of the waste as it pleases";[27] and, in theory, Munro triumphed. Nonetheless, rural realities, considered in Chapter Four, left waste in village mirasidar hands throughout most of the Company period. A collector of Chinglepet wrote to the Board in 1855 that "the Meerassidars have been in the habit of selling the waste lands in this collectorate and claiming Meerass in them, and they were suffered to do so until about a year ago."[28] The new policy alluded to by the collector was for Revenue to claim land not included in pattahs and to sell it on government's account. In 1856, the Court of Directors in London ordered that all waste land was at the disposal of Revenue authorities and should be offered for sale, first to local landowners and then to the public at large. After decades in which mirasidars had realized customary income by selling rights to uncultivated land in their villages, Munro finally prevailed, and subsequent mirasidar legal suits failed to overturn the Court of Director's order. The climactic suit, filed in the Sadr Adalat, received the following comment from the judges: "It has been repeatedly held by this court that as a general rule all lands which have been abandoned and left waste by the original cultivators are at the disposal of revenue authorities."[29] Rules for selling waste lands were published in 1864 and survey and settlement operations provided government the technical means to put the new policy into universal effect.[30]

Note the wording of the judges' comment, quoted above: "waste" was considered to have been abandoned by cultivators; that abandonment consisted of not paying for the land in their annual revenue assessment. In villages, "waste" included a wide variety of land types and land uses. Some had never been farmed: it was dry land for grazing, for firewood, for brick clay, and for future residential sites. Some might be land deprived of irrigation by a broken tank but not suitable for dry crops. Some might be used in long-fallow farming, planted once in as many as ten years. This land comprised a valuable village asset, all the more so when irrigation was scarce; it was at the very least land left in store for future generations. Expanding population and agriculture would have made it increasingly valuable, and government moved to realize as much of that value as possible in immediate revenue. To do so meant to abrogate customary ownership by mirasidar collectivities. The official intent was not to take the land away from mirasidars, only to make individual mirasidars pay for it by buying bits of the public domain for private ownership. Mirasidars with sufficient means obliged, after obstructing waste land auctions for as long as possible. They tried, of course, to lower the cost of their purchases below government expectations, and, having entered the land on their pattahs, often defaulted on tax payments in the hope of buying the land back at government auctions at an overall savings. This strategy inflated the volume of sales listed under the heading of "coercive process" in Madras districts, as mirasidars might buy the same land repeatedly.[31]

The course of events concerning property in "waste" demonstrates the style and timing of state direct action to alter property relations in village society. First, Munro's ryotwari theory laid legal bases for change in the meaning of circar land. Whereas before 1801 circar land had meant that over which kings had authority and claims to revenue without reference to poligars, after 1801 the Company consigned fixed stretches of land to zamindars and then redefined circar land to include a division between private and public domains. For most of the Company period, the state claim to own public land remained strictly a legal formulation. But in the 1840s, hunger for revenue and aggressive reform efforts pushed officials to realize state property rights in cash and physical control. Subsequent state investments in roads, irrigation, port facilities, and town buildings required both enhanced income and improved control over agrarian and urban space. The ideological impetus for this change in government's posture toward property appears in the words of reformers during the 1840s; the political will appears in proclamations from Madras, Calcutta, and London, in the 1850s; and the technical apparatus to define and secure state property rights throughout the countryside comes into place during legal conflicts and then survey and settlement, completed by 1880. At century's end, circar land included considerable tracts of road and railway right of way, irrigation infrastructure, and space inside villages and towns under the control of government bureaucrats. The state's proprietary power reflected its growth as a source of employment and funds for investment in public works. The Anglo-Indian imperial state thus evolved into an institutional arbiter of access to opportunity and mobility for its citizens in the Tirunelveli region. Its evolution whittled away at the property rights of mirasidar collectivities by dispossessing villages of land not contained in pattahs and by pushing individual mirasidars toward a strategy of land purchase to secure their rights through the symbol of the pattah, received in return for cash revenue payment.

But government did not constitute a wholly autonomous or exogenous force working on village property relations according to the dictates of the treasury. Our discussion of rural governance in Chapter Four established the role of mirasidars in securing the new regime in the countryside. Agreements between district officials and mirasidars that put Revenue on firm footing in irrigated villages depended upon state respect for mirasidar rights to property. Leading mirasidars sat at both sides of the table during negotiations that led to these agreements. Mirasidars administered government's grabbing of village "waste," and the success of government policy hinged on resourceful landowners buying up land sold at auction. Mirasidars thus themselves worked in their village milieus and in the widening world of opportunity that opened up during the nineteenth century to dismantle collective traditions of ownership in their communities.

Outside its concern for "waste," government pushed very feebly to restructure private property relations inside village communities. Revenue officials negotiated the olungu settlement in the Tinnevelly District in part to allay mirasidar fears that new procedures would undermine collective landholding traditions. In dry-farming tracts, village officers retained their powers to distribute assessments and pattahs through the 1870s. Nonetheless, by the time of survey and settlement, villages in the wet, dry, and mixed zones were characterized by local customs of property right founded on the authority of pattahs and on the principle that individual families owned rights to land. To understand this change in the regional property system we must look not only to the power of government, guided by ryotwari theory, to define rights by its issuance of pattahs and ownership of public land, but also to another force at work more immediately in village society: increasing commodity production.

The dramatic increase in market activity and the string of relatively good agricultural seasons after 1835 put more cash with which to buy pattahs in the hands of farming families. More competition for land encouraged all agricultural producers to secure their land ownership from competing claims. Though at first village leaders could increase their power over property by fighting to retain the political autonomy of their village domains, over time this became more difficult and less necessary. In dry villages, especially in cotton-growing tracts, inflows of cash replaced revenue receipts as the basis of export finance, thus providing monies to peasants to secure family property rights, at least in the eyes of official authority in town; survey and settlement made these rights more secure, and negotiable. As market power replaced military power in the village political economy of the dry zone, peasants could compete on terms in which the pattah provided a valuable asset, eagerly sought. Government in essence built institutional means to redefine farming-family rights to land. These rights characterized dry-village custom in 1801, but had to be recreated, during the nineteenth century, in market and bureaucratic terms, independent of patrimonial rights wielded by lineage heads and little kings; peasants proceeded to do so.

The internal dynamics of village society that redefined the rights to village land are much better documented for wet and mixed agricultural settings than for the dry. The reason is simple: competitors for land rights took their disputes to revenue officers and judges for arbitration and adjudication. In these disputes we see in close detail local efforts to reconstruct property custom as villagers participated in transactions with state authority and in agricultural commodity markets. We see, too, that disputes arose from local conflicts of interest that existed in 1801, the legacy of centuries of change in agrarian relations. Disputants knew one another well. They fought for rights in terms consistent with pangu and pattam principles enshrined in their own cultural traditions. But the conditions they faced changed perceptibly after 1801, and their strategies reflect their knowing pursuit of opportunities presented by the Anglo-Indian regime as well as by expanding markets.

Dry-farming peasants who lived in hamlets included within extended mirasidar domains, who in the Anglo-Indian lexicon became tenants, and who in many cases traced their ancestry to post-1300 migrations into the region, took the first initiatives. Although a few early collectors did issue pattahs to tenants in the mixed zone, the success of Munro's new settlement scheme rested on government's commitment to protect mirasidar rights, and, after 1820, government expressed no interest in tenant rights. Writing in 1908, a member of the governor's council in Madras, G. Stokes, expressed official orthodoxy when he wrote about a proposed bill to protect ryotwari tenants: "In my opinion, the longer this subject sleeps the better. No one wants the proposed legislation except some theorists in the Government of India and any legislation if effective is bound to stir up nothing but strife in our village life."[32] Yet tenants raised the issue themselves, from the outset of Company rule. They disputed with mirasidars the customary ownership of dry land not cultivated by mirasidars, on which peasants were nonetheless expected to pay the occupancy rental fee called swamibhogam. Surely, disputes over this land had antecedents long before 1801, but disputes now took on new meaning, for official decisions had to be made during annual revenue collections about who would receive pattahs, symbols of ownership.

A collector issued pattahs to tenants in 1805, and mirasidars sued him immediately.[33] Subsequently, revenue officials subsumed swamibhogam rents, during the course of collections before 1822, in revenues collected from mirasidars under village leases. Because mirasidars leased out whole villages, wet and dry lands included, they received pattahs for village lands as a whole.[34] This set precedent for later mirasidar claims to that land. But resistance to this arrangement plagued mirasidars and collectors alike during the decades before 1820. Tenants seem to have refused to pay their revenue through mirasidars, knowing that this would undermine their rights. Resistance by tenants became one of the insecurities that mirasidars faced during the leases, and, in fact, became one of the key issues during early negotiations over the new olungu system of revenue collections that began in 1819. Mirasidars insisted, with most force in the mixed zone, that collectors support mirasidar rights to tenant land. One collector was told that mirasidars would sign permanent cash lease agreements, despite their many objections to this arrangement,[35] if tenant lands would be permanently affirmed as mirasidar property and if collectors enforced rental payments.[36]

During negotiations over the olungu settlement, mirasidars demanded to be satisfied on the issue of rights to tenant land. The Board of Revenue responded, characteristically, in 1819 with the proclamation that "the parties with whom the new settlement should be made are the collective body of mirasidars in each village."[37] Nevertheless, the legal theory enshrined in ryotwari gave no ground for considering collective mirasidar rights to be permanent, for if this were done it would undermine the division of public and private domains built into Munro's plan. Legally, mirasidars had to be construed as individuals, and their rights squared with the terms of Munro's theory. The Board accordingly penned this order, in 1823:

> If Meerassidars possess the right of occupancy and either cultivate the land themselves or by means of the Ryots, the settlement should be made with them . . . but if they do not provide for the cultivation, the settlement should be made with the Ryots who are actually in possession and the Pattahs should be given to the cultivating Ryots.[38]

This order gave adequate scope for local interpretation, though literal adherence to its terms would have sabotaged negotiations with mirasidars throughout the mixed zone, where peasant farmers of dry land cultivated completely by their own means. The key phrase that gave collectors latitude was that which allowed the mirasidars to be given pattahs if they cultivated the land "by means of the Ryots," which in effect legitimized landlordism where mirasidars were understood to be in local control of the tenantry. Weighing the alternatives, the collector decided to order that pattahs be given on principle to mirasidars. He justified himself to the Board by saying, first, that previous collection procedures had given mirasidars implicit right to the land, and second, that any other course of action would generate countless court actions by mirasidars against revenue officials.[39] The Board concurred. When a later collector mistakenly gave pattahs to tenants, and mirasidars petitioned the Board, the collector received immediate orders from his superiors to stop.[40]

Tenants kept the issue alive. Revenue officials became arbiters in disputes that often allowed tenants to buy land rights and receive pattahs.[41] Records of these agreements dot Revenue Department documents during the 1830s, having been generated during negotiations to put the olungu system in place. For instance, Shanar cultivators in Dalapathisamudram and Maravas in Nanguneri received pattahs for dry land, with the consent of their respective communities of mirasidar shareholders.[42] By 1840, the regional picture of tenant land rights had become locally variegated, as we would expect. A collector reported that though much of the dry land continued to be entered in mirasidar pattahs, "without reference to the actual cultivator, . . . the remaining Punjah land is held and cultivated by the undertenants, in which they are protected by pattahs issued in their own names, containing a proviso that they are not entitled to sell or mortgage the land to the distress of the mirasidars."[43]

But struggles continued. Disputants used whatever means they could bring to bear to secure their rights, including violence. They used institutional means provided by government and turned dramatic moments at court and in revenue proceedings to their own benefit. Because proof relied on documents to show revenue payment and swamibhogam receipts, litigants often resorted to forgery and coercion. Because officials provided testimony considered trustworthy, competing claimants engaged in bribery and collusion. The conflicts between Revenue and Judicial departments that William Strange complained about gave contestants room to maneuver in the fight for rights. Revenue officials could assign pattahs and enforce swamibhogam payments, which were part of the revenue; but only judges could decide who legally owned land and whether swamibhogam payments were just.[44] Tenants and mirasidars could move from one court case and petition to the next, appealing and challenging decisions to bolster their claims. One official investigator bemoaned this state of affairs, in 1843: "at this hour our Revenue and Judicial officers are thwarting one another. . . . Wastelands which are given into the occupation of a Ryot are decreed away from him by a judge for the different views taken by the two authorities respecting mirasidar Right."[45] As this complaint makes clear, the question of tenant rights and state rights to "waste" interpenetrated one another. Both the state and mirasidars sought to strengthen their command of dry land surrounding irrigated fields. To support mirasidar rights would in principle weaken the state's property claim. To deny those rights would weaken state authority and undermine the alliance of interests connecting urban officials and mirasidars. How struggles that ensued in this legal and political conundrum were resolved would depend on mirasidar abilities to secure their rights over tenant land in terms consistent with law, given their powerful position in the regional ruling elite.

In the wet zone, mirasidars easily accomplished the task by converting once collective claims to all land—both wet and dry—into individual landownings embraced by pattahs. This meant mirasidars had to pay for tenant land in their pattahs, just as they would for "waste" land to be sold by government at auction. Such purchases were of little consequence in the wet zone, however, where dry land was of very low quality and rich mirasidars abounded. In the mixed zone, the challenge facing mirasidars posed more difficulty, for here dry lands were of relatively high value, their cultivators relatively more powerful in local society, and mirasidars more dependent on rental incomes. During the decades before 1860, moreover, mixed-zone mirasidars saw tanks dilapidate. Tenants saw the value of their land increase where it could support cotton and garden crops. To lose rights to good dry land threatened mirasidar and tenant real incomes, and rising fortunes among dry-land farmers put them in strong positions to fight for rights.

Battles became bitter. In some cases, documents laid rock-hard foundations for mirasidar claims. A Vellala tenant in Tippanampatti petitioned for a pattah in 1825, when pattahs were first issued. Denied because he had previously paid his revenue to mirasidars, he then refused to pay swamibhogam. Mirasidars influenced the tahsildar to obstruct the tenant's harvest, but the tenant again paid nothing in 1828 and sued again for a pattah. Denied again, but still refusing to pay his rent, he and other tenants were taken to court, where the mirasidars won, putting the matter to rest, as far as the records show. In this case and many others like it, mirasidars validated their claims by bringing to court rental agreements (*adaiyolai*) and receipts (*ethiradaiyolai*), which judges took to prove ownership, even if tenants had received pattahs from revenue officials. In one exceptional case, the shareholders of Mayamankurichi even produced documents to show that the dry land in question lay within boundaries specified by the original brahmadeya grant.[46]

Yet by the same token, lack of documentary proof in court could undermine mirasidar claims to tenant land, so that disputes among shareholders about their respective rights penetrated and complicated struggles between mirasidars and tenants. In several recorded cases, tenants sued successfully to block the collection of swamibhogam by mirasidars who had bought rights to this payment; tenants argued, and the court agreed, that the right to collect had been vested in the community of mirasidars or in a mirasidar family, neither of which could lawfully sell that right.[47] In some instances, mirasidars who sought to convert what had been collective sharehold claims to swamibhogam into private landlord rights met resistance from their own mirasidar neighbors, who feared that such enterprise would weaken sharehold custom. That is, the very shareholders who sought to secure mirasidar rights to tenant land were viewed by their peers as enemies of community shareholding and resisted as such in court.

This view was entirely justified. We have already seen that property rights inside mirasidar communities were never equally distributed.[48] Leading mirasidar families—about 10 percent of the mirasidar population, according to the 1823 census—held the lion's share of good irrigated land and reaped disproportionate profits from village land revenue and grain market operations. They fought successfully to prevent the introduction of a strict ryotwari settlement into their villages, and supplied the key actors in all official negotiations. Well endowed, they sought positions in government, and manned key positions in regional administration.[49] Incentives mounted after 1830 for such families to seek individual landowner status and to acquire each its own pattah. The new revenue system encouraged all mirasidars to register their own annual dues to government, and, by 1834, 82 percent of the 644 "mirasi" villages for which data exist had records to show which family owed how much land revenue.[50] Rising land values and market activity widened mirasidar scope for selling shares outside the old community of shareholders. The village of Vasudevanallur is perhaps an extreme example of a resulting mixed-caste mirasidar community: a Vaduga zamindar acquired half of all shares in 1849, and Muslims, Maravas, and Chettis owned fully 25 percent of the land under village tanks.[51] Caste boundaries around mirasidar shareholding had suffered breaches when markets in irrigated land rights were widened. Enterprising shareholders had good reasons to diminish collective control so as to increase their returns from farmland and from transactions in specific shares. And pattahs provided symbolic affirmation of their individual rights, independently of the sharehold community. Lesser mirasidars had little choice but to seek security by also acquiring pattahs. Slowly community sharehold customs crumbled under the initiative of leading mirasidars.

Enterprising enemies of mirasidar collectivity chiseled away at custom from within on the basis of individual rights established long before 1801. Even Pandya-era inscriptions reveal a huge array of transactions in shares that rested on individual land rights and depended on a market in shares.[52] But there is little doubt that the scope for enterprise increased during post-Pandya centuries; and, conversely, that despite a growing number of transactions in shares, customs constraining individual control of village land remained in force in 1801. Company records show various local arrangements to accommodate conflicting individual and collective rights. Some communities distinguished types of village assets so as to stimulate enterprise within the framework of collective village ownership. Families could thus buy land individually, but would share in collective rights to rents from dry land, to grazing and wooded land, and to irrigation works capitalized by the community fund.[53] Swamibhogam rights, like rights to "waste," seem generally to have fallen into the category of collective rights, and most agreements on record that document transfers of ownership from mirasidars to tenants were made with the consent of shareholders collectively, at least for legal purposes. Private claims to tenant land thus constituted a very pointed threat to poor shareholders, who could not afford to buy up either tenant land or "waste" on their own account, for these lands represented a stronghold of community rights and access to them was a valuable asset. Ironically, however, for mirasidar communities to maintain control over tenants would now legally require that some mirasidars and not others secure rights to tenant land by either registering it in pattahs or signing rental agreements, individually.

Officials devoted to the protection of mirasidar interests and to the security of landed property rights thus encouraged mirasidar families to maintain traditional power and authority by dismantling sharehold custom. Cash receipts from grain sales enabled commercially active mirasidars to do just that. Village efforts therefore converged with what became, after 1850, an official resolve, at least among the British, to end "the evils of the sharing system."[54]

Poor mirasidars, nonetheless, had good reason to fight to preserve collective ownership, and their defensive action received some support in court. They seem to have fought for tenant lands most bitterly and to have based their claims most consistently on traditions of community ownership. They engaged legal counsel, and as late as the 1860s courts ruled in specific cases in their favor. One Zillah Court judge ordered a set of individual shareholders to buy out collective village interests to establish legal claim to land; another dismissed individual mirasidar claims where collective rights were proven to his satisfaction.[55] In one very complex case, a collector and a judge combined to untangle claims to land purchased by one nonmirasidar investor, as part of a scheme, supported by the collector, to improve village irrigation.[56] In the 1830s, and again in the 1850s, the Zillah Court ruled that the rotation of individual lands in a village among shareholders should occur whenever a majority of mirasidars requested.[57] The Madras High Court decreed a similar defense of customary land rotation in 1863, in two cases in which a majority of mirasidars confronted a few recalcitrant shareholders.[58] The records of survey and settlement operations in Tinnevelly District abound with arbitration concerning division of land rights among mirasidars; dividing individual rights consumed much of the time and effort of survey and settlement officers.[59]

Most conflicts among mirasidars and between mirasidars and tenants seem to have resolved themselves amicably in negotiations within communities, between individuals, that allowed families to buy up land rights. Leading mirasidars were in general in strong positions to benefit from such procedures, being influential in government, skilled in the workings of state institutions, and financially endowed. Many court cases, however, indicate that local turmoil and brutality could ensue when competitors could not resolve who owned what land by purchase agreement.

The worst battles pitted relatively weak mirasidars against relatively strong tenants, each group being locked in a desperate struggle to maintain or improve its status in the property system against threats from the other. One long battle pitted three Shanar families against the mirasidars in the village of Konguvarayakurichi. The Shanars registered 300 acres of dry land with the tahsildar in 1801; but the mirasidars managed to change the registry and get pattahs issued in their name in 1825, by which time 1,691 productive palm trees and 3,500 newly planted palms grew on those 300 acres. The Shanars refused to pay swamibhogam. Mirasidars harassed them and, despite a court decision in favor of the Shanars in 1831, took forceful possession of the land the next year. Finally, the Shanars won legal recognition of their independent landowning status in two court cases that were supported by a collector's order in 1834.[60]

One recorded instance of sustained local conflict between mirasidars and tenants polarized the very large village of Varttiraya Iruppu for fifty years. Near Srivilliputtur, in the northern mixed zone, Vellala cultivators in this village farmed 8,000 acres of the best dry land in the northwest, on the western extremity of the cotton road. They paid the highest swamibhogam rates in the district to their mirasidars, and yet obtained pattahs for their own land under revenue leases before 1820.[61] They stopped paying swamibhogam in 1823, "having become," in the words of the collector, "the most substantial and strong-est party in the village." During the 1830s, their proprietary struggle began to affect the land revenue, so that the collector himself went to investigate twice in one year and discovered that officially reported cultivated acreage had declined drastically because the tahsildar and village accountant had become tenant partisans in the struggle. In 1836, he found that officials underreported tenant cultivation and obstructed mirasidar harvests by organizing Palla laborers and dis-rupting agricultural operations. During the decades of this conflict, tenants never once brought their case to court: they obviously felt that they stood on poor legal ground. But the mirasidars would not sell off their rights to tenant land. The tenants resorted to illegal means, and mirasidars responded in part by seeking government help. Col-lectors sacked two tahsildars and tahsildars sacked three village ac-countants for corruption and collusion with tenants. Mirasidars con-ducted survey and spying operations on their own to gather evidence against local officials. Violence became so commonplace that a special peshcar was assigned to the village to maintain law and order and secure the revenue. Still the revenue suffered. One mirasidar led a revenue boycott to protest government inefficiency. He stopped paying taxes, levied a battery of suits against the collector, and "excited and instigated others to follow the same example."[62] During the 1840s, when prices were very low, thousands of acres of good dry land lay uncultivated, according to official records.[63] Tenants kept their land off the books to invalidate mirasidar claims to swamibhogam.

Government took an increasingly strong stand, supporting mirasidar rights over tenant land. Backing up a collector's decision, a Zillah Court judge decreed in the 1840s that mirasidars could evict tenants.[64] This became law, and the High Court affirmed it during an early session with these words: "ryots may be entitled to perpetual occupancy of mirasi land, subject to the payment of the mirasidars' share, but such tenure generally depends upon long established usage and must be proven by satisfactory evidence."[65] Eviction would be justified for nonpayment of rent. Even beyond eviction, a collector ordered in 1858 that the mirasidars in Vilattikulam could attach tenant property and sell it for arrears of swamibhogam under the same regulation that allowed government and zamindars to undertake "coercive process."[66] But inflation after 1850 decreased dramatically the buying power of rental payments, always fixed in cash; and when mirasidars sought legal power to increase swamibhogam rates, they met disappointment. Collectors refused to grant such increases, because revenue officials had no means to enforce any more than customary rates.[67] By 1865, price movements had cooled off most conflicts between mirasidars and tenants, and an investigation revealed that most legal issues had been solved: "the respective rights of . . . different classes of tenants . . . are perfectly well known and have been defined and upheld by numberless decrees in the courts."[68] Survey and settlement completed the process of defining rights to land among mirasidars and tenants by dividing specific plots of land into holdings among owners, each with his own pattah. Even so, bitterness lingered in the village of Varttiraya Iruppu, where the division of holdings kindled old animosities, and the village had to be divided into four separate revenue villages to insure smooth local administration.[69]

Thus the champions of change in village property custom came from three camps. None provided a primary impetus that set the others in motion; their initiatives intersected and propelled one another. The new regime established in 1801 pressed for land revenue in cash, and its demands during the period of falling prices after 1820 pushed hard on the mirasidars who most depended on swamibhogam payments in the mixed zone.[70] Government also pressed for control of "waste" after 1840, and for powers to decide property disputes. By the end of Company Raj, many officials seem to have been committed to an orderly division of all collective rights into individual landholdings. But official activity does not explain the course of events concerning rights to village land. Local initiative established the agenda and the poles of antagonism in struggles for rights. In villages, upstart tenants took the lead. Their perception of their own interests and rights was based on a conflict between customs of mirasidar control and both tenant ideas about rightful ownership—according to principles of pangu and pattam—and tenant resolve to capture the material returns of family labor for themselves. Commercially successful peasants led the tenant fight: farmers with good dry land, wells, and stands of productive palmyra palms. Such tenants were counterparts in the vicinity of mirasidar villages of agricultural commodity producers in dry-zone villages, who sought to capitalize on land and to do so pursued better control of its output in the face of superior claims. Tenants could use government institutions in their fight, but could benefit from contradictions and weakness in the state, as well. Poor mirasidars, particularly in the mixed zone, hard-pressed by seasons and by revenue demands, became the tenants' most determined foes; they opposed, too, the leading mirasidars who sought to convert existing family sharehold claims into private property. During social conflict, state officers adjudicated disputes, many of which seem to have ended to the distress of poor tenants and poor mirasidars; and the state also enriched itself, as proprietor of the public domain. These three sets of actors—state officials, resourceful tenants, and leading mirasidars—defined a new set of customs and cultural understandings on property matters. As a result of their work, agrarian society came to construe farmland as private property and the public domain as state property.

DOMINANCE

The redefinition of rights to village land consumed the whole Company period and was not complete before survey and settlement. By mid-century, the determination of dominant-caste rights in the face of social upstarts and government bureaucrats became an urban issue, as well. After 1840, the conjuncture of relatively good seasons, expanding population, decreasing transport costs, increasing cotton exports, and growing government accelerated urbanization. More and more people came to towns, centers for government, commerce, travel, and worship. People came from all walks of life and for all social purposes, and more often they came to stay. Every state-sponsored innovation and every technological import emphasized the significance of towns. Roadway, railway, and port construction concentrated new opportunities in the two dozen major towns that censuses show to have grown so rapidly after 1881, and which must have grown more slowly, but steadily, before then, especially those that became railway junctions in the 1870s. These towns housed the region's major government offices, bankers, businessmen, popular deities, and educational institutions. They became centers of opportunity both for socially mobile country folk and for underemployed village workers in seasons of distress. Town space, much more than village space, lay in the public domain, and social relations in the growing towns were in flux after 1840, because of new arrivals and mobile participants in commodity markets.

A conflict in district headquarters, in 1858, marks a turning point. It pitted opponents passionately interested in customs regulating access to streets. We probably would not know so much about this particular fray had it not involved native Christians, with missionary backers whose involvement brought it to the attention of Parliament.[71] Its legal basis lay in a ruling by the Sadr Adalat, which proclaimed "public roads . . . open to all . . . for passing to and fro, whether dead or alive,"[72] and so for government it involved a matter of serious principle that the state should define rules concerning use of public space. This melee gains added significance for us because the course of events and the social forces lined up on either side were parallel to those in conflicts over village land taking place at the same time.[73] It marks a migration of social conflict over customary rights from village to town.

In every way Tirunelveli town epitomized its rural setting. The Nellaiyappa temple sat at the center of town, the Medai Delavoy Mudaliar palace directly behind, next to the tahsildar's office and central hospital. In this town of tiny lanes, broad streets on four sides of the temple facilitated sacred circumambulations of the deity, Nellaiyappa, on festival days. High-caste families, mostly Vellalas, lived on all four sides. Radiating out from the temple streets, the town center, major roads ran west toward the major market (pettai) and east toward the river and beyond to the fort and town of Palayamkottai. The whole town sat on a slender stretch of high ground squeezed between paddy fields; large irrigation channels ran immediately to the north and south of town; and large mirasidar villages enriched by Tambraparni waters lay in sight on all sides. Tirunelveli was an urban monument to the mirasidar way of life.

High-caste residents of Tirunelveli town understandably opposed the movement of low-caste corpses and attendant loud funeral processions along streets in front of their homes. No such movement could be imagined inside high-caste quarters of Tambraparni valley villages. The tahsildar himself and undoubtedly most of the families of the town owned land and imbibed expectations about appropriate routes for low-caste funerals in spatially segregated mirasidar villages nearby. Ideally, such processions would not touch town streets at all, but would move away to the cremation or burial ground, unseen, through paddy fields and irrigation ditches.

The dead man, a Palla, passed away in hospital, struck down by cholera as he attended government offices behind the Nellaiyappa temple.

Before this incident, people who died in the government hospital had passed without turmoil out of the town center through the new street (pudu teru) built at state expense to connect the pettai, the district headquarters, and Palayamkottai. Thirty-nine bodies had passed along this route during three years before 1858, and nineteen of these had been low-caste, but none, it appears, a Palla.

In this case, however, townspeople closed their shops and crowded into the streets to prevent the Palla's body from moving out along one side of the temple toward the new street. Hearing from the tahsildar that mobs obstructed the way, the collector ordered in a body of armed footsoldiers (sepoys). The sepoys proceeded to the hospital and departed with the corpse, not toward the new street, but rather around the temple, out the main gate of the town, and along the high road to Palayamkottai. This new route must have further excited the opposition. Why the troops took it Parliamentary evidence did not reveal, but they might have done so to avoid the thickest congregation of protestors. Nonetheless, sepoys fired shots to clear the way. At least ten people were killed and many more wounded.

High caste residents might have objected with such force to the Palla's body being moved through their streets for fear that this would set the precedent of allowing even the lowliest folk free access to town center streets, their streets. But, more probably, their vehemence derived from their success two weeks before, when residents' objections had altered the burial plans of a Christian weaver; and more generally from confidence that their just cause enjoyed government support, because a collector had in 1853 ordered that standing rules remain in place forbidding objectionable low-caste movement through town streets.

Despite the violence, despite prolonged uproar in the Madras press, and despite investigations that consumed several years, the town itself quickly returned to normal. Two days later an English officer observed, "I visited the town yesterday and again this morning; no excitement whatever appears; people wear their usual orderly and respectful demeanor and carry on their usual trades; in fact, it is almost beyond belief that such an unfortunate event has occurred."[74]

No similar incident happened again. Custom changed, at one stroke, to accommodate social forces that demanded freer access to town streets than would be customary in mirasidar villages, which were designed to segregate high-caste residential space from pollution. The demand had come from people whose physical mobility through the streets—laborers, artisans, and hawkers—underpinned their livelihoods, whose cause had been taken up by both English missionaries and by a reforming collector who nullified the collector's order of 1853. Resistance came from elites who sought to maintain their collective control over the use of what became as a result of this incident truly public space. Official resolve to open the streets no doubt derived from a desire to set a precedent ending the cumulative troubles with the question of access to roads and, more broadly, from the state's commitment to control public property. The logical convergence of opposing interests on this moment of riot apparently produced a resolution based, not on new ideas in South Indian society about pollution or social hierarchy, but on the henceforth accepted premise that the streets belong to the state, at least in town.

Like paying swamibhogam rent to mirasidars, carrying dead relatives through muddy ditches and fields instead of along paved streets expressed social inferiority. It affirmed dependent and subordinate rights in society. Customary ceremonial enactments, such as those at funerals, confirmed high-caste powers to delimit the rights of those below; and in the changing social climate upstarts and entrepreneurs looked to the power of the state to protect and extend their own rights. The state, at the same time, committed itself to protecting and extending its power to adjudicate and dictate conflict resolution and to control the public domain that it had defined. Whereas rights to agricultural means of production could be and were redefined through the social construction of commodity markets, caste dominance also rested on its ritual recognition by the state. Here commodity markets did not provide means for conflict resolution.

At the outset of Company Raj, officials quickly discovered the most powerful people in the country and brought them into negotiations to found the new regime. By the end of the Company period, however, economic and political development had progressed in large part through social initiatives that put established power relations into question. Conflict over the terms of social dominance ensued, and embroiled villagers and townspeople alike. Long before this conflict took modern political form, that is, in the organization of parties and articulation of platforms, it involved villagers and townsfolk in traditional dominant-caste domains, as described in Chapter Three. Because dominance had always entailed representations to the state and support by the state, competitors logically moved to establish and bolster their positions in the eyes of government, in its own bureaucratic and legal terms. Conflicts involved competing representations of social status and rights by prominent people who articulated positions for their putative constituencies, seeking thereby to establish the position of their constituents as a body and themselves as leaders in the eyes of government. Wealth obtained in commodity production made those representations possible. Organized resistance made them volatile.

Shanars embroiled themselves in a great many disputes, first over private property rights and then over access to temple honors. Enterprising upstarts of the first order, they inhabited agrarian settings of traditionally unstable caste dominion, where dominant-caste fortunes declined, in relative terms, during the nineteenth century; they lived outside secure caste domains in the wet and dry zones, where old dominant castes maintained political precedence and reaped the lion's share of new economic opportunity. Whereas, in wet and dry zones, the question of dominance turned on how much power would accrue to members of old dominant-caste alliances—Brahmans, Vellalas, and

Vadugas, primarily—Shanar success posed a much more serious challenge to Maravas and mirasidars in the northern and southern zones of Shanar caste concentration.

Before 1857, individual Shanar families took up the fight for tenant land rights. Throughout the mixed zone and on the fringes of Tambraparni irrigation in the southeast, Shanar hamlets dotted land on the outskirts of mirasidar villages. The inferior, dependent status of Shanars under mirasidar authority was customarily enacted not only in Shanar payments of swamibhogam, but also in Shanar payments of labor service, particularly at temple festivals such as that in Tiruchendur.[75] In their disputes with mirasidars, Shanars pursued rights by the same means and with much the same results as peasant tenants generally; but particularly in the southeast, Shanars found articulate alien allies who served them well. Missionaries supported Shanar efforts and Shanar conversions made the Tinnevelly District "one of the bright spots of the heathen world" for the Church Mission Society.[76] Village after village of Shanars converted to Christianity, and many converts celebrated their rejection of the rituals that constituted their subordination by tearing down temple idols, making churches where Hindu gods had reigned. Shanar converts established new self-sustaining communities with missionary help, sometimes on tracts of "waste" bought by missions from the government, the largest being Nazareth, near Sattankulam. Schools and self-help societies enabled Christian Shanars to develop whole new villages outside mirasidar control.[77]

In 1857, a schismatic Shanar convert named Sattampillai added something new to Shanar enterprise. The leader of a dissident band in Nazareth, Sattampillai deeply resented Bishop Robert Caldwell's published description of the Shanars as low, benighted members of Hindu society, and he proceeded to formulate a new countervision of the Shanars. In doing so, he reinterpreted the past and constructed an image of Shanar collective identity. His new church, called the Hindu Church of Jesus Christ, attracted few followers, but he compiled an impressive corpus during six decades of publishing before his death in 1918. Sattampillai refuted the dominant cultural conception of Shanars as lowly not by using Christian arguments but by proclaiming a new Shanar history. The heart of his message was that great Shanars had once ruled as proud kings in the southern Tamil country. They had born the title *nattar*, or *nadan*, but were toppled from power and subsequently oppressed by rulers who depended on wily Brahmans.

Sattampillai and his brethren got little respect outside their immediate circle. Contemporary Englishmen who composed ethnographic and historical accounts of Tirunelveli and its people, though well aware of the new Shanar history proclaimed by Sattampillai, discounted it and published accounts more in line with customary, less flattering images of Shanar tradition.[78] This became official wisdom. Sattampillai's vision of oppressed Shanars seeking their rightful place in society also achieved little importance for mirasidars and their supporters, who concentrated their wrath on missionary efforts to uplift Shanars and spread Christianity, stimulating heated conflicts in villages and in the press.[79]

Yet Sattampillai publicized an image of collective Shanar identity, glory, degradation, and aspiration. And despite their diversity—for Shanars lived in each agricultural zone and included very rich merchants in the north and dirt-poor palmyra climbers in the south—Shanars, because of their commercial and agricultural skills, did as a population experience the most dramatic upswing in their relative economic fortunes of any caste group in the region. This gave potentially wide meaning in the present to a new vision of the Shanar past, while the growth of government power and the implications of Sattampillai's message encouraged Shanars to look to the state to remedy their condition.

By far the greatest improvement in Shanar fortunes occurred in the north, in and around towns enriched by the cotton export trade.[80] Caste linked Shanar producers of cotton, palmyra products, and garden crops in northern villages to major Shanar merchant houses in town. Shanar fortunes no doubt rose most dramatically when compared to those of the two dominant groups who became notorious throughout the century for opposing Shanar aspirations, mirasidars and Maravas. Village Shanars dug wells, planted palmyra trees, produced garden crops and cotton, and sold their produce in growing town markets. Urban Shanar businessmen became major figures in towns on the cotton road and railway line, as changing economic geography favored Shanar merchant enterprise. The cotton road increased the importance of towns along its route to the port and thus that of businessmen in those towns. The railway concentrated its benefits in a smaller number of towns along the old trunk road, where Shanar merchants rose to their greatest heights. The railway also induced a small diaspora among Shanar businessmen. Sivakasi, on the cotton road but not on the railway (until 1928), declined in vigor and in Shanar population; emigrant Shanars relocated in growing centers—Madurai, Tuticoryn, and Madras—creating a web of connected Shanar business operations with widening reach.[81]

Social status became a preoccupation among economically prosperous but low-caste Shanar businessmen in the north. Their leaders exhorted aspiring Shanars to adopt customs of dress, marriage, and dining that expressed higher caste status. They petitioned government for the official designation of their caste to be changed in all public records, most importantly the Census of India, from Shanar to Nadan. They sued in court for access to temples, from which Shanar devotees were customarily excluded, so they could establish their new status in the patronage and worship of gods.

This last demand met fierce resistance, particularly from Maravas, who seem to have been most resentful of this Shanar attack on customary rules of access to sacred precincts in traditional Marava domains. At stake were the honors and status that Marava warriors had invested in dominion for centuries by building and patronizing temples. Conflicts centered around towns where Shanar businessmen prospered most visibly, and around villages where Marava and Shanar fortunes had moved in opposite directions for decades. Conflict over temple entry became increasingly tense during the great cotton boom of the 1860s, when Shanars must have done especially well. Using profits from cotton exports, Shanars in the village dug wells, and Shanars in town pushed their case on temple entry. In 1860, confrontations began between Marava and Shanar bands in cotton-growing Sattur taluk.

Decisions by judges constantly came to bear in temple disputes. Government, in the midst of a prolonged policy consideration of temple management, sought to settle disputes concerning Shanar access to temples, which threatened the peace.[82] To do so, courts had to decide whose claims were to be upheld by law. During the 1870s, court suits and street scenes flared when Shanars sought to worship deities in large temples in Madurai and Tiruchendur and in a small temple in Srivilliputtur. In 1878, a district munsif barred Shanars from entering Srivilliputtur temples but allowed Shanar processions on village streets; but when Shanars in Sattur taluk petitioned to take a procession along village streets, the local zamindar protested and officials ordered that the procession be limited to the Shanar quarter; a riot resulted. During the 1880s, violence became more common as Shanars demanded rights of procession and opponents resisted. The issue for judges was whether to legitimize Shanar entry into sacred precincts under state protection, and thus to recognize a Shanar social status that custom denied, government doubted, and Shanars asserted against higher caste opposition.

The complex, climactic upheaval occurred in 1899, in a season of severe agricultural distress in Tirunelveli and famine throughout Madras Presidency. Rich Shanar merchants petitioned to conduct a feast in a temple associated with the Madurai temple of Minakshi-Sundaresvaran, in the town of Kamudi within the zamindari estate of Ramnad, near the northern border of Tinnevelly District. The court battle that ensued ended to the distress of the Shanars, for the district judge, then the High Court, and finally the Privy Council upheld the customary exclusion of Shanars from internal temple precincts. The law thus upheld and redefined custom in imperial terms.

While this court case confronted the district judge, Shanars and Maravas confronted one another in the most serious riots ever to rock the region. Speculation in the aftermath of rioting held that the riots spreading out from towns to villages throughout the northwestern quadrant of the district were connected to the Kamudi temple court case by conspiracies among Maravas and Shanars, Maravas taking their lead from the Raja of Ramnad and Shanars taking theirs from town merchants. But the widely dispersed incidents of riot, during which Marava and Shanar gangs attacked and counterattacked for days and even weeks on end, suggest instead widespread local animosities, accumulated over decades. Rising Shanar fortunes in cash-crop production and trade would have given Shanars increasing control over commercial assets in villages and towns, which struggling Marava farmers, village police, and town laborers would have viewed as a more pointed threat to themselves during times of dearth and confrontation. Famine distress, during which Maravas sought jobs and food controlled disproportionately by Shanar merchants, at a time when Shanars enjoyed relative security both as merchant employees and as farming families, might have heightened Marava bitterness. When faced, further, with Shanar determination to invade temple precincts controlled by locally dominant Maravas, bitterness might well have triggered widespread but locally led Marava assaults on Shanars. Shanar resolve to reject any course of action that expressed obeisance and inferiority to Maravas could well have fueled Shanar attacks and counterattacks on Maravas. In Sivakasi town, local war broke out. Outside towns, the government was in no position to quell riots, depending as it did on an urban constabulary and largely Marava village police. Violence subsided slowly as the monsoon arrived and labor moved back to the land, in November and December 1899.[83]

By 1900, a century of conflict over the definition and distribution of rights had produced a new political environment in an Anglo-Indian imperial setting. Resentment simmered against upstart low castes, especially Shanars.[84] Riots broke out in cotton towns at least once again before 1920, pitting Shanar shopkeepers against Marava laborers during food shortages, in 1918.[85] The imperial system had by this time created a new political arena within which to compete for rights, precedence, and resources in the public domain. Caste political associations, following the model of the Nadar Mahajana Sangam, founded by rich cotton-town Shanar merchants, became a recognized institutional means for voicing demands in the media and in the urban context of government decision making.[86] Grievances and images of group identity increasingly centered, after 1900, on exclusion from and representation in halls of government. Economically successful participants in the social system of commodity production pursued rights to public assets—government jobs, education, and representation in policy-making bodies—by depicting themselves as leaders of constituencies unjustly denied their rights.

New visions of history became ideological weapons in struggles for rights in the public domain, and these visions permeated popular perceptions of social reality. Most powerful by far became the vision that Brahman domination prevented social mobility for all non-Brahman castes. This idea might well have arisen among struggling dry-land tenants during fights to wrest control of land from Brahman mirasidars, in villages like Varttiraya Iruppu. It assumed great importance for Shanar Christians under missionary influence, and pervaded Sattampillai's tracts. It entered the presidency political scene when high-caste politicians in Madras devised the credo of Non-Brahmanism, which animated the political party that would win presidency elections and share government power in the 1920s and 1930s, the Justice party.[87] The imperial state, for its part, rationalized this pattern of ideological order by representing civil society in South India according to caste blocks of political interest and social identity, codified not only in censuses but in official pronouncements about customary rights, such as the Kamudi temple-entry court case.[88] Opposition and factional alignments in presidency politics would revolve around visions of rising groups pitted against entrenched interests—Non-Brahmans versus Brahmans, Telugus versus Tamils, Indians versus British—throughout the subsequent history of South Indian nationalism.[89]

CULTURE

Conclusions about shifts in popular culture cannot easily be given a firm empirical grounding. Yet the people of the countryside in nineteenth-century Tirunelveli seem to have redefined the practical meanings of pangu and pattam, and reinterpreted the nature of rights in society in light of those new meanings. They did so in two overlapping phases. The first consumed the decades before 1880 and the second, the decades after 1850. During the first, rights to land and labor in villages preoccupied antagonists, and, during the second, rights to precedence in relation to state authority. The first phase produced a social system adapted to expanding commodity production, and the second a derivative set of social bases for political representation in the imperial state. Emergent leaders in groups relatively successful in the first phase brought their conceptions of right to bear in the second. Before 1880, initiatives by officers of state, leading landowners, and upstart peasants reformulated Tamil conceptions of property right to rationalize agrarian capitalism. After 1850, landowning commodity producers, merchants, and professionals reformulated Tamil ideas about public precedence in competing representations for status in the imperial state. Their cultural creativity produced a South Indian style of agrarian capitalism and nationalist politics.

The first phase concerned the generality of family farmers, instituted a lasting division between public and private domains, and produced the gulf between conflicts over the means of production and over state power that characterizes capitalist societies in general. Later battles for representation in the public arena would never threaten the underlying control over land and labor wielded by people endowed with private capital assets. People with sufficient means would enter political competition with increasing vigor toward the turn of the twentieth century, pushed, it seems, by declining prospects for enrichment in irrigated agriculture, and certainly pulled by improving prospects in urban centers. Back in the village, their assets and powers remained secure, because bases had been laid in popular culture and political economy for dominance by those who owned private property—people with land and money.

In the first phase, events in and around mirasidar villages, by far the best documented, provide the clearest evidence for semantic shifts and lexical innovations in popular discourse on the subject of rights. They also depict the clearest case of structural change in customary property relations. Groups embroiled in mirasidar conflicts, in addition, loom large in the annals of modern South Indian politics, so that mirasidar conflicts shed light on developments in political culture after 1880. Most important for this particular story, cultural shifts in and around irrigated villages on questions of right put the power of the British in proper perspective, because they highlight on record the causal role of local initiative.

In 1800, mirasidars held property rights (kani) that embraced all community assets, including land, labor, water, and surrounding dry lands; their rights derived from grants, actual or fictive, from Pandya royalty. Royal patronage during the centuries before 1500 had defined their rights on the pattam principle, and after 1500 they increasingly paid state officials in cash and grain for the reaffirmation of their property rights. Their wealth depended on royal protection, patronage, and arbitration. The state's share of the village harvest—melvaram—comprised a pool of grain and cash divided so as to feed royal authority and strengthen local leaders in and around mirasidar communities. Local officials were prominent mirasidars; in most cases they would have enjoyed superior shares of the village by customary rights established in original grants, on the pattam principle. Inside communities, all families shared village assets on the principle that each possessed a share—pangu—defined by family status in ranked caste strata and by family endowments within each stratum. Leading Palla families thus possessed superior status, income, and authority among their caste peers by their mirasi right to organize labor gangs. Village mirasidar families possessed superior claims to the harvest, land, labor, and village authority by virtue of originally granted or subsequently purchased shares. Both individual family property and the state's share of village wealth were thus construed in cultural terms that rooted both in mirasidar collective property right.

State officials and village families pursued their interests in mirasidar village property in these cultural terms well into the nineteenth century. Though for the British the pattah designated strictly private property rights, Company policy could not force this idea on mirasidars; and the olungu system, introduced during negotiations in the 1820s and 1830s, was a compromise between the Company demand for secure annual cash revenues and mirasidar demands for local control over the exact terms of revenue collection. Under the olungu system, in force until the 1850s, mirasidars pursued rights to property faced by competition from one another, from tenants, and from officials, in the context of increasing commodity production and state power.

By doing so, mirasidars and their competitors whittled away at the sharehold system, seeking security in the acquisition of pattahs. Company officials, committed to the protection of mirasidar property rights, interpreted that commitment in terms consistent with ryotwari and expressed it by issuing pattahs to individual landowners. Tenants who challenged mirasidar rights, as well as mirasidars who sought security for their own families, had little choice but to acquire pattahs; they did not abandon the cultural conception of collective rights but redefined the meaning of shares to rationalize family private land ownership distinct from community claims. The proprietary significance of the pangu thus shrank within boundaries redefined between families that possessed specified plots of land. The meaning of land and of ownership changed together, the first being divided up into plots of dirt distinguished from water, trees, and labor; and the second being divided into individual rights to plots of dirt. The property system in villages thus came into line with state law, as indigenous cultural conceptions of right were redefined in the context of two forces that had always affected decisions in mirasidar villages: state policy and market opportunity. Pangu was redefined to mean shares in a family estate, pattam to mean individual entitlement to property, symbolized by the pattah. Competitors for rights redefined pangu and pattam and thus enabled both commodity production and state power to grow as forces in village society, rationalized in indigenous cultural terms.

The smoothness of this transformation in property relations in most of the Tirunelveli region resulted from the Company's initial reliance on mirasidars as pillars of the new regime, and thus from the Company's commitment to protect mirasidar property rights. It depended, too, on the ability of individual mirasidars to change the meaning of pangu and pattam in village life without sacrificing dominance in property relations. By the end of the century, despite change in property culture, mirasidars—now as a body of individual landowners—retained their traditional dominance in most irrigated villages. And they moved into town and into the political arena from this rural stronghold.

Where the cultural reconstruction of rights created serious social conflict, it pitted factions caught in a contradiction between continued control of agrarian domains by dominant-case alliances and the increasing power of upstarts in the political economy. The contradiction did not emerge, except perhaps in undocumented fights between village headmen, lineage leaders, and upstart peasants, in dry villages dominated by Vadugas in the north or Shanars in the south. In the wet zone, it emerged in the abortive effort of townsfolk from mirasidar backgrounds to extend their customary control of village streets to town settings, where they faced decisive opposition from imperial officers who insisted that government would control the public domain. Conflicts, however, characterized the mixed zone throughout the century—first when mirasidars faced potential loss of land, and then when Maravas faced potential loss of status; both were traditionally dominant groups being threatened by economic upstarts who used state auspices to make claims for entitlement to key agrarian resources: land and temple honor. These conflicts, first in the village, then in town and village together, established cultural terms, strategies, and poles of opposition for modern politics, during the decades before the creation of presidency political parties and platforms.

CONCLUSION
PEASANT SOCIETY

Historians explore universals and constants in the particular and transitory, and styles of history take shape according to methods employed to that end. Like many other recent books, this one explores the changing structure of everyday life, and thus concerns pedestrian social settings, ordinary human experience, and mundane routines. Unlike actors in histories of great men and events, the key people in this story were not powerful or influential. Their individual decisions carried little weight. Their importance lies in their being ordinary. Their living conditions reflect those of others like them. Their lives shaped the world around them only in the aggregate. They lived predominantly in villages, as did most people in the world, during centuries before the industrial revolution. The story of their everyday lives constitutes a subtle and elusive drama. Even today, much that we see appears fixed and ageless, if only because we would lock reality in place to create solidity in a world of uncertainty and confusion; and fixity pervades "common sense" about the preindustrial past, if only because its realities are so alien from our own. The drama in social history comes precisely from the constant creativity and contingency that animate social routine, in the distant past and today, as people make decisions, both conscious and unconscious, about how to reproduce their world. The people who thus make and break the status quo do not become famous, yet their quiet innovations and conformities aggregate to make society—the human environment—what it is and what it is becoming. Their individual decisions interact to produce rhythms of inner motion that render societies dynamic. To hear those rhythms in recorded words and deeds from the past is the social historian's task. Often obscured by cataclysmic events, often very faint and chaotic, rhythmic undercurrents of social change need be amplified and simplified in scholarship; perhaps they can only make sense when considered over long stretches of time, when seeming fixity gives way to a sense of glacial movement, when the great events and deeds that punctuate, distort, accelerate, retard, or simply drown out faint rhythms can be set in perspective. In the very long term, dynamics within slowly changing agrarian societies produced the world of rapid change we know today.[1]

The village community that typifies agrarian social order is among the world's most enduring social forms. Its longevity and survival in poor countries today have been mistaken for immutability. The great preponderance of scholarship concerning villagers stresses their parochialism, traditionalism, superstition, and vulnerability to attacks on their way of life by the modern urban sector.[2] Such views of rustic folk took root in the modern mind as historians who studied great men and events located history's dynamic in the city and as social sciences studied village society with a prior scholarly commitment to structural models and synchronic analysis, so that the village came to embody social stasis in a rapidly changing world dominated by urban ideas, technologies, and people.[3] The task that confronts agrarian social historians is to discover, amplify, and analyze rhythms of motion within agrarian folk life. To that end, this book treats a small but diverse region over a very long period of time, in the hope that we will find clues in these South Indian village settings to the millennial dynamics of agrarian society that have produced today's peasantry.

Underlying epochal change in this agrarian society, the peninsular landscape and culture provide a substratum of continuity and constancy, yet even the land and culture underwent subtle transformations as peasants made critical decisions about how best to invest their time and energy. In villages, those peasant decisions produced rhythms of inner movement that altered the structure of rural society over generations, and decisive action did not occur in a vacuum. Gradual but, in the very long term, dramatic change in the context of peasant decision making altered the import of decisions which, in aggregate, recreated the Tamil landscape and Tamil culture alike.

Recalling the two maps of a peasant society discussed in the Introduction—our village and regional maps—it is immediately clear that one dimension of change in the context of peasant decision making is spatial. Concentric circles of social interaction surrounding villages multiplied in number, and the outer rings expanded tremendously, during the millennium after 900. During medieval times, peasants in Tirunelveli pursued their livelihood in a context maximally defined by Indic civilization. Post-medieval migrations expanded their maximal world of interaction to embrace most of Eurasia after 1300. Early modern explorations and conquests created, after 1500, a new world of circulation and exchange that stretched around the globe, to the Atlantic and the Pacific, and bore heavily on local conditions faced by Tirunelveli villagers.[4]

Epochal expansions in the extent of agrarian interaction brought new ideas, technologies, and actors into the Tirunelveli region, which conditioned peasant decisions both by imposing constraints and by opening new opportunities. As a result, people at work in South India, peasants and nonpeasants together, interacted to reconstruct the agrarian system.[5] They did so in part by carving up the land to make the most of its potential, and in part by competing with one another, in groups, to better family livelihood. As their social and agricultural environment slowly changed, so did their ideas about how best to pursue improved family living conditions. Working with analytical tools provided by their evolving culture, and living their lives within an institutional environment that shows striking continuities over centuries, peasants reinterpreted their world and altered their institutionalized relations within villages by shifting their sense of the relative value of symbolic assets provided in key social networks within their civilization. In medieval times, religious institutions and assets took primary place in the process of social change among Tamil villagers. In post-medieval centuries, the state became relatively much more prominent. State power grew during subsequent centuries until growth in the market outstripped it in significance for peasants. Thus villagers changed agrarian society locally because of epochal change in the whole of the peasant world. It thus befits our story of peasant history in South India to conclude with a brief survey of its context and comparative implications.

A medieval synthesis occurred in Europe and Asia during the centuries in which Pandyas and Cholas ruled in South India. Major historic events account for the end of the medieval era: Mongol expansion across the Eurasian steppeland marks the beginning of a clearly post-medieval environment in the thirteenth century, just as Europe's expansion overseas in the fifteenth century marks the start of an early-modern era. These later shifts in the spatial context of agrarian life in Eurasia involved great migrations, major technical innovations, and brutal wars that unified the world as millions died during long human surges across land and sea. But why the tenth century marks a fairly clear dividing line between pre-medieval and medieval conditions in the Eurasian peasant world remains unexplained. No events of the scope reflected in the careers of Marco Polo, Genghis Khan, Christopher Columbus, Vasco de Gama, and Hernando Cortez set in motion the medieval synthesis that came into place by the year 900.

The medieval centuries of China's T'ang and Sung dynasties, Europe's High Middle Ages, Middle Eastern postcaliphal states, and medieval kingdoms in India, among them that of the Cholas in the South, were times of dramatic agricultural expansion and consolidation.[6] Population increased throughout Eurasia at a rate perhaps twice that of the centuries just preceding 900.[7] Whether demographic expansions caused or were caused by the invention or spread of new technologies and institutions remains controversial, but indicators of growth moved ahead in unison.[8] Only in Europe did the geographical locus of growth move decisively north and west into colder climates at the periphery of the Roman Empire, as Europeans created that agrarian system called feudalism.[9] In both China and India, civilization moved south, into lands that had also been at the periphery of classical empires—into hot, humid domains of peasant life dominated by rice paddy cultivation. More than the European, these Asian medieval systems show striking continuities with classical forms of agrarian order; these were cultural transplantations in new agrarian settings.

China's population moved south of the Yangtze toward the mountainous tropics. By 1391, not only had China's total number of households risen from under nine million in the ninth century to nearly fifteen but key southern regions, which held fewer than one in every four householders in the ninth century, housed three in every five by the end of the fourteenth.[10] Increasing land productivity diversified avenues to opportunity, so that, in its transplanted setting, the imperial bureaucracy underwent a substantial change in structure: the empire drew its officials less from "a hereditary elite which specialized in government service" and more "from a broadly based gentry that viewed a bureaucratic career as only one of a variety of occupational choices."[11] As in Europe, subcontinental agrarian expansion in China proceeded by the production of more numerous and densely packed constituent regions. The land became more productive as it became more complexly organized, and as small-scale social and spatial units developed distant connections. Civilization expanded its reach. People produced the materials of civilized life in greater proportion to land area than ever before. As peasants worked the land in a widening sphere of civilization, agrarian society developed new forms of order.

South of the Himalayas, medieval population seems to have grown perceptibly faster during medieval times than before.[12] The classical agrarian system devised under the imperial Guptas in North India spawned numerous Gangetic kingdoms that succeeded the empire in densely settled regions of agricultural expansion.[13] In South as in East Asia, the old southern periphery attained prominence in the civilization for the first time, and by analogous technical innovations in rice farming and cultural transplantations. As in Europe, however, this old periphery in South India had by medieval times already established its cultural traditions, expressed in its language and literature, and embodied in ancient kinship and religious practices. The southern peninsula became during medieval times a clearly defined part of Indic civilization. New regions came to life in the Tamil-speaking south as people used technology to make drainage water productive in communities along drainage basins.

By the tenth century, a characteristically South Indian agrarian system had been born. It matured in densely settled patches of green, separated by expanses of dry land, near the coast. Its great centers were Kanchipuram in the north, Tanjavur in the Kaveri delta, and Madurai on the Vaigai, each an urban agglomeration of economic, political, and religious significance. The stone and metal inscriptions that form the bulk of our data concerning this epoch reveal the central organizational principles that held these dispersed centers and core agricultural zones together in one agrarian system. Given its geography, Burton Stein's description of the system as "segmentary" seems appropriate; even more so because, despite Chola imperial expansion, the whole of the system was never unified under one state. Expansion both within the core regions around royal capitals and across the peninsula progressed by the replication of small-scale units of order and by their ritual integration into a ceremonial complex that centered on the power of South Indian gods.[14] Some scholars have argued that Stein underestimates the power of Chola kings in the Chola heartland, and the significance of wealthy merchant towns in Chola statecraft.[15] Some have consequently characterized the small-scale units of agrarian order—the nadus—that typify medieval South India as administrative and marketing microregions, where Stein considers these to be ethnic units built by dominant peasants.[16] At the center of the Chola kingdom, the powers of kings and merchants might well have outstripped those of their counterparts elsewhere in the Tamil country; but certainly on the periphery of the Pandya and Chola domains, at the very tip of the peninsula, Stein's characterization is apt. Tamil literature makes it painfully clear that the foundations of the medieval synthesis were soaked in blood from battles that established the temple-centered, devotional, Brahmanical religious ceremonial practice at the center of agrarian order.[17] The medieval system demanded that kings rise above others in regions, just as peasant families rose above others in agricultural communities, by ceremonial social differentiation charged with religious meanings and constituted by religious rituals.

Religious networks clearly comprised the strongest threads in the fabric of agrarian order in medieval South India. Gods provided symbolic capital assets of paramount significance in peasant decisions concerning family livelihood. Temples and ceremonial events generated and distributed culturally valued symbols that dominated decisions about investment, if only because so many of the society's assets—its skill, technology, grain, arts, and organizational energy—flowed through temple precincts. Culturally, it seems that medieval Tamils conceived the control of nature and of society in religious terms, so that transactions between people and gods focused human energies during efforts to produce crops, subdue enemies, and suppress disruptive forces. Interactions between people and gods also tied disparate core agricultural zones one to another. Inscriptionally recorded diversity in names, titles, and commercial activity make dispersed zones seem very different from one another; it differentiates, as we have seen, even nadus within the Tirunelveli region. What holds the picture of medieval South India together is above all the set of ceremonial practices recorded in quite uniform ways in the ritually potent and highly Sanskritized language of the inscriptions. The Sanskritic and temple-centered character of Tamil verse during medieval times distinguishes it sharply from earlier epochs, and nurtures a popular belief in Tamil Nadu today that medieval South India succumbed to an invasion of Brahmans from the north.[18] Medieval peasants in their nadus expanded kinship networks and constituted family boundaries by applying principles of ritual hierarchy and separation; they achieved cultural control of their potentially disruptive Palla labor force by the same means. Temple deities evoked powerful emotions and linked powerful people in society into a system of order that replicated the dominance of village peasants in nadus within kingdoms.

Late medieval centuries brought significant change: the power of warrior kings seems to have grown, and warlords led movements outward from core zones in search of wealth. Chola armies moved south, while peasant contemporaries of Europe's First Crusaders fought their way into the upland dry areas adjacent to the Kaveri River, in what is today the Coimbatore District of Tamil Nadu.[19] As in Europe, late medieval warrior movements might have been propelled by population pressure in agricultural core zones; but whatever the cause, one result in South India and in Europe was that kings built bigger and more grandly to glorify god.[20] Late Chola monarchs and their successors in the Pandya country commanded larger armies than did earlier medieval kings; they built garrison towns, fortified capitals, and moved their armed might much more widely than had their predecessors. They announced their glory in splendid sacred works of architecture that foreshadow the monumental building of later imperial epochs.[21] Thus the last century of the medieval period seems to have seen the rise of increasingly powerful kings in command of more labor and skill in the countryside; their rise and related population movements appear to have been generated within medieval core zones;

and their increasing significance for peasants presages later trends, when, after 1300, massive movements triggered by events in Central Asia announced an epochal shift in the context of South Indian peasant life.

Warrior migrations by Mongols and Turks across the Central Asian steppe unified Eurasia as never before. Buffered by land—because Russian arms and dense forests thwarted steppe warfare to the west—Europe felt the shocks of postmedieval unification both very late and indirectly. The shock hit Europe from the south by sea, and quietly in an invasion of black plague bacillus, which had moved from Asia by ship to the Mediterranean, and which announced Eurasia's "unification by disease."[22] Unlike the wars of invasion attending Mongol and Turk expansion elsewhere, the plague left Europe's productive capital stock intact. That productive capacity fortified later European generations who confronted expansive Ottoman Turks. A dynastic grandchild of earlier movements from the steppe, the Ottoman "gunpowder empire" not only stimulated militant state development among its western competitors, but also, by capturing the eastern Mediterranean and North Africa, pushed European maritime enterprise away from the Levant and out into the Atlantic.[23] Europe's productive capacity, its militant rulers, and its seafaring adventures combined energies to accomplish the world's next great unification in 1492; their surge across the Atlantic in turn spelled mass death by disease and conquest, this time in the Americas.[24]

Thus in the course of two centuries after 1300, the two great events of world unification connect in a long chain of cause and effect. Each meant brutal invasion and mass death as people on the move united once distant spheres of civilization. Each human surge expanded the geographical scope of social interaction and propelled change in agrarian social order. Overland migratory conquest from Central Asia stimulated, above all, innovations in the exercise of state power. Canon, cavalry, fortress, and armed ship strengthened armies. By the sixteenth century, all across Eurasia distinctively early modern empires and states had arisen that outshone their medieval predecessors in their capacity to coerce. Their ability to extract surpluses and to protect trade at the same time widened the frontiers of commercial circulation, and no frontier surpassed the Americas. The transcontinental system of production, power, and trade across the Atlantic generated new economic opportunities that "turned the continents inside out" to face the sea.[25] Precious metals and crops from the New World, and commercial networks stretching across the Atlantic and Pacific, crisscrossing the Indian Ocean, touched the lives of people on every Old World coast. Eurasia's postmedieval epoch of warlord conquest gradually created stores of state power and merchant capital whose disposition would dominate the early modern epoch after 1500, when European seaborne empires and Eurasian land empires exerted their influence together on coastal regions in both the Old and New worlds.

From the Ottoman west to India, Turks pushed steadily into positions of state power in postmedieval agrarian societies. Throughout Asia's southern rim, Turks and Persians combined to generate major innovations in the means to exert and legitimate state power. Their efforts produced circuits of political discourse and military movement that stretched across the expanding Muslim world. At the same time, Muslim maritime enterprise expanded, centered in port cities strung like pearls on strings of trade, enriching Indian Ocean coastlines from East Africa to Southeast Asia.[26] As Muslim merchants brought the Indian Ocean and Mediterranean into one commercial world, Muslim empire builders made one political world of the land between Istanbul and Dacca.

The founding of a Turkic Sultanate at Delhi in 1206 marked the onset of centuries of innovation in statecraft in India, stimulated by competition both within the Muslim fold and between its frontiersmen and those in their path of expansion. A raid by Malik Kafur launched from Delhi disrupted political order in the farthest corner of South India by vanquishing the Pandyas at Madurai in the early 1300s. Waves of southerly migration followed, not of Muslims but rather of South Indian warriors and peasants under the umbrella of authority raised by conquerors who sought to erect a bulwark against Muslim expansion at "the city of victory," Vijayanagar. Conceived as a barrier against outsiders and hailed as a protector of tradition by its leaders, the Vijayanagar empire expressed South India's postmedieval integration into a truly subcontinental system of states, all of which, being composed of competing powers in an environment of mass human and technological circulation, adopted quite similar techniques for domination in an environment pervaded by war. For the whole of South India's Vijayanagar period, from the 1300s through the early 1500s, the Indian subcontinent witnessed mass migrations and dramatic movements outward from old core agricultural zones.[27] Politically, this was an era during which warriors on the move rose to prominence in far-flung localities and established foundations for tributary states; while, economically, agricultural diversification and expanding trade networks produced new potential for agrarian exchange and state finance.[28]

Vijayanagar emperors never subdued South India. But for two centuries after 1350, the Krishna-Godavari River confluence seethed with war, about 700 miles due north of the tip of India, and Vijayanagar remained the epicenter of South Indian politics; royal authority in all quarters felt the influence of Vijayanagar imperial expansion. Migrant warriors and peasants moving south from the capital dispersed agricultural and military technologies throughout the peninsula; they founded new communities, cleared tracts of land for plowing, subdued predatory tribes that inhabited tracts between irrigated medieval core agricultural zones. Militarily, migrants made the peninsula a continuous terrain of opportunity, as it had never been under medieval kings. Medieval mandalams disappeared as relevant units of political discourse; so did nadus, now surrounded by dry peasant farming communities and penetrated by powers from outside medieval domains. New competitors for wealth and power entered old realms of agrarian order. They came from outside the homeland of Tamil civilization, and many spoke languages other than Tamil, though closely akin to it—mostly Kannada and Telugu. These newcomers did worship South Indian gods, so that temple-centered royal activity established the legitimacy of imperial officers and adventurers throughout Vijayanagar's peninsular sphere.[29] This ideological and institutional continuation of medieval royal traditions facilitated major innovations in South Indian statecraft, which thrust military men and their powers to extract and protect into unprecedented prominence for peasants.

Postmedieval migrations and conquests altered the logic of capital accumulation in the South Indian agrarian system by increasing the power of military men to gather wealth through culturally legitimate coercion and protection. Temples to South Indian gods remained places where religious specialists produced highly prized cultural assets in the symbols of rank and honor bestowed during ceremonial events; but the people whose rank and honor achieved prominence were now warlord rulers, not leaders of agrarian alliances rooted in traditional nadus. In addition, warlords themselves became centers of ritual. Their extractive and redistributive powers became legitimate independently of the gods; this is manifested by the sixteenth century in a logic of sovereignty shared by Muslim Mughal emperors and their Hindu competitors alike, from Delhi to Madurai. Rulers during this age based their authority on powers to protect. By protecting landholders, artisans, merchants, and subordinated rulers, kings and emperors built the bases of tributary domains. Early modern rulers, like the Nayakas of Madurai, could trace the roots of their authority back, through their patronage for temples and support for brahmadeyas, to medieval times, and thus bolster their hold on tribute from the countryside. But the Nayakas' style of statecraft bore strong resemblance to that of Muslim rulers, with whom they shared one world of political discourse and technology. In its ability to channel market wealth and religious merit into the hands of state minions, the Nayaka warrior state resembled much more the contemporary Mughal empire than the medieval Pandya kingdom.

The Nayaka state was distinctly early modern also in the commercial foundations on which it depended; and, in politics as in economics, the postmedieval transformation, from the 1300s to the 1500s, set the stage for early modern cultural and institutional development, because the expanding agricultural frontier produced crops for local and regional trade as migrant warriors inserted themselves into agrarian polities. After 1600, the Nayaka state, like the Mughal empire, protected trade and depended on extraction and consumption that in turn stimulated production for market exchange, while overseas enterprise brought both supplies of new products and demand for indigenous crops, primarily spices and cotton cloth. Overseas demand set up circuits of exchange that connected hills and weaving towns to cotton-growing localities and coastal entrepots. Under the protection of kings and militant trading companies, circuits of trade stimulated agrarian society most where they converged in core areas of agricultural production, royal authority, and temple activity. Such areas dotted the Tamil coastal plain, one being the Tambraparni River valley.[30] As in other parts of Eurasia, therefore, in South India early modern states benefited from and facilitated an increase in the significance of trade among agrarian folk, particularly along the coast, where inland worlds of exchange, production, and power overlapped the world of seaborne enterprise.[31]

Having founded and sustained their domain at the tip of India on their ability to protect and extract commercial assets, the Nayakas after 1700 simply faced too many competitors to survive. Nevertheless, the logic of the early modern agrarian system, which promised state protection in return for tribute, survived the Nayaka demise as it did the contemporary decline of the Mughals. The entrenched cultural expectation among peasants and rulers alike that protection would buy a share of the crop fostered and financed military competition throughout the subcontinent; and Europeans emerged the major winners.

By the eighteenth century, the political economy of Indian states hinged on large-scale control of capital generated in agriculture and trade. As in the Americas and in Europe, eighteenth-century political turmoil in India thus centered on struggles for the fruits of merchant capital. England lost a prize in North America, but gained another in southern Asia; in the one sphere, old alliances broke apart, while in the other, new ones came into place. England's first empire crumbled under demands that taxation and commerce be freed from Crown authority; the second empire arose when Crown authority and European fighting technology built Asian domains within which Englishmen could tax profitably and Indians could profit in return for paying taxes.[32]

Military competition among armed contenders for the state's share of agrarian commercial assets in South Asia altered the subcontinent's geography of power. After 1740, the political center of gravity moved toward the coast, away from the inland center of the Mughal empire at Delhi. Along India's coast, entrepots connected inland and overseas commercial enterprise; near the coast, strategically situated military powers struggled for supremacy in a political system that lived on tribute extracted from stores of commercial wealth generated by exchanges in agricultural and artisan products. The British East India Company found powerful allies among city merchants and bankers; victories on the battlefield brought more tribute to invest in commerce and war, and more allies among the vanquished and those in search of protectors. The Company's most determined foes were men who pursued precisely the same goals; their most willing subjects were men who sought Company protection in order to maintain profits and local control of agrarian assets in the fact of real or potential threats, in an environment of catastrophic political uncertainty.

During the centuries after 900, every epoch brought imperialists to the tip of India. The Chola empire penetrated the Pandya realm and Chola minions set themselves in positions of power in Madurai and in favored Tambraparni nadus. The Vijayanagar empire swallowed the peninsula, lorded over the Pandyas, and sent south waves of warriors, protectors, little kings, and tributary agents. The Mughal empire expanded into the southern peninsula, but Aurangzeb died during the effort, and his empire crumbled during decades when a new imperial regime expanded inland from the coast, its southern capital at the port city of Madras. The British East India Company men who obtained authority in Madurai and Tirunelveli did so as mercantile imperialists in an age when merchant enterprise thrived with direct royal patronage, protection, and partnership. Like imperialists before them, Englishmen sought to seize the high ground in society, to attain a privileged position in the social process of capital accumulation. Cholas had sought booty, temple honor, and Brahman favor. Vijayanagar warriors had demanded land for their followers and tribute for their armies.

Streams of tribute generated under early modern regimes, such as that of the Nayakas, had provided stores of royal finance capital that attracted the Mughals and the Company alike to the Indian peninsula. Tribute depended on and financed trade; it fed the power of the Company and nawab, and now laid the foundation for Company Raj.

Imperialism changed substantially in every era. Its substance always reflected and derived from the evolving structure in South India's agrarian system; and the evolution of that system, in turn, resulted not from unilateral imperialist action but from the peninsula's integration into wider and wider spheres of interaction, influence, circulation, and exchange. Cholas based their power on ritual hegemony in a system of capital accumulation centered on temples and brahmadeyas. Vijayanagar warlords staked claims to tribute on protective and extractive coercion, which stimulated market exchange and provided more circulating commercial wealth. The Nayakas domesticated the warlord tributary state on Pandya soil, and benefited from the increasing stores of commercial wealth that attended both Nayaka state formation and increasing overseas trade. But unfortunately for Nayakas, the stores of royal and commercial finance capital that characterized early modern South India attracted more powerful competitors: Tipu Sultan, the nizam of Hyderabad, the nawab of Arcot, Marathas, and French and English merchant companies. The fateful alliance between the nawab and the English yoked the predatory aspirations of a southern Mughal offshoot prince with those of merchant warriors from Europe; both sought to capture streams of royal finance capital. Their rural support came from locals who needed protection and wanted profits. Loyalties to ancient indigenous rulers were by this time irrelevant; and neither the Muslim nawab nor the Christian English posed any imminent threat to local interests by virtue of their religion. The Company proved the stronger in this alliance and cast off the nawab as soon as possible. Already ample flows of tribute fed the Company rise to power, and the existence of local tax traditions allowed the Company men to enter positions of authority in Tirunelveli, as in most of South India, with little disruption to the status quo.

The first fruits of victory were land taxes and trade profits. Like imperialists before them, the English did their best to multiply first fruits for themselves and their allies. They coveted the most profitable niches in the political economy. They controlled export trade finance, revenue redistribution, the military, top government decision making, and the terms of trade between India and the rest of the world. The Company and then Crown did whatever possible to profit from their Indian connection, and the British almost certainly reaped profits in

India way out of proportion to their productive input.[33] They did so by making their regime as much as possible in the British image. Yet their means to accomplish that task remained limited to the end. To achieve success would always require alliances and compromises that would limit success; expedience would necessarily dominate policy implementation, for British policy ideals would always meet costly bottlenecks and cost-saving opportunities presented by the power of Indian people in the regime. Beneath the shiny façade of Queen Victoria's Indian empire, penetrating eyes would always find a political world and a division of imperial spoils that rewarded handsomely the key people in the countryside who made the regime work. Even far beneath the great heights of profit making in cities, occupied by urbanites of the realm—English and Indian alike—in small towns and in villages, land taxes, trade, and public works patronage would finance irrigation, roads, and widening entrepreneurship. From the ranks of those Indians who benefited most from the expansion of commodity production and government wealth would come the nationalists and regional politicians who sought to take the fruits of empire out of English hands.

Imperialism has conditioned the intellect so thoroughly that even nationalists have adopted an imperial sensibility. Modern Indian historiography stressed the work of imperial leaders and their adversaries from the beginning. Although Indian nationalists made major breakthroughs—putting the British adventure in India in new, critical light—they continued to illuminate the Indian past from the center of the empire, leaving the countryside in darkness. Looking out from the center, the imperial sensibility emphasizes the distinctive wholeness of Indian civilization in contrast to that other sphere of paramount importance, Europe. It highlights the issues most heatedly debated by British imperialists and Indian nationalists, and among these the issue of Indian unity stands out above all others. Analysts commonly attributed British military victory in India to the subcontinent's ageless political fragmentation, thus to an inherent absence of national feeling among the people of India; unity became a fixation among leaders of the Indian National Congress, for obvious reasons. The imperial view also spotlights great men and issues of aggregate, subcontinental significance; it hungers for lessons that pertain to the life cycles of empires and nations. For historians, of course, the most important questions concern change—who makes it happen, with what effects on a population, and with what opposition. On this score nationalists confronted imperialists head on, and their debates continue to echo in historical scholarship.[34] Both agree, however, that it was imperialists under Company and Crown who shook rural India out of centuries of quietude and immobility; both portray themselves as progressive and their opponents regressive; and both bolster their judgments above all by measurements of improvement, or development, in India under the guiding hand of ruling powers. Thus the central questions in the history of British India developed around debates over the impact of British policy on the well-being of the Indian population.[35]

Since Indian independence, scholars have challenged and to a considerable extent abandoned the imperial sensibility by subjecting its mythical, ahistoric images of the countryside, such as the self-sufficient village republic, to critical scrutiny, and by disaggregating India to constitute a vibrant, variegated history of a subcontinent as large, populous, and diverse as Europe.[36] Today, as do European studies, South Asian studies fix on major constituent cultural regions.[37] Local detail and regional potraits have supplanted subcontinental generalizations in the scholarly imagination.[38] From this perspective, Tamil Nadu appears afresh as a regional social order woven into the fabric of wide regions (including empires and nations), which today define the central problems for social history.

An alternative to the imperial sensibility, peasant history, in India as in Europe, portrays everyday rural conditions but trains our mind's eye out toward the peasants' wider world. Particularities in village milieus, and therefore diversity within regions, stand out. The unity of large regions and generalizations about them fade from view; and dramatic events at the center of states, in the cities, lose much of their import. The long-term and slow changes in everyday life, amid natural surroundings and movements over the landscape, pose key questions. Followers rather than leaders of mass movements walk to center stage in our sense of politics. We look for the logic of social reproduction that provides stability and continuity but still alters the structure of rural life over generations. From this perspective, the history of the Tirunelveli region looks quite different from an imperial view of it.

Considering, for instance, the impact of British rule from a very long-term view of peasant history, in Tirunelveli the most important conclusion of this book is that epochal transformations of peasant society during the centuries before 1800 help to explain both the foundation of the Anglo-Indian regime and village social change during imperial maturation. Commercial development before 1800 produced a village interest in both state and market growth, which fueled the expansion of government power and commodity production after 1800. Tamil culture had changed sufficiently since medieval times to rationalize and motivate social changes after 1800 that brought bureaucrats and capitalists into new local prominence, not without considerable conflict and local turmoil.

Cultural change that accompanied rural social initiatives during the nineteenth century make sense as part of a millennial process of reinterpretation and reevaluation of symbolic assets in the peasant world. Kinship, religion, state, and market networks generated stores of symbolic assets in 1900 as in 900; the attainment of symbolic capital in all four networks preoccupied Tamil villagers under the British as under the Pandyas. But as epochal outward shifts in the spatial context of peasant life brought new people, technologies, ideas, and competitors into the Tirunelveli region, peasants confronted a changing world and reassessed the relative value of symbolic assets in their own cultural milieu. Symbols of state power rose in relation to all others when military men pushed themselves into social prominence after the fall of the Pandyas; leadership in communities, security of subsistence, and improvement in social standing came to rest increasingly on one's position in networks of state power. After 1600, in pockets of commercialism, under state protection and stimulated by inland as well as overseas trade, market assets rose steadily in cultural significance. By 1800, both Englishmen and Tamils in Tirunelveli participated in a global system of social interaction based predominantly on market exchange, a worldwide capitalist social system. By 1800, though Englishmen and Tamils spoke different languages and hailed from quite different cultures, at the tip of India they shared assumptions about the state and the market that allowed negotiations over the specific character of the new regime.

In its evolution before 1900, the Tirunelveli region should not be equated with all of South India, or even Tamil Nadu. It is distinctive. Its particularities and, indeed, its internal diversity dominate its history. It is the one South India medieval core agricultural region to include both high-quality river irrigation and high-quality black cotton soil. This natural resource base, under the impetus of overseas demand for cotton cloth, gave it commercial advantages before 1800; and, under the impetus of demand for raw cotton, even more advantages after 1800—best illustrated, perhaps, by the fact that precious metal flowed into Tinnevelly District as it flowed out of Madras Presidency from the 1820s to the 1840s, when, nonetheless, prices in the district follow the downward presidency pattern, showing that district productivity kept pace with species imports. Yet though the region held unusual commercial potential throughout history, it was also off the beaten track of warring armies and invaders from the north. Its political history revolved around conquests of Madurai and subsequent battles

214

to subdue a region that would always come into the hands of warriors who held Madurai. Its peripheral location saved Tirunelveli incalculable suffering during periods of heavy fighting, best illustrated by the contrast between late eighteenth-century experience along the Tambraparni and in the Kaveri delta, when Tirunelveli wet zone mirasidars felt minimal disruption from war and their Tanjavur counterparts suffered dreadfully at the hands of invaders.[39] Socially and culturally, it is tempting to speculate what subtle influence the region's unique endowments might have had on the character of its inhabitants. They certainly have had more opportunity than most in South India to engage themselves profitably in trade. They might also have developed an unusual tolerance and adaptability when faced with social and cultural diversity, not only because of their proximity to Sri Lanka and Kerala and long contact with overseas merchants from the Middle East and Europe, but because of their internal diversity. At the tip of India, this region lies in a cul-de-sac that has held all variety of immigrants. New migrants in each wave found their place. Each brought new cultural elements and new connections to the wider world, which also found their place in regional society and culture.

Because the pecularities of the region hinge on commercial potential, Tirunelveli can be compared to many historical peasant social settings throughout Eurasia, but particularly on the coast, which benefited from comparative advantages in both agriculture and trade. Decreasing transport and transaction costs over the centuries transformed the world geography of trade, and some regions lost out in the process, having been favored in one period but deprived in the next. The rise and fall of the Silk Road and of Levantine trade provide dramatic examples of shifting conditions for trade and travel that hit regions hard which depended on trade through particular cross-continental routes. Political trends often propelled such shifts. Military turmoil in eighteenth-century India, for example, forced commercial and financial activity to concentrate in safe places, where the benefits of wartime speculation could be reaped and those of trade and agriculture preserved.[40] Coastal India was favored by eighteenth-century conditions. Peace could be maintained adequately to carry on overseas trade, safe from inland warrior competition. In fact, coastal India enjoyed steadily improving commercial significance during the centuries after 1500; political trends after 1700 moved the balance of power in the subcontinent in a direction in which economic trends had pushed the balance of wealth for some time. This slow shift in the geography of agrarian political economy parallels others of epochal significance, most importantly, perhaps, the shift that brought European countries bordering the Atlantic into such prominence after 1500. By the eighteenth century, coastal people throughout the world were connected by sinews of trade and state. The centuries after 1500 must have commercialized all cultures on the coast, where native agricultural assets and inland political conditions allowed, more than in the interior expanses of huge continents. Distant peasant cultures may well have moved on parallel courses that emphasized the relative value of market assets in the context of protective state power, in civilizations from East Asia to Western Europe.

The likelihood of long, slow, parallel transformations, across great cultural distances, suggests a global approach to the rise of capitalism and imperialism rather than the dominant approach today, which fixates on Europe's great transformation and European initiative around the world. The reasons for the rise of British power at the tip of India may parallel those behind the rise of European imperialism more generally. Perhaps the foundation of Britain's second empire, and of others like it, rested on alliances built in the coastal, commercialized milieus, spawned within agrarian civilizations by expanding seaborne enterprise. On these lines, we might reconceive the rise of capitalism and imperialism together, considering both in a global context and looking for cross-cultural interactions and alliances that brought both into being. Instead of understanding both as strictly European inventions, we might discover a global, cross-cultural process of invention, which involved many peoples—with Europeans as major innovators—tied by sea into one vast cultural and social system that spread its influence from the coast inland.[41]

Peasant history in Tirunelveli emphasizes the importance of long-term coastal commercialization, and at the same time casts into doubt the impenetrability of Indo-European cultural barriers that most scholars assume, for we find a number of cultural convergences and bridges, forged during the rise of state and market networks, in Europe and India alike during centuries after 1300. More importantly, the history of this region highlights peasant creativity, which in the final analysis animates epochal transformation in South India. From the beginning, village folk created diverse agrarian social settings and social roles. The term "peasant" itself fails to capture that diversity. Even to call this a "village society" obscures the range of village types in agricultural zones and the slow but steady process of change inside villages that reveals creative action by villagers in a changing world. From the beginning, inequality among family farmers and diversity among their communities hold the key to social identity among the peasantry and to the character of village society. Long-term cultural change can be understood in this light to result from creative action to reconstitute social inequality in diverse local settings amid changing regional circumstances; these circumstances of course include the arrival into the region of new competitors for power, but more importantly the arrival of new opportunities presented by declining transport and transaction costs in a widening world of movement and communication. Those country people who seized new opportunities in each period defined the social vanguard, working within one evolving cultural frame of reference, and changing that culture internally as they strove to better their family livelihood. Villagers through the ages generated those little transformations that in aggregate brought Europe and India into one orbit and helped to bring a colonial regime into existence.

Nineteenth-century documentation reveals that social vanguard in action and the little transformations in vivid detail. In the context of the European industrialization and Anglo-Indian imperialism, unique features of Tirunelveli again stand out. Its lush irrigated paddy fields proved to be fertile ground for a firm alliance between the British and a literate agrarian elite that provided the heart and soul of the state officer corps and sustained the treasury. Tambraparni River valley villages had always benefited most from years of peace and overseas trade; so much so that village, town, and city merged into one social setting, grounded in paddy production and crowned by the regional capital; in this milieu, mirasidars wielded control. Negotiations between mirasidars and Company men set the new regime on firm footing and strengthened leading mirasidars, who seized opportunity, dissolved collective sharehold traditions, filled professional ranks, ventured into business, and redefined the nature of rights in their society in their own cultural terms. Uniquely among districts in Madras Presidency, Tinnevelly also embraced high-quality cotton soil, good garden lands, and seaports, which, in the context of Anglo-Indian state stability, accentuated the local impact of world market trends. British demand for tinnies cotton triggered rapid growth in regional commodity production in villages, which in the context of state growth accelerated the growth of towns and of opportunities for profit throughout the economy. Upstart peasants—among whom Shanars stand out as a caste group—seized opportunities presented by expanding commodity production; they formed another social vanguard propelling change in village order and Tamil culture. The uniqueness of this region in its agrarian social history may best be captured in the diversity of its social vanguard and in their peculiar configurations of social conflict. In some parts of the presidency, such as Tanjavur, mirasidars held unchallenged sway; and in other, predominantly dry, regions, rich peasants and village officers turned military into commercial dominance.[42] In Tinnevelly District, wet- and dry-zone styles of social change interpenetrated one another; and commercialization in this relatively well-endowed agrarian setting spread opportunities for profit—hence social opportunism—more widely than in less advantaged and diverse parts of South India.

The best way to extrapolate from this case study is not to argue that the Tirunelveli pattern of peasant experience applies to the Indian subcontinent more generally, but rather to argue that it suggests peasant history in British India be studied comparatively.[43] Thinking of the Indian subcontinent not as an aggregate of administrative or large-scale cultural territories, but instead as a large set of small-scale agrarian milieus, the Tirunelveli case indicates that factors which most distinguished village experience were those that affected the customary social division of wealth and economic trends. Mixed-zone mirasidars faced quite different conditions from those of their counterparts in the wet zone. Good irrigation and economic opportunities for wet-zone mirasidars enabled them to reconstruct their dominance in new terms; whereas mixed-zone mirasidars experienced relative decline. Warrior peasants in the black-soil cotton country did considerably better than their counterparts in the red-soil tract. Change in village communities, therefore, cannot be understood primarily in terms of conditions that resulted from the policies of British imperial elites, nor can continuities be attributed primarily to pan-Indian cultural or social characteristics such as the predominance of caste hierarchy, as so many studies suggest. Locally, variables as diverse as rainfall, soil type, irrigation technology, transportation routes, settlement patterns, and market structures describe the environment that communities faced in the course of their history. In the end, it is this great local diversity and the importance of local dynamics in a changing world context that is the most generalized feature of peasant history in Tirunelveli.

The salience of diversity extends to any study of the historical experience of social aggregates such as caste groups, and to the study of cultural constructs such as the caste system. In a general sense, we can conclude that the reformulation of hierarchical caste relations during the development of agrarian capitalism in Tirunelveli reflects a particularly Indian, or South Indian, phenomenon. But it is far more important to emphasize that historical social relations in caste society differ in space and change over time according to their niches in a regional political economy. That mirasidars were predominantly high-caste Brahmans and Vellalas is, of course, critical, and makes sense only in light of general caste principles, but their dismantling of sharehold communities resulted from responses to opportunities presented in a nineteenth-century context of expanding commodity production and imperial bureaucracy. This context affected mirasidar communities differently, while it also affected people in all castes, including those lower-caste upstarts who pushed mirasidars to acquire private landholdings. General cultural principles of caste do not explain either the real social relations that evolved in and around mirasidar communities nor their pattern of change. The Shanars demonstrate, conversely, that a very diverse caste group embedded in a distinctive niche in the agrarian economy can have strong similarities in social experience across localities, despite its diversity. Yet the modern ideological invention of the Shanars as a caste with a history of its own in the regional caste system derived from the success of particular groups of Shanars in the nineteenth century, when some Shanars produced a new vision of the Shanar past for later appropriation by others. Commodity production, empire, and competition for rights produced a caste ideology in the modern political arena, as much as did caste cultural principles. The local upheavals attending Shanar social mobility, moreover, resulted not so much from Shanar caste group action as from Shanar families being upstarts in places where they faced dominant caste groups threatened with relative impoverishment and insecurity. Traditional caste antagonism does not explain upheavals that embroiled Shanars; neither does the Christianity of some Shanars. The explanation lies in the particular conditions Shanars faced as upstarts who challenged weak dominant caste families.

All this said, the particulars of a peasant society still turn our thoughts toward the wider world and its impact on peasant history. In Tirunelveli, after 1750 we find trends that pertain to peasant history throughout the Indian subcontinent and beyond. For seventy years after 1750, the dominant political theme was the building of military and administrative foundations for a new regime. The level of taxation and destruction, the policies of rulers, and the responses of locally dominant folk would be critical for peasants throughout India during these turbulent years. After 1820, a downward trend in prices, wars on the fringes of Company territory, and economic demands thrust on the Company by industrial interests in England generated pressure for more revenue that stimulated reform efforts during the 1840s throughout British India. The historical conjuncture that so deeply affected Tirunelveli during the forty years after 1835 impinged on the peasantry in various ways throughout the subcontinent. The mid-century transformation of governance and economic life affected peasants even more widely. The imperial order, which we have seen in one region, came into place by the 1880s in all of British India; analogous modern regimes came into place elsewhere, conditioning life for peasants whose local worlds would be shaped and studied evermore by imperial personnel who were devoted, above all, to the maintenance of empire. The economic doldrums that plagued Tirunelveli toward the turn of the twentieth century certainly impinged on life in much of India and the world. Though India did not suffer depression as severe as in some countries, the thirty years before World War I brought strikingly parallel economic and political trends in localities across five continents. In that context, local conflicts between upstart Shanars and hard-pressed Maravas, mirasidar movements into government service and politics, and Palla efforts to find jobs in town and overseas make sense as initiatives within not only British India but a world political economy. And finally, villagers in this region at the tip of India shared with rustic folk worldwide the fate of being relegated to obscurity and robbed of history by cosmopolitan intellectuals, working in metropolitan centers that dominated the world by nineteenth century's end.

NOTES

Introduction: A Peasant Millennium

1. Raymond Williams, *The Country and the City* (New York, 1973), treats pertinent English literary work.

2. Barrington Moore, *Social Origins of Dictatorship and Democracy* (Boston, 1966), especially pp. 463-83. Eric Wolf, *Peasant Wars of the Twentieth Century* (New York, 1969), pp. 276-302.

3. For two recent elaborations of the arguments presented by Barrington Moore and Eric Wolf, see James C. Scott, *The Moral Economy of the Peasant* (New Haven, 1976), and Ralph Thaxton, *China turned Rightside Up* (New Haven, 1983).

4. Fernand Braudel, *Capitalism and Material Life, 1400-1800* (New York, 1967), takes this point of departure, and quotes Karl Marx to add force (p. 373): "The contrast between town and country begins with the transition between barbarism and civilization, from the tribal regime to the state, from the individual locality to the nation, and recurs in all history until our own days." Philip Abrams, "Towns and Economic Growth: Some Theories and Problems," in Abrams and Wrigley, eds., *Towns in Societies* (Cambridge, 1978), pp. 9-33, criticizes this approach from the perspective of urban history.

5. Immanuel Wallerstein, *The Modern World System*, I, *Capitalist Agriculture and the Origins of the European World-Economy in the Sixteenth Century* (New York, 1974), pursues this idea to its logical extreme. E. P. Thompson, *The Making of the English Working Class* (New York, 1963), p. 405, puts it in perspective: "The Industrial Revolution, which drained the countryside of some of its industries and destroyed the balance between rural and urban life, created also in our own minds an image of rural isolation and 'idiocy.'"

6. This line of reasoning underlies the interdisciplinary field of peasant studies, which now boasts two journals, *Peasant Studies* and the *Journal of Peasant Studies*. For a useful survey of prominent ideas, see Sydel Silverman, "The Peasant Concept in Anthropology," *JPS*, 7:1 (1979), 49-69.

7. This line of thought guides area studies, whose dominant ideas find clear exposition in Marshall Sahlins, *Culture and Practical Reason* (Chicago, 1976). David Ludden, "Productive Power in Agriculture," in Desai, Rudolph, and Rudra, eds., *Agrarian Power and Agricultural Productivity in South Asia*, Bombay, 1984, pp. 51-99, surveys work on South Asian peasant history published before 1980.

8. Eric L. Jones, *Agriculture and the Industrial Revolution* (Oxford, 1974); see also J. D. Chambers and G. E. Mingay, *The Agricultural Revolution, 1750-1880* (New York), 1966; William Parker and Eric L. Jones, eds., *Eu-*

ropean Peasants and Their Markets: Essays in Agrarian Economic History (Princeton, 1975); and Cicely Howell, "Stability and Change 1300-1700," *JPS*, 2:2 (1975), 468-82, which exemplify this effort.

9. Eric Wolf, *Europe and the People without History* (Berkeley and Los Angeles, 1982).

10. Recently, some effort has gone to showing that Indian peasants did revolt when confronted with imperialist and capitalist assaults, contrary to Moore, *Social Origins*, pp. 314-412. See A. R. Desai, ed., *Peasant Struggles in India* (Bombay, 1979); D. N. Dhanagare, *Peasant Movements in India, 1920-1950* (Delhi, 1983); and Kathleen Gough, "Peasant Resistance and Revolt in South India," *PA*, 41 (1968-1969), 526-44. For Marx on India, see Shlomo Avineri, ed., *Karl Marx on Colonialism and Modernization* (Garden City, 1969), pp. 88-95, 99-108, 132-39.

11. Max Weber, *The Religion of India* (New York, 1958), especially pp. 329-43; Louis Dumont, *Homo Hierarchicus* (Chicago, 1970), pp. 1-20.

12. The Tirunelveli region today includes the Tirunelveli District of Tamil Nadu and western taluks of Ramanathapuram District, called Srivilliputtur and Sattur taluks when Ramanathapuram District was created in 1911. During the nineteenth century, the region was called Tinnevelly District. Throughout this book, I refer to the region and to its largest town as Tirunelveli.

13. Burton Stein, "Integration of the Agrarian System of South India," in Frykenberg, ed., *Land Control and Social Structure in Indian History* (Madison, 1969), pp. 175-216, laid groundwork for research on this line. For case studies that pursue it, see Arjun Appadurai, *Worship and Conflict under Colonial Rule* (New York, 1981); Carol A. Breckenridge, "The Sri Minakshi Sundaresvaran Temple," Ph.D. dissertation, Wisconsin, 1976; Nicholas B. Dirks, "Little Kingdoms of South India," Ph.D. dissertation, Chicago, 1981; and Pamela G. Price, "Resources and Rule in Zamindari South India, 1802-1903," Ph.D. dissertation, Wisconsin, 1979.

14. See Kathleen Gough, *Rural Society in Southeast India* (Cambridge, 1981), and John Harriss, *Capitalism and Peasant Farming* (Bombay, 1982), which consider villages in Tanjavur and Chengalpattu, respectively.

15. Charles Metcalfe penned the most famous lines about village India: "The village communities are little republics, having nearly everything they want within themselves, and almost independent of any foreign relations. They seem to last where nothing else lasts. Dynasty after dynasty tumbles down; revolution succeeds to revolution; Hindoo, Patan, Mogul, Mahratta, Sik, English are all masters in turn; but the village communities remain the same." Great Britain, Parliament, *Parliamentary Papers* (House of Commons), 1830-1831, vol. XI, "Report from the Select Committee on the Affairs of the East India Company," Appendix 84, "Minute of Charles Metcalfe," 7 November 1830, p. 331. For the history of this view, see Clive Dewey, "Images of the Village Community," *MAS*, 6:3 (1972), 291-328.

16. See Frank Perlin, "Of White Whale and Countrymen in the Eighteenth Century Maratha Deccan," *JPS*, 5:2 (1978), 172-237; Rajat and Ratnalekha

Ray, "The Dynamics of Continuity in Rural Bengal under the British Imperium," *IESHR*, 10:2 (1973), 103-29; and Ratnalekha Ray, *Change in Bengal Agrarian Society, 1760-1850* (Delhi, 1979).

17. See Frank Perlin, "Precolonial South Asia and Western Penetration in the 17th-19th Centuries," *Rev*, 4:2 (1980), 267-306.

18. See Eric Stokes, "The First Century of British Colonial Rule: Social Revolution or Social Stagnation," and "Dynamism and Enervation in North Indian Agriculture: The Historical Dimension," in Eric Stokes, *The Peasant and the Raj* (Cambridge, 1978), pp. 19-45, 228-42; Ludden, "Productive Power in Agriculture," pp. 62-82. For Eurasian trends, see Eric L. Jones, *The European Miracle* (Cambridge, 1981); Marshall Hodgson, *The Venture of Islam* (Chicago, 1974); William McNeill, *The Rise of the West* (Chicago, 1963); L. S. Stavrianos, *Global Rift* (New York, 1981); Wolf, *Europe and the People without History*.

19. See K. A. Nilakanta Sastri, *Sources of Indian History with Special Reference to South India* (Bombay, 1964).

20. See Noburu Karashima, "A Bibliography of South Indian Epigraphy," *JAAS*, 6 (1973), 1512-63; and Burton Stein's bibliography in his *Peasant State and Society in Medieval South India* (Delhi, 1980).

21. Daniel Thorner, "Peasantry," in Sills, ed., *International Encyclopedia of Social Science* (New York, 1968), 11: 503-11; Daniel Thorner, "Peasant Economy as a Category in Economic History," and Robert Redfield and Milton Singer, "City and Countryside," in Shanin, ed., *Peasants and Peasant Societies* (Harmondsworth, 1971), pp. 202-18, 337-66.

22. Sidney Mintz, "A Note on the Definition of Peasants," *JPS*, 1:1 (1973), 91-100; Teodor Shanin, "The Nature and Logic of Peasant Economy," *JPS*, 1:1 (1973), 63-80; Harriett Friedman, "Household Production and the National Economy," *JPS*, 7:2 (1980), 158-84; Rodney Hilton, "Reasons for Inequality among Medieval Peasants," *JPS*, 5:3 (1978), 271-84.

23. The notion that labor "humanizes the land" comes from Walter Rodney, *A History of the Guyanese Working People, 1881-1905* (Baltimore, 1981), pp. 1-59. See also Colin McEvedy and Richard Jones, *Atlas of World Population History* (Harmondsworth, 1978), pp. 343-51.

24. Bernard Cohn and McKim Marriott, "Networks and Centers in the Integration of Indian Civilization," *Journal of Social Research* (Ranchi), 1:1 (1958), 1-9; David Mandelbaum, *Society in India* (Berkeley and Los Angeles, 1970). See also Carol A. Smith, *Regional Analysis* (New York, 1976).

25. Henri Pirenne, *Mohamet et Charlemagne*, p. 219, quoted in C. R. Whittaker, "Late Roman Trade and Traders," in Garnsey, Hopkins, and Whittaker, eds., *Trade in the Ancient Economy* (Berkeley and Los Angeles, 1983), p. 163.

26. Irawati Karve, *Hindu Society—An Interpretation* (Poona, 1968); Pauline Kolenda, *Caste in Contemporary India* (Menlo Park, N.J., 1978).

27. *Capitalism and Material Life*, pp. 373-74.

Chapter 1: Sanctified Places

1. K. Kailasapathy, *Tamil Heroic Poetry* (London, 1968).

2. According to M. N. Srinivas, in peninsular India, "preference for marriage with certain near relatives such as cross cousin and cross niece (a man's elder sister's daughter) has a limiting effect on the social space of the peasant. Such relatives often live in the same or nearby village. The village is not an exogamous unit. Preference for marriage with certain relatives tends to multiply the bonds one has with the same body or bodies of people." M. N. Srinivas, ed., *India's Villages* (Bombay, 1955), p. 12. For an account of social situations described in Sangam poetry, see David Ludden and M. S. Pillai, *The Kuruntokai* (Madurai, 1976), pp. 1-37.

3. See George L. Hart, III, *Poets of the Tamil Anthologies* (Princeton, 1979), and V. S. Rajam, *"Anangu," JAOS*, forthcoming.

4. *Manimekalai*, edited by Ventakasami Nattar and Turaisami Pillai (Tirunelveli, 1946), chapters 8, 21, and 23. My study and translation of this text were funded by a grant from the National Endowment for the Humanities.

5. O.H.K. Spate and A.T.A. Learmonth, *India and Pakistan* (London, 1967), pp. 47-49; R. Ramamurthy, "A Study of a Hundred Years' Rainfall at Madras City," *IGJ*, 43 (December 1968-January 1969), 49-57; F. Blasco and P. Legris, "Originalité des climats secs du sud de l'Inde," *AG*, 82:450 (1973), 129-50; Emmanuel Adiceam, *La Géographie de l'irrigation dans le Tamilnad* (Paris, 1966), pp. 42-98; Jasbir Singh, *An Agricultural Atlas of India* (Kurukshetra, 1974).

6. *Statistical Atlas of Madras Presidency, Fasli 1350 (1940/41)* (Madras, 1941); *Statistical Atlas of Madras Presidency, Fasli 1360 (1950/51)* (Madras, 1951); A. J. Stuart, *A Manual of the Tinnevelly District* (Madras, 1879), Appendices No. 56, 57; *Madras District Gazetteers: Tinnevelly*, by H. R. Pate (Madras, 1917) (hereafter cited as Pate, *Gazetteer*), chapter 1 and p. 251; *Madras District Gazetteers: Tinnevelly. Statistical Abstract* (Madras, 1934), pp. 28-29, 97-98. On rainfall reliability, see *Census of India, 1961*, vol. 9, part 9.

7. David Ludden, "Patronage and Irrigation in Tamil Nadu: A Long-Term View," *IESHR*, 16:3 (1979), 347-65, gives an overview.

8. Jack Goody, *Cooking, Cuisine, and Class* (Cambridge, 1982), considers the social implications of high cuisine. In India, the elements of high cuisine have ecological and technological moorings.

9. Clarence Maloney, "Archaeology in South India: Accomplishments and Prospects," in Stein, ed., *Essays on South India*, p. 3.

10. S. Singaravelu, *Social Life of the Tamils* (Kuala Lumpur, 1966), p. 43; Maloney, "Archaeology in South India," p. 33; Lawrence S. Leshnik, *South Indian "Megalithic" Burials* (Weisbaden, 1974), pp. 1, 8, 59-72.

11. Joseph E. Schwartzberg, ed., *Historical Atlas of South Asia* (Chicago, 1978), p. 24.

12.   J. T. Kearns, "The Cairns of Tinnevelly," *Madras Journal of Literature and Science*, 21 (1859), 27-29.

13.   Good bibliographies of inscriptional material are in Karashima, "A Bibliography of South Indian Epigraphy," and Stein, *Peasant State*.

14.   Romila Thapar, *A History of India*, vol. 1 (Harmondsworth, 1966), p. 171.

15.   Ludden, "Patronage and Irrigation," p. 354.

16.   Similar uses of inscriptional data appear in Stein, *Peasant State*, chapter 4; Y. Subbarayulu, *Political Geography of the Chola Country* (Madras, 1973); and Brian Murton, "Some Propositions on the Spread of Village Settlement in Interior Tamil Nadu before 1750 A.D.," *IGJ*, 48:2 (1973), 56-72. Table 1 and my discussion of caste concentrations in 1881 are based on data in *Census of India, 1881. Tinnevelly District Taluk Tables* (Madras, 1883), summarized in David Ludden, "Agrarian Organization in Tinnevelly District, 800-1900 A.D.," Ph.D. dissertation, Pennsylvania, 1978, pp. 380-83.

17.   Revenue Department, "Census and Dehazada of the Province of Tirunelvelie," Sundries, No. 39, TNA (hereafter cited as "1823 Census"). This manuscript census, compiled during the introduction of the ryotwari system (see below, Chapter Four) is misdated in the TNA catalogue.

18.   See Chapter Two, below, for the post-1300 creation of the mixed and dry agricultural zones. I have calculated the "index of concentration" for each caste group from data in 1881 *Census of India*, taluk tables, by adding the absolute values of differences between the percent of each group in each taluk and the total population of each taluk. The index thus measures the degree to which a jati group is distributed differently from the population as a whole. A jati distributed in 1881 exactly as was the total population would have an index of zero. The index used here is derived from that used in Surinder Mehta, "Patterns of Residence in Poona (India) by Income, Education and Occupation (1937-1965)," *AJS*, 73 (1968), 496-508.

19.   Edgar Thurston, *Castes and Tribes of Southern India* (Madras, 1909), 6: 1-28, 77-119.

20.   K. A. Nilakanta Sastri, *The Pandyan Kingdom* (Madras, 1972), pp. 47, 50, 58, 74. Burton Stein, "Coromandel Trade in Medieval India," in Parker, ed., *Merchants and Scholars*, pp. 47-62, and "The State and the Agrarian Order in Medieval South India" in Stein, ed., *Essays on South India*, pp. 64-91; N. Subrahmanian, *The History of Tamilnad (to A.D. 1336)* (Madurai, 1972), p. 81; Thurston, *Castes and Tribes*, 6: 361-89.

21.   *SII*, vol. 5, inscription no. 446 (citations to inscriptions in this series hereafter appear in this form: *SII*, 5: 446) shows an example of the formula used in inscriptions to announce that a king "sits on the throne." The "Five Pandyas" occur in epigraphy whenever sovereignty is in doubt, indicating that a multiplicity of claimants to the throne are contending for legitimacy. See Nilakanta Sastri, *Pandyan Kingdom*.

22.   Nilakanta Sastri, *Pandyan Kingdom*, p. 112. *ARE*, 1916/17: no. 433

(citations to stone inscriptions in this series appear hereafter in this form: *ARE*, 1916/17: 433). *SII*, 14: 240.

23. For peninsular politics, see K. A. Nilakanta Sastri, *A History of South India* (Oxford, 1955). Under the Cholas and Vijayanagar, Pandyas continued to sit on the Madurai throne; see Chapter Two.

24. A. C. Burnell, *Elements of South Indian Paleontography* (London, 1878), p. 94, cited in A. Appadorai, *Economic Conditions in Southern India (1000 to 1500 A.D.)* (Madras, 1936), 1: 25-26; Nicholas B. Dirks, "Political Authority and Structural Change in Early South Indian History," *IESHR*, 13:2 (1976), 125-58.

25. *Tamil Lexicon* (Madras, 1934-1936), 1: 512 and 3: 1360.

26. *ARE*, 1929/30: Part II, p. 73; *ARE*, 1923/4: 217; *SII*, 14: 16A, 43, 44; K. V. Subrahmanya Aiyer, "Tiruchendur Inscription of Varaguna Maharaja II," *EI*, 21, 3 (July 1931), 101-15.

27. A. S. Ramanatha Ayyar, "Four Pandya Records from Ukkirankottai," *EI*, 23 (July 1936), 7-9; *SII*, 14: pp. ii-iii.

28. For examples of such titles as place-specific, see *SII*, 14: 40-41, 44, 157, 161, 194; and *ARE*, 1965/6: 285.

29. *SII*, 14: 4, 16A, 17, 40, 41, 43, 44, 91, 93, 96.

30. *SII*, 14: 43, 44.

31. *SII*, 14: 4, 16A, 40, 41, 91, 93.

32. *SII*, 14: 157.

33. See *SII*, 5: 419, 421, 451, for chiefs at work on their own account. *SII*, 14: 157, 161, and 194 are good examples of Chola-period grants, where officers of supervisor (*kankani*), protector (*nayaka*), and accountant (*kanakkan*) are specified.

34. *SII*, 14: 145, 226, 231. K. A. Nilakanta Sastri, *The Cholas* (Madras, 1955), p. 455.

35. *SII*, 14: 231; *ARE*, 1929/30: 340; *ARE*, 1965/6: 285. For a general discussion, see Appadorai, *Economic Conditions*, pp. 194-221.

36. *SII*, 14: 56, 61; *ARE*, 1916/17: 482, 524.

37. See Arjun Appadurai and Carol A. Breckenridge, "The South Indian Temple," *CIS*, NS 10:2 (1976), 187-209.

38. *ARE*, 1926/7: 587, and Part II, pp. 97-98.

39. *Census of India,* 1961, vol. 9, Part 11-D, "Temples of Madras State." For a full discussion of this data, see Burton Stein, "Temples in the Tamil Country, 1300-1750 A.D.," *IESHR*, 14:1 (1977), 11-46. Ludden, "Agrarian Organization," pp. 146-47 presents temple statistics for the Tirunelveli region.

40. T.K.T. Viraraghavacharya, "The Srivilliputtur Temple of Sudikkodutta Nachchiyar," *Tirupati-Tirumalai Devasthanam Monthly Bulletin,* 6 (1955), Nos. 3-11.

41. Ibid., pp. 2, 4.

42. David Shulman, *Tamil Temple Myths* (Princeton, 1980); Kamil Zvelibil, *The Smile of Murugan* (Leiden, 1973), p. 190.

43. The renowned "Nanadesittisai 1500" guild made a grant at Amba-

samudram, recorded in *SII*, 14: 146. See Stein, "Integration of the Agrarian System," for a discussion of guilds and their grants.

44. Appadorai, *Economic Conditions*, pp. 274-301. Burton Stein, "Economic Functions of the Medieval South Indian Temple," *JAS*, 19:2 (1960), 163-76; George W. Spencer, "Temple Moneylending and Livestock Redistribution in Early Tanjore," *IESHR*, 5:3 (1966), 277-93. The most detailed account of activity in a Tirunelveli region temple is R. Tirumalai, *Rajendra Vinnagar* (Madras, 1980). For much more detailed discussion of transactions surrounding temples and for an intensive treatment of local rights in the Chola country, see E. James Heitzman, "Gifts of Power: Temples, Politics, and Economy in Medieval South India." Ph.D. dissertation, University of Pennsylvania, 1985.

45. *ARE*, 1926/7: 52; *SII*, 14: 18.

46. *SII*, 14: 13, 16A.

47. *TLI*, vol. 3, pp. 1453-56, Nos. 80-81, 85f., 88-90 (citations to inscriptions in this series hereafter appear in this form: *TLI*, 3, 1453-56: 80-81, 85f., 88-90). See also *SII*, 14: 144-45, 148.

48. *ARE*, 1928/9: 21, and Part II, pp. 70-71; Nilakanta Sastri, *The Cholas*, pp. 541-42.

49. Appadorai, *Economic Conditions*, pp. 195-96, 215-19; *TLI*, 3, 1495: 449.

50. *SII*, 14: 191.

51. *ARE*, 1928/9: 21, and Part II, pp. 70-71. This is an inscription from Tiruppattur in Madurai District.

52. Eleven of sixteen localities listed in *SII*, 14: 16A, the Tiruchendur grant, were brahmadeyas, four were non-Brahman villages (*ur*), and one was a *pattinam*, a town.

53. Nilakanta Sastri, *The Cholas*, pp. 489ff.

54. *SII*, 14: 132; *TLI*, 3, 1449: 52; *SII*, 14: 67.

55. *TLI*, 3, 1457-58: 100-104. Tirumalai, *Rajendra Vinnagar*, p. 10, depicts the sabha's central role in managing the temple from its beginning, in Mannarkoil, a village in Rajamangalam (see below, note 72).

56. Subbarayulu, *Political Geography of the Chola Country*, pp. 56-57, establishes the "ethnic zone" argument that Stein develops in *Peasant State*, chapter 3.

57. See *SII*, 14: 44, 157, for examples.

58. Nilakanta Sastri, *The Cholas*, pp. 503-507; *ARE*, 1940/1: 34; *ARE*, 1929/30: 432, 451, 457-60, 462, 466.

59. See Appadorai, *Economic Conditions*, chapter 2, Parts 1, 5, 8, and 9, for a general discussion.

60. See *ARE*, 1916/17: 399, 405, for examples.

61. *SII*, 14: 424, 16A; *ARE*, 1916/17: 399, 402, 405; *ARE*, 1963/4: 304; *ARE*, 1932/3: 210.

62. Nilakanta Sastri, *Pandyan Kingdom*, pp. 35-36, 82-83, and "The Manur Inscription of Maranjadaiyan," *EI*, 22 (January 1933), 5-11. See also

SII, 14: 13, 16A, and p. i. The estimate of six dozen brahmadeyas includes subordinate brahmadeyas (see below and note 66) and is, like the whole of the discussion here, based solely on published inscriptional evidence. Much evidence remains unpublished.

63. K. V. Subrahmanya Aiyer, "Tinnevelly Inscription of Maravarma Sundara-Pandya II," *EI*, 22:1 (1933) 39-48; *TAS*, v. 1, pt. 6 (1911), pp. 61-88, 89-94, 106-14, 133-46; T. A. Gopinatha Rao, "The Krishapuram Plates of Sadasivaraya, Saka Samvat 1489," *EI*, 9 (1907-1908), 328-41; H. Krishna Sastri, "The Kuniyur Plates of the Time of Vengata II: Saka Samvat 1556," *EI*, 3 (1894-1895), 236-58.

64. Stein, *Peasant State*, chapter 4, which is also the basis of the following paragraph.

65. Nilakanta Sastri, *The Cholas*, pp. 492-93; Appadorai, *Economic Conditions*, pp. 113-15. Such payments seem implicit in most, if not all, *vellan vekai* records, such as *ARE*, 1916/17: 327, and *SII*, 14: 145, 160-61. Nilakanta Sastri, *The Cholas*, pp. 571-74, has a different interpretation.

66. *ARE*, 1916/17: 288-89, 564, 569, 571; *ARE*, 1929/30: 387-89, 393-435. Rajarajachaturvedimangalam (Rajamangalam) included the following villages: Kaderu (Alvar Kurichi) (*TLI*, 3, 1446-47: 30-35), Kallidaikurichi (*TLI*, 3, 1449: 52), Pappankulam (*TLI*, 3, 1455: 86), Tiruvalisvaram (*TLI*, 3, 1461: 30, and *SII*, 14: 170), Attanallur (*ARE*, 1916/17: 433), Pallakal (*ARE*, 1916/17: 288-89), Mannarkoil (*SII*, 14: 132; see also Tirumalai, *Rajendra Vinnagar*), and Iluppaikurichi (*ARE*, 1918/19: Appendix A, No. 1). These inscriptions date from different periods. Villages included under an extended brahmadeya in one century could be excluded in the next. See, for instance, the Attur brahmadeya inscriptions listed first in this note. The inscriptions from Mannarkoil, discussed in Tirumalai, *Rajendra Vinnagar*, suggest that Rajamangalam expanded over the course of later Pandya centuries. In 1477, it included sixteen urs, each with several hamlets (for example, Iluppaikurichi had six: *ARE*, 1916/17: 311).

67. *ARE*, 1916/17: 456-60, 524-25, 402; *ARE*, 1932/3: 229, 241.

68. *ARE*, 1916/17: 619, 700; *SII*, 14: 153, 157. Similar examples: *SII*, 14: 145, 160-61, 164, 194, 295.

69. Nilakanta Sastri, *The Cholas*, pp. 455, 595-96; *ARE*, 1916/17: 433; *TLI*, 3, 1453-56; *SII*, 14: 56, 81, 95, 146, 154, 245. See Tirumalai, *Rajendra Vinnagar*. That Mullinadu defined an area of central transactional importance for Cholas, and perhaps an area of Chola migratory colonization, is suggested by the fact that seven of every ten inscriptions from Chola times in *SII*, 14: 68-112 are from that nadu. The Cholas stationed one of their garrisons in Mullinadu (Nilakanta Sastri, *The Cholas*, p. 455). *SII*, 14: 167 shows another garrison at Attur. The eastern and western ends of the Tambraparni River valley thus seem to have been the key points on the Chola map of the Tirunelveli region. The central valley rose to importance after the Chola decline (see Chapter Two).

70. For the notion of symbolic capital, see Pierre Bourdieu, *Outline of a Theory of Practice* (Cambridge, 1977).

CHAPTER 2: FARMING FRONTIERS

1. *Census of India*, 1961, vol. 9, part 11-D, p. 242.

2. See *SII*, 5: 410-11, 431, 448, for examples.

3. Nellaiyappakoil inscriptions are summarized in *ARE*, 1894: 118-63; *ARE*, 1926/7: 42-87; and *TLI*, 3, 466-512; many have been published in *SII*, 5: 407-55.

4. Pate, *Gazetteer*, pp. 171-72; S. Kurukuhudasa Pillai, *Tirunelveli Cimai Carittiram* (Ettaiyapuram, 1931), p. 16; Ludden, "Patronage and Irrigation," p. 355; T. A. Gopinatha Rao, "The Krishnapuram Plates," p. 341. On Marudur, see below, Chapters Four and Five.

5. The number of inscriptions for each nadu recording transactions that brought supplies regularly into the Nellaiyappa temple are as follows: Kilvembanadu, 36; Melvembanadu, 12; Mullinadu, 7; Kilkalakurram 3; Amitagunavalanadu, 3; Murappanadu, 3; Asurnadu, 1; Anmanadu, 1; Ariyanadu, 1; Kallaganadu, 1; see citations in note 3 above. Inscriptions also show flows of supplies into the temple from parts of Pandyamandalam outside the Tirunelveli region. See note 3, above.

6. *ARE*, 1916/17: 311.

7. *TAS*, vol. 1, No. 6, pp. 99-100; *ARE*, 1916/17: 325 and Part II, p. 134.

8. George W. Spencer, "Religious Networks and Royal Influence in Eleventh Century South India," *JESHO*, 12: 1 (1969), 42-56, and "Royal Initiative under Rajaraja I," *IESHR*, 7:4 (1970), 431-42; Nilakanta Sastri, *The Cholas*, pp. 455 ff.; Stein, *Peasant State*, chapter 6.

9. S. Krishnasvami Aiyangar, *South India and Her Muhammadan Invaders* (Oxford, 1921), p. 157.

10. *TAS*, vol. 1, No. 6, pp. 43-44, 52, 61-88, 89-94, 106-14, 133-46.

11. Viraraghavacharya, "The Srivilliputtur Temple."

12. Maravas did not only do battle with Pandyas; for hints of Pandya-Marava alliances and other details of this period, see *ARE*, 1940/1: 300-309; Nilakanta Sastri, *Pandyan Kingdom*, pp. 214-25; S.A.Q. Husaini, *The History of the Pandya Country* (Karaikudi, n.d.), pp. 136-42; A. Sreedhara Menon, *A Survey History of Kerala* (Kottayam, 1967), pp. 234-42; and V. Rangacharya, "The History of the Naik Kingdom of Madurai, *IA*, 43 (September 1914), pp. 189-91.

13. Appadorai, *Economic Conditions*, 2: 552-59; Simon Digby, *War-horse and Elephant in the Delhi Sultanate* (Karachi, 1971), pp. 48-49, 61, 69-70.

14. *TAS*, vol. 1, No. 6, p. 62. The following provide glimpses of military history in this period: Appadorai, *Economic Conditions*, 1, chapter 9; Digby, *War-horse and Elephant*; Adam Watson, *The War of the Goldsmith's Daugh-*

ter (London, 1964); and Jagdish Narayan Sarkar, *Some Aspects of Military Thinking and Practice: Medieval India* (Calcutta, 1974).

15.   On professionalization of warfare as a counterpart of technological change, see Kieth Otterbein, *The Evolution of War* (Washington, D.C.: 1970).

16.   A. Krishnaswami, *The Tamil Country under Vijayanagar* (Annamalainagar, 1964), pp. 82-106.

17.   Stein points to the broad militarization of the agrarian system in "Integration of the Agrarian System," and in *Peasant State*, chapter 8.

18.   This interpretation was suggested to me by Arjun Appadurai and Carol A. Breckenridge.

19.   B. A. Saletore, "The Stanikas and Their Historical Importance," *Journal of the University of Bombay*, 7:1 (1938), 29-93.

20.   *ARE*, 1917/18: 718. Saletore cites more extreme examples of the influence of military men in his *Social and Political Life in the Vijayanagar Empire (A.D. 1346-A.D. 1646)* (Madras, 1934), 1: 183-88.

21.   *ARE*, 1935/6: 202; *ARE*, 1916/17: 602-606.

22.   Viraraghavacharya, "The Srivilliputtur Temple."

23.   Most Tamil Muslims are called "Lubbais" in British-period census records. They are said to be Tamil converts: Thurston, *Castes and Tribes*, 6: 198-205; Pate, *Gazetteer*; and *Census of India*, 1921, *Madras*, vol. 6, Part 2, pp. 27-29. Lubbais were 60 percent of the Tinnevelly District Muslim population in 1871: A. J. Stuart, *A Manual of the Tinnevelly District* (Madras, 1876), p. 164. The remainder of the region's Muslims were presumably of Arab extraction in port towns such as Kayalpatnam, and of Indian Muslim extraction from the north. Except for the Kayalpatnam Muslims, who migrated to the region by sea during the later Pandya period, we can assume that the rest of the region's Muslims would have histories of migration dating back to the seventeenth century or later.

24.   Pate, *Gazetteer*, pp. 205, 220-26; Robert Caldwell, *The Tinnevelly Shanars* (Madras, 1850), pp. 2-3, and *Lectures on the Tinnevelly Missions, Descriptive of the Field, the Work and the Results* (London, 1878); Robert Hardgrave, *The Nadars of Tamilnad* (Berkeley and Los Angeles, 1969).

25.   Robert Caldwell, *Records of the Early History of the Tinnevelly Mission* (Madras, 1881), p. 295; Hardgrave, *Nadars*, pp. 19-21.

26.   The earliest known record of Nadar transactions dates from the sixteenth century: *ARE*, 1940/1: 271. See also *ARE*, 1963/4: 306.

27.   *ARE*, 1917/18: 235, and Part II, p. 134.

28.   J. Hepburn, "Settlement Report," 17 October 1807, TCR,TNA, vol. 3582, 1807, p. 290. See also PBR,TNA, vol. 435, pp. 8501-30; and *Papers Relating to the Revenue Settlement of Tinnevelly*, TCR,TNA, pp. 83-97.

29. Shanars and Pariahs both show dramatic increases, which may be the result of repopulation following the famines of 1811-1813 and 1831-1833, or may be byproducts of census procedures if, for example, the census counts in the southwest were taken during times of seasonal immigration by Shanars to tap palmyra trees. See note 33 below.

30. Pate, *Gazetteer*, pp. 371-74.

31. The "six towns" are Sivakasi, Virudhunagar, Tirumangalam, Sattangudi, Palayampatti, and Aruppukkottai, all today in Ramanathapuram and Madurai districts. Sivakasi and Virudhunagar were in Tinnevelly District before 1911. Hardgrave, *Nadars*, pp. 95-97.

32. *ARE*, 1960/1: Copper Plates Nos. 27-28.

33. Thomas Turnbull, "Geographical and Statistical Memoir of Tinneveli and Its Zamindars," c. 1824, Revenue Department Sundries, No. 38, TNA, quoted in Hardgrave, *Nadars*, p. 98. Shanars as a percent of total taluk populations, in 1823 and 1881:

Taluk	1823	1881
Shankarankoil	5	7
Sattur + Srivilliputtur	11	14
Ottapidaram	na	10
Tenkasi	20	17
Nanguneri	3	20

Sources: "1823 Census" and 1881 *Census*, taluk tables.

34. Pate, *Gazetteer*, p. 338.

35. S. Kathirvel, "History of the Maravas, 1700-1801," Ph.D. dissertation, Madras, 1971, p. 26. Also see T. V. Mahalingam, *Mackenzie Manuscripts*, vol. 1 (Madras, 1972), pp. 236, 239, "Marava Jati Kaifiyat."

36. Mahalingam, *Mackenzie Manuscripts*, pp. 133-34, and, for similar accounts, pp. 129, 134, 161-62, 167-70. See also T. Chandrasekharan, *A Descriptive Catalogue of the Tamil Manuscripts in the Government Oriental Manuscripts Library, Madras*, vol. 9 (Madras, 1954), pp. 2942-43; and William Taylor, "Marava Jathi Vernanam," *Madras Journal of Literature and Science*, 4 (1836), 357-60.

37. Chandrasekharan, *Descriptive Catalogue*, pp. 2946-47. W. E. Ganapathi Pillai, *Ettaiyapuram Past and Present* (Madras, 1890), pp. 16-17; Pate, *Gazetteer*, pp. 374-75; National Archives of India, *National Register of Private Records*, No. 5, "Descriptive List of Documents Available in Bihar, Kerala, Madhya Pradesh, Punjab, Tamil Nadu, Uttar Pradesh, and the National Archives of India, New Delhi" (based on information received for 1963-1964) (New Delhi, 1973), pp. 190-92; Nicholas B. Dirks, "The Pasts of a Palaiyakarar," *JAS*, 41: 4 (1982), 655-83.

38. Kathirvel, "History of the Maravas," chapter 1; K. Rajayyan, *History of Madurai, 1736-1801* (Madurai, 1974); Louis Dumont, *Hierarchy and Marriage Alliance in South Indian Kinship* (London, 1957), pp. 17-18.

39. Rangacharya, "History of the Naik Kingdom of Madurai," *IA*, 43 (June 1914), 113-14. Telugu migrant bands should be considered as town-sized versions of the "moving cities" that were Vijayanagar armies, for which see Robert Sewell, *The Forgotten Empire* (London, 1924), pp. 332-34; Watson, *War of the Goldsmith's Daughter*; and especially Saletore, *Social and Political Life*, 1: 450-57.

40. Ganapathi Pillai, *Ettaiyapuram Past and Present*, pp. 17-24.

41. Stein makes this suggestion in *Peasant State*, chapter 8, citing "Some Suggestions for Madras Ryots" (by a special correspondent to the *Madras Mail*, 1906), p. 2.

42. Saletore, *Social and Political Life*, vol. 2, chapter 3.

43. "General Sketch of the History of the Southern Divisions of the Peninsula from the Commencement of Calleeyoogam to the Present Age" (Collected at Pavur in Tenkasi Taluk in Tirunelveli from the traditionary information of Aulabala Sastry and Yamen Achari—1801), IOL, Map Room MS No. 8.

44. Its data flawed by the exclusion of a large part of the Telugu tract (Ettaiyapuram zamindari), the "1823 Census" shows 2,490 of the district's 4,921 enumerated Telugu Smarta Brahmans living in the wet zone. No comparable breakdown of the regional population exists for 1881 (when, according to the 1881 census taluk tables, only 3 percent of the district's total Telugu population lived in the wet zone) or for later periods.

45. Ludden, "Patronage and Irrigation," pp. 353-57.

46. Statements showing numbers of tanks appear in Jamabandy Reports, Public Works proceedings, and in reports such as *List of Special and Other Works of Irrigation Performed in the Madras Presidency from 1836 to 1849* (Madras, 1852).

47. David Ludden, "Ecological Zones and the Cultural Economy of Irrigation in Southern Tamiladu," *SA*, NS 1:1 (1978), 1-13, presents an overview of the process of regional agricultural differentiation.

48. On soil types, see Spate and Learmonth, *India and Pakistan*, pp. 775-78; Stuart, *Manual*; and Pate, *Gazetteer*. See also S. P. Raychaudhuri, *Soils of India* (New Delhi, 1963); *Black Soils of India* (New Delhi, 1963); and "Classification of Soils in India," *International Geography Congress, 21st Meeting, Delhi, 1968, Selected Papers* (Delhi, 1968), 1: 450-80. For a graphic description of the sandy southeast, see Caldwell, *Lectures on the Tinnevelly Missions*, pp. 50-51.

49. Gathered during survey and settlement operations in 1876 (see Chapter Four), the cropping data in Stuart, *Manual*, pp. 168-77, are the most detailed for any one year in the nineteenth century. For statistics and computations behind Map 7, see Ludden, "Agrarian Organization," pp. 395-97. Concentrations are calculated for crops as for population (see Chapter One, note 18) by subtracting the percent of district cultivated acreage under each crop for one taluk from the percent of total cropped acreage for that taluk. For example, by this measure, Ambasamudram taluk had considerably more single- and double-cropped paddy acreage than its share of total cropped acreage in the district, but much less kambu, showing index values of $+16$, $+26$, and -6, respectively. Comparable values for the dry taluk of Ottapidaram were -25, -26, and $+29$. See Map 5 for taluk boundaries.

50. Half of 1 percent of Tinnevelly District rice in 1876 was grown on unirrigated land. To measure water depths in order to gauge supplies in the tank, builders sank stone pillars into the tank bed that are still visible and in

use. For aggregate patterns of irrigation and cropping, showing the intimate connections between rice and water control, see Emmanuel Adiceam, *La géographie de l'irrigation dans le Tamilnadu* (Paris, 1966), pp. 99-110, and M. N. Vasantha Devi, "Some Aspects of the Agricultural Geography of South India," *IGJ*, 39:1-2 (1964), 1-41; 39:3-4 (1964), 59-122.

51. For more detail, see Stuart, *Manual*, and Pate, *Gazetteer*, upon which this account is based. Good accounts of semi-arid agriculture include S. M. Shah, "Cropping Pattern in Relation to Irrigation," *IJAE*, 18 (January 1963), 154-60; C.W.B. Zacharias, *Madras Agriculture* (Madras, 1950); N. V. Kanitkar, *Dry Farming in India* (New Delhi, 1960); and P. A. Venkateswaran, *Agriculture in South India* (New Delhi, 1961).

52. British officials recognized these zones implicitly, and their accounts suggest that their native informants, most importantly revenue officials, divided the region on lines similar to my agricultural zones. See James Hepburn, *Collector's Report on the Decennial Lease*, 1812, TCR,TNA. Noazech Ahmed uses the idea of "ecological zones" in *The Development of Agriculture in Bangladesh* (Dacca, 1976), pp. 34-47. On the possibility that such zone designations may provide useful means for comparative generalization in agrarian history, see Ludden, "Productive Power," pp. 74-82.

53. Calculated from *Census of India*, 1881, *Villagewar Census Tables for Tinnevelly District* (Madras, 1883). For mapped densities in 1881, see Ludden, "Agrarian Organization," p. 45.

54. Michael Moffatt, in *An Untouchable Community in South India* (Princeton, 1979), p. 293, points to this long-term process when he says the caste system "does permit slow and micropolitically enacted tradeoffs between material gains and social rank. The system sets limits on such tradeoffs, however. It requires that certain people be available to play certain lowering roles, making Untouchables unlikely to cross the dividing line between untouchability and touchability. And it continually reproduces economic dominance in such a way that material success among the very low is strictly limited."

55. The 1881 census was the last to give detailed caste data, and did not tabulate caste information for Christians, many of whom were Shanars. I have assumed that half of Tirunelveli's Christians were Shanars, and added that figure to the 13.7 percent of the population that the 1881 census shows to be Shanars. Most of the rest of the district's Christians were Parava Catholics.

56. On dominant caste strategies: Brenda E. F. Beck, *Peasant Society in Konku* (Vancouver,1972); and McKim Marriott, "Hindu Transactions: Diversity Without Dualism," in Kapferer, ed., *Transactions and Meaning* (Philadelphia, 1976), pp. 125-26. On dominant castes in general: Dumont, *Homo Hierarchicus*, pp. 152-66; Mandelbaum, *Society in India*, 2: 358-80; and, especially relevant here because of its mapping effort, Brenda E. F. Beck, "Centers and Boundaries of Regional Caste Systems," in Smith, ed., *Regional Analysis* (New York, 1976), pp. 255-88.

57. For the ambiguities in Shanar caste ranking, see Hardgrave, *Nadars*, pp. 21-24.

58. K. Ishwaran, "Kinship and Distance in Rural India," in Piddington, ed., *Kinship and Geographical Mobility* (Leiden, 1965), pp. 81-94.

CHAPTER 3: TRIBUTARY STATE

1. R. Satyanatha Aiyer, *History of the Nayaks of Madurai* (Madras, 1924), chapter 2; A. Krishnaswami, *The Tamil Country under Vijayanagar*, pp. 196-216; William Taylor, *Oriental Historical Manuscripts* (Madras, 1835), "History of the Carnatic Governors Who Ruled over the Pandya Mandalam"; K. Rajayyan, *Rise and Fall of the Poligars of Tamilnadu* (Madras, 1974), and *History of Madurai*. ARE, 1940 1: 300-309, and Part II, pp. 252-53.

2. Susan Lewandowski, "Changing Form and Function in the Ceremonial and the Colonial Port City in India," *MAS*, 11:2 (1977), 183-212; Rangacharya, "History of the Naik Kingdom," *IA*, 44 (April 1915), 59-66, 69-73. Breckenridge, "Sri Minakshi Sunderasvaran Temple," chapter 1; Dennis Hudson, "Siva, Minakshi, Vishnu: Reflections on a Popular Myth in Madurai," *IESHR*, 14:1 (1977), 107-18.

3. K. Appadurai, *Talavay Ariyanatha Mutaliyar* (Madras, 1950); Taylor, *Oriental Historical Manuscripts*, 2: 113-16.

4. Taylor, *Oriental Historical Manuscripts*, 2: 215.

5. Kathirvel, "History of the Maravas," pp. 46, 96-97. Also Taylor, *A Catalogue Raisonée of Oriental Manuscripts*, 3 (Madras, 1862), 356-60; Mahalingam, *Mackenzie Manuscripts*, 1: 167ff.; Satyanatha Aiyer, *History of the Nayaks*, pp. 246-48.

6. Saletore, *Social and Political Life*, 1: 208, 210, 215.

7. For histories of particular little kingdoms, see Dirks, "Little Kingdoms of South India," and "Pasts of a Palaiyakarar"; and Price, "Resources and Rule."

8. About 15 percent of all villages listed in the "1823 Census" in Nellaiyambalam, Shermadevi, and Brahmadesam taluks had more than one Marava subjati in residence. On kilais and subjatis today, see Louis Dumont, "The Distribution of Some Maravar Sub-Castes," in Bala Ratnam, *Anthropology on the March* (Madras, 1963), pp. 299-301, and *Hierarchy and Marriage Alliance*, pp. 17-18.

9. Kathirvel, "History of the Maravas," pp. 27-40.

10. Dumont, "Distribution of Some Maravar Sub-Castes," pp. 305-306. The six are Chokkampatti, Uttumalai, Auvudiapuram, Pariyur, Naduvakurichi, and Vandai.

11. Pate, *Gazetteer*, p. 373; Rangacharya, "History of the Naik Kingdom," *IA*, 43 (July 1914), 135-37; O.S. #5, Tinnevelly Zillah Court, 1851, Transferred District Court records, Bundle 92, TNA (hereafter court records will be cited in this format: O.S. #5, 1851, Zillah Court, TDCR, 92).

12. For example, Gopinatha Rao, "The Krishnapuram Plates."

13. Pate, *Gazetteer*, pp. 98-99. This latter practice is still visible in early nineteenth-century records.

14.   Clarence Maloney, "The Paratavar: 2000 Years of Cultural Dynamics of a Tamil Caste," *MI*, 48: 3 (1969), 224-40. Robert Caldwell, *A Political and General History of the District of Tinnevelly* (Madras, 1881), p. 71. C. R. De Silva, "The Portugese and Pearl Fishing off South India and Sri Lanka," *SA*, NS 1:1 (1978), 14-28.

15.   Caldwell, *History*, pp. 70-83; Satyanatha Aiyer, *History of the Nayaks*, pp. 90-91; *Selections from the Dutch Records of the Government of Ceylon*, No. 5, "Memoir of Jan Shroeder, Governor of Ceylon, delivered to ... Lubbert Van Ech on March 17, 1762," translated by E. Riemers (Colombo, 1946), pp. 33-47. The major treaties were signed in 1669, 1685, 1690, and 1711.

16.   Frank Perlin, "Proto-industrialization and Pre-colonial South Asia," *PP*, 98 (1983), 30-95, emphasizes connections between overseas trade and inland economic life through monetary circulation. For South Indian coastal commercialization in this period, see A. I. Chicherov, *Indian Economic Development in the 16th-18th Centuries: Outline History of Crafts and Trade* (Moscow, 1971); and articles by L. B. Alaev in Tapan Raychaudhuri and Irfan Habib, eds. *The Cambridge Economic History of India*, vol. 1, *c.1200-c.1750* (Cambridge, 1982), pp. 226-34, 315-24.

17.   Schwartzberg, ed., *Historical Atlas*, pp. 49-50. See also Ashin Das Gupta, "Trade and Politics in Eighteenth Century India," in D. S. Richards, ed., *Islam and the Trade of Asia* (Philadelphia, 1970), pp. 181-214, and his article in Raychaudhuri and Habib, eds., *Cambridge Economic History*, 1:407-33.

18.   Holden Furber, *Rival Empires of Trade in the Orient, 1600-1800* (Minneapolis, 1976).

19.   The "1823 Census" shows concentrations of artisans, especially weavers, in towns, in the wet zone, and on the road from Tenkasi to Madurai. The largest concentrations were not at the coastal export centers, of which Tuticoryn was the most important. Aggregations of weavers were largest in the vicinities of Ambasamudram and Tirunelveli towns, where rice, patronage, and inland demand were strong, and protection secure.

20.   PBR,IOL, 19 March 1798, pp. 2142-253. TCR,TNA, vol. 3598, 1803, pp. 45-51, 200-207; PBR,TNA, 11 July 1803, vol. 351, pp. 7408-40; S. Lushington, *Report Regarding the Tinnevelly Poligars and Sequestered Pollams, 1799-1800* (Tinnevelly, 1916), TCR,TNA, p. 12.

21.   See the "1823 Census," "Sources from which revenues derive."

22.   TCR,TNA, vol. 3587, 1807, pp. 120-25, and vol. 3582, 1807, pp. 267-69. In 1830, sources list 586 different rates of assessment for land classified as irrigated but planted with dry crops and 928 rates for land irrigated with well water. In 1835, government taxed irrigated land at 146 different rates, and, in 1855, dry land at 497 rates. All this diversity in rates can be attributed to pre-1800 tax procedures, which were highly localized and generated distinct local revenue traditions, carried over into the nineteenth century by Company officials as a matter of course (see Chapter Four). Jamabandy

Report F. 1239; TCR,TNA, vol. 7971, 1843, pp. 229-68; Pate, *Gazetteer*, pp. 286, 288.

23. Lushington, *Report Regarding the Tinnevelly Poligars*, p. 9.

24. PBR,IOL, 19 March 1798, pp. 2142-53; M. Hodgson, "Report on the Province of Tinnevelly, 24 September 1804," TCR,TNA (hereafter: Hodgson, "Report of 1804").

25. Jamabandy Report F. 1238; Stuart, *Manual*, pp. 161, 182, 194.

26. James Hepburn, *Collector's Report on the Triennial Lease* (Tinnevelly, n.d.), TCR,TNA; Hodgson, "Report of 1804."

27. TCR,TNA, vol. 3582, 1807, pp. 58-60; PBR,TNA, 2 February 1807, vol. 439, p. 879.

28. O.S. #1, 1851, Zillah Court, TDCR, 91.

29. TCR,TNA, vol. 3641B, pp. 7-14.

30. PBR,TNA, 21 May 1812, vol. 571, pp. 5163-64.

31. Hepburn, *Collector's Report*; Hodgson, "Report of 1804"; Jamabandy Report F. 1217.

32. Pate, *Gazetteer*, p. 338; Caldwell, *The Tinnevelly Shanars*; Kathirvel, "History of the Maravas," p. 17; K. Ramachandran, "Vadamalaipuram, Ramnad District," in Slater, ed., *Some South Indian Villages* (Madras, 1918), p. 32.

33 TCR,TNA, vol. 7983, pp. 68-70. PBR,TNA, 9 November 1829, vol. 1213, pp. 12326-28; *Selections from the Records of Madras Government*, vol. 6, "Correspondence Relative to Proposals for Organizing a Permanent Corps of Coolies" (Madras, 1855), pp. 2-10.

34. For family cycles as a source of local stratification, see Max Weber, *General Economic History* (New York, 1927), pp. 8-9; Daniel Thorner, Basil Kerblay, and R.E.F. Smith, eds. *Theory of Peasant Economy* (Homewood, Ill., 1966).

35. TCR,TCO, "Ettaiyapuram Received, 1869-1878," letter to the Collector dated 20 February 1874.

36. PBR,TNA, 27 April 1812, vol. 569, pp. 4210-83.

37. Ibid.

38. Computed from *Settlement Registers. Descriptive Memoirs of Tinnevelly District*, dated 1873-1877, TNA, produced during survey and settlement operations (see below, Chapter Four). The sample villages were in Srivilliputtur and Ottapidaram taluks. For details, see Ludden, "Agrarian Organization," p. 167. On the subject of inams under the Raj, see R. E. Frykenberg, ed., *Land Tenure and Peasant in South Asia* (New Delhi, 1977), pp. 37-80.

39. PBR,TNA, 10 March 1817, vol. 747, pp. 3046-60.

40. S. Lushington, "Settlement Report, 29 December 1800," reprinted in W. H. Bayley and W. Hudleston, eds., *Papers on Mirasi Right Selected from the Records of the Madras Government* (Madras, 1862), pp. 77-84.

41. See Chapter One, note 63.

42. Hodgson, "Report on 1804," as quoted in Bayley and Hudleston,

Papers on Mirasi Right, p. 106. H. H. Wilson, *A Glossary of Judicial and Revenue Terms* (London, 1855, rpt. ed. Bombay, 1966), p. 342.

43. A.S. #10, 1849, Auxilliary with Zillah Court, TDCR, 17.

44. A. T. Arundel, "Settlement of Srivilliputtur," 18 March 1878, in *Papers Related to the Settlement of Tinnevelly*, TCR,TNA, p. 248.

45. TCR,TNA, vol. 7977, 1849, pp. 163-76; A.S. #108, 1848, Zillah Court, TDCR, 91; PBR,TNA, 2 January 1822, vol. 934, pp. 279-91; A.S. #3, 1834, Auxilliary Court, TDCR, 4.

46. A.S. #43, 1840, Auxilliary Court, TDCR, 65. The share concerned is from Nettur, on the banks of the Chittar, where the share was valued at Rs. 603 in 1773-1776, Rs. 1,590 in 1816, and Rs. 3,254 in 1837. Prices fluctuated without comparable increase in this period (Figure 5).

47. H. J. Stokes, "The Custom of 'Kareiyid' or Periodic Redistribution of Land in Tanjor," *IA*, 3 (1874), 65-69.

48. Bayley and Hudleston, *Papers on Mirasi Right*, pp. 78-79.

49. "List of Records Showing the Nature and Volume of Suits in the Tinnevelly Adalat Court," Catalogue to TDCR,TNR.

50. TCR,TNA, vol. 7967, 1837, pp. 118-19.

51. Krishna Shastri, "The Kuniyur Plates," pp. 255-57.

52. TCR,TNA, vol. 7977, 1849, pp. 163-76.

53. James Hepburn, *Collector's Report on the Decennial Lease*, 5 December 1812 (Tinnevelly, n.d.), TCR,TNA; Jamabandy Report F. 1235. "Leading Mirasidars" also received separate enumeration in the "1823 Census."

54. TCR,TNA, vol. 3582, 1807, p. 285. PBR,TNA, 27 April 1812, vol. 569, pp. 4210-83.

55. For data on increase in the capital component of production with new irrigation today, see Edward J. Clay, "Equity and Productivity Effects of a Package of Technical Innovations and Changes in Social Institutions," *IJAE*, 30:4 (1975), 74-87. For increasing labor demand in irrigated agriculture in Tamil Nadu, see Z.W.B. Zacharias, *Studies in the Economics of Farm Management in Madras* (Delhi, 1954-1957), 1: 110-16 and 2: 137-58.

56. *Idangai valangai jatiyar varalaru*, Mackenzie Manuscripts, Madras Oriental Manuscripts Library MS No.R-1572, cited in Stein, *Peasant State*, p. 184.

57. For examples, see TCR,TNA, vol. 7971, 1843, pp. 292-316, 321-40; and TCR,TNA, vol. 7977, 1849, pp. 163-79.

58. See Ernst Wiegt, "Der Trockene Sudosten Indiens: Mensch und Wirtschaft im Tambraparni Tal," *Geographische Rundshau*, 20:11 (November 1968), pp. 405-14; Kathleen Gough, "Caste in a Tanjore Village," in E. R. Leach, *Aspects of Caste in South India, Ceylon and Northwest Pakistan* (Cambridge, 1971), pp. 11-60. See below, Chapter Six.

59. Hepburn, *Collector's Report on the Decennial Lease*, pp. 9-10; W. Robinson, *Minute on the Proposed Settlement of Tinnevelly*, 1868, TCR,TNA, pp. 3, 14; O.S. #1, 1851, Zillah Court, TDCR, 91.

60. A.S. #10, 1849, Auxilliary with Zillah Court, TDCR, 17; A.S. #3,

1817, Zillah Adalat Court, TDCR, 75; A.S. #126, 1851, Auxilliary Court, TDCR, 17.

61. *Mukkudal Pallu*, edited by N. Setukumaran (Madras, 1973).

62. V. Krishnan, "Tambraparni Ryot (A Study of the Rural Economy of the Tirunelveli District)," Gokhale Prize Award Thesis, University of Madras, 1931.

63. Lushington, "Report," in Bayley and Hudleston, *Papers on Mirasi Right*, pp. 78-79. See also the sale deed, ibid., Appendix 4, pp. ix-xxxiv. For "rights in persons," see Suzanne Miers and Igor Kopytoff, eds., *Slavery in Africa* (Madison, 1977), pp. 7-11.

64. For British attitudes and legislation, see Benedicte Hjejle, "Slavery and Agricultural Bondage in South India in the Nineteenth Century," *SEHR*, 15:1-2 (1967), 71-126. The study of bonded labor in premodern agriculture is still underdeveloped. For general approaches and comparisons, see Miers and Kopytoff, *Slavery in Africa*, and Orlando Patterson, *Slavery and Social Death* (Cambridge, 1982). For an economist's line of attack, see Robert J. Evans, Jr., "Some Notes on Coerced Labor," *JEH*, 30:4 (1970), 861-66. For a spatial approach, see Carol A. Smith, "Exchange Systems and the Spatial Distribution of Elites: The Organization of Stratification in Agrarian Societies," in Carol A. Smith, ed., *Regional Analysis*, 2 (New York: 1976) 326-33. For a case study stressing cultural forces in the political economy of servitude, see Gyan Prakash, "Production and the Reproduction of Bondage: Kamias and Maliks in South Bihar, India, c. 1300-1930," Ph.D. dissertation, Pennsylvania, 1984.

65. *TAS*, vol. 1, No.6, pp. 43-44, 52, 61-88, 89-94, 106-14, 133-46.

66. This is my rough translation of an Anglo-Indian term that was part of common official vocabulary in nineteenth-century Tirunelveli. See Chapters Four and Six, and Glossary, below.

67. For instance, the case of Tippanampatti, whose history is sketched in O.S. #41, 1828, Auxilliary Court, TDCR, 2.

68. To be more precise, I have not found cases in which such claims were contested in court or before revenue officers in the nineteenth century. This does not prove that no such claims survived, but it is suggestive, given the number and wide distribution of cases contesting swamibhogam. See Chapter Six.

69. Satyanatha Aiyer, *History of the Nayaks*, gives details. Also, see S. Thananjayarajasingham, *A Critical Study of a Seventeenth Century Tamil Document Relating to a Commercial Treaty* (Perandeniya, 1968), p. 7, lines 229-30, and p. 18; and Price, "Resources and Rule," p. 5.

70. Rajayyan, *Rise and Fall of the Poligars*, pp. 42-43.

71. For war stories, see Rajayyan, *History of Madurai*, and Caldwell, *History*.

72. Kathirvel, "History of the Maravas," pp. 124-25, quoting a report from the Collector of Poligar Peshcash, 23 June 1892; S. Lushington, "Settlement Report of 28 May 1802," TCR,TNA, pp. 2-3; Caldwell, *History*, chapter five; *Selections from the Dutch Records*, pp. 42-47; PBR,IOL, 21

October 1793, pp. 6860-69; Caldwell, *History*; and Kathirvel, "History of the Maravas."

73. Hodgson, "Report of 1804," paragraphs 5-6. Thomas Munro criticized this view: A. J. Arbuthnot, *Major General Sir Thomas Munro* (London, 1881), I: 248.

74. Rajayyan, *Rise and Fall*, p. 26; Taylor, *Catalogue*, 3: 355-63. TCR,TNA, vol. 3583, 1808, pp. 309-11. The Company lowered Chokkampatti's revenue demand in 1787-1797, presumably in the belief that it had been raised beyond the poligar's ability to pay; and, perhaps, to keep his people away from the Company's opposition. PBR,IOL, 21 October 1793, pp. 6869-902. Nevertheless, Chokkampatti remained a problem for years to come: see Chapters Four and Six, below.

75. S. Lushington, "Settlement Report of 28 May 1802." An abstract of this report appears in "The Fifth Report of the Select Committee of the House of Commons on the Affairs of the East India Company," *Parliamentary Papers, East Indies* (rpt. Irish University Press, Shannon, 1969), vol. 3.

76. K. Rajayyan, *Administration and Society in the Carnatic (1701-1801)* (Tirupati, 1966), pp. 43-55; Caldwell, *History*, p. 104; Rajayyan, *Rise and Fall*, pp. 16-17; S. Lushington, "Report on Desacaval," 16 October 1800, PBR,TNA, vol. 264, pp. 8764-811.

77. These conclusions are based on taluk temple data summarized in Ludden, "Agrarian Organization," Table 8, p. 147. Note that the 1961 census data on temples only considers major temples still in use in 1961. It is possible that a decline in Marava fortunes after 1800 (see Chapter Five) allowed for the decay of working temples. It is also possible, though unlikely, that temples were destroyed in warfare.

78. Caldwell's *History* has the most detailed battle narratives.

79. Madras Government, Foreign Department Sundries, TNA, "Mr. Hodgson's Report on the Dutch Settlements, dated 23 March 1818," Appendix B, "Extract from a letter from Mr. Irwin, dated 28 April 1783," p. 7; also Jamabandy Report F. 1217. John Gurney, "The Debts of the Nawab of Arcot," Ph.D. dissertation, Oxford, 1968; see also Jamabandy Report F. 1245. PBR,IOL, 23 September 1793, pp. 5815-19. Also PBR,IOL, 25 September 1793, pp. 956-70, and PBR,IOL, 8 August 1793, pp. 4882-89.

80. Lushington, "Settlement Report of 28 May 1802."

81. PBR,IOL, 13 June 1793, pp. 3196-205; TCR,TNA, vol. 3641B, 1790, pp. 35-36; PBR,TNA, 17 May 1831, vol. 1280, pp. 2914-17.

CHAPTER 4: ANGLO-INDIAN EMPIRE

1. For official administrative history, see Pate, *Gazetteer*, pp. 270-357. Robert E. Frykenberg, *Guntur District, 1788-1848* (London, 1965), first established the role of local administration in the politics of Company Raj.

2. The District Collectorate Records include correspondence from tahsildars to collector, from collector to Board, from London to the Board and

from the Board to collector on district affairs, as well as numerous other reports, for example, by engineers and judges, as well as petitions from citizens and letters to the collector from English businessmen and missionaries. These records represent the most detailed documentary resource for the study of local history in South India. Annual volumes reside in the Tamil Nadu Archives for years before 1860, and in the district record room for later years. The series ends in the 1870s, for reasons discussed in this chapter.

3. For revenue system development, see R. C. Dutt, *The Economic History of India*, 2 vols. (Calcutta, 1901; rpt. New Delhi, 1960). Ludden, "Productive Power," gives bibliography.

4. See Arbuthnot, *Sir Thomas Munro*; T. H. Beaglehole, *Thomas Munro and the Development of Administrative Policy in Madras, 1792-1818* (Cambridge, 1962); and Nilmani Mukherjee, *The Ryotwari System in Madras, 1792-1827* (Calcutta, 1962). Dharma Kumar, *Land and Caste in South India* (Cambridge, 1965), traces the development of the ryotwari system during the nineteenth century.

5. See Dirks, "Little Kingdoms in South India," and Price, "Resources and Rule."

6. See Frykenberg, *Guntur District*; Eugene Irschick, *Politics and Social Conflict in Tamilad* (Berkeley and Los Angeles, 1969); and R. Suntharalingam, *Politics and Nationalist Awakening in South India* (Tuscon, 1974).

7. The names of tahsildars were published in annual Jamabandy Reports, from 1825 to 1855. Deputy collector appointments were similarly recorded from 1863 to 1890. Brahman domination of educational opportunities and public office preoccupied politicians during the twentieth century. See Irschick, *Politics and Social Conflict*, pp. 27-55, 218-74 ff.; David Washbrook, *The Emergence of Provincial Politics* (Cambridge, 1976), pp. 261-87; and Marguerite Ross Barnett, *The Politics of Cultural Nationalism in South India* (Princeton, 1976). See Chapter Six, below.

8. "Report on the Landholdings of the Native Establishment," in PBR,TNA, vol. 2291, 3 July 1851, pp. 9079-102, and annual supplements in Jamabandy Reports after 1863 provide the data for this discussion, an earlier version of which appeared in David Ludden, "Who Really Ruled Madras Presidency?" *IESHR*, 15:4 (1978), 517-21.

9. TCR,TNA, vol. 7968, 1838-1839, pp. 175-76.

10. This comparison is based on holdings and assessments per pattah for the general population and per estate for officeholders. For details, see Ludden, "Agrarian Organization," p. 265. All officers were not required to report their holdings: those with monthly pay below Rs.5 were exempted. F. Lushington, *Comparative Tables of the Provincial Civil Establishment of the Madras Presidency for 1857* (Madras, 1858), gives details on offices and pay. Of officers listed for Tinnevelly District in Lushington, *Comparative Tables*, 55 percent reported owning land and appear in the "Report on the Landholdings of the Native Establishment."

11.   Eric Stokes, *English Utilitarians and India* (London, 1959), traces connections between theory and practice in ryotwari.

12.   Hodgson, a member of the Tanjore Commission, wrote special reports to the Board of Revenue on Coimbatore, Tinnevelly, and Dindigul prior to the triennial lease. His last major minute as a member of the Board was dated 8 December 1819, and is reprinted in the "Fifth Report of the Select Committee of the House of Commons on the Affairs of the East India Company." See Mukherjee, *The Ryotwari System*, pp. 33-35, 112. About Tinnevelly District, Hodgson wrote that "during the time of the Mohammadan government . . . a fixed sum was in general demanded for rent of the poonjah lands, which the inhabitants assessed upon the cultivated land amongst themselves according to local circumstances" (TCR,TNA, vol. 3582, 1807, p. 244). He also wrote that "to establish a Ryotwari rent in a district of which the land is all Punjah or nearly so is . . . only methodizing and ameliorating the ancient practice of fixing the rent on the land" ("Report of 1804," paragraph 18).

13.   TCR,TNA, vol. 3599, 1804, pp. 14-23, 44-51. PBR,TNA, 11 July 1803, vol. 351, pp. 7408-41.

14.   The "1823 Census" even includes zamindari villages, with the exception of Ettaiyapuram. For more on the exceptional character of Ettaiyapuram, see below.

15.   TCR,TNA, vol. 3599, 1804, pp. 57-60, and vol. 3581, 1806, p. 95.

16.   Jamabandy Report F. 1235.

17.   In 1801, collector Lushington "took the amount of the former actual collections and made the inhabitants divide their land into four different classes upon which the revenue was divided." TCR,TNA, vol. 3582, 1807, p. 244. Jamabandy Report F. 1235 contains an extended critique of settlement procedures under ryotwari, which simply translated old revenue rates into formal ryotwari terms. For a comparable case, see Neil Rabitoy, "System vs. Expediency: The Reality of Land Revenue Administration in the Bombay Presidency, 1812-1820," *MAS*, 9:4 (1975), 539-46.

18.   Jamabandy Report F. 1245.

19.   Jamabandy Report F. 1235.

20.   Arbuthnot, *Sir Thomas Munro*, 1:281-86.

21.   Ellis, collector of Chinglepet, wrote an influential series of minutes on mirasi rights, reprinted, along with the Board's considerations, in Bayley and Hudleston, *Papers on Mirasi Right*, pp. 172-344. Both Ellis and Hodgson opposed Munro's ryotwari scheme for irrigated villages.

22.   TCR,TNA, vol. 3596, 1819, pp. 107-10.

23.   PBR,TNA, 21 May 1812, vol. 571, pp. 5163-64. Revenue Department, *General Report of the Board of Revenue for 1815* (Madras, n.d.), p. 351. TCR,TNA, vol. 3595, 1818, pp. 323-25. Jamabandy Report F. 1228. See Figure 5 for price data; details not available for 1808-1812. Collectors put villages back under the division of grain heap (amani) system when no one could be found to pay security for the revenue in advance of the harvest. See

John Cotton, *Settlement Report for Fasli 1225* (Tinnevelly, n.d.), TCR,TNA. TCR,TNA, vol. 3597, 1820, pp. 41-42, and vol. 3596, 1819, pp. 512-21.

24. TCR,TNA, vol. 4696, 1822, pp. 117-26, 173.

25. Pate, *Gazetteer*, pp. 282-83. TCR,TNA, vol. 3594, 1817, pp. 142-44, 319-21, 378-80; vol. 3595, 1818, pp. 240-41, 329-30; and vol. 3596, 1819, pp. 540-62. PBR,TNA, 15 November 1819, vol. 839, pp. 10196-97.

26. The Board made two major policy statements, on 5 January 1818 and on 15 November 1819, in which it exempted mirasidar villages in Tanjore, Tinnevelly, and parts of Trichnopoly districts from the terms of ryotwari, laying the groundwork for the development of the olungu system. The Board's conclusions contain the following statements about mirasidar villages: "everything is variable except the number of shares into which the village was divided on its first establishment. . . . Under such a system it is obviously impossible to establish any assessment on each field or on each ryot without dissolving the unity of interest which pervades the whole and forms the basis of this tenure. . . . Under these considerations, the Board are under the opinion that the extension of field assessments to Tanjore, or to the wetlands of Tinnevelly and Trichnopoly, is no less impracticable than inexpedient; and think that the parties with whom the settlement ought to be made are the collective body of the Meerasidars in each village. . . . The proportion of the total assessment to be paid . . . may be clearly defined by assessing it upon the lands held by each, or . . . by apportioning it upon the shares held by each." PBR 5 January 1818, extracted in Bayley and Hudleston, *Papers on Mirasi Right*, pp. 392-93, and PBR,TNA, 15 November 1819, vol. 839, pp. 10196-97, 10200.

27. Bayley and Hudleston, *Papers on Mirasi Right*, pp. 392-93.

28. Pate, *Gazetteer*, pp. 283-84. The olungu system was first proposed in a letter from the Board to the collector, in 1821. TCR,TNA, vol. 3576, 1821, pp. 263-66, 277-79. For more details on setting olungu prices, see TCR,TNA, vol. 7983, 1856, pp. 91-94, and vol. 1784, 1857, pp. 69-72. Also TCR,TCO, To Board 1858, Letter No. 338, n.p.

29. This "underplot of the settlement," by which leading mirasidars retained their role as financial middlemen between farmers and Revenue, was discussed in Jamabandy Report F. 1235, which also described how the new assessments were simply adjustments of actual collections.

30. TCR,TNA, vol. 4363, 1821-1835, pp. 79-83.

31. Jamabandy Report F. 1236; TCR,TNA, vol. 4700, 1820, pp. 142-43.

32. More detail on negotiations that put the olungu system in place can be found in Ludden, "Agrarian Organization," chapter 6.

33. Annual variation in kar cultivated acreage during the years 1843-1854, the only ones for which they are available, were twice as high for Srivaikuntam Taluk as for up-river Brahmadesam and Nellaiyambalam taluks: 24 percent, 12 percent, and 14 percent, respectively. These were years of relatively good monsoons and general agricultural expansion in the Tambraparni River valley (see Chapter Five). Variations are calculated by taking the standard deviation

of cultivated acreage for the period as a percent of the mean (see Chapter Five, note 52).

34. Public Works Department, *Construction of the Srivaikuntam Anicut across the Tambraparni River*, Reprints of Old Government Records (Madras, 1920).

35. Jamabandy Report F. 1243. TCR,TNA, vol. 7968, 1838-1839, pp. 77-79.

36. PBR,TNA, 17 May 1831, vol. 1280, pp. 2914-17.

37. Jamabandy Reports, F. 1235-1247. See Ludden, "Agrarian Organization," p. 222.

38. Scott, *Moral Economy of the Peasant*, pp. 1-113, describes a head-on clash of peasant and state moral economies under colonialism. The same clash has been highlighted for South India by R. E. Frykenberg and D. A. Washbrook. In irrigated Tinnevelly District, however, irrigation created a bridge between village and state moral economies during precolonial centuries that remained in place under the Company. In dry zone Tinnevelly District, moreover, revenue demand remained within customary bounds, while village officers retained customary power. Negotiations between villagers and state officials did not comprise, therefore, a struggle between villagers and state power itself, as these and other authors have suggested, but rather a struggle over the terms of a moral and political interdependence between village elites and state authorities. For a critique of Scott, see Pierre Borcheux, "Moral Economy or Political Economy? The Peasants Are Always Rational," *JAS*, 42:4 (1983), 791-804.

39. For prices, see Figures 5 and 6; Ludden, "Agrarian Organization," pp. 387-90; Kumar, *Land and Caste*, p. 91; and A. Sarada Raju, *Economic Conditions in Madras Presidency, 1800-1850* (Madras, 1941), pp. 225-33. Note that the 1830s trend parallels prices in Britain: see B. R. Mitchell, *Abstract of British Historical Statistics*, (Cambridge, 1962), pp. 471-72. See Jamabandy Reports F. 1251 and 1252; Also TCR,TNA, vol. 7971, 1843, pp. 240-45, and vol. 7970, 1842, pp. 104-109.

40. See the Public Works Department, *First* and *Second Report of the Commissioners Appointed to Enquire into Public Works* (Madras, 1852, 1853); *Torture Commission Report* (Madras, 1855); *Selections from the Records of the Madras Government*, vol. 52 (Madras, 1858), and vol. 54 (1863); Revenue Department, *Reports and Other Papers with a View to Recasting the Revenue Laws of the Madras Presidency* (Madras, 1856); J. D. Bourdillon, *Remarks on the Ryotwari System of Land Tenure* (Madras, 1853); J.W.B. Dykes, *Salem: An Indian Collectorate* (Madras, 1853); J. B. Norton, *The Administration of Justice in Madras Presidency* (Madras, 1853), and *A Letter to Robert Lowe* (Madras, 1854); W. Holloway, *Notes on Madras Judicial Administration* (Madras, 1853); P. Smolett, *Madras: Its Civil Administration* (London, 1958); and T. L. Strange, *A Letter . . . On Judicial Reform* (Madras, 1860).

41. Suntharalingam, *Politics and Nationalist Awakening*, pp. 45-57.

42. TCR,TNA, vol. 7970, 1842, pp. 2-5, 104-19; vol. 7971, 1843, pp. 229-68, 292-316; vol. 7972, 1844, pp. 40-49; and vol. 7976, 1848, pp. 43-44, 49-55, 69-72, 220-23, 230-38 ff. E. B. Thomas served as acting collector in 1842, and as collector in 1843 and 1848. Pate, *Gazetteer*, p. 319.

43. TCR,TNA, vol. 7970, 1842, pp. 2-5; vol. 7971, 1843, pp. 229-68, 292-301; and vol. 7972, 1844, pp. 40-49. See Chapter Five.

44. Calculated from data in Jamabandy Reports F. 1235-1260. Once again, collectors were caught between the Board's order to end favorable tax rates and their inability to raise tax rates at will. Effective rates must have gone up on some of the district's worst irrigated land as a result of the ending of nunjah-mel-punjah rates; but no aggregate increase is apparent from taluk revenue accounts.

45. TCR,TNA, vol. 7972, 1842, pp. 40-49.

46. Kumar, *Land and Caste*, pp. 80-81; PBR,TNA, vol. 7970, 1842, pp. 104-109.

47. See, for comparison, Mitchell, *Abstracts of British Historical Statistics*, pp. 471-72; and for context, Michelle Burge McAlpin, "Price Movements and Fluctuations in Economic Activity (1860-1947)," in Kumar, ed., *The Cambridge Economic History of India*, Vol. 2. C. 1757-1970 (Cambridge, 1983), pp. 878-904.

48. Pate, *Gazetteer*, p. 292.

49. No adequate account of the post-1850 transformation in Indian governance has yet been written. For pieces of the puzzle, see Washbrook, *Emergence of Provincial Politics*, pp. 51-63; Suntharalingam, *Politics and Nationalist Awakening*, pp. 58-192; Hugh Tinker, *The Foundations of Local Self-Government in India, Pakistan and Burma* (London, 1954); Elizabeth Whitcombe, *Agrarian Conditions in Northern India*. Vol. 1. *The United Provinces under British Rule, 1860-1900* (Berkeley and Los Angeles, 1972); T. R. Metcalf, *The Aftermath of Revolt* (Princeton, 1964); and Daniel Headrick, *Tools of Empire* (New York, 1981).

50. From Jamabandy Reports F. 1265-1290. Sales for arrears of land revenue averaged Rs.351 annually from 1825 to 1850: PBR,TNA, 5 January 1852, vol. 2313, pp. 370-75.

51. *Manual of the Administration of the Madras Presidency* (Madras, 1885), 1:481-87; Stuart, *Manual*, pp. 199, 208-209; Washbrook, *Emergence of Provincial Politics*, p. 52; *Annual Report on the Administration of Madras Presidency for 1944/5*, (Madras, 1945).

52. Stuart, *Manual*, p. 211; Suntharalingam, *Politics and Nationalist Awakening*, pp. 95 ff. Anil Seal, *The Emergence of Indian Nationalism* (Cambridge, 1968), p. 18. Stuart, *Manual*, p. 211.

53. For an overview of the process, see *Manual of Administration*, 1:99-111.

54. For more details on Tinnevelly District's survey and settlement operations, see Stuart, *Manual*, pp. 124-31; Pate, *Gazetteer*, pp. 293-301; and *Papers Relating to the Revenue Settlement of Tinnevelly District*, TCR,TNA.

55. PBR,IOL, 26 October 1865, pp. 6062-71. *Papers Relating to the Revenue Settlement*, pp. 22-23. Stuart, *Manual*, p. 127.

56. W. Robinson, *Minute on the Proposed Settlement*.

57. Pate, *Gazetteer*, p. 299. Kumar, *Land and Caste*, p. 90, provides data on the total change in revenue demand (Tinnevelly demand was up 6.4 percent) drawn from the *Manual of Administration*.

58. Stuart, *Manual*, pp. 213, 219, 245-47.

59. *Annual Report on the Administration of Madras Presidency for 1871/2*, p. 89.

60. *Annual Report on the Administration of Madras Presidency* for various years.

61. *Papers Relating to the Sale of Waste Lands or Redemption of the Land Tax in India*, East Indies (Waste Lands), Return Ordered Printed by the House of Commons, 6 April 1864, pp. 198-200; Pate, *Gazetteer*, p. 301.

62. See Revenue Department, *Salt Works in the Madras Presidency*, Revenue Sundries No. 43, TNA, pp. 401-25.

63. Ganapathi Pillai, *Ettaiyapuram Past and Present*, pp. 120-27 ff., 132.

64. Revenue Department Consultations, 20 February 1869, quoted in TCR,TCO, "Ettaiyapuram Received, 1869-1876," n.p.

65. *Selections from Old Records, Papers Relating to Zamindars, Mittahs, etc. of Tinnevelly District*. (Madras, 1934). Proceedings of the Court of Wards, 4 October 1871, letter from Puckle dated 29 August 1871, in TCR,TCO, "Ettaiyapuram Received, 1869-1876," n.p.

66. Proceedings of the Court of Wards, 18 November 1871, letter from Puckle dated 10 October 1971, in TCR,TCO, "Ettaiyapuram Received, 1869-1876," n.p. The Court of Wards routinely took zamindaris under its control in the late nineteenth century, put zamindars in government schools, revamped estate administration, and invested zamindar surplus revenue in government bonds. For a case study, see Anand Yang, "An Institutional Shelter," *MAS*, 13:2 (1979), 247-64; and for context, Ludden, "Productive Power," pp. 64-72.

67. The Raja of Singampatti still had a forest case pending in 1975 (personal interview).

68. *Papers Relating to the Revenue Settlement*, pp. 59-260.

69. J. H. Garstin, *Report on the Revision of the Revenue Establishment in the Madras Presidency* (Madras, 1883), p. 2.

70. PBR,TNA, 21 September 1837, vol. 1574, pp. 11451-73.

71. TCR,TNA, vol. 7979, 1852, pp. 71-77, 145-49, and vol. 7982, 1885, pp. 77-88.

72. R. K. Puckle, "Settlement Report," in *Papers Relating to the Revenue Settlement of Tinnevelly*, n.d., TCR,TNA.

73. Puckle, "Settlement Report."

74. PBR,TNA, 3 July 1851, vol. 2291, p. 9079.

75. Also Kallars: see Stuart H. Blackburn, "The Kallars: A Tamil 'Criminal

Tribe' Reconsidered," *SA*, NS 1:1 (March 1978), 38-51. On the general in-stitutionalization of "criminal" categories in British India, see Anand Yang, ed. *Criminality and Control in British India* (Tucson, in press). This institu-tionalization rested, in turn, on what Bernard Cohn has called a "colonial sociology," by which administrative authorities divided up the population of the empire according to characteristics salient in the imperial scheme. See Bernard Cohn, "Representing Authority in Victorian India," in Hobsbawm and Ranger, eds. *The Invention of Tradition* (Cambridge, 1983), pp. 165-209.

76. PBR,TNA, 24 September 1832, vol. 1340, pp. 9977-82; PBR,TNA, 24 October 1835, vol. 1476, pp. 13958-84; PBR,TNA, 21 September 1857, vol. 1574, pp. 11451-71; TCR,TNA, vol. 7982, 1855, pp. 360-67. Puckle, "Settlement Report," pp. 262-63.

77. The Superintendent of Police wrote these words on the Marava prob-lem in 1945: "To attempt to abolish kaval without filling the economic gap which this would entail would be to repeat history and to produce results in crime which can well be imagined." Quoted from TNA, G.O. 626, 24 April 1945, in Blackburn, "The Kallars," p. 47. Pate makes similar remarks on the situation as of 1917, in *Gazetteer*, pp. 336-37.

78. Washbrook, *Emergence of Provincial Politics*, provides the best over-view of the period before 1920. For later years, see Christopher J. Baker, *The Politics of South India, 1920-1937* (Cambridge, 1976); and Barnett, *The Politics of Cultural Nationalism.*

79. For a related argument, see Douglas Earll Haynes, "Conflict and Cul-tural Change in Urban India," Ph.D. dissertation, Pennsylvania, 1982.

Chapter 5: Commodity Production

1. See Headrick, *Tools of Empire*, and Wolf, *Europe and the People with-out History*, pp. 310-84.

2. Pate, *Gazetteer*, pp. 499-500.

3. Thomas Turnbull, "Geographical and Statistical Memoir of Tirunelvelie and its Zamindaries," Revenue Department Sundries, No. 38, TNA. Stuart, *Manual*, pp. 94-95. Pate, *Gazetteer*, pp. 104, 215-17.

4. Arbuthnot, *Sir Thomas Munro*, 2:232.

5. "1823 Census."

6. For petty trades, see TCR,TNA, vol. 7973, 1845, pp. 316-17. Details for interzonal trade come from the "1823 Census"; Turnbull, "Memoir"; and "Report on Inland Customs," in PBR, especially PBR,TNA, 26 October 1837, vol. 1553, pp. 13572-91. Additional sources are Moturpha Reports, especially TCR,TNA, vol. 7971, 1843, pp. 292-316; and incidental accounts, such as those in *Salt Works in the Madras Presidency* (which describes salt trading), and Caldwell, *The Tinnevelly Shanars* (which describes palmyra product trade). For a helpful account of interzonal trade in the twentieth century, see V. Krishnan, "Trade Centers in the Tinnevelly District," *JMGA*, 15:3 (1940),

271-77. Early nineteenth-century prices, by village, are tabulated for F. 1233, 1823-1824, in PBR,TNA, 14 July 1825, vol. 1026, pp. 5979-6071; and monthly, at Tinnevelly Town, for 1809-1826, in "Statement of Price Current of Grains in several districts during Faslis 1218-1235 (1809-1826)," Board of Revenue Misellaneous Volumes, No. 241, TNA.

7. PBR,TNA, 26 October 1837, vol. 1553, pp. 13572-91. PBR,TNA, 22 October 1838, vol. 1630, pp. 13565-77 shows annual road expenditures for all Madras districts for the years from 1818 to 1838. TCR,TNA, vol. 7967, 1837, pp. 66-67 shows that thirty-seven choultries were built at various times for an average cost of Rs.5,000, the largest for Rs.30,000. TCR,TNA, vol. 7968, 1838-1839, pp. 85-86.

8. He also built and endowed an English medium school named after his boss, the collector: TCR,TNA, vol. 7969, 1840, p. 79, and vol. 7971, 1842, p. 75.

9. Stuart, *Manual*, pp. 258-89. Sixty-one working choultries are reported in TCR,TNA, vol. 7969, 1838-1839, p. 16, fifty-one of which had inam grants for their maintenance. No new inams were granted after 1818, which helps to explain why so few were built until the 1840s, when the government began again to help defray the cost of their construction and maintenance.

10. Stuart, *Manual*, p. 208.

11. Pate, *Gazetteer*, p. 243. TCR,TNA, vol. 7978, 1851, pp. 65-67. Of the Rs.50,000 the government spent on the northern trunk road between 1827 and 1850, 70 percent was spent after 1841; and the government spent another Rs.50,000 on the road before 1854. TCR,TNA, vol. 8023, 1850, p. 146; vol. 7979, 1852, pp. 159-62; and vol. 7982, 1855, pp. 101-105. *Salt Works in the Madras Presidency*, pp. 410-25.

12. Sarada Raju, *Economic Conditions*, p. 220.

13. Stuart, *Manual*, pp. 140-47.

14. Puckle, "Report on the Settlement," and TCR,TNA, vol. 7982, 1855, pp. 101-105.

15. For this and other transport improvements that complemented railway construction in British India, see Tom G. Kessinger, "Regional Economy (1757-1857): North India," in Kumar, ed., *Cambridge Economic History*, 2:258-59.

16. PBR,TNA, 1 March 1804, Back Nos. 7-8. For the China trade, see Michael Greenberg, *British Trade and the Opening of China* (Cambridge, 1951), and Vincent T. Harlow, *The Founding of the Second British Empire* (Oxford, 1964), chapter 8.

17. TCR,TNA, vol. 3582, 1807, p. 250, and vol. 3683, 1808, p. 284.

18. TCR,TNA, vol. 3599, 1804, pp. 100-13, and vol. 3572, 1811, pp. 240-60.

19. TCR,TNA, vol. 3572, 1811, pp. 240-60.

20. TCR,TNA, vol. 3596, 1818, pp. 107-19, and vol. 3596, 1819, pp. 235-38. Revenue Department, "Report on the External and Internal Commerce of Madras Presidency, 1820/1."

21. J. Forbes Royle, *On the Culture and Commerce of Cotton in India and Elsewhere* (London, 1851), pp. 9-11.

22. Gavin Wright, "Cotton Competition and the Post-Bellum Recovery of the American South," *JEH*, 34 (September 1974), p. 611, table based on Thomas Ellison, *The Cotton Trade of Great Britain* (London, 1866).

23. Computed from Sarada Raju, *Economic Conditions*, pp. 304-305, 310.

24. Computed from annual "Reports on External and Internal Commerce of the Madras Presidency," 1820-1864.

25. Tinnevelly District export and import data referred to here are from Stuart, *Manual*, pp. 213-17; annual "Reports on Internal and External Commerce" (to 1864); and (after 1864) Revenue Department, *Annual Volume of Trade and Navigation in Madras Presidency*, IOL.

26. Ludden, "Agrarian Organization," gives more statistics.

27. Cotton dropped from 77 percent to 63 percent of the total Tinnevelly sea exports between 1870/1 and 1880/1. See note 25 above.

28. For Madras Presidency data, see Sarada Raju, *Economic Conditions*, pp. 3, 6-7. See note 25, above.

29. Railway freight and passenger statistics are from Stuart, *Manual*, pp. 245-47. Town population data are from *Census of India, 1921*, Vol. 13, Imperial Table No. 4.

30. TCR,TNA, vol. 7971, 1843, pp. 292-316. Puckle, "Settlement Report."

31. PBR,TNA, 6 March 1843, vol. 1849, pp. 3393-94.

32. R. K. Puckle, "Report on the More Important Projects for Extending Irrigation in the Tinnevelly District," in TCR,TCO, "To Board, 1868," dated 6 March 1868, n.p.

33. TCR,TNA, vol. 3582, 1807, pp. 94-97, and vol. 3683, 1808, pp. 70-77.

34. TCR,TNA, vol. 4368, 1826-1835, pp. 20-25.

35. "Official Diary of the Proceedings of the Superintendent of Tank Repairs and Water Courses, 1808," Board of Revenue Miscellaneous Volumes, TNA, and Puckle, "Report on the More Important Projects."

36. Puckle, "Report on the More Important Projects."

37. See "Memorandum of the Chief Engineer for Irrigation," in Proceedings of the Madras Government, Public Works Department, 26 October 1868, No. 549, IOL; H. C. Prendergast, *Memorandum on the Srivaikuntam Anicut Project and Its Subsidiary Works* (Madras, 1868); Robert Buckley, *The Irrigation Works of India and Their Financial Results* (London, 1880); and Puckle, "Report on the More Important Projects."

38. S. Y. Krishnaswami, *Rural Problems in Madras* (Madras, 1947), pp. 88-89, 236-37. Whitcombe, *Agrarian Conditions in North India*, p. 12, makes a similar point.

39. Ludden, "Patronage and Irrigation," pp. 358-60.

40. PBR,TNA, vol. 2039, pp. 161081-84.

41. TCR,TNA, vol. 4368, 1825-35, p. 13, and vol. 8025, 1825, p. 405.

42. For details on irrigation expenditure, see "Miscellaneous Correspondence" volumes in TCR,TNA, which give figures for each work sponsored by government, such as TCR,TNA vol. 8013, 1840, p. 85.

43. A. T. Arundel, *Irrigation and Communal Labour in Madras Presidency* (Madras, 1879), pp. 10-14.

44. TCR,TNA, vol. 8022, 1849, p. 27, and vol. 8023, 1850, p. 391.

45. TCR,TNA, vol. 8025, 1852, No. 1040, n.p., "Official Diary of the Superintendent of Tank Repairs and Water Courses." Puckle, "Report on the More Important Projects." Tamil Nadu, Directorate of Information and Publicity, *Patinaintu Catanaikal*, No. 5, *Tirunelveli* (Madras, 1966), p. 25.

46. Nilakanta Sastri, "The Manur Inscription"; TCR,TNA, vol. 8025, 1852, No. 1040, n.p.

47. Well counts were exaggerated, after 1842, by the removal of the well tax that year from wells classified as "new," that is, built after 1842; this exclusion sent farmers rushing to have their wells classified as "new." Presumably this distortion would have diminished by the 1850s and certainly by the 1860s. During the 1860s, however, survey and settlement teams might have discovered wells left off the books altogether. The settlement records employ a second "new" vs. "old" well distinction, setting 1854 as the dividing line. For statistics, see Ludden, "Agrarian Organization," pp. 50-55. Statistics for 1823 include all wells, not only "agricultural wells," as do later counts.

48. I amassed this sample from *Descriptive Memoirs*, TNA, compiled during survey and settlement.

49. Ludden, "Agrarian Organization," pp. 402-403.

50. Calculated from "1823 Census" and Stuart, *Manual*, p. 178.

51. See descriptions of north Tinnevelly towns in Pate, *Gazetteer*, and Stuart, *Manual*.

52. The periods and subperiods in Tables 5-10 are statistically necessary because of data discontinuities in Jamabandy Reports, TNA, on which tables are based, and from which six values have been computed: 1. mean cultivated acreage; 2. the percent of each cultivation category to total acreage, irrigated acreage, etc.; 3. the variability in cultivated acreage, that is, the standard deviation as a percent of the mean; 4. the slope of the regression line formed by regressing cultivated acreage onto years for each subperiod, so that the slope, b, represents the number of acres of change as we move from year x to $x+1$; 5. the growth rate in cultivated acreage, expressed by taking the slope of the regression line as a percent of the mean cultivated acreage for each subperiod; and 6. the correlation, computed with Pearson's R, which depicts the degree to which statistical data points conform to the linearity of the regression trend line, showing thus how much growth trends are linear. The maximum value for Pearson's R is 1.0. For more statistical detail (e.g., on cultivation data by taluk, 1825-1854), see Ludden, "Agrarian Organization," pp. 391-403. All data pertain only to circar territory, not zamindaris.

53. The small decline in per capita cultivated acreage between 1825-1837 and 1843-1854 probably results from census undercounts in the earlier years.

54. Ludden, "Agrarian Organization," p. 345.

55. In 1820, the average assessment on wet land stood as Rs.11/acre and dry land at Rs.0.5/acre, a ratio of 20 to 1. In 1875 the ratio stood at less than 10 to 1, mostly because of increasing relative rates on good dry in comparison to poor irrigated land. Computed from Stuart, *Manual*, pp. 180-85.

56. Puckle, "Report on the Most Important Projects."

57. TCR,TNA, vol. 8024, 1851, No. 42, n.p., and PBR, 1 December 1879, No. 3256, pp. 10522-23.

58. TCR,TNA, vol. 8023, 1850, p. 391.

59. Revenue Dapartment, *Resettlement Report of Tinnevelly District, Ambasamudram and Tenkasy Taluks*, G.O. No. 304, 31 January 1918. See also V. Krishnan, "Tambraparni Ryot."

60. Pate, *Gazetteer*, pp. 170, 180-85. Government of Tamil Nadu, *Season and Crop Report*, for years 1956-1975. District cultivation data, 1880-1956, is from *Season and Crop Reports*. See also Christopher J. Baker, *An Indian Rural Economy, 1880-1955: The Tamil Nadu Countryside* (Bombay, 1984), pp. 135-232.

61. See Hugh Tinker, *A New System of Slavery* (London, 1974); Wolf, *Europe and the People without History*, pp. 354-84; Ravindra K. Jain, *South Indians on the Plantation Frontier in Malaya* (New Haven, 1970); and R. Jayaratnam, "Indian Emigration to Ceylon," *IESHR*, 4:4 (1967), 320-59.

62. Note that England's agricultural advancement during the eighteenth and nineteenth centuries also rested on traditional technology: Chambers and Mingay, *The Agricultural Revolution*, pp. 1-15 ff.

63. *Census of India, 1921*, vol. 13, *Madras Imperial Tables*, No. 4 (Madras, 1921).

64. Revenue Department, "Papers Relating to the Protection of Undertenants in Ryotwari Tracts" (hereafter: "Papers on Undertenants"), Confidential, G.O. No. 3494-95, 9 December 1914, pp. 106-107. Krishnan, "Tambraparni Ryot," pp. 26-27.

65. Revenue Department, *Resettlement Report of Tinnevelly, Ambasamudram, and Tenkasy Taluks*, appended petition.

66. Kumar, *Land and Caste*, p. 166.

67. On the importance of such investment, see Theodore Schultz, *Investing in People* (Berkeley and Los Angeles, 1981), pp. 1-40.

68. Krishnaswamy, *Rural Problems*, pp. 94-96 ff.

69. *Parliamentary Papers, Accounts and Papers*, 1847, vol. 42, "Papers in the Possession of the East India Company showing measures that have been taken since 1846 to promote the cultivation of cotton in India . . . ," pp. 305-420. *Parliamentary Papers, Reports from Committees, 1847-8 Session*, vol. 9, "Report of the Select Committee on the Cultivation of Cotton in India." *Parliamentary Papers, Accounts and Papers, Session 2, 1857*, vol. 30, part 1, "Selection of Papers showing measures taken since 1847 to promote the cultivation of cotton in India," Part 2, Madras. Sarada Raju, *Economic Con-*

ditions, pp. 75-101. J. Talboys Wheeler, *Handbook for the Cultivation of Cotton in the Madras Presidency* (Madras, 1862). J. Forbes Royle, *On the Culture and Commerce of Cotton.* Pate, *Gazetteer,* pp. 158-67.

70. See note 25 above.

71. As in early revenue policy making, Englishmen who observed the Indian system of trade often blamed what J. Talboys Wheeler called its "vicious system," which put too much power into the hands of unscrupulous (native) middlemen standing between cotton growers and exporters. Wheeler, *Handbook,* pp. 33 ff. Mr. Finnie's exploits are recorded ibid. chapter 4, and in *Parliamentary Papers* cited in note 69 above.

72. Wheeler complains that Finnie, "as a patriotic American planter," and thus in a conflict of interest when in India to improve Indian cotton exports to England, "systematically endeavoured to throw cold water upon the objects in view," technological change in Indian farming and ginning. *Handbook,* p. 91.

73. How the railway facilitated agency house penetration of inland marketing centers and elimination of vexatious middlemen is explained fully in J. S. Ponniah, "Production and Marketing of Raw Cotton in the Madras Presidency, with Special Reference to the Six Districts of Bellary, Kurnool, Coimbatore, Madurai, Ramnad, and Tinnevelly," Ph.D. dissertation, Madras, chapter 2.

74. This is conjecture based on town population, and economic and political trends. On the last of these, see Chapter Six.

75. Personal observations and interviews. See Washbrook, *Emergence of Provincial Politics,* pp. 64-146, for political implications.

76. Ponniah, "Production and Marketing of Raw Cotton," pp. 94-95. Gilbert Slater, *Some South Indian Villages* (Madras, 1918), p. 32.

Chapter 6: Changing Tradition

1. See Nicholas Dirks, "From Little King to Landlord," California Institute of Technology, Humanities Working Paper No. 84. The "1823 Census" records extant "Kaval shares" in several taluks, a good indication of sharehold traditions among Maravas.

2. See above, Chapter Two.

3. See above, Chapter Two.

4. Recent research suggests that legal codification did not underpin adjudication in pre-British South India. Scholars now look for the means of dispute settlement instead in ritualized events, such as temple ceremonies and royal darbars, which provided the locus and lexicon for the social creation of rights to resources, comparable to courts in Europe. See especially Appadurai, *Worship and Conflict.*

5. See above, Chapter Three.

6. In a recent survey of wells in Tamil Nadu, all katcha wells, that is, those not lined with stone, were owned by individuals, whereas 46 percent

of all pucca wells, more costly, deeper, and lined with stone, were jointly owned: Planning Commission, Programme Evaluation Organization, *Study of Problems of Minor Irrigation* (New Delhi, 1961), p. 32.

7. See above, Chapter Two.

8. See above, Chapter One.

9. See Chapter Four, note 4.

10. TDCR,TNA indexes give subjects of disputes. On the importance of district munsifs for property disputes, see Strange, *Letter*, pp. 9-11 and Appendix pp. vi, vii, ix.

11. Strange, *Letter*, Appendix, p. lxxxix. Holloway, *Notes on Judicial Administration*, pp. ii-iv. Court costs and their distribution are given for most cases retained in TDCR.

12. Strange, *Letter*, p. xiv.

13. Ibid., pp. 11-14.

14. Ibid., pp. 9-11.

15. "List of Records Showing the Nature and Volume of Suits," TDCR.

16. PBR,TNA, 2 September 1830, vol. 1251, pp. 9092-96. TCR,TNA, vol. 4363, 1821-1835, pp. 308-16. A.S. #27, 1847, Zillah Court, TDCR, 69.

17. Bayley and Hudleston, *Papers on Mirasi Right*, pp. 77-84, 165-66. Jamabandy Report F. 1253 summarizes rights in these two types of villages according to Revenue rules. Collectors recognized that "mirasi" villages were not all sharehold villages, and vice versa. See TCR,TNA, vol. 7966, 1836, pp. 139-49, and the case discussed in the next paragraph.

18. TCR,TNA, vol. 7966, 1836, pp. 139-49; vol. 7968, 1838, pp. 179-90; vol. 8010, 1837, pp. 168-69. PBR,TNA, 31 March 1845, vol. 1961, pp. 4231-309. A.S. #56, 1845, Zillah Court, TDCR, 10. See note 44.

19. Jamabandy Reports F. 1252 and 1253. TCR,TNA, vol. 7974, 1846, pp. 52-116.

20. TCR,TNA, vol. 4363, 1821-1835, pp. 26-63.

21. TCR,TNA, vol. 7970, 1842, pp. 58-74.

22. TCR,TNA, vol. 4368, 1825-1836, pp. 20-25. *Selections from the Records of the Madras Government. Correspondence Relative to . . . A Permanent Corps of Coolies*, pp. 2-10. See also Chapter Five, above, on irrigation construction.

23. A.S. #13, 1817, Zillah Court, TDCR, 75.

24. A.S. #125, 1821; A.S. #337, 1826 and A.S. #10, 1827; A.S. #31, 1844; A.S. #126, 1851; A.S. #81, 1853: all Zillah Court, TDCR: 1, 7, 17, 30, 77, respectively.

25. A.S. #13, 1845, Zillah Court, TDCR, 9.

26. A.S. #10, 1949, Zillah Court, TDCR, 17.

27. Arbuthnot, *Sir Thomas Munro*, p. 245.

28. Bayley and Hudleston, *Papers on Mirasi Right*, Document No. 92 (extracted from PBR, 14 May 1856), and p. 245.

29. Bayley and Hudleston, pp. 556-57, 589.

30. *Papers Relating to the Sale of Waste Lands*, pp. 10-11, 200-34.

31. Ibid., pp. 10-11. Moffatt, *An Untouchable Community*, pp. 48-50, points out that, in some localities, former landless laborers, many of them untouchables, succeeded in buying land under the new rules. In Tinnevelly District, such purchases must have been most important in the mixed zone, there perhaps being part of ongoing mirasidar-tenant land purchase transactions, for which see below.

32. "Papers on Undertenants," Appendix, p. 13.

33. Jamabandy Report, F. 1235. TCR,TNA, vol. 4365, 1827-1835, pp. 71-86.

34. Hodgson, "Report of 1807." The village of Varttiraya Iruppu (see below) was an exception to this rule. See also Bayley and Hudleston, p. 168.

35. For their objections, see above, Chapter Four.

36. Hepburn, *Collector's Report on the Decennial Lease*, pp. 9-10.

37. PBR,TNA, 15 November 1819, vol. 839, p. 10200.

38. PBR, 16 January 1823, extracted in TCR,TNA, vol. 3576, 1820-1823, p. 31.

39. Jamabandy Report F. 1235.

40. A.S. #11, 1830, and A.S. #17, 1830, Zillah Court, TDCR, 7.

41. For examples, see TCR,TNA, vol. 7969, 1840-1841, pp. 276-77, and A.S. #85, 1847, Zillah Court, TDCR, 14.

42. A.S. #108, 1848, and A.S. #45, 1851, Zillah Court, TDCR, 92. TCR,TCO, To Board, 1858, letters No. 25 and 273, n.p.

43. TCR,TNA, vol. 7968, 1838-1839, pp. 267-72; vol. 7979, 1852, pp. 34-39; vol. 7980, 1853, pp. 76-77. PBR,TNA, 31 March 1845, vol. 1961, pp. 4231-309. TCR,TCO, To Board, 1868, Letter No. 279, 18 June 1868, n.p.

44. See "Hukumnamah of 1835," in TCR,TNA, vol. 4709, 1835, p. 373; and TCR,TCO, To Board, 1868, Letter No. 271, 10 June 1868, which quotes the district munsif of Brahmadesam, who in turn cites a sadr ameen decision in A.S. #1, 1802, as follows: "that in suits instituted for pattahs the court can only declare the title of the land." Only the collector could issue a pattah; under a court order to do so, the collector, in the Bommiapuram case, discussed above, had to appeal the court decision at his own expense. See note 18.

45. PBR,TNA, 6 March 1843, vol. 1849, pp. 3402-403.

46. A.S. #32, 1828; A.S. #11 and #17, 1830; A.S. #23, 1851: all Zillah Court, TDCR, 2, 7, 23, respectively.

47. A.S. #85, 1847, Zillah Court, TDCR, 14. See also A.S. #17, 1846, Zillah Court, TDCR, 77.

48. See above, Chapter Three.

49. See above, Chapter Four.

50. Jamabandy Reports F. 1235 and 1244.

51. TCR,TNA, vol. 7977, 1849, pp. 49-54. Other similarly mixed-caste villages included Kadaiyanallur, Nettur, Kodaganallur, and Konguvaraya-kurichi, for which see PBR,TNA, 2 January 1822, vol. 1934, pp. 279-91. See also A.S. #3, 1834, and A.S. #43, 1840, Zillah Court, TDCR, 65.

52. See above, Chapter One.

53. For example, A.S. #134, 1853, Zillah Court, TDCR, 30. Note the parallel between the breakup of collective shareholding in South India and the enclosure movement in England, which also progressed by a combination of local initiatives and national legislative action. See Chambers and Mingay, *The Agricultural Revolution*, pp. 77-105.

54. *Papers on the Settlement of Tinnevelly*, pp. 160-74.

55. O.S. #44, 1819, and A.S. #22, 1845, Zillah Court, TDCR, 9, 76, respectively.

56. TCR,TNA, vol. 7977, 1849, pp. 49-54, 163-74.

57. A.S. #3, 1834; A.S. #51, 1839; and A.S. #8, 1851; Zillah Court, TDCR, 2, 20, 65, respectively.

58. *Reports on Cases Decided in the High Court* (Madras, 1866), vol. 1, pp. 1-6, 17-18.

59. *Papers on the Settlement of Tinnevelly*, pp. 9, 17 ff.

60. A.S. #39, 1834, Zillah Court, TDCR, 4. See also cases cited in notes 46 and 47 above.

61. *Papers on the Settlement of Tinnevelly*, pp. 237-80; Bayley and Hudleston, p. 168.

62. Jamabandy Report F. 1245. TCR,TNA, vol. 7967, 1837, pp. 17-21; vol. 7968, 1838-1839, pp. 6-7; vol. 7971, 1843, pp. 79-93; vol. 7972, 1844, pp. 21-28; vol. 7974, 1846, pp. 104-12; and vol. 7975, 1847, pp. 316-17.

63. TCR,TNA, vol. 7974, 1846, pp. 104-14.

64. A.S. #16, 1848, Zillah court, TDCR, 15. A.S. #2, 1853, Zillah Court, TDCR, 29 is the same sort of suit.

65. *Reports on Cases in the High Court*, 1: 264-69.

66. *Reports on Cases in the High Court*, 2: 171-73. TCR,TCO, To Board, 1858, Letter No. 47, 29 January 1858, n.p.

67. TCR,TCO volumes are filled with such cases, one being the case cited in the previous note.

68. "Papers on Undertenants," quoting an 1865 Revenue G.O.

69. *Papers on the Settlement of Tinnevelly*, pp. 160-74.

70. See above, Chapter Five.

71. *Parliamentary Papers, 1860, House of Commons*. Sessional Paper No. 733, vol. 52, No. 89. East India (Disturbances in Tinnevelly), cited in Robert E. Frykenberg, "On Roads and Riots in Tinnevelly," *SA*, NS 4:2 (1982), 34-52, from which my account of the riot is drawn.

72. Extract from the Proceedings of the Sessions Court in Tinnevelly, 11 December 1858, quoted in Frykenberg, "Roads and Riots," p. 38.

73. For further parallels with more notorious communal riots in North India, see Sandria Freitag, "Sacred Symbol as Mobilizing Ideology," and Anand Yang, "Sacred Symbol and Sacred Place in Rural India," *MAS*, 22:4 (1980), 397-425, 576-96.

74. Frykenberg, "Roads and Riots," p. 40.

75. Robert E. Frykenberg, "The Impact of Conversion and Social Reform

upon Society in South India during the Late Company Period," in Philips and Wainwright, eds. *Indian Society and the Beginnings of Modernization, c. 1830-1850* (London, 1976), pp. 187-243.

76. Church Mission Society, South India (Madras Mission), Correspondence: 1830-42. South Asia Microfilm Project, Center for Research Libraries, Microfilm, Reel No. 1, p. 67.

77. See Paul Appaswamy, *The Centenary History of the C.M.S. in Tinnevelly* (Palayamcottai, 1923); R. E. Frykenberg, "The Impact of Conversion"; and Hardgrave, *Nadars*, pp. 43-71.

78. Hardgrave, *Nadars*, pp. 89-90.

79. See Frykenberg, "The Impact of Conversion."

80. Connections between late nineteenth-century events in the north and earlier conflicts in the south are controversial. Hardgrave, *Nadars*, posits a direct connection, based on supposed caste consciousness of the Shanars in both north and south, and on their nineteenth-century migrations from the south into the north. Washbrook, *Emergence of Provincial Politics*, pp. 141-45 ff., posits instead a conscious effort by northern Shanar town-based merchants to create a myth of caste political identity for British consumption, without any real connection to the bulk of the Shanar population, especially in southern Tinnevelly District. Hardgrave's proposition of Shanar migrations northward during the century is very dubious (see Chapter Two, above); and, like Washbrook, I see no direct connections between rich merchant Shanars in the north and poor palmyra tappers in the south. All Shanars, however, experienced a relative rise in their economic fortunes, during the century; and, given their similarities, though they have no direct connection to one another, they responded culturally and politically in similar ways in the rural south and urban north. They developed ideological stances and politicized strategies consonant with economic mobility in caste society. See, for a similar case, Michael Roberts, *Caste Conflict and Elite Formation* (Cambridge, 1982), which also has an excellent bibliography and discussion of the debate surrounding Washbrook's work on caste politics.

81. Hardgrave, *Nadars*, pp. 104-105; 1921 *Census*.

82. My account of events preceding 1899 comes from Hardgrave, *Nadars*, pp. 109-16. For government temple administration policy, see Appadurai, *Worship and Conflict*.

83. Judicial Department, "Report of Mr. Hammick . . . on the Disturbances in Madura and Tinnevelly," G.O. Nos. 2017-18 (Confidential), 12 December 1899.

84. A.R.E. 1916/17, Part 1, p. 134, editor's comment on the inscription concerning *vellai nadans* (see Chapter Two).

85. David Arnold, "Looting, Grain Riots, and Government Policy in South India," *PP*, 84 (1979), 111-45.

86. See Washbrook, *Emergence of Provincial Politics*, pp. 261-329; David Arnold, Robin Jeffrey, and James Manor, "Caste Associations in South India,"

IESHR, 12:3 (1976), 353-74; and Lloyd I. Rudolph and Susanne Hoeber Rudolph, *The Modernity of Tradition* (Chicago, 1967), pp. 15-154.

87. Irschick, *Politics and Social Conflict*, pp. 171-356; Washbrook, *Emergence of Provincial Politics*, pp. 288-329; Baker, *Politics in South India*.

88. On colonial sociology and its intellectual foundations, see Cohn, "Representing Authority in Victorian India."

89. For good accounts of Tamil nationalism and Non-Brahmanism see Washbrook, *Emergence of Provincial Politics*, pp. 261-88; and Barnett, *The Politics of Cultural Nationalism*.

CONCLUSION: PEASANT SOCIETY

1. Sigfried Kracauer, *History: The Last Things before the Last* (New York, 1969), chapter 5, "The Structure of the Historical Universe," pp. 104-38, helps situate the social history I describe philosophically; Fernand Braudel, "History and Social Science: The *Long Duree*," in his *On History* (Chicago, 1980), pp. 25-54, does so methodologically. Eric Jones, *European Miracle*, and Eric Wolf, *Europe and the People without History* set the global perspective. Anthony Giddens, *Central Problems in Social Theory* (Berkeley and Los Angeles, 1979), pp. 49-130, pinpoints the importance of structural dynamics inside routines of social reproduction.

2. Richard Critchfield, *Villages* (New York, 1983), epitomizes this attitude and cites relevant literature.

3. Giddens, *Central Problems*, pp. 198-233, specifies the limits of synchronous social theory and social science. For pertinent views of peasants, see Eric Wolf, *Peasants* (Englewood Cliffs, 1966), and Silverman, "The Peasant Concept in Anthropology."

4. See Alfred Crosby, *The Columbian Exchange* (Westport, Conn., 1972); and Wolf, *Europe and the People without History*, pp. 127-262.

5. The "agrarian system" is an open-ended concept that Irfan Habib and Daniel Thorner introduced into Indian historical studies to capture the range of social connections between actors in an agricultural production milieu. They used "agrarian system," instead of "mode of production," but retained the wholistic view of agricultural society embedded in the latter phrase. See Burton Stein, "Integration of the Agrarian System," which is the first attempt to trace the process of change in a system over centuries.

6. See Mark Elvin, *The Pattern of the Chinese Past* (London, 1973); Gerald Hodgett, *A Social and Economic History of Medieval Europe* (London, 1972); Marshall Hodgson, *The Venture of Islam* (Chicago, 1974), vol. 2; and Romila Thapar, *A History of India*, vol. 1 (Harmondsworth, 1966).

7. McEvedy and Jones, *Atlas of World Population*, pp. 346-48.

8. Jones, *European Miracle*, pp. 45-69; Elvin, *Pattern of the Chinese Past*; Robert M. Hartwell, "Demographic, Political, and Social Transformations of China, 750-1550," *HJAS*, 42:2 (1982), 365-442.

9. Hodgett, *Medieval Europe*, pp. 22-23: "The picture that emerges be-

tween c. 500 and 1000 is a picture of a modestly expanding rural economy. Expansion and change were greater in the north than in the south where the economy stood still or tended to decline. In the temperate zone the development of virgin lands or lands that had been little cultivated meant that the balance of production was tipped in favor of the north which became the area of experiment and challenge in early medieval farming practice."

10.   Hartwell, "Transformations of China," pp. 369, 375.

11.   Ibid., pp. 365-66.

12.   McEvedy and Jones, *Atlas of World Population*, p. 185.

13.   Thapar, *History of India*, pp. 221-65.

14.   See Stein, *Peasant State and Society*.

15.   Stein's work must be set against the classic, Nilakanta Sastri, *The Cholas*, which argues for a powerfully centralized Chola empire, as does Kathleen Gough, *Rural Society in Southeast India*, pp. 105-13. See Stein, "The State and the Agrarian Order," and R. Champakalakshmi, "Peasant State and Society in Medieval South India," *IESHR*, 18:3-4 (1981), 411-27. Kenneth Hall, "Peasant State and Society in Chola Times: A View from Tiruvidaimardur Urban Complex," *IESHR*, 18:3-4 (1981), 393-410, and idem, *Trade and Statecraft in the Age of the Cholas* (New Delhi, 1980).

16.   In this Stein follows Subbarayulu, *Political Geography of the Chola Country*.

17.   The Tamil poet Tirunanasambantar is said to have executed 8,000 Jains upon winning the heart of the Pandya king to the love of Shiva. See Kamil Zvelebil, *Tamil Literature* (Leiden, 1974), pp. 139-40.

18.   See Barnett, *The Politics of Cultural Nationalism*, for a good account of such ideas in action.

19.   The upland region due west of Tanjavur, up the Kaveri River basin, is the best documented and largest zone of frontier settlement in this period. See Brian Murton, "Some Propositions on the Spread of Village Settlement in Interior Tamil Nadu before 1750 A.D.," *IGJ*, 48:2 (1973), 56-73, and idem, "The Evolution of the Settlement Structure in Northern Kongu to 1800 A.D.," in Beck, ed., *Perspectives on a Regional Culture* (Delhi, 1979), pp. 7-43. On the drainage basin in historical human geography, see C. T. Smith, "The Drainage Basin as an Historical Basis for Human Activity," in Chorley, ed., *Water, Earth, and Man* (London, 1969), pp. 101-12.

20.   Jones, *European Miracle*, p. 53. On the Cholas, see Spencer, "Religious Networks," and idem, "Royal Initiatives under Rajaraja I," *IESHR*, 7:4 (1970), 431-42.

21.   Monumental building became the hallmark of Vijayanagar and later Mughal emperors. Christopher A. Bayly, *Rulers, Townsmen, and Bazaars* (Cambridge, 1983), makes a powerful case for the importance of royal consumption in political and economic integration.

22.   Emmanuel Le Roy Ladurie, *The Mind and Method of the Historian* (Chicago, 1981), pp. 275-77; Jones, *European Miracle*, pp. 75-80.

23.   Hodgson, *Venture of Islam*, vol. 3, considers "gunpowder empires."

See also McNeill, *Rise of the West*, pp. 484-564, and Jones, *European Miracle*, pp. 75-95.

24. See Crosby, *Columbian Exchange*.

25. See Ralph Davis, *The Rise of the Atlantic Economies* (Ithaca, 1973). The quote is from Derent S. Whittlesey, *The Earth and State: A Study in Political Geography* (New York, 1944), quoted in Jones, *European Miracle*, p. 80. See also Pierre Vilar, *A History of Gold and Money, 1450-1920* (London, 1976); William S. Atwell, "International Bullion Flows and the Chinese Economy *circa* 1530-1650," *PP*, 95 (1982), 68-90; Charles Issawi, "The Decline of the Middle Eastern Trade, 1100-1850," in Richards, ed., *Islam and the Trade of Asia* (Philadelphia, 1970), pp. 245-66; Neils Steensgaard, *The Asian Trade Revolution of the Seventeenth Century* (Chicago, 1973); and Philip D. Curtin, *Cross-Cultural Trade in World History* (New York, 1984), pp. 109-78.

26. See Curtin, *Cross-Cultural Trade*, pp. 129-58.

27. See Stein, "Integration," pp. 188-96, and his article on Vijayanagar in Raychaudhuri and Habib, *Cambridge Economic History*, pp. 48-77, 102-24.

28. For comparisons of European and Asian militarism in the process of market development, see Jones, *European Miracle*, pp. 104-26, 159-71, 225-39.

29. K. A. Nilakanta Sastri, *A History of South India from Prehistoric Times to the Fall of Vijayanagar* (Madras, 1955), is the best overview of shifting political centers of gravity in the peninsula as a whole. See also Thapar, *History of India*.

30. These were medieval core zones of Pandya, Chola, and Pallava power. On the west, in the Chera country, now Kerala, the pepper trade was of great importance for interior economic life: see Curtin, *Cross-Cultural Trade*, pp. 146-48.

31. Perlin, "Proto-industrialization and Pre-colonial South Asia"; Raychaudhuri and Habib, eds., *Cambridge Economic History*, pp. 382-433. J. S. Richards, "Mughal State Finance and Premodern World Economy," *CSSH*, 23:2 (1981), 285-308.

32. The importance of merchant capital in politics during the transition to colonial rule has been emphasized in many recent researches. See Karen Leonard, "The 'Great Firm' Theory of the Decline of the Mughal Empire," *CSSH*, 21: 2 (1979), 151-67; Richards, "Mughal State Finance"; and Bayly, *Rulers, Townsmen, and Bazaars*, pp. 164-96.

33. On imperial financial problems after World War I, see B. R. Tomlinson, *The Political Economy of the Raj, 1914-1947* (London, 1976).

34. See Neil Charlesworth, *British Rule and the India Economy* (London, 1982).

35. See, for instance, the discussion of famine and government policy in Michelle Burge McAlpin, *Subject to Famine: Food Crises and Economic Change in Western India, 1860-1920* (Princeton, 1983).

36. Milton Singer, *When a Great Tradition Modernizes* (New York, 1972), p. 258; M. N. Srinivas, *India's Villages* (Bombay, 1960), p. 11. Philip Curtin discussed the importance of geographical perspectives in world history in his presidential address to the American Historical Association, "Depth, Span, and Relevance," *AHR*, 89:1 (1984), 1-9.

37. Schwartzberg, *Historical Atlas*, p. 50, depicts cultural regions in detail.

38. See Ludden, "Productive Power in Agriculture."

39. See above, Chapter Three, and Gough, *Rural Society*, pp. 117-18.

40. Ashin Das Gupta, "Trade and Politics," and Bayly, *Rulers, Townsmen, and Bazaars*, pp. 110-63.

41. Curtin argues that trade diasporas generated cultural change during efforts in cross-cultural trade. See *Cross-Cultural Trade*, pp. 1-15, where the argument of "cultural blends" has much in common with that made by Wolf, *Europe and the People without History*, pp. 385-92.

42. See Washbrook, *Emergence of Provincial Politics*, pp. 64-167; John Harriss, *Capitalism and Peasant Farming* (Bombay, 1982); and Bruce Robert, "Economic Change and Agrarian Organization in 'Dry' South India, 1890-1940," *MAS*, 17:1 (1983), 59-78. The debate on this continues.

43. For more on this argument, see Ludden, "Productive Power."

GLOSSARY

Abbreviations

HJ   Henry Yule and A. C. Burnell, *Hobson Jobson* (London, 1886)
HW   H. H. Wilson, *A Glossary of Judicial and Revenue Terms* (London, 1855)
(Ar)   from Arabic
(H)   from Hindi
(K)   from Kannada
(Per)   from Persian
(San)   from Sanskrit
(Tam)   from Tamil
NOTE: All italicized terms appear with *Tamil Lexicon* definitions.

abayam	refuge
aḍaiyōlai	a document (*ōlai*) serving as evidence of a pledge
adalat	court of law (*see* Sadr Adalat)
agapat	(Tam?) a revenue term designating a channel-fed tank
amāni	(Ar?) something held in trust or deposit, applied especially to lands under direct government revenue management (HW, p. 21)
amildār	(H) a collector of or contractor for revenue (a pre-1800 usage in South India) (HJ, p. 23)
amīn	(also: ameen) (Ar) "trustworthy person"; official inspector or intendent (HJ, p. 17)
anicut	(Tam: *aṇaikkaṭṭu*) dam
āṇmai	controlling power, manliness, courage, conquest
bhakti	(Tamil: *pakti*) devotion to god, piety
brahmadēya	a village granted to Brahmans and inhabited by them
cawnie	(Tam) Anglo-Indian English for *kāṇi*, q.v.
chain	(?) a dry land measure used in nineteenth-century revenue records, equal to 3.64 acres
chattram	(Tam) a place where food is given out gratuitously, especially to Brahmans (HW, p. 104)

261

chōḷam	great millet, sorghum (Hindi: *jowar*)
choultry	(?) a travelers' resting place (HJ, pp. 211-12)
circār	(also: sircar, sarcar) (H) government, the state; used to differentiate land under direct government authority from that under poligars or zamindars (HJ, p. 235)
collector	the chief administrative officer in an Indian zillah, district, or collectorate, also holding magisterial powers (HJ, p. 236)
curnam	(also: karnam, kurnam, etc.) (K) (Tamil: *kaṇak-kuppiḷḷai*) a village accountant (HJ, p. 281)
darkhast	(?) a petition
delavoy	(Tamil: *taḷavāy*) (K) the commander-in-chief, hence also the prime minister under Vijayanagar and Mysore rulers (HW, p. 121)
dēsakāval	protection (*kāval*) of the country (*dēsam*), referring to an area wider than a village
dēvadāna	a gift to god, hence to temples
district	an Indian administrative division under British rule
ēri	an irrigation tank
ethiraḍaiyōlai	a receipt given to acknowledge an *aḍaiyōlai*
firka	a subdivision of a taluk
ghāts	(H) path of descent, a mountain pass, hence a mountain chain as in the Eastern and Western Ghats of peninsular India (HJ, p. 369)
gōmāstāh	(Per) an agent, steward, or representative (HW, p. 189)
headman	the chief civil officer of a village (HW, p. 370), titled variously in local usage (patel, monigar, nattanmaigar, etc.)
hūzūr	(also: huzoor) (Ar) "the presence," a respectful form of address referring to government officers, hence denoting leading officials and their head-quarter stations (HJ, p. 431)
īnām	(Ar) a gift from superior to inferior, especially applied to tax-free grants of land by rulers to subjects (HW, pp. 217-18)

262

iṟai	duty, obligation, tax
iṟaivan	king, chief, lord, master
jajmāni	(H) a village system of customary payments, in kind, at harvest time, from landowning patrons (jajmāns) to clients who perform services for them throughout the year (HW, p. 226)
jamabandy	(H) the annual settlement of revenue accounts in an estate, village, or district (HW, p. 228)
jāti	kind, class, species, caste
kaḍamai	duty, obligation, tax
kambu	bullrush, spiked, or pearl millet (Hindi: *bajra*)
kambu-aḍi-kambu	an agricultural practice in which land is specially prepared and manured for cultivation with *kambu* year after year
kaṇakkan	accountant
kaṇakkuppiḷḷai	village accountant
kāṇi	the fraction one-eighth; a land measure (1.32 acres); land in general; landed property or hereditary possessions; rights of possession or hereditary right in general
kāṇikkaḍan	land tax
kāṇiyātchi	control (*ātchi*) of rights of possession, especially in land; hence landownership
kāṇiyātchikkāran	one who controls rights of possession; hence landowner
kaṇkāṇam	supervision
kaṇkāṇi	supervisor
kār	rain; the rainy season; the rainy-season paddy crop
kārāḷar	farmer, Vellala
kārāṇmai	inscriptional usage for *kāṇiyātchi*, q.v.
karṇam	*see* curnam, *kaṇakkuppiḷḷai*
kaṭṭumaṟam	catamaran
kāval	protection
kāvalkāran	watchman, especially village watchman or police officer

kiḷai	a branch, hence branch of genealogical tree, kindred, relations, or sub-*jāti* division
kiḷavan	owner, lord, master, chief of agricultural tract
koṭṭai	fort, castle, also a grain measure and hence an area of land planted by one such measure of seed grain (1.62 acres of paddy land)
kōvil	(also: *kōyil*) temple
kuḍi	resident, tenant; place of residence
kudimaramat	(Tam + Ar) seasonal repairs (*maramat*) to irrigation channels by villagers (*kudi*) (HW, p. 299)
kuḍivāram	the cultivators' share of the crop, in contrast to government's share (*mēlvāram*, q.v.)
kuḷam	a tank, reservoir, or pond
kuṭumban	headman of the Palla caste in a village
lakh	(H) one hundred thousand, especially of rupees
malaimakkaḷ	people (*makkaḷ*) of the mountain (*malai*)
maṇḍalam	circle, sphere, orbit; a division of the country
maniyam	(Tam) superintendence or management of village affairs, especially revenue affairs (HW, p. 329)
māniyam	land held either rent-free or at low tax rates in consideration of services to the village
maramat	(Ar) mending, repairing (HW, p. 331); especially, in Madras Presidency, the construction or repair of irrigation works (HJ, p. 558)
maṭam	hermitage, monastery
mēḍai	a raised platform
mēlvāram	the superior (*mēl*) portion of the crop, claimed by the landlord or by government, in contrast to the cultivator's share, *kuḍivāram*
mirāsi	(Ar: *mīrās*, "to inherit") inheritance, inherited property or right (HW, p. 342)
mirāsidār	the holder of a *mirāsi*, especially village shareholders (HW, pp. 342-43; HJ, p. 565)
muchilka	(also: muchalka, etc.) (H) a written obligation or agreement (HW, p. 348)
mufti	(Ar) a Muslim judicial officer (HW, p. 349), hence a judicial officer in Mughal and Company territory

mufti sadr amin	a judicial officer ranking above the village munsif and below the zillah judge in nineteenth-century Madras Presidency
mūnsif	(also moonsiff, etc.) (H) native civil judge of the lowest rank under British rule; also called village munsif (HJ, p. 581; HW, p. 356)
nādalvān	ruler of a nadu
nāḍu	country, district, province; an agricultural tract; a division of the Tamil country
nāḍumakkaḷ	people (makkaḷ) of an agricultural tract (nāḍu)
nanjai	(Tamil sp. nansey) irrigated fields or crops
nanjai-mēl-punjai	the agricultural practice of planting dry (punjai) crops, millets, on irrigated (nanjai) land, to secure a harvest in a year of low rainfall
nāṭṭānmaikkāran	the leader of a village or agricultural tract, hence village headman
nāṭṭār	the leaders of a nāḍu
nāṭṭōm	an inscriptional usage: "we of the nāḍu"
nāyaka	(also nayak, naik) warrior chief, ruler
nunjah	Anglo-Indian English for nanjai, q.v.
nunjah-mel-punjah	Anglo-Indian English for nanjai-mēl-punjai, q.v.
ōlai	a palm-leaf strip used as a writing surface, hence a manuscript or document in general
olungu	(Tam: oḷungu, "order," "regularity") a system of revenue settlement applied to irrigated parts of Madras Presidency
pākam	share, portion
pāḷaiyakkāran	a military chief, commander of a fortress (pāḷaiyam)
pāḷaiyam	war camp, fortress
pallakkāḷ	an irrigation channel
pallakkuḍi	a Palla caste person
pallam	lowness
panchāyat	(H) a native court of arbitration (HW, p. 394)
pangu	share, portion
patham	(Tam) a concessionary tax assessment rate

pattah	(also: pottah, etc.) a lease, deed, contract, receipt, or official document of certification; specifically, a document specifying the land revenue due from a piece of land or a person (HW, pp. 408-10)
pattahdār	one who holds a pattah, hence landowner
paṭṭam	certificate, authorization, degree
pattam	a fixed-money rental tenure
paṭṭinam	town, city, commercial center
pēṭṭai	a fortified market town
pisānam	a variety of paddy; a season of paddy cultivation, beginning with the northeast monsoon and ending in February or March
poligar	a *pāḷaiyakkāran*, q.v.
pollam	(Tam) the estate of a poligar (HJ, pp. 718-19)
ponakulam	nineteenth-century revenue term for a rainfed tank
punjah	Anglo-Indian for *punjai*, q.v.
punjai	(Tamil sp. *punsey*) unirrigated fields or crops
qanungo	(also: canungo, kanungo, etc.) (Per) a revenue officer (HW, p. 260)
rāgi	(Tamil sp. *irāgi*) a variety of foodgrain, eleusine coracana (HJ, p. 753)
renter	contractors for revenue collection, who pay in advance into the treasury for authorization to collect from a specified territory
ryot	(also: raiyat) (Ar) a subject, but especially a cultivator, farmer, or peasant (HW, p. 433)
ryotwāri	(also: raiyetwar, rayetwar, etc.) a system of land tax collection in which state officers collect directly from farmers, without intermediary renters or zamindars (HJ, p. 778)
sabhā	the assembly of a *brahmadēya*
sadr	eminence, superiority, hence the highest or foremost (HW, p. 450)
Sadr Adalat	the chief court of justice under the East India Company's authority (HW, pp. 450-51)
sāmai	little millet

sangam	gathering, convocation; hence the earliest period of Tamil history, named for a mythical gathering of poets at Madurai
sangu	chank, conch; large convoluted shell used for making jewelry
seed cottai	a nineteenth-century term for the area of land that would be planted with one *kottai* of seed paddy (1.62 acres)
sepoy	(Per) a foot soldier (HJ, pp. 809-11)
sērvaikkāran	commander of an army
sherishtādār	(?) head ministerial officer of a court, hence a head native officer in district headquarters (HJ, p. 826)
sowkar	(also: soukar, savukar) banker (HJ, p. 858)
sthanikar	temple manager
swāmibhōgam	(San) rent paid to *mirāsidār* (HW, p. 496)
tahsildār	(H) a native revenue official; in Madras Presidency, the chief administrative officer of a taluk (HW, p. 500; HJ, p. 894)
talaivan	headman
tālūk	(also: talook) (Ar) an administrative subdivision of a district (HJ, p. 894)
tēri	sand hill, sandy tract
tinai	place, region, situation
Tinnies	a variety of cotton grown in Tinnevelly, Ramnad, and Madurai districts of Madras Presidency
ūr	a village; a non-Brahman village and the inhabitants' assembly
vaduga	(Tamil sp. *vadugar*) northerner, hence Telugu- and Kanada-speakers in Tamil country
vamsāvali	genealogical account
vanpyre	(Tam: *vanpayir*) cultivation using well water
varagu	kodo millet
vāram	share, portion
vāykkāl	an irrigation channel
vēlālar	Vellala
vēlan	one with a spear (*vēl*); warrior, chief

267

veḷḷāḷar	Vellala
watchman	a village officer in charge of police duties
zamīndār	(also: zemindar) under British rule, an owner of an estate under permanent settlement (HW, pp. 562-64; HJ, p. 980)
zillah	an administrative district

BIBLIOGRAPHY

ARCHIVAL RECORDS

Madras Presidency Board of Revenue Proceedings, TNA, IOL.
Madras Presidency Settlement Registers and Descriptive Memoirs, TNA.
Madras Presidency Transferred District Court Records, TNA.
Settlement Registers. Descriptive Memoirs of Tinnevelly District. n.d. (c.1877), TNA.
Tinnevelly Collectorate Records, TNA.
Tinnevelly Zillah Court Records, TCO.
Tinnevelly District Jamabandy Reports:

Fasli	Source
1211	Lushington, "Report," TCR.
1212	TCR,TNA, v.3598, 1803, pp. 92-111.
1213	TCR,TNA, v.3598, 1803, pp. 200-207.
1214	TCR,TNA, v.3599, 1804, pp. 82-95.
1215	TCR,TNA, v.3581, 1806, pp. 92-97.
1216	TCR,TNA, v.3582, 1807, pp. 167-72.
1217	TCR,TNA, v.3583, 1808, pp. 41-63.
1218	n.a.
1219	Hepburn, *Report on the Triennial Lease*, TCR.
1220	n.a.
1221	n.a.
1222	Hepburn, *Report on the Decennial Lease*, TCR.
1223	TCR,TNA, v.3691, 1814, pp. 257-63.
1224	n.a.
1225	Cotton, *Settlement Report F.1225*, TCR.
1226	n.a.
1227	TCR,TNA, v.3595, 1818, pp. 323-25.
1228	TCR,TNA, v.3596, 1819, pp. 512-21.
1229	TCR,TNA, v.3597, 1820, pp. 110-17.
1230	TCR,TNA, v.3576, 1820-1825, pp. 225-35.
1231	TCR,TNA, v.4696, 1822, pp. 93-104.
1232	TCR,TNA, v.3576, 1820-1825, pp. 479-84.
1233	PBR,TNA, 14 July 1825, v.1011, pp. 5,979-6,073.
1234	TCR,TNA, v.4698, 1824, pp. 144-57.
1235	PBR,TNA, 17 Oct. 1826, v.1089, pp. 638-753.
1236	PBR,TNA, 29 Oct. 1827, v.1123, pp. 12,723-97.

1237   PBR,TNA, 9 Oct. 1828, v.1162, pp. 9,845-992.
1238   PBR,TNA, 22 Oct. 1829, v.1210, pp. 10,996-11,101.
1239   PBR,TNA, 11 Nov. 1830, v.1263, pp. 13,130-248.
1240   PBR,TNA, 24 Nov. 1831, v.1302, pp. 10,069-183.
1241   PBR,TNA, 6 Sept. 1832, v.1337, pp. 9,018-133.
1242   PBR,TNA, 11 Nov. 1833, v.1388, pp. 14,097-231.
1243   PBR,TNA, 24 Nov. 1834, v.1430, pp. 12,986-133.
1244   TCR,TNA, v.4709, 1835, pp. 419-500.
1245   PBR,TNA, 24 Nov. 1836, v.1535, pp. 16,944-17,138.
1246   PBR,TNA, 26 Oct. 1837, v.1579, pp. 13,423-571.
1247   PBR,TNA, 24 Dec. 1838, v.1641, pp. 17,343-507.
1248   PBR,TNA, 2 Jan. 1840, v.1690, pp. 66-258.
1249   PBR,TNA, 19 Nov. 1840, v.1730, pp. 16,177-361.
1250   PBR,TNA, 22 Nov. 1841, v.1781, pp. 17,171-331.
1251   PBR,TNA, 18 Nov. 1842, v.1818, pp. 10,412-598.
1252   PBR,TNA, 25 Jan. 1844, v.1901, pp. 1,666-868.
1253   PBR,TNA, 16 Dec. 1844, v.1948, pp. 17,815-18,151.
1254   PBR,TNA, 24 Nov. 1845, v.1999, pp. 10,657-11,263.
1255   PBR,TNA, 17 Dec. 1846, v.2055, pp. 16,336-537.
1256   PBR,TNA, 21 Feb. 1848, v.2120, pp. 2,535-733.
1257   PBR,TNA, 30 July 1849, v.2205, pp. 11,640-867.
1258   PBR,TNA, 17 Jan. 1850, v.2225, pp. 771-1,014.
1259   PBR,TNA, 13 Jan. 1851, v.2269, pp. 757-998.
1260   PBR,TNA, 4 Jan. 1851, v.2309, pp. 15,892-16,118.
1261   PBR,TNA, 7 Feb. 1853, v.2360, pp. 1,553-801.
1262   PBR,TNA, 3 Apr. 1854, v.2413-14, pp. 4,802-950.
1263   PBR,TNA, 7 May 1855, v.2471, pp. 7,256-387.
1264   PBR,TNA, 8 Dec. 1855, v.2504, pp. 19,670-921.

Faslis 1265 to 1310: Madras Presidency, Revenue Department, *Report on the Settlement of the Land Revenue of the Provinces under the Madras Presidency.*

GOVERNMENT PUBLICATIONS AND MANUSCRIPTS

British Parliamentary Papers
House of Commons, 1830-31. Vol. 11, "Report from the Select Committee on the Affairs of the East India Company." *Parliamentary Papers, East Indies.* Shannon: Irish University Press, 1969. Vol. 3.
Accounts and Papers, 1847. Vol. 42, "Papers in the possession of the East India Company showing measures that have been taken

since 1846 to promote the cultivation of cotton in India . . . ,"
pp. 305-420.

Reports from Committees, 1847-1848 Session. Vol. 9, *"Report of
the Select Committee on the Cultivation of Cotton in India."*

Accounts and Papers. Session 2, 1857. Vol. 30, pt. 1, "Selection of
Papers showing measures taken since 1847 to promote the
cultivation of cotton in India," part 2, "Madras."

House of Commons, 1860. Sessional Paper no. 733. Vol. 52, No.
89, *East India (Disturbances in Tinnevelly).*

Censuses

"Census and Dehazada of the Province of Tirunelvelie," Revenue
Department Sundries, No. 39. TNA.

*Census of India, 1881. Villagewar Census Tables for Tinnevelly
District.* Madras, 1883.

Census of India, 1881. Tinnevelly District Taluk Tables. Madras,
1883.

Census of India, 1921, Madras. Vols. 6, 12. Madras, 1921.

Census of India, 1961. Vol. 9. New Delhi, 1961.

Dutch Records

Selections from the Dutch Records of the Government of Ceylon,
No. 5. "Memoir of Jan Shroeder, Governor of Ceylon." Translated by E. Riemers. Colombo, 1946.

Epigraphy

Archaeological Survey of India. *Annual Report on South Indian
Epigraphy.* 1894-1965.

Archaeological Survey of India. *South Indian Inscriptions.* Vols. 5,
14.

Government of Travancore. *Travancore Archaeological Series.* Vol.
1, 1911.

Mackenzie Manuscripts

"General Sketch of the History of the Southern Divisions of the
Peninsula from the Commencement of Calleeyoogam to the
Present Age, Collected at Pavur in Tenkasi Taluk in Tirunelveli
from the traditionary information of Aulabala Sastry and Yamen Achari, 1801." IOL, Map Room, Manuscript No. 8.

Madras Presidency

Annual Report on the Administration of Madras Presidency. Madras, 1871-1945.

District Gazetteers. Tinnevelly District. Vol. 1, by H. R. Pate. Madras, 1917. Vol. 2, *Statistical Supplement*, by K. N. Krishnaswami Aiyer. Madras, 1934.

Epidemic Fevers: The Medical, Geographic and Agricultural Report of a Committee Appointed by the Madras Government to Enquire into the Causes of the Epidemic Fever Which Prevailed in the Provinces of Coimbatore, Madras, Dindigul and Tinnevelly During the Years 1809, 1810, and 1811. London, 1816.

Foreign Department. "Mr. Hodgson's Report on the Dutch Settlements, dated 23 March 1818." Foreign Department Sundries, TNA.

Forest Department. *Centenary of the Forest Department in Madras, 1856-1956.* Madras, 1959.

Judicial Department. "Report of Mr. Hammick . . . on the Disturbances in Madura and Tinnevelly." Confidential. G.O. Nos. 2017-18, 12 December 1899.

High Court. *Decrees in Appeal Suits, Sadr Adalat, 1805-1847.* Madras, 1860.

High Court. *Reports on Cases Decided in the High Court, 1864-1866.* Madras, 1866.

Manual of Administration of the Madras Presidency. 2 vols. Madras, 1885.

Planning Commission, Programme Evaluation Organization. *Study of Problems of Minor Irrigation.* New Delhi, 1961.

Provincial Banking Enquiry Committee. *Written Evidence.* Vols. 2-3. Madras, 1930.

Public Works Department. *Construction of the Srivaikuntam Anicut Across the Tambraparni River.* Reprints of Old Records. Madras, 1920.

Public Works Department. *First Report of the Commissioners Appointed to Enquire into Public Works.* Madras, 1852.

Public Works Department. *List of Special and Other Works of Irrigation Performed in the Madras Presidency from 1836 to 1849.* Madras, 1852.

Public Works Department. *Memorandum on the Srivaikuntam Anicut Project and Its Subsidiary Works.* By H. C. Prendergast. Madras, 1868.

Public Works Department. *Second Report of the Commissioners Appointed to Enquire into Public Works.* Madras, 1853.

Report of the Committee on Local Self Government in Madras. Madras, 1882.

Report of the Taxation Inquiry Committee, 1924-1925. Vol. 1. Madras, 1926.

Revenue Department. *Annual Volume of Trade and Navigation in Madras Presidency.* 1864-1905.

Revenue Department. *General Report of the Board of Revenue for 1815.* n.d.

Revenue Department. "Geographical and Statistical Memoir of Tirunelvelie and Its Zamindaries." By Thomas Turnbull. Revenue Department Sundries, No. 38.

Revenue Department. *Minute on the Proposed Settlement of Tinnevelly.* By W. Robinson. Madras, 1868.

Revenue Department. "Official Diary of the Proceedings of the Superintendent of Tank Repairs and Water Courses, 1808." TNA.

Revenue Department. "Papers Relating to the Protection of Under-tenants in Ryotwari Tracts." Confidential. G.O. No. 3494-95, 9 December 1914.

Revenue Department. "Report on the External and Internal Commerce of Madras Presidency." IOL, 1820-1864.

Revenue Department. *Report on the Revision of the Revenue Establishment in the Madras Presidency.* By J. H. Garstin. Madras, 1883.

Revenue Department. *Reports and Other Papers with a View to Recasting the Revenue Laws of the Madras Presidency.* Madras, 1856.

Revenue Department. *Resettlement Report of Tinnevelly District, Ambasamudram and Tenkasy Taluks.* G.O. No. 304, 31 January 1918.

Revenue Department. *Salt Works in the Madras Presidency.* Revenue Sundries, No. 43.

Sanitary Commissioner. *List of Fairs and Festivals Occurring Within the Limits of the Madras Presidency.* Madras, 1868.

Selections from Old Records, Papers Relating to the Zamindars, Mittahs, etc. of Tinnevelly District. Madras, 1934.

Selections from the Records of the Madras Government.

Vol. 4. "Correspondence Relative to the Establishment of a Permanent Corps of Coolies." Madras, 1855.

Vol. 25. "Reports on Important Works of Irrigation for 1854." Madras, 1856.

Vol. 29. "Replies to the Collective Memorandum on Public Works in the Madras Presidency. Madras, 1856.

Vols. 52, 54. "Papers Relating to the General Revenue Survey of Madras Presidency." Madras, 1858, 1863.

Selections from the Records of the Madras Government. New Series, No. 1. "Collections of Papers Relating to Inam Settlement in Madras." Madras, 1906.

Statistical Atlas of Madras Presidency for Fasli 1340 (1930/1). Madras, 1931.

Statistical Atlas of Madras Presidency for Fasli 1350 (1940/1). Madras, 1941.

Statistical Atlas of the Madras Presidency for Fasli 1360 (1950/51). Madras, 1951.

Torture Commission Report. Madras, 1855.

National Archives of India

National Register of Private Records. No. 5, "Descriptive List of Documents Available in Bihar, Kerala, Madhya Pradesh, Punjab, Tamil Nadu, Uttar Pradesh, and the National Archives of India, New Delhi." New Delhi, 1973.

Tamil Nadu

Directorate of Information and Publicity. *Patinaintu Catanaikal.* No. 5, *Tirunelveli.* Madras, 1966.

Directorate of Information and Publicity. *Season and Crop Report.* Annual.

Tinnevelly District Collectorate Records, TNA

Cotton, John. *Settlement Report for Fasli 1225.*

Hepburn, James. *Collector's Report on the Decennial Lease.* 1812.

———. *Collector's Report on the Triennial Lease.* n.d.

Hodgson, M. "Report on the Province of Tinnevelly, 24 September 1804."

Lushington, S. *Report Regarding the Tinnevelly Poligars and Sequestered Pollams, 1799-1800.* Rpt. Tinnevelly, 1916.

———. "Settlement Report of 28 May 1802."

Papers Relating to the Revenue Settlement of Tinnevelly. n.d. (c.1877).

Robinson, W. *Minute on the Proposed Settlement of Tinnevelly.* Madras, 1868.

BOOKS AND ARTICLES

Abrams, Philip. "Towns and Economic Growth: Some Theories and Problems." In Philip Abrams and E. A. Wrigley, eds., *Towns in*

Societies: Essays in Economic History and Historical Sociology, pp. 9-33. Cambridge, 1978.

Adiceam, Emmanuel. *La Géographie de l'irrigation dans le Tamilnad.* Paris, 1966.

Ahmed, Noazech. *The Development of Agriculture in Bangladesh.* Dacca, 1976.

Alaev, L. B. "South India." In Kumar, ed., *Cambridge Economic History,* pp. 226-34, 315-24.

Appadorai, A. *Economic Conditions in South India (1000-1500 A.D.).* 2 vols. Madras, 1936.

Appadurai, Arjun. *Worship and Conflict under Colonial Rule: A South Indian Case.* New York, 1981.

———, and Carol A. Breckenridge. "The South Indian Temple: Authority, Honour and Redistribution." *CIS,* NS 10:2 (1976), 187-209.

Appadurai, K. *Talavay Ariyanatha Mutaliyar.* Madras, 1950.

Appaswamy, Paul. *The Centenary History of the C.M.S. in Tinnevelly.* Palayamkottai, 1923.

Arasaratnam, Sinnappah. "Dutch Commercial Policy and Interests in the Malay Peninsula, 1750-1795." In Blair Kling and M. N. Pearson, eds., *The Age of Partnership: Europeans in Asia Before Dominion,* pp. 159-90. Honolulu, 1979.

———. "Indian Commercial Groups and European Traders, 1600-1800: Changing Relationships in Southeastern India." *SA,* NS 1:2 (1978), 42-54.

———. "Weavers, Merchants and the Company: The Handloom Industry in Southeastern India, 1750-1790." *IESHR,* 17:3 (1980), 257-82.

Arbuthnot, A. J. *Major General Sir Thomas Munro.* London, 1881.

Arnold, David. "Looting, Grain Riots, and Government Policy in South India." *PP,* 84 (1979), 111-45.

———, Robin Jeffrey, and James Manor. "Caste Associations in South India: A Comparative Analysis." *IESHR,* 12:3 (1976), 353-74.

Arundel, A. T. *Irrigation and Communal Labour in Madras Presidency.* Madras, 1879.

Atwell, William S. "International Bullion Flows and the Chinese Economy *circa* 1530-1650." *PP,* 95 (1982), 68-90.

Avineri, Shlomo, ed. *Karl Marx on Colonialism and Modernization.* Garden City, 1969.

Baack, Ben. "The Development of Exclusive Property Rights to Land in England." *EH,* 22:1 (1979), 63-74.

275

Baker, Christopher J. *An Indian Rural Economy, 1880-1955: The Tamil Nadu Countryside*. Bombay, 1984.

———. "Madras Headmen." In Chaudhuri and Dewey, ed. *Economy and Society*, pp. 26-52.

———. *The Politics of South India, 1920-1937*. Cambridge, 1976.

Baliga, B. S. *Studies in Madras Administration*. Madras, 1960.

Barnett, Marguerite Ross. "Creating Political Identity: The Emergent South Indian Tamils," *Ethnicity*, 1:3 (1974), 237-60.

———. *The Politics of Cultural Nationalism in South India*. Princeton, 1976.

Barnett, Richard B. *North India Between Empires: Awadh, the Mughals, and the British, 1720-1801*. Berkeley and Los Angeles, 1980.

Bates, Crispen. "The Nature of Social Change in Rural Gujerat: The Kheda District, 1818-1918." *MAS*, 15:4 (1981), 415-54.

Bayly, Christopher A. "Local Control in Indian Towns: The Case of Allahabad, 1880-1920." *MAS*, 5:4 (1971), 289-312.

———. *The Local Roots of Indian Politics: Allahabad 1880-1920*. Oxford, 1975.

———. *Rulers, Townsmen, and Bazaars: North Indian Society in the Age of British Expansion, 1770-1870*. Cambridge, 1983.

Bayley, W. H., and Hudleston, W. *Papers on Mirasi Right Selected from the Records of the Madras Government*. Madras, 1862.

Baynes, C. R. *The Civil Law of the Madras Presidency*. Madras, 1852.

Beaglehole, T. H. *Thomas Munro and the Development of Administrative Policy in Madras, 1792-1818*. Cambridge, 1966.

Beck, Brenda E. F. "Centers and Boundaries of Regional Caste Systems: Toward a General Model." In Carol A. Smith, ed. *Regional Analysis*, 2:255-88. New York, 1976.

———. *Peasant Society in Konku. A Study of Right and Left Subcastes in South India*. Vancouver, 1972.

Béteille, André. *Caste, Class, and Power*. Berkeley and Los Angeles, 1971.

———. *Studies in Agrarian Social Structure*. Delhi, 1974.

Blackburn, Stuart H. "The Kallars: A Tamil 'Criminal Tribe' Reconsidered," *SA*, NS 1:1 (March 1978), 38-51.

Blasco, F., and P. Legris. "Originalité des climats secs du sud de l'Inde." *AG*, 82:450 (1973), 129-50.

Bloch, Marc. *Feudal Society*. Chicago, 1961.

———. "Toward a Comparative History of European Societies." In F. C. Lane and J. C. Riemersma, eds. *Enterprise and Secular Change*, pp. 494-521. Homewood, Ill., 1953.

Boserup, Ester. *The Conditions of Agricultural Growth*. Chicago, 1965.

Bourdieu, Pierre. *Outline of a Theory of Practice*. Cambridge, 1977.

Bourdillon, J. D. *Remarks on the Ryotwari System of Land Tenure*. Madras, 1853.

Braudel, Fernand. *Capitalism and Material Life, 1400-1800*. New York, 1967.

———. *On History*. Chicago, 1980.

Breckenridge, Carol A. "The Śrī Mīṇākshi Sundarēsvaran Temple: Worship and Endowments in South India, 1833-1925." Ph.D. dissertation, Wisconsin, 1976.

Brenner, Robert. "Agrarian Class Structure and Economic Development in Pre-Industrial Europe: The Agrarian Roots of European Capitalism." *PP*, 97 (1982), 16-113.

Bronger, Dirk. "Der Sozial Geographische Einfluss der Kastenwesens auf Siedlung und Agrarstruktur im Sudlichen Indien." *Erdkunde*, 24:2 (1970), 89-106, and 24:3 (1970), 194-207.

Buckley, Robert. *The Irrigation Works of India and Their Financial Results*. London, 1880.

Caldwell, Robert. *Lectures on the Tinnevelly Missions, Descriptive of the Field, the Work and the Results*. London, 1857.

———. *A Political and General History of the District of Tinnevelly in the Presidency of Madras, from the Earliest Period to Its Cession to the English Government in A.D. 1801*. Madras, 1881.

———. *Records of the Early History of the Tinnevelly Mission*. Madras, 1881.

———. *The Tinnevelly Shanars: A Sketch of Their Religion and Their Moral Condition, and Characteristics as a Caste*. Madras, 1849.

Calkins, Phillip B. "The Formation of a Regionally Oriented Ruling Group in Bengal, 1700-1740." *JAS*, 29:4 (1970), 799-806.

Chambers, J. D., and G. E. Mingay. *The Agricultural Revolution, 1750-1880*. New York, 1966.

Champakalakshmi, R. "Peasant State and Society in Medieval South India." *IESHR*, 18:3-4 (1981), 411-27.

Chandrasekharan, T. *A Descriptive Catalogue of the Tamil Manuscripts in the Government Oriental Manuscripts Library, Madras*. Vols. 9-10. Madras, 1954-1955.

Charlesworth, Neil. *British Rule and the Indian Economy*. London, 1982.

Chatterjee, S. S. *Review of Work Done on Water Requirements of Crops in India*. New Delhi, 1967.

Chaudhuri, K. N. "European Trade with India." In Raychaudhuri and Habib, *Cambridge Economic History*, 1:382-406.

———. *The Trading World of Asia and the English East India Company, 1660-1760*. Cambridge, 1978.

———, and C. J. Dewey, eds. *Economy and Society: Essays in Indian Economic and Social History*. Delhi, 1979.

Chicherov, A. I. *Indian Economic Development in the 16th-18th Centuries: Outline History of Crafts and Trade*. Moscow, 1971.

Church Mission Society. South India. Madras Mission. "Correspondence: 1830-1842." (Center for Research Libraries. South Asia Microfilm Project Microfilm.)

Clay, Edward J. "Equity and Productivity Effects of a Package of Technical Innovations and Changes in Social Institutions: Tubewells, Tractors and High-Yielding Varieties." *IJAE*, 30:4 (1975), 74-87.

Cohn, Bernard S. "Political Systems in Eighteenth Century India: The Benares Region." *JAOS*, 83 (1962), 312-20.

———. "Representing Authority in Victorian India." In E. J. Hobsbawm and T. O. Ranger, eds. *The Invention of Tradition*. Cambridge, 1983, pp. 165-209.

———. "Society and Social Change under the Raj." *SAR*, 4:1 (1970), 27-49.

———, and McKim Marriott. "Networks and Centers in the Integration of Indian Civilization." *Journal of Social Research* (Ranchi), 1:1 (1958), 1-9.

Conaway, H. "An Analysis of Irrigation and Basic Agricultural Patterns." M.A. thesis, Pennsylvania, 1977.

Critchfield, Richard. *Villages*. New York, 1983.

Crosby, Alfred W. *The Columbian Exchange: The Biological and Cultural Consequences of 1492*. Westport, Conn., 1972.

Curtin, Philip D. *Cross-Cultural Trade in World History*. New York, 1984.

———. "Depth, Span, and Relevance." *AHR*, 89 (1984), 1-9.

Danvers, F. C. *A Century of Famine*. Madras, 1877.

Das Gupta, Ashin. "Indian Merchants and the Trade in the Indian Ocean." In Raychaudhuri and Habib, *Cambridge Economic History*, 1:407-33.

———. "Trade and Politics in Eighteenth Century India." In D. S. Richards, ed. *Islam and the Trade of Asia*. Philadelphia, 1970, pp. 181-214.

Davis, Ralph. *The Rise of the Atlantic Economies*. Ithaca, 1973.

Desai, A. R., ed. *Peasant Struggles in India*. Bombay, 1979.

De Silva, C. R. "The Portuguese and Pearl Fishing off South India and Sri Lanka." *SA*, NS 1:1 (1978), 14-28.

Dewey, Clive. "The Government of India's 'New Industrial Policy,' 1900-1925: Formation and Failure." In Chaudhuri and Dewey, eds. *Economy and Society*, pp. 215-57.

————. "Images of the Village Community: A Study in Anglo-Indian Thought." *MAS*, 6:3 (1972), 291-328.

————, and A. G. Hopkins, eds. *The Imperial Impact: Studies in the Economic History of Africa and India*. London, 1978.

Dhanagare, D. N. *Peasant Movements in India, 1920-1950*. Delhi, 1983.

Digby, Simon. *War-horse and Elephant in the Delhi Sultanate: A Study of Military Supplies*. Karachi, 1971.

Dirks, Nicholas B. "From Little King to Landlord: Property, Law, and Gift under the Permanent Settlement." California Institute of Technology, Humanities Working Paper No. 84. June 1983.

————. "Little Kingdoms of South India: Political Authority and Social Relations in the Southern Tamil Countryside." Ph.D. dissertation, Chicago, 1981.

————. "The Pasts of a Palaiyakarar: The Ethnohistory of a South Indian Little King." *JAS*, 41:4 (1982), 655-83.

————. "Political Authority and Structural Change in Early South Indian History." *IESHR*, 13:2 (1976), 125-58.

————. "The Structure and Meaning of Political Relations in a South Indian Little Kingdom." California Institute of Technology, CIS, NS, 13:2 (1979), 169-206.

Djurfeldt, Goran, and Staffen Lindberg. *Behind Poverty: The Social Formation in a Tamil Village*. London, 1975.

Dumont, Louis. "The Distribution of Some Maravar Sub-Castes." In K. Bala Ratnam, ed. *Anthropology on the March*. Madras, 1963, pp. 197-306.

————. *Hierarchy and Marriage Alliance in South Indian Kinship*. London, 1957.

————. *Homo Hierarchicus: The Caste System and Its Implications*. Chicago, 1970.

————. *Une sous-caste de l'Inde du sud, organisation sociale et religion des Pramalai Kallar*. Paris, 1957.

Dutt, Romesh Chandra. *The Economic History of India*. 2 vols. Calcutta, 1901, rpt. New Delhi, 1960.

Dykes, J.W.B. *Salem: An Indian Collectorate*. Madras, 1853.

Elvin, Mark. *The Pattern of the Chinese Past*. London, 1973.

Evans, Robert J., Jr. "Some Notes on Coerced Labor." *JEH*, 30 (1970), 861-66.

Friedman, Harriett. "Household Production and the National Economy: Concepts for the Analysis of Agrarian Formations." *JPS*, 7:2 (1980), 158-84.

Freitag, Sandria B. "Religious Rites and Riots: From Community Identity to Communalism in North India, 1870-1940." Ph.D. dissertation, California, Berkeley, 1980.

———. "Sacred Symbol as Mobilizing Ideology: The North Indian Search for a 'Hindu' Community." *MAS*, 22:4 (1980), 397-425.

Frykenberg, Robert Eric. "Caste, Morality, and Western Religion under the Raj." *MAS*, in press.

———. "Conversion and Crises of Conscience under Company Raj in South India." In Marc Gaborieau and Alice Thorner, eds. *Asie du sud, traditions et changements. 5th European Conference on South Asian Studies*, pp. 311-21. Paris, 1978.

———. "Education as an Instrument of Imperial Integration During the Company's Raj in South India." In Cyril Henry Philips, ed. *Policy and Practice in the Indian Empire, c. 1820-1860*. London, in press.

———. *Guntur District, 1788-1848: A History of Local Influence and Central Authority in South India*. London, 1965.

———. "The Impact of Conversion and Social Reform upon Society in South India during the Late Company Period: Questions Concerning Hindu-Christian Encounters with Special Reference to Tinnevelly." In Cyril Henry Philips and Mary Doreen Wainwright, eds. *Indian Society and the Beginnings of Modernisation, c. 1830-1850*, pp. 187-243. London, 1976.

———. "On the Study of Conversion Movements: A Review Article and a Theoretical Note," *IESHR*, 17:1 (1980), 121-38.

———. "On Roads and Riots in Tinnevelly: Radical Change and Ideology in Madras Presidency during the Nineteenth Century." *SA*, 4:2 (1982), 34-52.

———. "The Roots of Modern Education in South India, 1784-1854: An Analysis of Its Role as an Instrument of Socio-Political Integration under Company Raj." *AHR*, forthcoming.

———. "The Silent Settlement in South India, 1793-1836: An Analysis of the Role of Inams in the Rise of the Indian Imperial System." In R. E. Frykenberg, ed. *Land Tenure and Peasant in South Asia*, pp. 37-53. Delhi, 1977.

———. "Traditional Processes of Power and Administration in South India: An Historical Analysis of Local Influence." *IESHR* 1:2 (1963), 1-21.

Furber, Holden. *Rival Empires of Trade in the Orient, 1600-1800.* Minneapolis, 1976.

Ganapathi Pillai, W. E. *Ettaiyapuram Past and Present.* Madras, 1890.

Giddens, Anthony. *Central Problems in Social Theory: Action, Structure and Contradiction in Social Analysis.* Berkeley and Los Angeles, 1979.

———. *New Rules of Sociological Method: A Positive Critique of Interpretive Sociology.* New York, 1976.

Gilmartin, David. "Religious Leadership and the Pakistan Movement in the Punjab." *MAS,* 13:3 (1979), 485-517.

Goody, Jack. *Cooking, Cuisine, and Class: A Study in Comparative Sociology.* Cambridge, 1982.

Gopinatha Rao, T. A. "The Inscriptions of the Later Pandyas." *TAS,* 1 (1910), 43-152, 251-82.

———. "The Krishnapuram Plates of Sadasivaraya, Saka Samvat 1489," *EI,* 9 (1907-1908), 328-41.

Gough, Kathleen. "Caste in a Tanjore Village." In E. R. Leach, ed. *Aspects of Caste in South India, Ceylon and Northwest Pakistan,* pp. 11-60. Cambridge, 1971.

———. "Peasant Resistance and Revolt in South India," *PA,* 41 (1968-1969), 526-44.

———. *Rural Society in Southeast India.* Cambridge, 1981.

Greenberg, Michael. *British Trade and the Opening of China.* Cambridge, 1951.

Grover, B. R. "An Integrated Pattern of Commercial Life in the Rural Society of North India during the 17th and 18th Centuries." In *Proceedings of the 37th Session of Indian Historical Records Commission,* 37:121-25. Delhi, 1966.

Gurney, John. "The Debts of the Nawab of Arcot." Ph.D. dissertation, Oxford, 1968.

Habib, Irfan. *The Agrarian System of Mughal India, 1556-1707.* Bombay, 1963.

———. "Potentialities of Capitalistic Development in the Economy of Mughal India." *JEH,* 29:1 (1969), 32-78.

Hall, Kenneth R. "Peasant State and Society in Chola Times: A View from the Tiruvidaimurudur Urban Complex." *IESHR,* 18:3-4 (1981), 393-410.

Hall, Kenneth R. *Trade and Statecraft in the Age of the Cholas.* New Delhi, 1980.

Hardgrave, Robert. *The Nadars of Tamilnad: The Political Culture of a Community in Change.* Berkeley and Los Angeles, 1969.

Harlow, Vincent T. *The Founding of the Second British Empire, 1763-1793.* 2 vols. London, 1964.

Harriss, John. *Capitalism and Peasant Farming: Agrarian Structure and Ideology in Northern Tamil Nadu.* Bombay, 1982.

Hart, George L., III. *Poets of the Tamil Anthologies.* Princeton, 1979.

Hartwell, Robert M. "Demographic, Political, and Social Transformations of China, 750-1550," *HJAS*, 42:2 (1982), 365-442.

Haynes, Douglas Earll. "Conflict and Cultural Change in Urban India: The Politics of Surat City, 1850-1924." Ph.D. dissertation, Pennsylvania, 1982.

Headrick, Daniel. *Tools of Empire: Technology and European Imperialism in the Nineteenth Century.* New York, 1981.

Heitzman, E. James. "Gifts of Power: Temples, Politics, and Economy in Medieval South India." Ph.D. dissertation, Pennsylvania, 1985.

Henningham, Stephen. "Bureaucracy and Control in India's Great Landed Estates: The Raj Darbhanga of Bihar, 1879-1950." *MAS*, 17:1 (1983), 35-58.

Hill, S. C. *Yusuf Khan: The Rebel Commandant.* London, 1914.

Hilton, Rodney. "Reasons for Inequality among Medieval Peasants." *JPS*, 5:3 (1978), 271-84.

Hjejle, Benedicte. "Slavery and Agricultural Bondage in South India in the Nineteenth Century." *SEHR*, 15:1-2 (1967), 71-126.

Hodgett, Gerald. *A Social and Economic History of Medieval Europe.* London, 1972.

Hodgson, Marshall. *The Venture of Islam: Conscience and History in a World Civilization.* 3 volumes. Chicago, 1974.

Holloway, W. *Notes on Madras Judicial Administration.* Madras, 1853.

Howell, Cicely. "Stability and Change, 1300-1700: The Socio-Economic Context of the Self-Perpetuating Family Farm in England." *JPS*, 2:2 (1975), 468-82.

Hudson, Dennis. "Siva, Minakshi, Vishnu: Reflections on a Popular Myth in Madurai." *IESHR*, 14:1 (1977), 107-18.

Hunter, William Wilson. "Tinnevelli." In W. W. Hunter, ed. *The Imperial Gazetteer of India*, 13:297-311. London, 1887.

Hurd, John. "Railways." In Kumar, ed. *Cambridge Economic History*, 2:737-61.

Husaini, S.A.Q. *The History of the Pandya Country.* Karaikudi, n.d.

Irschick, Eugene F. *Politics and Social Conflict in Tamilnad.* Berkeley and Los Angeles, 1969.

Ishwaran, K. "Kinship and Distance in Rural India." In Ralph Piddington, ed. *Kinship and Geographical Mobility,* pp. 81-94. Leiden, 1965.

Issawi, Charles. "The Decline of the Middle Eastern Trade, 1100-1850." In D. S. Richards, ed. *Islam and the Trade of Asia,* pp. 245-66. Philadelphia, 1970.

Jain, Ravindra K. *South Indians on the Plantation Frontier in Malaya.* New Haven, 1970.

Jayaratnam, R. "Indian Emigration to Ceylon: Some Aspects of the History and Social Background of the Migrants." *IESHR,* 4:4 (1967), 320-59.

Jones, Eric L. *Agriculture and the Industrial Revolution.* Oxford, 1974.
————. *The European Miracle: Environments, Economies, and Geopolitics in the History of Europe and Asia.* Cambridge, 1981.

Kailasapathy, K. *Tamil Heroic Poetry.* Oxford, 1968.

Kanitkar, N. V. *Dry Farming in India.* New Delhi, 1960.

Karashima, Noburu. "A Bibliography of South Indian Epigraphy." *JAAS,* 6 (1973), 1512-63.

Karve, Irawati. *Hindu Society—An Interpretation.* Poona, 1968.

Kathirvel, S. "History of the Maravas, 1700-1801." Ph.D. dissertation, Madras, 1971.

Kaufmann, S. B. "A Christian Caste in Hindu Society: Religious Leadership and Social Conflict among the Paravas of Southern Tamilnadu." *MAS,* 15:2 (1981), 203-34.

Kearns, J. T. "The Cairns of Tinnevelly." *Madras Journal of Literature and Science,* 21 (1859), 27-29.

Kessinger, Tom G. "Regional Economy (1757-1857): North India." In Kumar, ed. *Cambridge Economic History,* 2:242-69.
————. *Vilyatpur 1848-1968: Social and Economic Change in a North Indian Village.* Berkeley and Los Angeles, 1974.

Kolenda, Pauline. *Caste in Contemporary India: Beyond Organic Solidarity.* Menlo Park, N.J., 1978.

Kolliner, Andrew. "The Structure of Rural Credit in the Ceded Districts of the Madras Presidency with Particular Reference to Kurnool District, 1880-1930." M.A. thesis, Pennsylvania, 1975.

Kracauer, Sigfried. *History: The Last Things before the Last.* New York, 1969.

Krishnamurty, J. "The Occupational Structure." In Kumar, ed. *Cambridge Economic History,* 2:533-52.

Krishnan, V. "Tambraparni Ryot (A Study of the Rural Economy of the Tirunelveli District)." Gokhale Prize Award Thesis, Madras, 1931.

——. "Trade Centers in the Tinnevelly District." *JMGA*, 15:3 (1940), 271-77.

Krishna Sastri, H. "The Kuniyur Plates of the Time of Vengata II: Saka Samvat 1556," *EI*, 3 (1894-1895), 236-58.

Krishnasvami Aiyangar, S. *A History of Tirupati.* Tirupati, 1941.

——. *South India and Her Muhammadan Invaders.* Oxford, 1921.

Krishnaswami, A. *The Tamil Country under Vijayanagar.* Annamalainagar, 1964.

Kulke, Hermann. "Fragmentation and Segmentation versus Integration? Reflections on the Concepts of Indian Feudalism and the Segmentary State in Indian History." *SH*, 4:2 (1982), 237-64.

Kumar, Dharma, ed. *The Cambridge Economic History of India.* Volume 2, *c.1757-c.1970.* Cambridge, 1983.

——. *Land and Caste in South India.* Cambridge, 1965.

——. "Landownership and Equality in Madras Presidency, 1853-4 to 1946-7." *IESHR*, 12:3 (1975), 229-62.

——. "South India." In Kumar, ed. *Cambridge Economic History*, 2:352-75.

Kurukuhudasa Pillai, S. *Tirunelveli Cimai Carittiram.* Ettaiyapuram, 1931.

Leach, E. R. "Hydraulic Society in Ceylon." *PP*, 15 (1959), 2-25.

——. *Pul Eliya: A Village in Ceylon.* Cambridge, 1968.

Leonard, Karen. "The 'Great Firm' Theory of the Decline of the Mughal Empire." *CSSH*, 21:2 (1979), 151-67.

——. "The Hyderbad Political System and Its Participants," *JAS*, 30:3 (1971), 569-82.

Le Roy Ladurie, Emmanuel. *The Mind and Method of the Historian.* Chicago, 1981.

Leshnik, Lawrence S. *South Indian "Megalithic" Burials: The Pandukal Complex.* Wiesbaden, 1974.

Lewandowski, Susan. "Changing Form and Function in the Ceremonial and the Colonial Port City in India: An Historical Analysis of Madurai and Madras." *MAS*, 11:2 (1977), 183-212.

Ludden, David. "Agrarian Organization in Tinnevelly District, 800-1900 A.D." Ph.D. dissertation, Pennsylvania, 1978.

——. "Dimensions of Agrarian Political Economy: Focus on Tamil Nadu, India," *PS*, 8:4 (1979), 19-30.

——. "Ecological Zones and the Cultural Economy of Irrigation in Southern Tamilnadu." *SA*, NS 1:1 (1978), 1-13.

------. "Patronage and Irrigation in Tamil Nadu: A Long-term View." *IESHR*, 16:3 (1979), 347-65.

------. "Productive Power in Agriculture: A Survey of Work on the Local History of British India." In Meghnad Desai, Susanne H. Rudolph, and Ashok Rudra, eds. *Agrarian Power and Agricultural Productivity in South Asia*, pp. 51-99. New Delhi, 1984.

------. "The Terms of Ryotwari: Semantics and Disputes over Property Rights in Madras Presidency, 1800-1885." In Pauline Kolenda, ed. *South Indian Studies: An Anthology of Critical Essays on Recent Scholarship*. Madras, in press.

------. "Who Really Ruled Madras Presidency?" *IESHR*, 15:4 (1978), 517-21.

------, and M. S. Pillai. *The Kuruntokai: An Anthology of Classical Tamil Love Poetry in Translation*. Madurai, 1976.

Lushington, F. *Comparative Tables of the Provincial Civil Establishment of the Madras Presidency for 1857*. Madras, 1858.

Mahalingam, T. V. *Administration and Social Life under Vijayanagar*. Madras, 1940.

------. *Economic Life in the Vijayanagar Empire*. Madras, 1951.

------. *Mackenzie Manuscripts: Summaries of the Historical Manuscripts in the Mackenzie Collection*. 2 vols. Madras, 1972-1976.

Maloney, Clarence. "Archaeology in South India: Accomplishments and Prospects." In Stein, ed. *Essays on South India*, pp. 1-41.

------. "The Paratavar: 2000 Years of Cultural Dynamics of a Tamil Caste." *MI*, 48:3 (1969), 224-40.

Mandelbaum, David. *Society in India: Continuity and Change*. 2 vols. Berkeley and Los Angeles, 1970.

Manimekalai. Edited by N. M. Ventakasami Nattar and A. S. Turaisami Pillai. Tirunelveli, 1946.

Marriott, McKim. "Hindu Transactions: Diversity without Dualism." In Bruce Kapferer, ed. *Transaction and Meaning: Directions in the Anthropology of Exchange and Symbolic Behavior*, pp. 109-42. Philadelphia, 1976.

------, ed. *Village India: Studies in the Little Community*. Chicago, 1955.

Mayer, Adrian. "The Dominant Caste in a Region of Central India." *SJA*, 14:4 (1958), 407-27.

McAlpin, Michelle Burge. "Price Movements and Fluctuations in Economic Activity (1860-1947)." In Kumar, ed. *Cambridge Economic History*, 2:878-904.

------. *Subject to Famine: Food Crises and Economic Change in Western India, 1860-1920*. Princeton, 1983.

McEvedy, Colin, and Richard Jones. *Atlas of World Population History*. Harmondsworth, 1978.

McNeill, William. *Plagues and Peoples*. Garden City, 1976.

——. *The Rise of the West: A History of the Human Community*. Chicago, 1963.

Mehta, Surinder K. "Patterns of Residence in Poona (India) by Income, Education and Occupation (1937-1965)." *AJS*, 73 (1968), 496-508.

Meinzen-Dick, Ruth Suseela. "Local Management of Tank Irrigation in South India: Organization and Operation." M.A. thesis, Cornell, 1983.

Meister, Michael W. ed. *Encyclopedia of Indian Temple Architecture, South India, Lower Dravidadesam, 200 B.C.-A.D. 1324*. 2 vols. Philadelphia, 1983.

Mencher, Joan P. *Agriculture and Social Structure in Tamil Nadu*. Durham, 1978.

——. "Kerala and Madras: A Comparative Study of Ecology and Social Structure." *Ethnology*, 5:2 (1966), 135-71.

Metcalf, Thomas R. *The Aftermath of Revolt: India 1857-1870*. Princeton, 1964.

——. "Estate Management and State Records in Oudh." *IESHR*, 4:2 (1967), 99-108.

——. *Land, Landlords, and the British Raj: Northern India in the Nineteenth Century*. Berkeley and Los Angeles, 1979.

Miers, Suzanne, and Igor Kopytoff, eds. *Slavery in Africa: Historical and Anthropological Perspectives*. Madison, 1977.

Mintz, Sidney. "A Note on the Definition of Peasants." *JPS*, 1:1 (1973), 91-100.

Mitchell, B. R. *Abstract of British Historical Statistics, 1750-1970*. Cambridge, 1962.

Moffatt, Michael. *An Untouchable Community in South India: Structure and Consensus*. Princeton, 1979.

Moore, Barrington. *Social Origins of Dictatorship and Democracy: Lord and Peasant in The Making of the Modern World*. Boston, 1966.

Mudaliar, C. Y. *The Secular State and Religious Institutions in India: A Study of the Administration of Hindu Religious Trusts in Madras*. Wiesbaden, 1974.

Mukherjee, Nilmani. *The Ryotwari System in Madras, 1792-1827*. Calcutta, 1962.

Mukkudal Pallu. Edited by N. Setukumaran. Madras, 1973.

Murton, Brian. "Agrarian System Dynamics in Interior Tamil Nadu Before 1800 A.D." *NGJI*, 21:3-4 (1975), 151-65.

———. "The Evolution of the Settlement Structure in Northern Kongu to 1800 A.D." In Brenda E. F. Beck, ed. *Perspectives on a Regional Culture: Essays about the Coimbatore Region of South India*, pp. 7-43. Delhi, 1979.

———. "Key People in the Countryside: Decision-makers in Interior Tamilnadu in the Late Eighteenth Century." *IESHR*, 10:2 (1973), 157-80.

———. "Land and Class: Cultural, Social and Biophysical Integration in Interior Tamil Nadu in the Late 18th Century." In R. E. Frykenberg, ed. *Land Tenure and Peasant in South Asia*, pp. 81-99. Delhi, 1977.

———. "Some Propositions on the Spread of Village Settlement in Interior Tamil Nadu before 1750 A.D." *IGJ*, 48:2 (1973), 56-72.

———. "Some Sources for the Geography of South India, 1763-1843." *Pacific Viewpoint*, 11 (1970), 181-87.

Nilakanta Sastri, K. A. *The Cholas*. Madras, 1955.

———. *Foreign Notices of South India, from Megasthenes to Ma Huan*. Madras, 1939.

———. *A History of South India from Prehistoric Times to the Fall of Vijayanagar*. Madras, 1955.

———. "The Manur Inscription of Maranjadaiyan." *EI*, 22 (January 1933), 5-11.

———. *The Pandyan Kingdom, from the Earliest Times to the Sixteenth Century*. Rpt. Madras, 1972.

———. *Sources of Indian History with Special Reference to South India*. Bombay, 1964.

Norton, J. B. *The Administration of Justice in Madras Presidency*. Madras, 1853.

———. *A Letter to Robert Lowe*. Madras, 1854.

Obeyesekere, Gananath. *Land Tenure in Village Ceylon: A Sociological and Historical Study*. London, 1967.

Otterbein, Keith F. *The Evolution of War: A Cross-Cultural Study*. Washington, D.C., 1970.

Parker, William, and Eric L. Jones, eds. *European Peasants and Their Markets: Essays in Agrarian Economic History*. Princeton, 1975.

Patterson, Orlando. *Slavery and Social Death: A Comparative Study*. Cambridge, 1982.

Perlin, Frank. "Of White Whale and Countrymen in the Eighteenth Century Maratha Deccan: Extended Class Relations, Rights, and the Problem of Rural Autonomy under the Old Regime," *JPS*, 5:2 (1978), 172-237.

———. "Precolonial South Asia and Western Penetration in the 17th-19th Centuries: A Problem of Epistemological Status." *Rev*, 4:2 (1980), 267-306.

———. "Proto-industrialization and Pre-colonial South Asia." *PP*, 98 (1983), 30-95.

Ponniah, J. S. "Production and Marketing of Raw Cotton in the Madras Presidency, with Special Reference to the Six Districts of Bellary, Kurnool, Coimbatore, Madurai, Ramnad, and Tinnevelly." Ph.D. dissertation, Madras, 1944.

Prakash, Gyan. "Production and the Reproduction of Bondage: Kamias and Maliks in South Bihar, c. 1300-1930." Ph.D. dissertation, Pennsylvania, 1984.

Price, Pamela G. "Rajadharma in Ramnad: Land Litigation and Largess," *CIS*, NS 13:2 (1979), 207-39.

———. "Resources and Rule in Zamindari South India, 1802-1903: Sivagangai and Ramnad as Little Kingdoms under the Raj." Ph.D. dissertation, Wisconsin, 1979.

———. "Warrior Caste 'Raja' and Gentleman 'Zamindar': One Person's Experience in the Late Nineteenth Century." *MAS*, 17:4 (1983), 563-90.

Rajam, V. S. "*Anangu*: A Notion Semantically Reduced to Signify Female Sacred Power." *JAOS*, forthcoming.

Rajayyan, K. *Administration and Society in the Carnatic (1701-1801).* Tirupati, 1966.

———. *History of Madurai, 1736-1801.* Madurai, 1974.

———. *Rise and Fall of the Poligars of Tamilnadu.* Madras, 1974.

———. *South Indian Rebellion: The First War of Independence, 1800-1801.* Mysore, 1971.

———. "Travancore's Dispute with the Carnatic over Kalakkad." *JIH*, 44 (1966), 289-96.

Ramakrishna, K. C. "Financing and Forced Sales of Produce." *IJE*, 10:3 (1930), 217-30.

Ramamurthy, R. "A Study of a Hundred Years' Rainfall at Madras City." *IGJ*, 43 (December 1968-January 1969), 49-57.

Ramanatha Ayyar, A. S. "Four Pandya Records from Ukkirankottai." *EI*, 23 (July 1936), 7-9.

Ramanujan, A. K. *The Interior Landscape: Love Poems from a Classical Tamil Anthology.* Bloomington, Ind., 1966.

Rangachari, V. "The History of the Naiks of Madura," *IA*, 43 (1914), 1-16, 27-36, 43-48, 111-18, 133-42, 153-58, 187-94, 217-20,

229-32, 253-62; 44 (1915), 37-40, 59-66, 69-73, 113-18; 45 (1916), 32-36, 54-56, 69-76, 81-92, 100-108, 116-20, 130-40, 147-54, 161-70, 178-88, 196-204; 46 (1917), 22-28, 36-46, 57-63, 74-78, 96-105, 119-24, 156-63, 183-89, 209-19, 327-47, 272-75.

—————. *Topographical List of Inscriptions of the Madras Presidency, Collected till 1919.* 3 vols. Madras, 1919.

Ray, Rajat, and Ratnalekha Ray. "The Dynamics of Continuity in Rural Bengal under the British Imperium: A Study of Quasi-Stable Equilibrium in Underdeveloped Societies in a Changing World." *IESHR*, 10:2 (1973), 103-29.

Ray, Ratnalekha. *Change in Bengal Agrarian Society, 1760-1850.* Delhi, 1979.

Raychaudhuri, S. P. *Black Soils of India.* New Delhi, 1963.

—————. "Classification of Soils of India." In *International Geographical Congress, 21st Meeting, Delhi, 1968, Selected Papers*, 1:450-58. Delhi, 1968.

—————. *Soils of India.* New Delhi, 1963.

Raychaudhuri, Tapan. "Inland Trade." In Raychaudhuri and Habib, *Cambridge Economic History*, 1:325-59.

—————. "The Mughal Empire." In Raychaudhuri and Habib, *Cambridge Economic History*, 1:172-92.

—————, and Irfan Habib, eds. *The Cambridge Economic History of India.* Volume 1, *c.1200-c.1750.* Cambridge, 1982.

Redfield, Robert, and Milton Singer. "City and Countryside: Cultural Interdependence." In Teodor Shanin, ed. *Peasants and Peasant Societies, Selected Readings*, pp. 202-18. Harmondsworth, 1971.

Richards, John S. "Mughal State Finance and Premodern World Economy." *CSSH*, 23:2 (1981), 285-308.

Robert, Bruce. "Economic Change and Agrarian Organization in 'Dry' South India, 1890-1940: A Reinterpretation." *MAS*, 17:1 (1983), 59-78.

Roberts, Michael. *Caste Conflict and Elite Formation: The Rise of a Karava Elite in Sri Lanka, 1500-1931.* Cambridge, 1982.

Rodney, Walter. *A History of the Guyanese Working People, 1881-1905.* Baltimore, 1981.

Royle, J. Forbes. *On the Culture and Commerce of Cotton in India and Elsewhere.* London, 1851.

Rudolph, Lloyd I., and Susanne Hoeber Rudolph. *The Modernity of Tradition.* Chicago, 1967.

Russel, A.J.H. *A Geographical Survey of Cholera in the Madras Presidency from 1818 to 1927.* Madras, 1929.

Sahlins, Marshall. *Culture and Practical Reason*. Chicago, 1976.

Saletore, B. A. *Social and Political Life in the Vijayanagar Empire (A.D. 1346-A.D. 1646)*. Madras, 1934.

———. "The Stanikas and Their Historical Importance." *Journal of the University of Bombay*, 7:1 (1938), 29-93.

Sarada Raju, A. *Economic Conditions in Madras Presidency, 1800-1850*. Madras, 1941.

Sarkar, Jagdish Narayan. *Some Aspects of Military Thinking and Practice: Medieval India*. Calcutta, 1974.

Satyanatha Aiyer, R. *History of the Nayaks of Madurai*. Oxford, 1924.

Saunders, A. J. "The Saurashtra Community of Madurai." *Journal of Madras University*, 1 (1928), 69-92.

Schultz, Theodore. *Investing in People: The Economics of Population Quality*. Berkeley and Los Angeles, 1981.

Schwartzberg, Joseph E., ed. *A Historical Atlas of South Asia*. Chicago, 1978.

Scott, James C. *The Moral Economy of the Peasant: Rebellion and Subsistence in Southeast Asia*. New Haven, 1976.

Sewell, Robert. *The Forgotten Empire*. London, 1924.

Shah, S. M. "Cropping Pattern in Relation to Irrigation." *IJAE*, 18 (January 1963), 154-60.

Shanin, Teodor. "The Nature and Logic of Peasant Economy." *JPS*, 1:1 (1973), 63-80.

Silverman, Sydel. "The Peasant Concept in Anthropology." *JPS*, 7:1 (1979), 49-69.

Singaravelu, S. *Social Life of the Tamils: Classical Period*. Kuala Lumpur, 1966.

Singer, Milton. *When a Great Tradition Modernizes: An Anthropological Approach to Indian Civilization*. New York, 1972.

Singh, Jasbir. *An Agricultural Atlas of India*. Kurukshetra, 1974.

Slater, Gilbert, ed. *Some South Indian Villages*. Madras, 1918.

Smith, C. T. "The Drainage Basin as an Historical Basis for Human Activity." In R. J. Chorley, ed. *Water, Earth and Man*. London, 1969, pp. 101-12.

Smith, Carol A. "Exchange Systems and the Spatial Distribution of Elites: The Organization of Stratification in Agrarian Societies." In Carol A. Smith, ed. *Regional Analysis*, 2:309-74. New York, 1976.

Smolett, P. B. *Madras: Its Civil Administration*. London, 1858.

Sopher, D. E. "The Swidden/Wet Rice Transition Zone in the Chittagong Hills." *AAAG*, 54 (1964), 107-26.

Spate, O.H.K., and A.T.A. Learmonth. *India and Pakistan: A General and Regional Geography.* London, 1967.

Spear, Percival. *Twilight of the Mughals.* London, 1951.

Spencer, George W. "Religious Networks and Royal Influence in Eleventh Century South India." *JESHO,* 12:1 (1969), 42-56.

―――. "Royal Initiative under Rajaraja I," *IESHR,* 7:4 (1970), 431-42.

―――. "Temple Moneylending and Livestock Redistribution in Early Tanjore." *IESHR,* 5:3 (1968), 277-93.

Sreedhara Menon, A. *A Survey History of Kerala.* Kottayam, 1967.

Srinivas, M. N., ed. *India's Villages.* Bombay, 1955.

―――, and A. M. Shah. "The Myth of the Self-sufficient Indian Village." *Economic Weekly,* 12 (1960), 1375-78.

Srinivasan, C. R. *Rice Production and Trade in Madras.* Madras, 1934.

Stavrianos, L. S. *Global Rift: The Third World Comes of Age.* New York, 1981.

Steensgaard, Neils. *The Asian Trade Revolution of the Seventeenth Century: The East India Companies and the Decline of the Caravan Trade.* Chicago, 1973.

Stein, Burton. "Brahman and Peasant in Early South Indian History." *Adyar Library Bulletin,* 31-32 (1967-1968), 229-69.

―――. "Circulation and the Historical Geography of Tamil Country." *JAS,* 37:1 (1977), 7-26.

―――. "Coromandel Trade in Medieval India." In John Parker, ed., *Merchants and Scholars,* pp. 47-62. Minneapolis, 1965.

―――. "Economic Functions of the Medieval South Indian Temple." *JAS,* 19:2 (1960), 163-76.

―――, ed. *Essays on South India.* Honolulu, 1975.

―――. "The Far South." In Raychaudhuri and Habib, eds., *Cambridge Economic History,* 1:452-58.

―――. "Historical Ecotypes in South India." In R. E. Asher, ed., *Proceedings of the Second International Conference Seminar of Tamil Studies,* pp. 284-88. Madras, 1971.

―――. "Integration of the Agrarian System of South India." In R. E. Frykenberg, ed., *Land Control and Social Structure in Indian History,* pp. 175-216. Madison, Wisc., 1969.

―――. *Peasant State and Society in Medieval South India.* Delhi, 1980.

―――. "The South." In Raychaudhuri and Habib, eds., *Cambridge Economic History,* 1:203-13.

Stein, Burton. "South India: Some General Considerations of the Region and Its Early History." In Raychaudhuri and Habib, eds., *Cambridge Economic History,* 1:14-44.

———, ed. *South Indian Temples: An Analytical Reconsideration.* New Delhi, 1978.

———. "The State and the Agrarian Order in Medieval South India: A Historiographical Critique." In Stein, ed., *Essays on South India,* pp. 64-91.

———. "Temples in the Tamil Country, 1300-1750 A.D." *IESHR,* 14:1 (1977), 11-46.

———. "Vijayanagara, c. 1350-1564." In Raychaudhuri and Habib, eds., *Cambridge Economic History,* 1:102-124.

Stokes, Eric. *The English Utilitarians and India.* London, 1959.

———. *The Peasant and the Raj: Essays in Agrarian Society and Peasant Rebellion in Colonial India.* Cambridge, 1978.

Stokes, H. J. "The Custom of 'Kareiyid' or Periodical Redistribution of Land in Tanjore." *IA,* 3 (1874), 65-69.

Strange, T. L. *A Letter . . . on Judicial Reform.* Madras, 1860.

Stuart, A. J. *A Manual of the Tinnevelly District.* Madras, 1876.

Subbarayalu, T. *Political Geography of the Chola Country.* Madras, 1973.

Subrahmanian, N. *The History of Tamilnad (to A.D. 1336).* Madurai, 1972.

———. *Sangam Polity.* Bombay, 1966.

Subrahmanya Aiyer, K. V. "The Ancient History of the Pandya Country." In K. V. Subrahmanya Aiyer, *Historical Sketches of the Ancient Dekhan.* 3 vols. 1:73-182. Madras, 1917-1919.

———. "Tinnevelly Inscription of Maravarman Sundara-Pandya I," *EI,* 22:1 (January 1933), 39-48.

———. "Tiruchendur Inscription of Varaguna Maharaja (II)," *EI,* 21:3 (July 1931), 101-15.

Suntharalingam, R. *Politics and Nationalist Awakening in South India.* Tucson, 1974.

Tamil Lexicon. Madras, 1935-1937.

Taylor, William. *A Catalogue Raisonée of Oriental Manuscripts in the Library of the (Late) College, Fort St. George.* 3 vols. Madras, 1857-1862.

———. " 'Marava Jathi Vernanam' from unpublished Mackenzie Manuscripts in possession of the Asiatic Department of the Madras Literary Society." *Madras Journal of Literature and Science,* 4 (1836), 357-60.

————. *Oriental Historical Manuscripts in the Tamil Language, Translated with Annotations.* 2 vols. Madras, 1935.

Thananjayarajasingham, S. *A Critical Study of a Seventeenth Century Tamil Document Relating to a Commercial Treaty.* Perandeniya, 1968.

Thapar, Romila. *A History of India.* Vol. 1. Harmondsworth, 1966.

Thaxton, Ralph. *China Turned Rightside Up: Revolutionary Legitimacy in the Peasant World.* New Haven, 1983.

Thomas, P. J. *The Problem of Rural Indebtedness.* Madras, 1934.

————. *Some South Indian Villages: A Resurvey.* Madras, 1940.

Thompson, E. P. "The Grid of Inheritance: A Comment." In Jack Goody, Joan Thirsk, and E. P. Thompson, eds., *Family and Inheritance: Rural Society in Western Europe, 1200-1800,* pp. 328-60. Cambridge, 1976.

————. *The Making of the English Working Class.* New York, 1963.

————. *Whigs and Hunters: The Origins of the Black Act.* New York, 1975.

Thorner, Daniel. "Peasant Economy as a Category in Economic History." In Teodor Shanin, ed., *Peasants and Peasant Societies,* pp. 202-18. Harmondsworth, 1971.

————. "Peasantry." In David Sills, ed., *International Encyclopedia of Social Science,* 11:503-11. New York, 1968.

————, Basil Kerblay, and R.E.F. Smith, eds. *The Theory of Peasant Economy.* Homewood, Ill., 1966.

Thurston, Edgar. *Castes and Tribes of Southern India.* 6 vols. Madras, 1909.

Tinker, Hugh. *The Foundations of Local Self-Government in India, Pakistan and Burma.* London, 1954.

————. *A New System of Slavery: The Export of Indian Labour Overseas, 1830-1920.* London, 1974.

Tirumalai, R. *Rajendra Vinnagar.* Madras, 1980.

Tomlinson, B. R. *The Political Economy of the Raj, 1914-1947: The Economics of Decolonization.* London, 1976.

Vasantha Devi, M. N. "Some Aspects of the Agricultural Geography of South India." *IGJ,* 39:1-2 (1964), 1-41; and 39:3-4 (1964), 59-122.

Venkateswaran, P. A. *Agriculture in South India.* New Delhi, 1961.

Vilar, Pierre. *A History of Gold and Money, 1450-1920.* London, 1976.

Viraraghavacharya, T.K.T. *History of Tirupati, The Tirvengadam Temple.* 2 vols. Tirupati, 1953.

Viraraghavacharya, T.K.T. "The Srivilliputtur Temple of Sudikko-dutta Nachchiyar." *Tirupati-Tirumalai Devasthanam Monthly Bulletin*, 6 (1955), 1-11.

Wallerstein, Immanuel. *The Modern World System, I, Capitalist Agriculture and the Origins of the European World-Economy in the Sixteenth Century*. New York, 1974.

Washbrook, David A. *The Emergence of Provincial Politics: The Madras Presidency, 1870-1920*. Cambridge, 1976.

————. "Law, State and Agrarian Society in Colonial India," *MAS*, 15:3 (1981), 649-721.

Watson, A. *The War of the Goldsmith's Daughter*. London, 1964.

Weber, Max. *General Economic History*. New York, 1927.

————. *The Religion of India: The Sociology of Hinduism and Buddhism*. New York, 1958.

Wheeler, J. Talboys. *Handbook for the Cultivation of Cotton in the Madras Presidency*. Madras, 1862.

Whitcombe, Elizabeth. *Agrarian Conditions in Northern India*. Vol. 1. *The United Provinces under British Rule, 1860-1900*. Berkeley and Los Angeles, 1972.

Whittaker, C. R. "Late Roman Trade and Traders." In P. Garnsey, K. Hopkins, and C. R. Whittaker, eds. *Trade in the Ancient Economy*. Berkeley and Los Angeles, 1983.

Wiegt, Ernst. "Der Trockene Sudosten Indiens: Mensch und Wirtschaft im Tambraparni Tal." *Geographische Rundshau*, 20:11 (November 1968), 405-14.

Williams, Raymond. *The Country and the City*. New York, 1973.

Wilson, H. H. *A Glossary of Judicial and Revenue Terms*. London, 1855.

Winks, Robin, ed. *Slavery: A Comparative Perspective*. New York, 1972.

Wiser, William H. *The Hindu Jajmani System*. Lucknow, 1958.

Wolf, Eric. *Europe and the People without History*. Berkeley and Los Angeles, 1982.

————. *Peasant Wars of the Twentieth Century*. New York, 1969.

————. *Peasants*. Englewood Cliffs, 1966.

Yang, Anand, ed. *Criminality and Control in British India*, Tucson, in press.

————. "An Institutional Shelter: The Court of Wards in Late Nineteenth Century Bihar." *MAS*, 13:2 (1979), 247-64.

————. "Sacred Symbol and Sacred Place in Rural India: Community Mobilization in the 'Anti-Cow Killing' Riot of 1893." *MAS*, 22:4 (1980), 576-96.

Yule, H., and A. C. Burnell. *Hobson-Jobson: A Glossary of Colloquial Anglo-Indian Words and Phrases*. London, 1886.

Zacharias, C.W.B. *Madras Agriculture*. Madras, 1950.

———. *Studies in the Economics of Farm Management in Madras*. 3 vols. Delhi, 1954-1957.

Zvelebil, Kamil. *The Smile of Murugan*. Leiden, 1973.

———. *Tamil Literature*. Wiesbaden, 1974.

INDEX

Adaichani tank, 146-47, 155
adaiyolai, 182
Adichanallur, 21
agency houses, 133, 159-63
agrarian system, 7, 10-11, 13-14, 256:
  early modern (post-1500), 42, 68-100,
  209-11; long-term change, 15-18, 39-
  41; medieval, 24, 40-41, 203-204. *See
  also* social networks
agrestic servitude. *See* labor, coercion
agricultural zones: changing property
  rights, 178-88; commercial crops,
  137, Map 7; cropping, 56-59; customary rights, 167-70; development,
  214; dominant caste domains, 65-67;
  geography, Map 8; investment climates, 141-42, 149-51; populations,
  63-67; village types, 81-96; social
  change, 156-63, 217-18; trade between, 132-34; wet-mixed-dry continuum, 60-63
agriculture: commercialization, 56, 58,
  62-63, 65, 68, 130-41, 165, 178 (in
  long term, 73-74); commercialism and
  property rights, 184; finance, 93, 144;
  fixed capital in, 81, 83-84, 94, 96,
  159, 176 (in dry zone: 81, 162, 193);
  frontier, 42, 56, 82, 168; growth
  trends, 43, 80, 113-14, 121, 147-56;
  investment climates, 149-51; medieval,
  18-22, 52; "net product," 121; post-
  medieval development, 52-58; productivity and seasons, 16-17, 20, 22, 110,
  214; productivity and power, 156-63;
  and religion, 32-34, 37, 205; statistics,
  249; technology, 16-17, 20, 22, 156.
  See also crops; irrigation; technology
alliances: Anglo-Indian, 13, 101-102,
  123, 128-29, 213; against British-Na-
  wabi forces, 97; against Nayakas, 69;
  Christian, 192; Compay-nawab, 211;
  dominant-caste alliances, 81; military
  power and medieval alliances, 28;
  marriage and kinship, 9, 15, 33; kin-

ship, 71-72; marriage alliances in
  caste settlement, 63-64; marriage alliances and localism, 66; political, in
  medieval political stability, 17, 26-30
——Vellala-Brahman alliance: rise, 36-
  41; stability, 45, 65-67; maps, 11-13,
  72, 77-81, 84-94, 102-107, 109-14,
  166; decline, 115-29, 159
Alvar Tirunagari, 111
amani, 78, 112
Ambasamudram, 22-23, 33-34, 37, 48,
  95, 134, 148, 158, 226-27. *See also*
  Ilangokudi; Rajamangalam
Ambattans, 25
American Civil War and world cotton
  trade, 139
Americas in world trade, 7, 206
anaikkattu, *see* dams
Andal (Sudikkodutta Nachiyar), 31-32,
  43, 46, 95, 168
Anglo-Indian English, 103
anicuts, *see* dams
anmai, 39
Anmanadu, 30
anthropology, 4, 11
Arab merchants, 131
Arabian Sea, 19
Arapangu Maravas, 50
arbitration, 112
Arcot, 76
Ariyanayakipuram dam, 52, 69
artisans, 25, 51, 74
Arundel, A. T., 146
Asian studies, peasants in, 4
Attur, 30, 33; tank, Map 18
Aurangzeb, 97

Balijas, 25, 52
bankers and poligar peshcash, 99
barbers, 25, 64
Bengal, 170
betel, 20, Map 7
bhakti, 31-32, 36, 204-205
blacksmiths, 64

laborers (*cont.*)
90-91; bondage, 93; female, 92; loss
of mirasi rights, 164, 174-75; mobility, 190; pollution and immobility,
91-92; real income, 158, 220
land: auctions, 118, 123, 176; conception and classification, 15, 20-21, 26,
35, 44, 63, 76-81, 84, 85-88, 114,
116, 120-21, 198; demarcation, 108,
120; records, 108; transactions (gift
and market), 34-40, 183. *See also* agriculture; soils; state revenue; surveys
land revenue, *see* state revenue
landlordism, 104, 173, 180. *See also*
swamibhogam; tenancy
landowners: and state, 28-29, 79-81,
126, 173, 177-78, 199; and irrigation,
144; and urban employment, 158. *See
also* mirasidars; village society
landownership: and labor, 167-70; distribution, 105-107; records, 122; titles, 81-96, 104. *See also* property;
rights to resources; village society
landowning collectivities, 109, 111; demise and irrigation, 146-47. *See* mirasidar villages; mirasidars; pangus;
shareholding
language and social strata, 103, 115
little kings, 70, 105, 125, 163
local chiefs: under Pandyas, 28-29, 90;
Pandya legacy, 70
local funds, 136
localism: Pandyan, 30; and marriage,
15; and religion, 31-33; material de-
terminants, 34-35; localization of divine power, 32, 46; decline, 115-29,
135-41, 178, 183
low castes, 24
Lubbais, 230
"lump sum" settlement, 117

Mackenzie Manuscripts, 49, 91, 98,
165-66
Madras City, 76, 80
Madras Presidency, 5, 7, 101-104, Map
2; constabulary, 128; irrigation expenditure, 145; intellectual climate,
115-16; reform, 116-17; rice prices,
117; "Report on Inland Customs,"
133; "Report on the External and In-

ternal Commerce," 134; shipping, 141
Madurai, 15, 21, 23, 42, 45, 48, 51, 68,
96; warfare, in and around, 26, 51,
96-97; center of regional order, 26,
69-70, 99, 136, 158, 194, 204
Madurai Sultanate, 44
magistrates, 171
maistries, 145
Malaysia, 156
Malik Kafur, 44-45, 207
mandalams, 18, 68-69, Map 3
Manimekalai, 17, 18, 224
maniyamdars, 77-78
Manur, 147, 227
Marathas, 97
Maravas, 25, 44, 46, 49-51, 65-66, 82-
83, 96, 98, 114, 128-29, 157, Maps
8, 17; and Pandyas, 229; and swa-
minbhogam, 181; conflict with Shanars, 191-96, 199, 220; decline, 156-
57, 193-94; unstable dominance, 67,
94-96, 195-96, 231; sub-jatis, 71-72.
See also kaval; village officers
market networks, 9-14: and temples, 33-
34, 38, 40; elaboration under Nayakas, 73-75; and revenue, 81; English power, 129. *See also* merchants,
towns
marriage, 15, 33; in caste settlement, 63-
64; exclusion of vellai nadans, 48
Marudappadevar, 49
Marudur dam, 42, 52, 113, 142, 147,
155
Marx, Karl, 4-5
Mayamankurichi, 182
measures, 76, 108, 120-21
Medai Delavoy Mudaliar family, 69, 70,
80, 99, 189
medieval dynasties, South India, 7, 13,
15-42, 202, 204-205; collapse of, 13,
42-45
medieval period, Eurasia, 201-205
Mel Kadaiyam, 30
Melaseval, 45
melvaram, 37, 76, 78-79, 110-11, 197;
grain sales, 81
merchant capital, 207, 210
merchants, 25-26, 28, 33, 40, 46, 51;
human geography, 52, 64; native and
European, 129-30, 156-63

LIBRARY OF CONGRESS CATALOGING IN PUBLICATION DATA

Ludden, David E.
PEASANT HISTORY IN SOUTH INDIA.

Bibliography: p.　　Includes index.

1. Peasantry—India—Tirunelveli (District)—History.　I. Title.
HD1537.I4L83　1985　　305.5′63　　85-42692
ISBN 0-691-05456-8 (alk. paper)

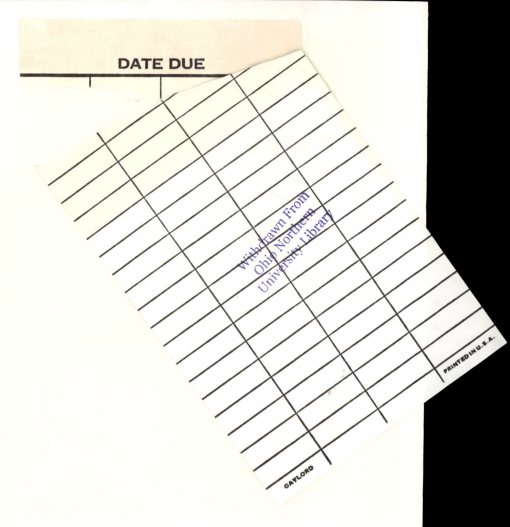